R. Gupta's®

BANKING AWARENESS

A Treasure of Banking Industry Knowledge with Concise Study Material & 1000+ Solved MCQs

Useful for

◆ IBPS-PO/Clerks ◆ SBI-PO/Clerks ◆ RBI ◆ NABARD ◆ IDBI/SIDBI ◆ Regional Rural Banks (RRBs) ◆ Bank of Baroda–PGDBF ◆ Credit Officers & All Other Banking Recruitment Exams

by

RPH Editorial Board

Ramesh Publishing House, New Delhi

Published by
O.P. Gupta *for* Ramesh Publishing House

Admin. Office
12-H, New Daryaganj Road, Opp. Officers' Mess,
New Delhi-110002 ✆ 23275224, 23245124

E-mail: info@rameshpublishinghouse.com
For Online Shopping: www.rameshpublishinghouse.com

Showroom
• Balaji Market, Nai Sarak, Delhi-110006 ✆ 23282525 📱 9354373464
• 4457, Nai Sarak, Delhi-110006

Book Code: R-1849

13th Edition: January 2026

ISBN: 978-93-5012-882-4

Price: ₹ 280

Printed at: B.K. Offset, Delhi

CONTENTS

❑❑❑

Banking Awareness

1 Introduction to Banking

As far as the origin of the present banking system in the world is concerned, the first bank called the "Bank of Venice" is believed to be established in Italy in the year 1157. The first bank in India was started in the year 1770 by the Alexander & Co., an English Agency as "Bank of Hindustan" which failed in 1782 due to the closure of the Agency House in India. The first bank in the modern sense was established in the Bengal Presidency as "Bank of Bengal" in the year 1806.

According to G. Crowther, the modern banking has three ancestors in the history of banking in this world :-

(*i*) The Merchants

(*ii*) The Goldsmiths

(*iii*) The Money Lenders

(*i*) The Merchants: It were the merchant who first evolved the system of banking as the trading activities required remittances of money from one place to another place which is one of the important functions of a bank even now. Because of the possibility of theft of money during physical transportation of money, the traders began to issue the documents which were taken as titles of money. This system gave rise to the institution of "Hundi" which means a letter of transfer whereby a merchant directs another merchant to pay the bearer of Hundi the specified amount of money in the Hundi and debit this amount against the drawer of Hundi.

(*ii*) The Goldsmiths: The second stage in the growth of banking was the role of goldsmiths. The business of goldsmiths was such that he had to secure safe to protect the gold against theft and take special precautions. In a period when paper was not in circulation and the money consisted of gold and silver, the people started leaving their precious bullion and coins in the custody of goldsmiths. As this practice spread, the goldsmiths started charging something for taking care of the gold and silver. As the evidence of receiving valuables, he stared to issue a receipt. Since the gold and silver coins had no mark of the owners, the goldsmiths started lending them. The goldsmiths were prepared to issue an equal amount of gold or silver money to the receipt holder, the goldsmith receipts became like cheques as a medium of exchange and a means of payment by one merchant to the other merchant.

(*iii*) The Money Lenders: The third stage in the growth of banking system is the changing of the character of goldsmiths into that of the money lenders. With the passing of time and on the basis of experience, the goldsmiths found that the withdrawals of coins were much less than the deposits with them and it was not necessary to hold the whole of the coins with them. After keeping the contingency reserve, the goldsmiths started advancing the coins on loan by charging interest. In this way, the goldsmith money lender became a banker who started performing two important functions of the modern banking system, that of accepting deposits and advancing loans. The only difference is that now it is the paper money and then its was gold or silver coins.

MEANING AND DEFINITION OF A BANK

It is very difficult to give a precise definition of a bank due to the fact that a modern bank performs a variety of functions. Ordinarily a 'Bank' is an institution which deals with the money and credit in such a manner that it accepts deposits from the public and makes the surplus funds available to those who need them, and helps in remitting money from one place to another safely. Different economists have given different definition of a bank. Some of the important definitions are as under:

"A bank collects money from those who have it to spare or who are saving it out of their incomes, and it lends this money to those who require it." **G. Crowther**

"Banking means the accepting for the purpose of Indian companies lending or investment, of deposits of money from the public, repayable on demand or otherwise, and withdrawable by cheque, draft or otherwise."

The Banking Companies (Regulation) Act, 1949

An ideal definition of a bank can be given as under:

"A bank is a commercial establishment which deals in debts and aims at earning profits by accepting deposits from general public at large, which is repayable on demand or otherwise through cheques or bank drafts and otherwise which are used for lending to the borrowers or invested in Government securities."

TYPES OF BANKS

Banks are of various types and can be classified :

A. On the basis of Reserve Bank Schedule
B. On the basis of ownership
C. On the basis of domicile
D. On the basis of functions
E. On the basis of economic structure

ON THE BASIS OF RESERVE BANK SCHEDULE

Bank can be of the following two types on the basis of Second Schedule of the Reserve Bank of India Act, 1934 :

(*i*) **Scheduled Banks:** All those banks which are included in the list of Schedule Second of the Reserve Bank of India are called the Scheduled Bank. Only those banks are included in the list of scheduled banks which satisfy the following conditions:

(*a*) That it must have a paid up capital and reserves of ₹ 5 lakhs.

(*b*) That it must ensure the Reserve Bank that its operations are not detrimental to the interest of the depositors.

(*c*) That it must be a corporation or a co-operative society and not a single owner firm or a partnership firm.

(*ii*) **Non-scheduled Banks:** The banks which are not included in the second schedule of the Reserve Bank of India Act, 1934 are called non-scheduled banks. They are not included in the second schedule because they does not fulfill the three pre-conditions laid down in the Act to qualify for the induction in the second schedule.

ON THE BASIS OF OWNERSHIP

Banks can be classified on the basis of ownership in the following categories:

(*i*) **Public Sector Banks:** The banks which are owned or controlled by the Government are called "Public Sector Banks". In 1955, the first public sector commercial bank was established by passing a special Act of Parliament which is known as State Bank of India. Subsequently, the Government took over the majority of shares of other State Banks which were operating at the state levels namely State Bank of Patiala, State Bank of Bikaner & Jaipur, State bank of Travancore, State Bank of Mysore, State Bank of Indore, State Bank of Saurashtra and State Bank of Hyderabad working as subsidiaries of State Bank of India. The subsidiaries of SBI have been merged with SBI on April 1, 2017.

10 Public Sector Banks Merged into Four: The Union Cabinet has approved the merger of 10 public sector banks into four, paving the way for the largest consolidation among the state-owned lenders.

According to the plan: • Punjab National Bank has taken over Oriental Bank of Commerce and United Bank. • Canara Bank has taken over Syndicate Bank. • Union Bank of India has taken over Andhra Bank and Corporation Bank. • Indian Bank has been merged with Allahabad Bank.

The merger has become effective from April 1, 2020. Consolidation among public sector banks has been on the agenda for the National Democratic Alliance since 2014, when it first came into power. In 2018, it decided to merge Bank of Baroda with Vijaya Bank and Dena Bank. The government also allowed Life Insurance Corporation of India to take over IDBI bank.

After the merger of these banks total number of public sector banks is now 12:

1. State Bank in India	2. Punjab National Bank
3. Bank of Baroda	4. Canara Bank
5. Union Bank of India	6. Indian Bank
7. Bank of Maharashtra	8. Punjab and Sindh Bank
9. Indian Overseas Bank	10. United Commercial Bank
11. Central Bank of India	12. Bank of India

(*ii*) **Private Sector Banks:** On the contrary, Private Sector Banks are those banks which are owned and controlled by the private sector *i.e.,* private individuals and corporations. The private sector played a strategic role in the growth of joint stock banks in India. In 1951, there were in all 566 private sector banks of which 92 banks were scheduled banks and the remaining 474 were non-scheduled banks. At the time, there was not even a single public sector bank. With the nationalization of banks in 1969 and 1980 their role in commercial banking had declined considerably. Since then the number of private sector banks is decreasing and the number of public sector banks is increasing.

(*iii*) **Co-operative Banks:** The word 'co-operative' stands for working together. Therefore, co-operative banking means an institution which is established on the principle of co-operation dealing in ordinary banking business. Co-operative banks are special type of banks doing ordinary banking business in which the members cooperate with each other for the promotion of their common economic interests.

Features of Co-operative Banking

Following are the distinguishing main features of a co-operative bank:

(*i*) Membership of Co-operative Banks is voluntary.
(*ii*) Functions of a Co-operative Bank are common banking functions.
(*iii*) Organization and management of a Co-operative Bank is based on democratic principles.
(*iv*) Main objectives of a Co-operative Bank are to promote economic, social and moral development of its members.
(*v*) Basic principle of Co-operative Bank is equality.

Therefore, we can conclude and define a co-operative bank as under:

"Co-operative Bank is an institution established on co-operative basis which deals in ordinary banking business for the promotion of economic, social and moral development of its members on the principle of equality."

The short-term agriculture credit institutions cater to the short-term financial needs of the agriculturists which have the following three tier federal structure in co-operative:

(*a*) At the Village level : Primary Agricultural Credit Societies

(*b*) At the District level : Central Co-operative Banks

(*c*) At the State level : State Co-operative Banks

ON THE BASIS OF DOMICILE

The banks can be classified into the following two categories on the basis of domicile:

(*i*) Domestic Banks

(*ii*) Foreign Banks

(*i*) Domestic Banks: Those banks which are incorporated and registered in India are called domestic banks.

(*ii*) Foreign Banks: Foreign Banks are those banks which are set up in a foreign country with their control and management in the hands of head office in their country of origin but having business branches in India. Foreign Banks are also known as Foreign Exchange Banks or Exchange Banks. Traditionally, these banks were set up for financing the foreign trade in India and discounting the foreign exchange bills. But, now these banks are also accepting deposits and making advances like other commercial banks in India

ON THE BASIS OF FUNCTIONS

The banks can be classified on the basis of functions in the following categories:

(*i*) Commercial Banks

(*ii*) Industrial Banks

(*iii*) Agricultural Banks

(*iv*) Exchange Banks

(*v*) Central Bank

(*i*) Commercial Banks: Commercial Banks are those banks which perform all kinds of banking business and functions like accepting deposits, advancing loans, credit creation, and agency functions for their customers. Since their major portion of the deposits are for the short period, they advance only short-term and medium-term loans for business, trade and commerce. Majority of the commercial banks are in the public sector. Of late they have started giving long-term loans also to compete in the commercial money market. These commercial banks are also called joint stock banks because they are constituted and organized in the same manner as the joint stock companies are constituted.

(*ii*) Industrial Banks: The Industrial banks are those banks which provide medium-term and long-term finance to the industries for the purchase of land and building, plant and machinery and other industrial equipment. They also underwrite the shares and debentures of the industries and also subscribe to them. The main functions of an Industrial Banks are as follows:

(*i*) They provide long-term finance to the industries to purchase land and buildings, plant and machinery and construction of factory buildings.

(*ii*) They also accept long-term deposits.

(*iii*) They underwrite the shares and debentures of the industry and sometimes subscribe to them.

In India, there are number of financial institutions which perform the function of an Industrial Bank. Major financial institutions are as under:

(*i*) Industrial Development Bank of India (IDBI)

(*ii*) Industrial Finance Corporation of India (IFCI)

(*iii*) Industrial Credit and Investment Corporation of India (ICICI) and

(*iv*) State Industrial Development Corporation such as Haryana State Industrial Development Corporation (HSIDC).

(*iii*) Agriculture Banks: The needs of agricultural credit are different from that of industry, business, trade and commerce. Commercial banks and industrial banks do not deal with agriculture credit financing. An agriculturist has both type of needs:

(*i*) He requires short-term credit to purchase seeds, fertilizers and other inputs, and

(*ii*) He also requires long-term credit to purchase land, to make permanent improvement on land, to purchase agricultural machinery and equipment such as tractors etc.

Agricultural credit is generally provided in India by the Co-operative institutions. The Co-operative Agricultural Credit Institutions are divided into two categories:

(A) Short-term agricultural credit institutions, and

(B) Long-term agricultural credit institutions.

A. Short-term Agricultural Credit Institutions

The short-term agricultural credit institutions cater to the short-term financial needs of the agriculturists which have the following three tier federal structure:

(*a*) At the Village level : Primary Agricultural Credit Societies

(*b*) At the District level : Central Co-operative Banks

(*c*) At the State level : State Co-operative Banks

B. Long-term Agricultural Credit Institutions

The long-term agricultural credit is provided by the Land Development Banks which were earlier known as Land Mortgage Banks. The land development banks provide long-term to agriculturists for a period ranging from 5 years to 25 years.

(*iv*) Exchange Banks: The exchange banks are those banks which deal in foreign exchange and specialised in financing the foreign trade. Therefore, they are also called foreign exchange banks. Foreign Exchange Banks are those banks which are set up in a foreign country with their control and management in the hands of head office in their country of origin but having business branches in India.

(*v*) Central Bank: The Central Bank is the apex bank of a country which controls, regulates and supervises the banking, monetary and credit system of the country. The Central Bank is owned and controlled by the Government of the country. The Reserve Bank of India is the Central Bank in India. The important function of central bank are as follows:

(*i*) It acts as banker to the Government of the country.

(*ii*) It also acts as agent and financial advisor to the Government of the country.

(*iii*) It has the monopoly to issue currency of the country.

(*iv*) It serves as the lender of the last resort.

(*v*) It acts as the clearing house and keeps cash reserves of commercial banks.

ON THE BASIS OF ECONOMIC STRUCTURE

Different countries adopt different types of banking system depending upon their economic structure.

1. Unit Banking System: Under this type of banking system, an individual bank operates through an single office. The size and area of operation is much smaller than in other types of banking system. It was originated and grew in USA. The main reason for the development of unit banking system in America is the fear of emergence of monopoly in banking business.

2. Branch Banking System: In this type of banking system, a big bank as a single ownership operates through a network of branches spread all over the country. This type of banking system was initially developed in England. Later on, it become popular in other countries like Canada, India and Australia etc.

3. Group Banking System: This banking system refers to the system of banking in which two or more banks are directly controlled by a corporation or an association or a business trust. The holding company may or may not be a banking company. In this system, each bank maintains its separate identity. Its business is managed by the holding company. This type of banking system was popular in USA.

4. Chain Banking System: It is another form of group of banking. It refers to the system in which two or more banks are brought under common control by a device other than the holding company. They have common management and policies. The management may consist of group of persons through stock ownership or otherwise.

5. Deposit Banking System: Commercial banks are the best examples for deposit banking. Deposit bank will have to maintain liquidity *i.e.*, enough cash reserve to meet withdrawals. Deposit bank is those banks which accept deposits of short-term and loans will also be for short-term periods. The business in this type of banking system is less risky. The loans provided by deposit bank are in the form of overdraft, cash credit and discounting bills of exchange.

6. Investment Banking System: These banks are those financial institutions which provide long-term finance to business. They invest in capital market *i.e.,* stocks & shares of different companies. These banks act as intermediaries between savers and investors. These investment bankers are classified into various categories such as underwriters and retailers. An investment banker performs highly useful services to the co-operative bodies by supplying long-term capitals. They also provide services to small investors. They mobilize the investment through shares, stocks and mutual funds.

7. Correspondent Banking System: It is another important type of banking system. A correspondent bank is one which connects the two banks under unit banking system. The best examples of correspondent bank in India are RBI or central bank.

8. Mixed Banking System: If the banks provide both short-term and long-term loans to the industries, it is called as mixed banking system. German banks are the best examples of this type of banking system. These banks accept both short-term and long-term deposits. Therefore, they are able to provide both short- and long-term loans required by the industry. The banks were facilitated to invest the surplus funds for the industrial development of the country in this type of banking system.

UNIT BANKING VS BRANCH BANKING

The banking system in different countries vary substantially from one another. Broadly speaking, however, there are two important types of banking systems, viz., unit banking and branch banking.

A. Unit Banking

'Unit banking' means a system of banking under which banking services are provided by a single banking organisation. Such a bank has a single office or place of work. It has its own governing body or board of directors. It functions independently and is not controlled by any other individual, firm or body corporate. It also does not control any other bank. Such banks can become member of the clearing house and also of the Banker's Association. Unit banking system originated and grew in the U.S.A. Different unit banks in the U.S.A. are linked with each other and with other financial centres in the country through "correspondent banks."

Advantages of Unit Banking

Following are the main advantages of unit banking:

1. Efficient Management: One of the most important advantages of unit banking system is that it can be managed efficiently because of its size and work. Co-ordination and control becomes effective. There is no communication gap between the persons making decisions and those executing such decisions.

2. Better Service: Unit banks can render efficient service to their customers. Their area of operation being limited, they can concentrate well on that limited area and provide best possible service. Moreover, they can take care of all banking requirements of a particular area.

3. Close Customer-banker Relations: Since the area of operation is limited, the customers can have direct contact. Their grievances can be redressed then and there.

4. No Evil Effects due to Strikes or Closure: In case there is a strike or closure of a unit, it does not have much impact on the trade and industry because of its small size. It does not affect the entire banking system.

5. No Monopolistic Practices: Since the size of the bank and area of its operation are limited, it is difficult for the bank to adopt monopolistic practices. Moreover, there is free competition. It will not be possible for the bank to indulge in monopolistic practices.

6. No Risks of Fraud: Due to small size of the bank, there is stricter and closer control of management. Therefore, the employees will not be able to commit fraud.

7. Closure of Inefficient Banks: Inefficient banks will be automatically closed as they would not be able to satisfy their customers by providing efficient service.

8. Local Development: Unit banking is localised banking. The unit bank has the specialised knowledge of the local problems and serves the requirement of the local people in a better manner than branch banking. The funds of the locality are utilised for the local development and are not transferred to other areas.

9. Promotes Regional Balance: Under unit banking system, there is no transfer of resources from rural and backward areas to the big industrial and commercial centres. This tends to reduce regional imbalance.

Disadvantages of Unit Banking

1. No Economies of Large Scale: Since the size of a unit bank is small, it cannot reap the advantages of large scale viz., division of labour and specialisation.

2. Lack of Uniformity in Interest Rates: In unit banking system there will be large number of banks in operation. There will be lack of control and, therefore, their rates of interest would differ widely from place to place. Moreover, transfer of funds will be difficult and costly.

3. Lack of Control: Since the number of unit banks is very large, their co-ordination and control would become very difficult.

4. Risks of Bank's Failure: Unit banks are more exposed to closure risks. Bigger unit can compensate their losses at some branches against profits at the others. This is not possible in case of smaller banks. Hence, they have to face closure sooner or later.

5. Limited Resources: Under unit banking system, the size of bank is small. Consequently, its resources are also limited. Hence, they cannot meet the requirements of large scale industries.

6. Unhealthy Competition: A number of unit banks come into existence at an important business centre. In order to attract customers they indulge in unhealthy competition.

7. Wastage of National Resources: Unit banks concentrate in big metropolitan cities whereas they do not have their places of work in rural areas. Consequently, there is uneven and unbalanced growth of banking facilities.

8. No Banking Development in Backward Areas: Unit banks, because of their limited resources, cannot afford to open uneconomic branches in smaller towns and rural areas. As such, these areas remain unbanked.

9. Local Pressure: Since unit banks are highly localised in their business, local pressures and interferences generally disrupt their normal functioning.

B. Branch Banking System

It means a system of banking in which a banking organisation works at more than one place. The main place of business is called head office and the other places of business are called branches. The head office controls and co-ordinates the work at branches. The day-to-day operations are performed by the branch manager as per the policies and directions issued from time to time by the head office.

This system of banking is prevalent throughout the world. In India also, all the major banks have been operating under branch banking system.

Advantages of Branch Banking

1. Better Banking Services: Such banks, because of their large size can enjoy the economies of large scale viz., division of work and specialisation. These banks can also afford to have the specialised services of bank personnel which the unit banks can hardly afford.

2. Extensive Service: Branch banking can provide extensive service to cover large area. They can open their branches throughout the country and even in foreign countries.

3. Decentralisation of Risks: In branch banking system, branches are not concentrated at one place or in one industry. These are decentralised at different places and in different industries. Hence, the risks are also distributed.

4. Uniform Rates of Interest: In branch banking, there is better control and co-ordination of the central bank. Consequently, interest rates can be uniform.

5. Better Cash Management: In branch banking, there can be better cash management as cash easily be transferred from one branch to another. Therefore, there will be lesser need to keep the cash idle for meeting contingencies.

6. Better Training Facilities to Employees: Under branch banking, the size of the bank is quite large. Therefore, such banks can afford to provide better training facilities to their employees. Almost every nationalised bank in India has its separate training college.

7. Easy and Economical Transfer of Funds: Under branch banking, a bank has a widespread of branches. Therefore, it is easier and economical to transfer funds from one branch to the other.

8. Better Investment of Funds: Such bank can afford the services of specialised and expert staff. Therefore, they invest their funds in such industries where they get the highest return and appreciation without sacrificing the safety and liquidity of funds.

9. Effective Central Bank Control: Under branch banking, the central bank has to deal only with a few big banks controlling a large number of branches. It is always easier and more convenient to the central bank to regulate and control the credit policies of a few big banks, than to regulate and control the activities of a large number of small unit banks. This ensures better implementation of monetary policy.

10. Contacts with the Whole Country: Under branch banking, the bank maintains continual contacts with all parts of the country. This helps it to acquire correct and reliable knowledge about economic conditions in various parts of the country. This knowledge enables the bank to make a proper and profitable investment of its surplus funds.

11. Greater Public Confidence: A bank, with huge financial resources and number of branches spread throughout the country, can command greater public confidence than a small unit bank with limited resources and one or a few branches.

Disadvantages of Branch Banking

Following are the disadvantages of branch banking:

1. Difficulties of Management, Supervision and Control: Since there are hundreds of branches of a bank under this system, management, supervision and control became more inconvenient and difficult. There are possibilities of mismanagement in branches. Branch managers may misuse their position and misappropriate funds. There is great scope for fraud. Thus, there are possibilities of fraud and irregularities in the financial management of the bank.

2. Lack of Initiative: The branches of the bank under this system suffer from a complete lack of initiative on important banking problems confronting them. No branch of the bank can take decision on important problems without consulting the head office. Consequently, the branches of the bank find themselves unable to carry on banking activities in accordance with the requirements of the local situation. This makes the banking system rigid and inelastic in its functioning. This also leads to "red-tapism" which means "official delay."

3. Monopolistic Tendencies: Branch banking encourages monopolistic tendencies in the banking system. A few big banks dominate and control the whole banking system of the country through their branches. This can lead to the concentration of resources in the hands of a small number of men. Such a monopoly power is a source of danger to the community, whose goal is a socialistic pattern of society.

4. Regional Imbalances: Under the branch banking system, the financial resources collected in the smaller and backward regions are transferred to the bigger industrial centres. This encourages regional imbalances in the country.

5. Continuance of Non-profitable Branches: Under branch banking, the weak and unprofitable branches continue to operate under the protection cover of the stronger and profitable branches.

6. Unnecessary Competition: Branch banking is delocalised banking, under branch banking system, the branches of different banks get concentrated at certain places, particularly in big towns and cities. This gives rise to unnecessary and unhealthy competition among them. The branches of the competing banks try to tempt customers by offering extra inducements and facilities to them. This naturally increases the banking expenditure.

7. Expensiveness: Branch banking system is much more expensive than the unit banking system. When a bank opens a number of branches at different places, then there arises the problem of co-ordinating their activities with others. This necessitates the employment of expensive staff by the bank.

8. Losses by Some Branches Affect Others: When some branches suffer losses due to certain reasons, this has its repercussions on other branches of the bank.

Thus, branch banking system as well as unit banking system suffer from defects and drawbacks. But the branch banking system is, on the whole, better than the unit banking system. In fact, the branch banking system has proved more suitable for backward and developing countries like India. Branch banking is very popular and successful in India. A comparison between unit banking and branch banking is essentially a comparison between small-scale and large-scale operations.

BALANCE SHEET OF THE BANK

The balance sheet of a commercial bank is a statement of its assets and liabilities. Assets are what others owe the bank, and what the bank owes others constitutes its liabilities. The business of a bank is reflected in its balance sheet and hence its financial position as well. The balance sheet is issued usually at the end of every financial year of the bank.

The balance sheet of the bank comprises of two sides: the assets side and the liabilities side. It is customary to record liabilities on the left side and assets on the right side. The following is the proforma of a balance sheet of the bank.

Balance Sheet of the Bank

Liabilities	Assets
1. Capital	1. Cash
a. Authorised capital	a. Cash on hand
b. Issued capital	b. Cash with central bank and other banks
c. Subscribed capital	
d. Paid-up-capital	
2. Reserve fund	2. Money at call and short notice
3. Deposits	3. Bills discounted
4. Borrowings from other banks	4. Bills for collection
5. Bills payable	5. Investments
6. Acceptances and endorsements	6. Loans and advances
7. Contingent liabilities	7. Acceptances and endorsement
8. Profit and loss account	8. Fixed assets
9. Bills for collection	

Liabilities

Liabilities are those items on account of which the bank is liable to pay others. They denote other's claims on the bank. Now, we have to analyse the various items on the liabilities side.

1. Capital: The bank has to raise capital before commencing its business. Authorised capital is the maximum capital upto which the bank is empowered to raise capital by the Memorandum of Association. Generally, the entire authorised capital is not raised from the public. That part of authorised capital which is issued in the form of shares for public subscription is called the issued capital. Subscribed capital represents that part of issued capital which is actually subscribed by the public. Finally, paid-up capital is that part of the subscribed capital which the subscribers are actually called upon to pay.

2. Reserve Fund: Reserve fund is the accumulated undistributed profits of the bank. The bank maintains reserve fund to tide over any crisis. But, it belongs to the shareholders and hence a liability on the bank. In India, the commercial bank is required by law to transfer 20 per cent of its annual profits to the Reserve fund.

3. Deposits: The deposits of the public like demand deposits, savings deposits and fixed deposits constitute an important item on the liabilities side of the balance sheet. The success of any banking business depends to a large extent upon the degree of confidence it can instill in the minds of the depositors. The bank can never afford to forget the claims of the depositors. Hence, the bank should always have enough cash to honour the obligations of the depositors.

4. Borrowings from Other Banks: Under this head, the bank shows those loans it has taken from other banks. The bank takes loans from other banks, especially the central bank, in certain extraordinary circumstances.

5. Bills Payable: These include the unpaid bank drafts and telegraphic transfers issued by the bank. These drafts and telegraphic transfers are paid to the holders thereof by the bank's branches, agents and correspondents who are reimbursed by the bank.

6. Acceptances and Endorsements: This item appears as a contra item on both the sides of the balance sheet. It represents the liability of the bank in respect of bills accepted or endorsed on behalf of its customers and also letters of credit issued and guarantees given on their behalf. For rendering this service, a commission is charged and the customers to whom this service is extended are liable to the bank for full payment of the bills. Hence, this item is shown on both sides of the balance sheet.

7. Contingent Liabilities: Contingent liabilities comprise of those liabilities which are not known in advance and are unforeseeable. Every bank makes some provision for contingent liabilities.

8. Profit and Loss Account: The profit earned by the bank in the course of the year is shown under this head. Since the profit is payable to the shareholders it represents a liability on the bank.

9. Bills for Collection: This item also appears on both the sides of the balance sheet. It consists of drafts and hundies drawn by sellers of goods on their customers and are sent to the bank for collection, against delivery documents like railway receipt, bill of lading, etc., attached thereto. All such bills in hand at the date of the balance sheet are shown on both the sides of the balance sheet because they form an asset of the bank, since the bank will receive payment in due course, it is also a liability because the bank will have to account for them to its customers.

Assets

According to Crowther, the assets side of the balance sheet is more complicated and interesting. Assets are the claims of the bank on others. In the distribution of its assets, the bank is governed by certain well defined principles. These principles constitute the principles of the investment policy of the bank or the principles underlying the distribution of the assets of the bank. The most important guiding principles of the distribution of assets of the bank are liquidity, profitability and safety or security. In fact, the various items on the assets side are distributed according to the descending order of liquidity and the ascending order of profitability.

Now, we have to analyse the various items on the assets side.

1. Cash: Here, we can distinguish cash on hand from cash with central bank and other banks cash on hand refers to cash in the vaults of the bank. It constitutes the most liquid asset which can be immediately used to meet the obligations of the depositors. Cash on hand is called the first line of defence to the bank.

In addition to cash on hand, the bank also keeps some money with the central bank or other commercial banks. This represents the second line of defence to the bank.

2. Money at Call and Short Notice: Money at call and short notice includes loans to the brokers in the stock market, dealers in the discount market and to other banks. These loans could be quickly converted into cash and without loss, as and when the bank requires. At the same time, this item yields income to the bank. The significance of money at call and short notice is that it is used by the banks to effect desirable adjustments in the balance sheet. This process is called 'Window Dressing'. This item constitutes the 'third line of defence' to the bank.

3. Bills Discounted: The commercial banks invest in short-term bills consisting of bills of exchange and treasury bills which are self-liquidating in character. These short-term bills are highly negotiable and they satisfy the twin objectives of liquidity and profitability. If a commercial bank requires additional funds, it can easily rediscount the bills in the bill market and it can also rediscount the bills with the central bank.

4. Bills for Collection: As mentioned earlier, this item appears on both sides of the balance sheet.

5. Investments: This item includes the total amount of the profit yielding assets of the bank. The bank invests a part of its funds in government and non-government securities.

6. Loans and Advances: Loans and advances constitute the most profitable asset to the bank. The very survival of the bank depends upon the extent of income it can earn by advancing loans. But, this item is the least liquid asset as well. The bank earns quite a sizeable interest from the loans and advances it gives to the private individuals and commercial firms.

7. Acceptances and Endorsements: As discussed earlier, this item appears as a contra item on both sides of the balance sheet.

8. Fixed Assets: Fixed assets include building, furniture and other property owned by the bank. This item includes the total volume of the movable and immovable property of the bank. Fixed assets are referred to as 'dead stocks'. The bank generally undervalues this item deliberately in the balance sheet. The intention here is to build up secret reserves which can be used at times of crisis.

Balance sheet of a bank acts as a mirror of its policies, operations and achievements. The liabilities indicate the sources of its funds; the assets are the various kinds of debts incurred by a bank to its customers. Thus, the balance sheet is a complete picture of the size and nature of operations of a bank.

MULTIPLE CHOICE QUESTIONS

1. The terms drawer, drawee and payee are associated with:
A. Cheques B. Promissory notes
C. Delivery order D. Hundies
E. None of these

2. A depositor can withdraw money from the bank any number of time in.............
A. Fixed deposit B. Savings bank
C. Current a/c D. Recurring deposit
E. None of these

3. The system of banking attracting deposits and lending for short period is called:
A. Mixed banking B. Deposit banking
C. Credit system D. Lending system
E. None of these

4. The banker will refuse payment against:
A. Post dated cheque
B. Mutilated cheque
C. Insufficient fund in a/c
D. All of these
E. None of these

5. The best example of pure commercial banking is:
A. British banking B. German banking
C. Indian banking D. Japanese banking
E. None of these

6. Which country's banking is regarded as best example of mixed banking?
A. Germany B. USA
C. Britain D. India
E. None of these

7. .... bank is one which specialise in financing foreign trade of a country.
A. Unit B. Branch
C. Overseas D. Exchange
E. None of these

8. "A central bank is an institution charged with responsibility of regulating supply and cost of money in the interest of general public". This definition was made by:

A. H L Hart B. Keynes
C. John Paget D. Dudley Johnson
E. None of these

9. Commercial bank can be either unit banking type or .... banking type.

A. Central B. Branch
C. Specialised D. Rural
E. None of these

10. Unit banks are linked with bigger banks by a system called.......

A. Mixed banking
B. Group banking
C. Correspondent banking
D. Network banking
E. None of these

11. .... is "Pay later product":

A. Debit card B. ATM card
C. Credit card D. Both A & B
E. None of these

12. .... is "Pay now product":

A. Debit card B. ATM card
C. Credit card D. Charge card
E. None of these

13. Another name of credit card is.......

A. Debit card B. Money card
C. Plastic money D. Card money
E. None of these

14. Credit card was first time launched in the world by.........

A. British bank B. Bank of America
C. HSBC D. SBI
E. None of these

15. The first bank in the world is:

A. Bank of America B. Federal Reserve bank
C. Bank of Venice D. Bank of Hindustan
E. None of these

16. First purely Indian bank is:

A. Allahabad Bank B. Punjab National Bank
C. Nedungadi Bank D. Bank of Hindustan
E. None of these

17. The first international credit card was introduced in India by:

A. SBI B. Canara Bank
C. Andhra Bank D. Bank of Baroda
E. None of these

18. .... deposits generally do not carry any interest.

A. Savings B. Recurring
C. Current D. Fixed
E. None of these

19. .... is a form of bank governance that occurs when a small group people control three or more banks that are independently incorporated.

A. Unit banking B. Branch banking
C. Group banking D. Chain banking
E. None of these

20. .... is a bank located outside the country of residence of the depositor:

A. Off-shore bank B. Unit bank
C. Foreign bank D. All of these
E. None of these

21. .... was originally the home of commercial banking.

A. U.S.A. B. England
C. Britain D. Germany
E. None of these

22. Commercial banks to expand deposit through expanding their loans and advances is known as:

A. Credit creation B. Trade discount
C. Deposit D. Bank advances
E. None of these

23. The German banking system is the best example for:

A. chain banking B. mixed banking
C. branch banking D. unit banking
E. None of these

24. Those banking have large scale operations and geographical spreading of risks:

A. mixed banking B. unit banking
C. branch banking D. chain banking
E. None of these

25. Unit banking is referred to as:

A. local banking B. branch banking
C. mixed banking D. central bank
E. None of these

26. Off Shore Banking Unit is:

A. a unit which is situated in Foreign country
B. a unit which is situated in Special Economic Zones and deals in foreign currency only
C. a unit which is actively participating in lending foreign currency loans and in joint ventures
D. None of the above
E. All of the above

27. Securitization is:

A. non-performing loans are acquired from banks and financial institutions at a discounted value and security receipts issued to them so that these loans are removed from their balance sheet enabling them to reduce the provision in respect of such loans and improve profitability
B. converting the illiquid loans of banks and financial institutions by Securitization Companies into tradable securities, after they are acquired and sold to the investors

C. a process of acquisition of non-performing loans from banks by a Securitization company and covert them into tradable securities and sold to the investors
D. All of the above
E. None of the above

28 Which category of accounts are opened under Financial Inclusion?
A. Senior Citizens Deposit
B. Super Saver Accounts
C. No-Frill Accounts
D. SBI Vishesh
E. None of these

29. While opening a current account, an introductory reference is absolutely necessary?
A. the introducer can be held responsible if the account becomes irregular
B. this is required under directions from the Reserve Bank of India
C. if it is not taken, the bank may be held responsible for being negligent and may, therefore, lose statutory protection available under Section 131 of the Negotiable Instruments Act, 1881
D. All of these
E. None of the above

30. The term ''kite flying'' in banking refers to:
A. drawing a cheque without providing sufficient funds to meet it
B. drawing and acceptance of a bill of exchange without consideration with a view to accommodate the other party
C. the pracuce of paying usance bills before they become due
D. drawing a post-dated cheque
E. None of these

31. A scheduled bank is one:
A. which conforms to the requirements of schedule III of the Banking Regulation Act, 1949
B. which has been declared as a scheduled bank by the Government of India
C. which has deposits exceeding ₹ 10 crore
D. which has its name added to the second schedule of the Reserve Bank of India Act, 1934
E. None of these

32. Invoice is a:
A. Accounting document
B. Legal document
C. Commercial document
D. All of these
E. None of these

33. Banking Sector will fall under which of the following?
A. Agricultural Sector B. Service Sector
C. Manufacturing Sector D. Industrial Sector
E. None of these

34. Which of the following sources of income for a bank is most significant?
A. service charges B. loans
C. deposits D. fees
E. None of these

35. Factors influencing customer behaviour in banking are:
A. location and range of services
B. safety and return
C. customer service
D. both B and C
E. None of these

36. Services associated with banking, insurance and securities are called:
A. Financial Services B. Banking Services
C. Credit Services D. Debt Services
E. None of these

37. The concept of ''Narrow Banking'' was recommended by:
A. Khan Committee
B. Nayak Committee
C. Sodhani Committee
D. Tarapore & Narasimham Committee
E. None of these

38. Banks would prefer to mobilize deposits under Savings Bank accounts, because:
A. account holders will be motivated to save since savings account offer interest also
B. it is a low cost deposit for the bank and banks can profitably deploy such funds
C. banks want to inculcate the savings habit among the public
D. All of the above
E. None of these

39. PAN number is required for all transactions above:
A. ₹ 25,000 B. ₹ 50,000
C. ₹ 1 lac D. ₹ 10 lacs
E. None of these

40. Bank can issue a duplicate of a lost demand draft at the request of the:
A. payee B. holder
C. purchaser D. either A or C
E. None of these

41. Counter-Guarantee is obtained when:
A. a Bank Guarantee is issued
B. a Fixed Deposit is issued
C. a Bond is issued
D. None of the above
E. All of these

42. Scheduled Commercial banks maintain an account with every office of the Reserve Bank of India primarily with a view to:
A. conforming to the requirements of the Reserve Bank of India Act, 1934

B. conducting business on Government Account
C. facilitating borrowings from the Reserve Bank of India
D. facilitating inter-bank clearing and transfer of funds from one centre to another
E. None of these

43. Which of the following is a form of ''Small Savings Bank'' popular among the poor or children?
A. Core Banking B. Credit Banking
C. Debit Card D. Piggy Banking
E. None of these

44. Personal Banking includes:
A. Deposits B. Insurance
C. Investment D. Above all
E. None of these

45. Non Banking assets include:
A. Property seized by the bank
B. Auction sale of the customer's property
C. Band Building
D. Both A and B
E. None of these

46. Which among the following terms describe the 'universal banking'?
A. Branches of Bank in all major form of the world
B. A bank providing services in all geographical territories of its country
C. A bank providing combination of commercial banking and investment banking
D. None of these
E. All of these

47. Loan and Advances of a bank come under which of the following category?
A. Assets B. Liabilities
C. Costs D. None of these
E. All of these

48. A Saving Bank Deposit Account is one where:
A. Amounts are deposited and are withdrawan as per requirement of the customers
B. The deposits are made only once in a year
C. Periodical Fixed amount are deposited month wise and withdrawals are allowed after a fixed period
D. All of the above
E. None of these

49. ''Door Step Banking'' facilities to Corporate customers/ Government Departments/ PSUs provide for delivery of cash at customers' place:
A. against telephonic instructions
B. against cheque deliverable at customer's place
C. against cheque delivered at the Bank
D. All of the above
E. None of these

50. Commercial banks are unique among financial institutions in that they:
A. advance loans to business
B. provide insurance to depositors
C. create demand deposits
D. hold saving deposits
E. None of these

51. Financial year in banks is a period from:
A. January to December B. May to June
C. April to March D. January to April
E. None of these

52. Nominee's Signature is to be obtained on:
A. Account Opening Form
B. Nomination Form
C. Speciman Signature Card
D. Need not to be obtained
E. None of these

53. The term "dormant accounts" means:
A. accounts showing an average balance of less than ₹ 100 during a half year
B. accounts which remains inoperative for an extended period of time
C. accounts which have been blocked under the exchange control regulations
D. loan/cash credit/overdraft accounts which are considered irrecoverable
E. None of these

54. As we know commercial banks accept deposits from the public. What do banks do with this money?
A. This is a type of credit creation. Bank gives this on loan.
B. This is an income for the bank.
C. Banks give this money directly to the govt. for developmental projects.
D. This money is deposited with the RBI who in turn gives some interest on it to banks.
E. None of these

55. Which of the following terms is used in banking?
A. Vacuum B. Power
C. Density D. Credit Card
E. None of these

56. Banks do not provide which of the following services?
A. Issuing Bank Drafts
B. Depositing Money
C. Sale of post cards and postal stamps
D. Lockers for valueable items/documents
E. None of these

57. Which of the following is not a part of the scheduled banking structure in India?
A. Money Lenders
B. Public Sector Banks
C. Private Sector Banks
D. Regional Rural Banks
E. None of these

58. One of the sources of income of banks is to charge fee for certain services. What are some of the services provided by the banks for which they charge fee?
1. Issuing Demand Drafts/Pay Orders
2. Issue of ATM/Credit/Debit Cards
3. Electronic Transfer of Money

A. Only 1 B. Only 2
C. Only 3 D. Only 1 & 2
E. All of these

59. As we all know, the major source of income of the banks is lending money (providing credit) and earning interest on it. In normal circumstances, the demand of the credit comes mainly from which of the following sectors?
1. Personal Loans
2. Priority Sector Lending & Bailout Packages
3. Project Finance

A. Only 1 B. Only 2
C. Only 3 D. All of these
E. None of these

60. India has different categories of Commercial Banks. Which of the following is NOT one such category?
A. Private Banks B. Commodity Banks
C. Nationalized Banks D. Co-operative Banks
E. None of these

61. Banking comes under:
A. Agriculture Sector B. Rural Sector
C. Service Sector D. Finance Sector
E. None of these

62. Which of the following is correct:
A. Bank don't manufacture products or extract natural resources from earth
B. A bank is a business
C. Bank sell financial services such as loans, home mortgage Loans, business loans, checking accounts, credit card services, certificates of deposit and individual retirement accounts.
D. All of above
E. None of these

63. When a person publicly announces that he can not repay loans, it is called .... in banking language:
A. Poor Credit worthiness
B. Bankruptcy
C. Willful Defaulter
D. Worst Creditor
E. None of these

64. Which of the following is not a banking term?
A. Letter of credit B. MIBOR
C. Factoring services D. Entry load
E. None of these

65. One single statement that depicts the financial position of a Bank and / or Business enterprise at a given point of time is called:
A. Statement of product details
B. Foreign exchange
C. Balance Sheet
D. Balance of payment
E. Trading and Manufacturing account

66. The usual deposit accounts of banks are?
A. Current accounts, electricity accounts and insurance premium accounts.
B. Current accounts, post office savings, bank accounts and term deposit accounts.
C. Loan accounts, savings bank accounts and term deposit accounts.
D. Current accounts, savings bank accounts and term deposit accounts.
E. Current bill accounts and term deposit accounts.

67. .... are Local Institutions functioning like Banks
A. Local Area Banks B. Indigenous Banks
C. Private Banks D. Financial Institutions
E. All the above

68. The 'No Frill Accounts' facility provided by the banks is aimed at which of the following categories of people?
A. Corporate world
B. Senior citizens
C. Current account holders
D. Poor people
E. Government employees

69. Working Capital Gap means—
A. Total current assets minus Total current liabilities
B. Total assets minus intangible assets
C. Total liabilities minus terms liabilities.
D. Total current assets minus current liabilities (other than bank borrowing)
E. None of these

70. .... constitute the largest source of funds for the banks.
A. Cash B. Loan
C. Deposit D. Agency service
E. None of these

71. .... banks are those banks which are incorporated outside India and their head office are also situated outside India.
A. Foreign exchange
B. Schedule
C. Non-scheduled
D. Commercial
E. None of these

72. .... is a system of banking in which one bank carries on its business through a network of branches spread all over the country.
A. Chain banking B. Unit banking
C. Branch banking D. Channel banking
E. None of these

73. The definition of 'banking is given in
   A. Negotiable Instruments, Act 1981
   B. RBI Act, 1934
   C. Banking Regulation Act, 1949
   D. Contract Act
   E. None of these

74. Which of the following is a borrowing facility?
   A. Term finance
   B. Performance guarantee
   C. Bills received under letter of credit
   D. All the above
   E. None of these

75. A set of institutions, instruments and markets which encourage savings and channelise them for productive purposes
   A. Stock Exchange B. Financial market
   C. Financial System D. Derivative market
   E. None of these

76. Financial year in banks is period between
   A. January to December
   B. March to April
   C. April to March
   D. July to June
   E. None of these

ANSWERS

1	**2**	**3**	**4**	**5**	**6**	**7**	**8**	**9**	**10**
A	C	B	D	A	A	D	D	B	C
11	**12**	**13**	**14**	**15**	**16**	**17**	**18**	**19**	**20**
C	A	C	B	C	B	C	C	D	A
21	**22**	**23**	**24**	**25**	**26**	**27**	**28**	**29**	**30**
D	A	B	C	A	B	D	C	C	B
31	**32**	**33**	**34**	**35**	**36**	**37**	**38**	**39**	**40**
D	C	B	C	C	A	D	D	B	D
41	**42**	**43**	**44**	**45**	**46**	**47**	**48**	**49**	**50**
A	D	D	D	D	C	A	A	C	A
51	**52**	**53**	**54**	**55**	**56**	**57**	**58**	**59**	**60**
C	D	B	A	D	C	A	E	D	B
61	**62**	**63**	**64**	**65**	**66**	**67**	**68**	**69**	**70**
C	D	B	D	C	D	B	D	D	C
71	**72**	**73**	**74**	**75**	**76**				
A	C	C	A	C	C				

2

Evolution of Banking in India

The banking history is interesting and reflects evolution in trade and commerce. It also throws light on living style, political and cultural aspects of civilized mankind. The strongest faith of people has always been religion and God. The seat of religion and place of worship were considered safe place for money and valuables. Ancient homes didn't have the benefit of a steel safe, therefore, most wealthy people held accounts at their temples. Numerous people, like priests or temple workers were both devout and honest, always occupied the temples, adding a sense of security. There are records from Greece, Rome, Egypt and Ancient Babylon that suggest temples loaned money out, in addition to keeping it safe. The fact that most temples were also the financial centers of their cities and this is the major reason that they were ransacked during wars. The practice of depositing personal valuables at these places which were also functioning as the treasuries in ancient Babylon against a receipt was perhaps the earliest form of "Banking".

Gradually, as the personal possession got evaluated in term of money, in form of coins made of precious metal like gold and silver, these were being deposited in the temple treasuries. As these coins were commonly accepted form of wealth, 'lending' activity to those who needed it and were prepared to 'borrow' at an interest began. The person who conducted this 'lending' activity was known as the "Banker" because of the bench he usually set. It is also observed that the term 'bankrupt' got evolved then as the irate depositors broke the bench and table of the insolvent banker.

With the expansion of trade, the concept of banking gained greater ground. The handling of "banking" transcended from individual to groups to companies. Issuing currency was one of the major functions of the banks. The earliest from of money – coins, were a certificate of value stamped on a metal, usually gold, silver, and bronze or any other metal, by an authority, usually the king. With the increasing belief and faith in such authority of their valuation and the necessities of wider trade a substitute to metal was found in paper. The vagaries of monarchial rule led to the issues of currency being vested with the banks since they enjoyed faith, controlled credit and trading. All forms of money were a unit of value and promised to pay the bearer of specified value. Due to failure on account of unwise loans, to rule and organize, a stable banking system arose. The word's earliest bank currency notes were issued in Sweden by Stockholms Banco in July 1661.

HISTORY OF BANKING IN INDIA

The story of Indian coinage itself is very vast and fascinating, and also throws tremendous light on the various aspects of life during different periods. The *Rig Veda* speaks only gold, silver, copper and bronze and the later *Vedic* texts also mention tin, lead, iron and silver. Recently iron coins were found in very early levels at Attranji Kheri(U.P.) and Pandu Rajar Dhibi (Bengal). A money economy existed in India since the days of Buddha.

In ancient India during the Maurya dynasty (321 to 185 BC), an instrument called adesha was in use, which was an order on a banker desiring him to pay the money of the note to a third person, which corresponds to the definition of a bill of exchange as we understand it today. During the Buddhist period, there was considerable use of these instruments. Merchants in large towns gave letters of credit to one another.

Trade guilds acted as bankers, both receiving deposits and issuing loans. The larger temples served as bankers and in the south, the village communities economically advanced loans to peasants. There were many professional bankers and moneylenders like the sethi, the word literally means "chief". It has survived in the North India as seth. Small purchases were regularly paid for in cowry shells (varataka), which remained the chief currency of the poor in many parts of India. Indigenous banking grew up in the form of rural money lending with certain individuals using their private funds for this purpose. The scriptures singled out the vaishyas as the principal bankers. The earliest form of Indian Bill of Exchange was called "Hundi". Exports and import were regulated by barter system.

Kautilya's Arthasastra mentions about a currency known as panas and even fines paid to courts were made by panas. E. B. Havell in his work: The History of Aryas Rule in India says that Muhammad Tughlaq issued copper coin as counters and by an imperial decree made them pass at the value of gold and silver. The people paid their tribute in copper instead of gold, and they bought all the necessaries and luxuries they desired in the same coin.

However, the Sultan's tokens were not accepted in counties in which his decree did not run. Soon the whole external trade of Hindustan come to a standstill. When as last the copper tankas had become more worthless than clods, the Sultan in a rage repealed his edict and proclaimed that the treasury would exchange gold coin for his copper ones. As a result of this thousands of men from various quarters who possessed thousand of these copper coins bought them to the treasury and received in exchange gold tankas. The origin of the word "rupee" is found in the Sanskrit *rupya* "shaped; stamped, impressed; coin" and also from the Sanskrit word "rupa" meaning silver. The standardisation of currency unit as Rupee in largely is due to Sher Shah in 1542.

The English traders that came to India in the 17th century could not make much use of the indigenous bankers, owing to their ignorance of the language as well the inexperience indigenous people of the European trade. Therefore, the English Agency Houses in Calcutta and Bombay began to conduct banking business, besides their commercial business, based on unlimited liability. The Europeans with aptitude of commercial pursuit, who resigned from civil and military services, organized these agency houses.

A type of business organization recognizable as managing agency took form in a period from 1834 to 1847. The primary concern of these agency houses was trade, but they branched out into banking as aside line to facilitate the operations of their main business. The English agency houses, that began to serve as bankers to the East India Company had no capital of their own, and depended on deposits for their funds. They financed movements of crops, issued paper money and established joint stock banks. Earliest of these was Hindustan Bank, established by one of the agency houses in Calcutta in 1770.

Banking in India originated in the last decades of the 18th century. The first banks were The Bank of Hindustan, which started in 1770, and General Bank of India, which started in 1786; both are now defunct. The oldest bank in existence in India is the State Bank of India, which originated in the Bank of Calcutta in June 1806, which almost immediately became the Bank of Bengal. This was one of the three presidency banks, the other two being the Bank of Bombay and the Bank of Madras, all three of which were established under charters from the British East India Company. For many years, the Presidency banks acted as quasi-central banks, as did their successors. The three banks merged in 1921 to form the Imperial Bank of India, which, upon India's independence, became the State Bank of India.

Indian merchants in Calcutta established the Union Bank in 1839, but it failed in 1848 as a consequence of the economic crisis of 1848-49. The Allahabad Bank, established in 1865 and still functioning today, is the oldest Joint Stock bank in India.

Foreign banks too started to arrive, particularly in Calcutta, in the 1860s. The Comptoire d'Escompte de Paris opened a branch in Calcutta in 1860, and another in Bombay in 1862; branches in Madras and Pondicherry, then a French colony, followed. HSBC established itself in Bengal in 1869. Calcutta was the most active trading port in India, mainly due to the trade of the British Empire, and so became a banking centre.

The next was the Punjab National Bank, established in Lahore in 1895, which has survived to the present and is now one of the largest banks in India. The presidency banks dominated banking in India but there were also some exchange banks and a number of Indian joint stock banks. All these banks operated in different segments of the economy. The exchange banks, mostly owned by Europeans, concentrated on financing foreign trade. Indian joint stock banks were generally undercapitalized and lacked the experience and maturity to compete with the presidency and exchange banks.

SWADESHI MOVEMENT

The period between 1906 and 1911, saw the establishment of banks inspired by the Swadeshi movement. The Swadeshi movement inspired local businessmen and political leaders to found banks for the Indian community. A number of banks established then have survived to the present such as Bank of India, Corporation Bank, Indian Bank, Bank of Baroda, Canara Bank and Central Bank of India.

Ammembal Subbarao Pai founded "Canara Bank Hindu Permanent Fund" in 1906. Central Bank of India was established in 1911 by Sir Sorabji Pochkhanawala and was the first commercial Indian bank completely owned and managed by Indians. In 1923, it acquired the Tata Industrial Bank.

The fervour of Swadeshi movement lead to establishing of many private banks in Dakshina Kannada and Udupi district which were unified earlier and known by the name South Canara (South Kanara)district. Four nationalized banks started in this district and also a leading private sector bank. Hence, undivided Dakshina Kannada district is known as "Cradle of Indian Banking".

DEVELOPMENT AFTER FREEDOM

The second milestone in the history of Indian banking was India becoming a sovereign republic. The Government of India initiated measures to play an active role in the economic life of the nation, and the Industrial Policy Resolution adopted by the government in 1948 envisaged a mixed economy. This resulted into greater involvement of the state in different segments of the economy including banking and finance. The banking sector also witnessed the benefits; Government took major steps in this Indian Banking Sector Reform after independence.

- First major step in this direction was nationalization of Reserve Bank in 1949.
- Enactment of Banking Regulation Act in 1949.
- Reserve Bank of India Scheduled Banks' Regulations, 1951.
- Nationalization of Imperial Bank of India in 1955, with extensive banking facilities on a large scale especially in rural and semi-urban areas.
- Nationalization of SBI subsidiaries in 1959.

Government of India took many banking initiatives. These were aimed to provide banking coverage to all section of the society and every sector of the economy.

The Industrial Credit and Investment Corporation of India Limited (ICICI) was incorporated at the initiative of World Bank, the Government of India and representatives of Indian industry, with the objective of creating a development financial institution for providing medium-term and long-term project financing to Indian businesses.

NATIONALIZATION PROCESS

Nationalization of banks in India was an important phenomenon. Despite the provisions, control and regulations of Reserve Bank of India, banks in India except the State Bank of India or SBI, continued to be owned and operated by private persons. By the 1960s, the Indian banking industry had become an important tool to facilitate the development of the Indian economy. At the same time, it had emerged as a large employer, and a debate had ensued about the nationalization of the banking industry. Indira Gandhi, then Prime Minister of India, expressed the intention of the Government of India in the annual conference of the All India Congress Meeting in a paper entitled *"Stray thoughts on Bank Nationalization."* The meeting received the paper with enthusiasm.

Thereafter, her move was swift and sudden. The Government of India issued an ordinance and nationalized the 14 largest commercial banks with effect from the midnight of July 19, 1969. Within two weeks of the issue of the ordinance, the Parliament passed the Banking Companies (Acquisition and Transfer of Undertaking) Bill, and it received the presidential approval on 9 August 1969.

A second dose of nationalization of 6 more commercial banks followed in 1980. The stated reason for the nationalization was to give the government more control of credit delivery. With the second dose of nationalization, the Government of India controlled around 91% of the banking business of India. Later on, in the year 1993, the government merged New Bank of India with Punjab National Bank and in April 2019 Vijaya and Dena Bank have been merged in Bank of Baroda. It was the merger between nationalized banks and resulted in the reduction of the number of nationalized banks from 20 to 17. Currently there are 12 nationalized commercial banks.

ECONOMIC LIBERALIZATION

The second major turning point in this phase was Economic Liberalization in India. After Independence in 1947, India adhered to socialist policies. The extensive regulation was sarcastically dubbed as the "License Raj". The Government of India headed by Narasimha Rao decided to usher in several reforms that are collectively termed as liberalization in the Indian media with Manmohan Singh whom he appointed Finance Minister. Dr. Manmohan Singh, an acclaimed economist, played a central role in implementing these reforms.

In the early 1990s, the then Narasimha Rao government embarked on a policy of liberalization, licensing a small number of private banks. These came to be known as *New Generation tech-savvy banks*, and included Global Trust Bank (the first of such new generation banks to be set up), which later amalgamated with Oriental Bank of Commerce, Axis Bank (earlier as UTI Bank), ICICI Bank and HDFC Bank. This move, along with the rapid growth in the economy of India, revitalized the banking sector in India, which has seen rapid growth with strong contribution from all the three sectors of banks, namely, government banks, private banks and foreign banks.

Currently, banking in India is generally fairly mature in terms of supply, product range and reach-even though reach in rural India still remains a challenge for the private sector and foreign banks. In terms of quality of assets and capital adequacy, Indian banks are considered to have clean, strong and transparent balance sheets relative to other banks in comparable economies in its region. The Reserve Bank of India is an autonomous body, with minimal pressure from the government. The stated policy of the Bank on the Indian Rupee is to manage volatility but without any fixed exchange rate-and this has mostly been true.

With the growth in the Indian economy expected to be strong for quite some time especially in its services sector-the demand for banking services, especially retail banking, mortgages and investment services are expected to be strong.

MULTIPLE CHOICE QUESTIONS

1. Second nationalisation of commercial banks (6 banks) was held in the year:

A. 1979 B. 1980
C. 1984 D. 1976
E. None of these

2. Bank of England was established in the year:

A. 1586 B. 1612
C. 1694 D. 1656
E. None of these

3. Origin of banking is said to be closely connected with:
A. Arabs B. Romans
C. Indians D. Jews
E. None of these

4. The first development bank in India is:
A. IDBI B. IFCI
C. ICICI D. SIDBI
E. None of these

5. Central Land Mortgage Bank was started in Madras in:
A. 1920 B. 1921
C. 1922 D. 1928
E. 1929

6. The first bank in India was started in the year:
A. 1825 B. 1770
C. 1912 D. 1840
E. None of these

7. Regional rural banks are sponsored by ....
A. Foreign exchange banks
B. Nationalized banks
C. Industrial banks
D. All of these
E. None of these

8. The first bank of India
A. RBI B. SBI
C. Bank of Hindustan D. HDFC
E. None of these

9. The first nationalization of banks in India was held in the year:
A. 1969 B. 1980
C. 1991 D. 1985
E. None of these

10. The first Women bank in India is
A. RRB B. BMS
C. LAB D. Either A or C
E. None of these

11. The first joint stock bank in India is ....
A. IDBI B. ICICI
C. Imperial Bank D. Allahabad Bank
E. None of these

12. RBI introduced .... scheme in 1969.
A. SAA B. Village adaption
C. Lead bank D. DIR
E. None of these

13. The first chartered bank was established at ....
A. Japan B. Philadelphia
C. India D. France
E. None of these

14. The first chartered bank was established in the year ....
A. 1781 B. 1775
C. 1870 D. 1881
E. None of these

15. India's first bank was:
A. Bank of Hindustan B. Bank of Hind
C. BOI D. Bank of Delhi
E. None of these

16. Bank of Hindustan was established at ....
A. Bombay B. Chennai
C. Kolkata D. Bengal
E. None of these

17. General Bank of India was established in ....
A. 1771 B. 1775
C. 1786 D. 1780
E. None of these

18. Upper bank of India was established in ....
A. 1860 B. 1870
C. 1863 D. 1865
E. None of these

19. Second phase of Indian banks were nationalized in:
A. 1960 B. 1969
C. 1970 D. 1869
E. None of these

20. The third phase of development banking in India started in early:
A. 1980 B. 1990
C. 1960 D. 1965
E. None of these

21. The government of India passed the SFC Act in ....
A. 1951 B. 1960
C. 1945 D. 1950
E. None of these

22. REPO rate was introduced in:
A. 1990 B. 1992
C. 1982 D. 1980
E. None of these

23. The statutory definition of the term ''banking'' is given in:
A. The Negotiable Instruments Act, 1881
B. The Reserve Bank of India Act, 1934
C. The Companies Act, 1956
D. The Banking Regulation Act, 1949

24. The term ''Licensed banks'' means:
A. Banks licensed to deal in foreign exchange business under the Foreign Exchange Regulation Act, 1973
B. Banks licensed to participate in the ''Clearing house''
C. Foreign banks which are licensed to establish branch officers in India
D. Banks licensed by the Reserve Bank of India under Section 22 of the Banking Regulation Act, 1949 for carrying on or commencing banking business in India
E. None of these

25. When was the first commercial bank in India named 'Hindustan Bank' set up in Calcutta (now Kolkata)?
A. 1690 B. 1750
C. 1805 D. 1890
E. 1770

26. Modern commercial banking in India begins with the setting up of the first Presidency Bank, The Bank of Bengal in ...... in Calcutta (now Kolkata).
A. 1790 B. 1806
C. 1825 D. 1910
E. 1625

27. Regional Rural Banks were established in the year:
A. 1968 B. 1970
C. 1976 D. 1977
E. 1975

28. Consequent upon the recommendations of the Working Group on Rural Banks, 5 Rural Regional Banks were initially set up in the year:
A. 1973 B. 1974
C. 1975 D. 1976
E. 1978

29. Six banks were nationalised because:
A. they were grossly mismanaged
B. the election manifest of Congress (I) contained such a commitment
C. the Government intended to enlarge the flow of bank credit to the economically weaker sections of the society
D. the measure was a part of restructuring the Indian banking system
E. None of these

30. Which among the following is correct regarding Bank of Hindustan?
A. The bank was established at Calcutta under European management
B. It was liquidated on 1829-32
C. Both of Above
D. The bank was governed by British Crown
E. None of the above

31. .... bank was established in 1786:
A. General Bank B. Reserve Bank of India
C. Bank of Bengal D. Bank of Calcutta
E. None of the above

32. The Largest and Oldest Bank, still in existence is:
A. Punjab National Bank
B. Reserve Bank of India
C. State Bank of India
D. Allahabad Bank
E. None of the above

33. Which among the following is correct?
A. State Bank of India originated as the Bank of Calcutta in June 1806
B. "Bank of Calcutta" was renamed as "Bank of Bengal"
C. Both of above
D. "Bank of Calcutta" was named as "Bank of India"
E. None of the above

34. Which among the following banks form the "Imperial Bank of India" in 1921?
A. Bank of Bombay
B. Bank of Madras
C. Bank of Bengal
D. All of the above
E. None of the above

35. When was the first nationalization of many banks were conducted?
A. 19 August, 1969 B. 19 October, 1969
C. 19 July, 1969 D. 05 June, 1967
E. None of the above

36. The Basic criteria that was considered while nationalisation of banks in 1969 was the liability base of banks is more than:
A. 30 crores or more
B. 40 crores or more
C. 50 crores or more
D. 60 crores or more
E. None of the above

37. Which public sector bank of India is the first fully Indian bank, established by the Indian national?
A. Allahabad Bank
B. Central Bank of India
C. State Bank of India
D. Punjab National Bank
E. Bank of Baroda

38. Which was the first Bank corporated by the Indians? (1881)
A. Imperial Bank of India
B. State Bank of India
C. Avadh Commercial Bank(oudh)
D. Reserve Bank of India
E. None of these

39. Bank is an institution which deals with ....
A. money B. treatment
C. education D. communication
E. None of these

40. The word meaning of Banco is ....
A. heap B. gold
C. deposit D. loan
E. None of these

41. Bank of Hindustan was established at ....
A. Bombay B. Chennai
C. Kolkatta D. Bengal
E. None of these

42. Consortium means ....
A. partnership B. owner
C. manager D. individual
E. None of these

43. Banking with a conscience is ....
A. tele banking B. social banking
C. SMS banking D. M-banking
E. None of these

44. Ethical Banking is ....
A. tele banking B. social banking
C. SMS banking D. M-banking
E. None of these

45. Alternative Banking is ....
A. tele banking B. social banking
C. SMS banking D. M-banking
E. None of these

46. Civic Banking is ....
A. tele banking B. social banking
C. SMS banking D. M-banking
E. None of these

47. Sustainable Banking is ....
A. tele banking B. social banking
C. SMS banking D. M-banking
E. None of these

48. The German banking system is the best example for
A. chain banking B. mixed banking
C. branch banking D. unit banking
E. None of these

49. Those banking have large scale operations and geographical spreading of risks
A. mixed banking
B. unit banking
C. branch banking
D. chain banking
E. None of these

50. Unit Banking is referred to as
A. local banking B. branch banking
C. mixed banking D. central bank
E. None of these

51. Lead Bank Scheme was introduced in
A. 1965 B. 1969
C. 1981 D. 1992
E. 1985

52. DFHI started its business in
A. 1975 B. 1988
C. 1991 D. 1999
E. 1995

53. The latest public sector bank in India is
A. Federal Bank
B. State Bank of Travancore
C. ICICI Bank
D. IDBI Bank
E. None of these

ANSWERS

1	2	3	4	5	6	7	8	9	10
B	C	D	B	E	B	B	C	A	B
11	**12**	**13**	**14**	**15**	**16**	**17**	**18**	**19**	**20**
C	C	B	A	A	C	C	C	B	B
21	**22**	**23**	**24**	**25**	**26**	**27**	**28**	**29**	**30**
A	B	D	D	E	B	E	C	C	C
31	**32**	**33**	**34**	**35**	**36**	**37**	**38**	**39**	**40**
A	C	C	D	C	C	D	C	A	A
41	**42**	**43**	**44**	**45**	**46**	**47**	**48**	**49**	**50**
C	A	B	B	B	B	B	B	C	A
51	**52**	**53**							
B	B	D							

3

Indian Banking Structure

The structure of banking in India consists of following components:

1. Central Bank – Reserve Bank of India (RBI)
2. Commercial Banks
   (*a*) Public sector Banks
   (*b*) Private Banks
   (*c*) Foreign Banks
3. Co-operative Banks
   (*a*) Primary Credit Societies
   (*b*) Central Co-operative Banks
   (*c*) State Co-operative Banks
4. Regional Rural Banks
5. Development Banks
6. Specialized Banks
   (*a*) Export Import Bank of India
   (*b*) Small Industries Development Bank of India
   (*c*) National Bank for Agricultural and Rural Development
7. Microfinance institutions
8. Development financial institutions

INDIAN BANKING SYSTEM

Reserve Bank of India, commercial banks, co-operative banks and regional rural banks broadly make up the banking system in India. There are two more types of banks, namely development banks and specialized banks for some particular purposes.

Central Bank – Reserve Bank of India (RBI)

The Reserve Bank of India (RBI), the central bank of India, which was established in 1935, has been fully owned by the government of India since nationalization in 1949. Like the central bank in most countries, Reserve Bank of India is entrusted with the functions of guiding and regulating the banking system of a country.

Commercial Banks

Commercial banks have been in existence for many decades. They mobilise savings in urban areas and make them available to large and small industrial and trading units mainly for working capital requirements. After 1969 commercial banks are broadly classified into nationalized or public sector banks and private sector banks. The State Bank of India along with another 18 banks are the public sector banks. The private sector banks include a small number of Indian scheduled banks which have not been nationalized and branched of foreign banks operating in India. They are commonly known as foreign exchange banks.

Public Sector Banks

- Allahabad Bank
- Andhra Bank
- Bank of Baroda
- Bank of India
- Bank of Maharashtra
- Canara Bank
- Central Bank of India
- Corporation Bank
- Indian Bank
- Indian Overseas Bank
- Oriental Bank of Commerce
- Punjab & Sind Bank
- Punjab National Bank
- Syndicate Bank
- UCO Bank
- Union Bank of India
- United Bank of India
- State Bank of India
- IDBI Bank Ltd.

Private Banks

Private banks are banks that the majority of share capital is held by private individuals. In private sector, small scheduled commercial banks and newly established banks with a network of 36124 branches are operating. To encourage competitive efficiency, the setting up of new private bank is now welcomed.

Examples of old private sector banks are:

- Bank of Rajasthan
- Catholic Syrian Bank
- Dhanalakshmi Bank
- Federal Bank
- ING Vysya Bank
- Karnataka Bank
- Karur Vysya Bank
- Lakshmi Vilas Bank
- Lord Krishna Bank
- South Indian Bank
- Tamilnad Mercantile Bank

Examples on new generation private sector banks are:

- Bank of Punjab
- Centurion Bank
- HDFC Bank
- ICICI Bank
- IndusInd Bank
- Kotak Mahindra Bank
- UTI Bank
- Yes Bank

Foreign Banks

Foreign banks are registered and have their headquarters in a foreign country but operate their branches in India. Apart from financing of foreign trade, these banks have performed all functions of commercial banks and they have an advantage over Indian banks because of their vast resources and superior management.

Examples of foreign bank functioning in India are:

- ABM Amro Bank
- Bank of America
- Bank of Bahrain & Kuwait
- Bank of Ceylon
- Barclays Bank
- BNP Paribas
- Ceylon Bank
- Citibank
- Hongkong & Shanghai Banking Corporation (HSBC)
- JP Morgan Chase Bank
- Sonali Bank
- Standard Chartered Bank

Though there are three types of commercial banks, yet their functions as commercial banks are very similar.

Co-operative Banks

Co-operative banks are banks incorporated in the legal form of co-operatives. Any co-operative society has to obtain a license from the Reserve Bank of India before starting banking business and has to follow the guidelines set and issued by the Reserve Bank of India. Currently, there are 54 co-operatives banks in India.

There are three types of co-operatives banks with different functions:

Primary Credit Societies: Primary Credit Societies are formed at the village or town level with borrower and non-borrower members residing in one locality. The operations of each society are restricted to a small area so that the members know each other and are able to watch over the activities of all members to prevent frauds.

Central Co-operative Banks: Central co-operative banks operate at the district level having some of the primary credit societies belonging to the same district as their members. These banks provide loans to their members (*i.e.*, primary credit societies) and function as a link between the primary credit societies and state co-operative banks.

State Co-operative Banks: These are the highest level of co-operative banks in all the states of the country. They mobilize funds and help in its proper channelization among various sectors. The money reaches the individual borrowers from the state co-operative banks through the central cooperative banks and the primary credit societies.

Regional Rural Banks

The M. Narisaman committee in 1975 after studying the impact of the Lead Bank Scheme recommended the establishment of rural banks in each district that may be dedicated to rural development. The first Gramin Bank started functioning on 2nd October 1975 under an ordinance and subsquently the Regional Rural Banks Act was passed in 1976. The management of Regional Rural banks was with a public sector bank, generally the lead bank of the district. The Regional Rural Bank operates within a given geographical area. The Capital for these banks was contributed by the Central Government (50%), the Sponsor Bank (35%) and the State Government (15%). As on March 31, 2020; 56 RRBs with 21848 branches are working in India. Out of which 70.2% branches are working in rural areas.

Regional rural banks perform the following two types of functions:

1. Granting of loans and advances to small and marginal farmers, agricultural workers, cooperative societies including agricultural marketing societies and primary agricultural credit societies for agricultural purposes or agricultural operations or related purposes.
2. Granting of loans and advances to artisans small entrepreneurs engaged in trade, commerce or industry or other productive activities.

Development Banks

Development Banks are banks that provide financial assistance to business that requires medium and long-term capital for purchase of machinery and equipment, for using latest technology, or for expansion and modernization. A development bank is a multipurpose institution which shares entrepreneurial risk, changes its approach in tune with industrial climate and encourages new industrial projects to bring about speedier economic growth. These banks also undertake other development measures like subscribing to the shares and debentures issued by companies, in case of under subscription of the issue by the public.

There are three important national level development banks. They are:

Industrial Development Bank of India (IDBI)

The IDBI was established on July 1, 1964 under an Act of Parliament. It was set up as the central co-ordinating agency, leader of development banks and principal financing institution for industrial finance in the country. Originally, IDBI was a wholly owned subsidiary of RBI. But it was delinked from RBI w.e.f. Feb. 16, 1976.

IDBI is an apex institution to co-ordinate, supplement and integrate the activities of all existing specialised financial institutions. It is a refinancing and re-discounting institution operating in the capital market to refinance term loans and export credits. It is in charge of conducting techno-economic studies. It was expected to fulfil the needs of rapid industrialisation.

On 29 June, 2018, Life Insurance Corporation of India (LIC) got a technical go-ahead from the Insurance Regulatory and Development Authority of India (IRDAI) to increase stake in IDBI Bank up to 51%. LIC completed the acquisition of 51% controlling stake on 21 January, 2019 making it the majority shareholder of the IDBI Bank.

Industrial Finance Corporation of India (IFCI)

The IFCI is the first Development Financial Institution in India. It is a pioneer in development banking in India. It was established in 1948 under an Act of Parliament. The main objective of IFCI is to render financial assistance to large scale industrial units, particularly at a time when the ordinary banks are not forth coming to assist these concerns. Its activities include project financing, financial services, merchant banking and investment.

Till 1993, IFCI continued to be Developmental Financial Institution. After 1993, it was changed from a statutory corporation to a company under the Indian Companies Act, 1956 and was named as IFCI Ltd with effect from October 1999.

Industrial Credit and Investment Corporation of India (ICICI)

ICICI was set up in 1955 as a public limited company. It was to be a private sector development bank in so far as there was no participation by the Government in its share capital. It is a diversified long-term financial institution and provides a comprehensive range of financial products and services including project and equipment financing, underwriting and direct subscription to capital issues, leasing, deferred credit, trusteeship and custodial services, advisory services and business consultancy.

The main objective of the ICICI was to meet the needs of the industry for long-term funds in the private sector.

Apart from this, the Industrial Reconstruction Corporation of India (IRCI) established in 1971 with the main objective of revival and rehabilitation of viable sick units and was converted in to the Industrial Reconstruction Bank of India (IRBI) in 1985 with more powers.

Development banks have been established at the state level too. At present in India, 18 State Financial Corporation's (SFCs) and 26 State Industrial Investment/Development Corporations (SIDCs) are functioning to look over the development of banking in respective areas /states.

Specialized Banks

In India, there are some specialized banks, which cater to the requirements and provide overall support for setting up business in specific areas of activity. They engage themselves in some specific area or activity and thus, are called specialized banks. There are three important types of specialized banks with different functions:

Export Import Bank of India (EXIM Bank): The Export-Import (EXIM) Bank of India is the principal financial institution in India for coordinating the working of institutions engaged in financing export and import trade. It is a statutory corporation wholly owned by the Government of India. It was established on January 1, 1982 for the purpose of financing, facilitating and promoting foreign trade of India. This specialized bank grants loans to exporters and importers and also provides information about the international market. It also gives guidance about the opportunities for export or import, the risks involved in it and the competition to be faced, etc.

The main functions of the EXIM Bank are as follows:

(*i*) Financing of exports and imports of goods and services, not only of India but also of the third world countries

(*ii*) Financing of exports and imports of machinery and equipment on lease basis

(*iii*) Financing of joint ventures in foreign countries

(*iv*) Providing loans to Indian parties to enable them to contribute to the share capital of joint ventures in foreign countries

(*v*) To undertake limited merchant banking functions such as underwriting of stocks, shares, bonds or debentures of Indian companies engaged in export or import

(*vi*) To provide technical, administrative and financial assistance to parties in connection with export and import.

Small Industries Development Bank of India

This specialized bank grant loan to those who want to establish a small-scale business unit or industry. Small Industries Development Bank of India (SIDBI) was established in October 1989 and commenced its operation from April 1990 with its Head Office at Lucknow as a development bank, exclusively for the small scale industries. It is a central government undertaking. The prime aim of SIDBI is to promote and develop small industries by providing them the valuable factor of production finance. Many institutions and commercial banks supply finance, both long-term and short-term, to small entrepreneurs. SIDBI coordinates the work of all of them.

Functions of Small Industries Development Bank of India (SIDBI):

(*i*) Initiates steps for technology adoption, technology exchange, transfer and upgradation, and modernisation of existing units.

(*ii*) SIDBI participates in the equity type of loans on soft terms, term loan, working capital both in rupee and foreign currencies, venture capital support, and different forms of resource support to banks and other institutions.

(*iii*) SIDBI facilitates timely flow of credit for both term loans and working capital to SSI in collaboration with commercial banks.

(*iv*) SIDBI enlarges marketing capabilities of the products of SSIs in both domestic and international markets.

(*v*) SIDBI directly discounts and rediscounts bills with a view to encourage bills culture and helping the SSI units to realise their sale proceeds of capital goods/equipment and components etc.

(*vi*) SIDBI promotes employment oriented industries especially in semi-urban areas to create more employment opportunities so that rural-urban migration of people can be checked.

National Bank for Agricultural and Rural Development

It was established on 12 July 1982 by a special Act by the parliament. This specialized bank is a central or apex institution for financing agricultural and rural sectors. It can provide credit, both short-term and long-term, through regional rural banks. It provides financial assistance, especially, to co-operative credit, in the field of agriculture, small-scale industries, cottage and village industries handicrafts and allied economic activities in rural areas. Its important functions are:

(*a*) Takes measures towards institution building for improving absorptive capacity of the credit delivery system, including monitoring, formulation of rehabilitation schemes, restructuring of credit institutions, training of personnel, etc.

(*b*) Co-ordinates the rural financing activities of all institutions engaged in developmental work at the field level and maintains liaison with Government of India, State Governments, Reserve Bank of India (RBI) and other national level institutions concerned with policy formulation.

(*c*) Undertakes monitoring and evaluation of projects refinanced by it.

(*d*) NABARD refinances the financial institutions which finances the rural sector.

(*e*) The institutions which help the rural economy, NABARD helps to develop.

(*f*) NABARD also keeps a check on its client institutes.

(*g*) It regulates the institution which provides financial help to the rural economy.

(*h*) It provides training facilities to the institutions working the field of rural upliftment.

(*i*) It regulates the cooperative banks and the RRB.

Indian Bank-like Financial Institutions

In India, there are some bank-like financial institutions that provide financial services. There are two types of such institutions that are important to the development of India:

1. Microfinance Institutions: Microfinance Institutions are bank-like financial institutions that providing financial services, such as microcredit, microsavings or micro insurance to poor people.

In addition, they also perform the following important functions:

1. Provide financing facilities, with or without collateral security, in cash or in kind, for such terms and subject to such conditions as may be prescribed, to poor persons for all types of economic activities including housing, but excluding business in foreign exchange transactions.
2. To buy, sell and supply on credit to poor persons industrial and agricultural inputs, livestock, machinery and industrial raw materials.
3. To provide professional advice to poor persons regarding investments in small business and such cottage industries as may be prescribed;

2. Development Financial Institutions (DFIs): DFIs are specialized financial institutions the Government established to promote investments in the manufacturing and agricultural sectors.

Their functions include:

1. Extending financial assistance in the form of medium- and long-term loans, participating in equity capital, underwriting and wherever relevant, acting as issuing house for public shares issues and providing guarantees for loans.

2. Specialize in medium- and long-term financing in addition to supplying financial services not normally provided by commercial banks and finance companies.
3. In addition, they help in identifying new projects, participate in their promotion, and where appropriate, provide ancillary financial, technical and managerial advice.

Banks, Year of Establishment and Head Office

Name of the Banks	Year of Establishment	Head Office
Allahabad Bank	24 April, 1865	Kolkata, West Bengal
Andhra Bank	20 November, 1923	Hyderabad, Andhra Pradesh
Bank of Baroda	20 July, 1908	Vadodara, Gujarat
Bank of India	7 September, 1906	Mumbai, Maharashtra
Bank of Maharashtra	16 September, 1935	Pune, Maharashtra
Bank of Rajasthan	1943	Udaipur, Rajasthan
Canara Bank	1906	Bengaluru, Karnataka
Central Bank of India	21 December, 1911	Mumbai, Maharashtra
Corporation Bank	12 March, 1906	Mangalore, Karnataka
Dena Bank	26 May, 1938	Mumbai, Maharashtra
Federal Bank	1945	Kerala
HDFC Bank	August, 1994	Mumbai, Maharashtra
ICICI Bank	June, 1994	Mumbai, Maharashtra
IDBI Bank	July, 1964	Mumbai, Maharashtra
Indian Bank	15 August, 1907	Chennai, Tamil Nadu
Indian Overseas Bank	10 February, 1937	Chennai, Tamil Nadu
J & K Bank	1 October, 1938	Sri Nagar, J & K
Karur Vysya Bank	1916	Karur, Tamil Nadu
Lakshmi Vilas Bank	3 November, 1926	Karur, Tamil Nadu
Oriental Bank of Commerce	19 February, 1943	Gurgaon, Haryana
Punjab and Sind Bank	24 June, 1908	New Delhi, India
Punjab National Bank	19 May, 1894	New Delhi, India
State Bank of India	1 July, 1955	Mumbai, Maharashtra
State Bank of Hyderabad	8 August, 1941	Hyderabad, Andhra Pradesh
State Bank of Mysore	2 October, 1913	Bengaluru, Karnataka
State Bank of Patiala	1917	Patiala, Punjab
State Bank of Travancore	12 September, 1945	Trivandrum, Kerala
South Indian Bank	1929	Thrissur, Kerala
Syndicate Bank	1925	Manipal, Karnataka
UCO Bank	6 January, 1943	Kolkata, West Bengal
Union Bank of India	11 November, 1919	Mumbai, Maharashtra
United Bank of India	1950	Kolkata, West Bengal
Vijaya Bank	1931	Bengaluru, Karnataka
Yes Bank	2004	Mumbai, Maharashtra

Bank and Tagline

BANKS	TAGLINES
Allahabad Bank	A TRADITION OF TRUST
Andhra Bank	FOR ALL YOUR NEEDS
Axis Bank	BADHTI KA NAAM ZINDAGI
Bank of Baroda	INDIA'S INTERNATIONAL BANK
Bank of India	RELATIONSHIP BEYOND BANKING
Bank of Maharashtra	ONE FAMILY ONE BANK
Bandhan Bank	AAPKA BHALA, SABKI BHALAI
Canara Bank	TOGETHER WE CAN
Central Bank of India	CENTRAL TO YOU SINCE 1911
Corporation Bank	PROSPERITY FOR ALL
Dena Bank	TRUSTED FAMILY BANK
Federal Bank	YOUR PERFECT BANKING PARTNER
HDFC Bank	WE UNDERSTAND YOUR WORLD
IDBI Bank	BANKING FOR ALL
Indian Bank	YOUR TECH-FRIENDLY BANK
Indian Overseas Bank	GOOD PEOPLE TO GROW WITH
IDFC First Bank	BANKING HATKE
Kotak Mahindra Bank	LET'S MAKE MONEY SIMPLE
OBC	WHERE EVERY INDIVIDUAL IS COMMITTED
PNB	THE NAME YOU CAN BANK UPON
SBI	PURE BANKING NOTHING ELSE, WITH YOU-ALL THE WAY
Syndicate Bank	YOUR FAITHFUL AND FRIENDLY FINANCIAL PARTNER
UCO Bank	HONOURS YOUR TRUST
Union Bank of India	GOOD PEOPLE TO BANK WITH
United Bank of India	THE BANK THAT BEGINS WITH "U"
Yes Bank	EXPERIENCE OUR EXPERTISE

MULTIPLE CHOICE QUESTIONS

1. Allahabad Bank was founded on .... by a group of Europeans at Allahabad:
A. July 19, 1865 B. October 2, 1865
C. April 24, 1865 D. October 7, 1961
E. None of these

2. In 1923, the Head Office of the bank was shifted to .... on business considerations:
A. Calcutta B. Chennai
C. Darjeeling D. Patna
E. None of these

3. Allahabad Bank was nationalized on:
A. November 1980 B. 19 July, 1969
C. 15 January, 1971 D. 1 October, 1969
E. None of these

4. In October 1989 .... bank was merged with Allahabad Bank:
A. United Industrial Bank Limited
B. Unit Trust of India Bank Limited
C. New India Bank Limited
D. HDFC Bank Ltd.
E. None of these

5. Headquarter of Allahabad Bank is situated at:
A. New Delhi
B. Allahabad, Uttar Pradesh
C. Kolkata, West Bengal
D. Bhagalpur, Bihar
E. None of these

6. Slogan of Allahabad Bank is:
A. Together We Prosper
B. A Tradition of Trust
C. A Long Tradition of Trust
D. Come with Me
E. None of these

7. In ...., Allahabad Bank has implemented CBS in all its branches:
A. March, 2011 B. March, 2012
C. March, 2013 D. March, 2015
E. None of these

8. Which among the following is correct about the vision and mission of Allahabad Bank?
A. To put the bank on a higher growth path by building a strong customer base through Talent Management, induction of state-of-the-art Technology and through Structural Re-organization
B. To ensure anywhere and any time banking for the customer with latest state-of-the-art technology and by developing effective customer centered relationship and to emerge as a world class service provider through efficient utilization of Human Resources and product innovation.
C. Both of above
D. Either A or B
E. None of these

9. Syndicate Bank was established in .... in Udupi.
A. 1926 B. 1900
C. 1925 D. 1902
E. None of these

10. Udupi is related to abode of Lord ....
A. Hanuman B. Shiva
C. Krishna D. Ganesha
E. None of these

11. Who among the following founded the Syndicate Bank?
A. Upendra Ananth (A businessman)
B. Vaman Kudva (An engineer)
C. T M A Pai (A physician)
D. All of the above
E. None of these

12. The Logo of Syndicate Bank contains picture of:
A. Elephant B. Lion
C. Dog D. Puma
E. None of these

13. Which among the following is correct?
A. Picture of Dog in logo, symbolizing the tradition of faithfulness and friendliness
B. In the logo, orange colour denotes power, energy, enthusiasm, creativity, thoughtfulness and sincerity
C. Yellow colour in the logo, denotes acquisition of knowledge, it is best colour to create enthusiasm for life and can awaken greater confidence and optimism, it helps with decision making as it relates to clarity of thoughts and ideas and it is non - emotional coming from the head rather than the heart.
D. All of the above
E. None of these

14. Headquarter of Syndicate Bank is now situated at:
A. Shimla, Himachal Pradesh
B. Dispur, Assam
C. Manipal, Karnataka
D. Bhopal, Madhya Pradesh
E. None of these

15. Slogan of Syndicate Bank is:
A. You can Faith on us
B. Your Faithful and Friendly Financial Partner
C. Faithfulness Banking
D. At Your Doorstep
E. None of these

16. The Syndicate Bank was nationalized on:
A. 14 November, 1969 B. 19 July, 1969
C. 2 October, 1969 D. 24 May, 1968
E. None of these

17. Which among the following is correct?
A. Syndicate Manipal School of Banking (SMSB) is a joint venture between Syndicate Bank and Manipal Global Education (MAGE).
B. Recently, Syndicate Bank tied up with MAGE for a post graduate diploma course in banking and finance.
C. Under this, bank will select the candidates and they will be completing a 1 year PGDBF course. After the successful completion of the course, these candidates will be appointed as a Scale 1 officer with the bank.
D. All of the above
E. None of these

18. Oriental Bank of Commerce was founded on:
A. 20 February, 1943 B. 19 February, 1943
C. 21 February, 1943 D. 21 February, 2011
E. None of these

19. Headquarter of Oriental Bank of Commerce (OBC) is located at:
A. New Delhi B. Udaypur, Rajasthan
C. Gurgaon, Haryana D. Airoli, Navi Mumbai
E. None of these

20. Slogan of Oriental Bank of Commerce is:
A. Working for a better tomorrow
B. Where every individual is committed
C. We understand your world
D. Belief in Commitment
E. None of these

21. OBC was founded in 1943 in:
A. Lahore B. Rawalpindi
C. Gujjarpur D. Peshawar
E. None of these

22. .... was the first chairman and one of the founder of the OBC:
A. Rai Chand Ram Bahdur
B. Rai Bahadur Lala Sohan Lal
C. Lala Rai Bahadur Singh
D. Either A or C
E. None of these

23. After partition in 1947, OBC had to close down its branches in the newly formed Pakistan and shift its registered office from Lahore to ....
A. Jalandhar B. Amritsar
C. Patiala D. Delhi
E. None of these

24. The bank was nationalized on:
A. 25 August, 1951 B. 19 July, 1969
C. 15 April, 1980 D. 21 July, 1969
E. None of these

25. In 1997, which among the following bank was acquired by OBC?
A. Bari Doab Bank
B. Punjab Cooperative Bank
C. Both of the Above
D. Gramin Bank
E. None of these

26. OBC amalgamated .... bank:
A. Global Trust Bank B. Global Unit Bank
C. Global Standard Bank D. Universal Bank
E. None of these

27. Which among the following products and services are provided by oriental bank of commerce?
A. Insurance Products B. Self-Banking Halls
C. Internet Banking D. ATMs
E. All of the above

28. UTI Bank Limited was actually founded on:
A. 1990 B. 1991
C. 1992 D. 1924
E. None of these

29. Axis Bank was formerly known as:
A. Hind Bank Limited
B. UTI Bank Limited
C. United India Bank Limited
D. Either A or C
E. None of these

30. Headquarter of Axis Bank is located at:
A. Hyderabad, Andhra Pradesh
B. New Delhi
C. Mumbai, Maharashtra
D. Patna, Bihar
E. None of these

31. Slogan of Axis Bank is:
A. Badhti Ka Naam Zindagi
B. Good People to Bank with
C. Hum Hai Na
D. Come with Me
E. None of these

32. Axis Bank was incorporated on .... and get certificate of business on 14th December.
A. 3rd December 1993 B. 15th December 1993
C. 10 December 1993 D. 2 May, 1984
E. None of these

33. .... was the first private sector bank to get a license under the new guidelines issued by the RBI on that time in 1993.
A. SBI
B. Axis Bank
C. Punjab and Sind Bank
D. Canara Bank
E. None of these

34. UTI Bank (Axis Bank) have come together to launch an international cobranded credit card under the .... umbrella.
A. Visa Card B. Master Card
C. Rupay D. Either A or C
E. None of these

35. In .... company name has been changed from UTI Bank Limited to Axis Bank Limited.
A. 2006 B. 2007
C. 2005 D. 2004
E. None of these

36. Axis Bank is a:
A. Private Sector Bank
B. Public Sector Bank
C. Wholly Government Bank
D. Semi Government Bank
E. None of these

37. Axis Bank was the .... Indian private sector bank to set up a branch in China.
A. First B. Second
C. Third D. Sixth
E. None of these

38. Punjab & Sind Bank was founded on:
A. 24 July, 1908 B. 24 June, 1908
C. 19 July, 1908 D. 11 June, 1908
E. None of these

39. Headquarter of Punjab & Sind Bank is located at:
A. New Delhi B. Patiala
C. Chandigarh D. Jaipur
E. None of these

40. Among the following person, major founder of Punjab & Sind bank was:
A. Bhai Vir Singh
B. Sir Sunder Singh Majitha
C. Sardar Tarlochan Singh
D. None of these
E. All of the above

41. The bank was founded on the principle of:
A. Social Commitment to help the weaker section of the society to raise their standard of life.
B. Enhancement and Development of people of punjab only.
C. To collect deposits and use it against british management for patriotic activities.
D. All of the above
E. None of these

42. On .... Punjab & Sind Bank was among six banks that the Government of India nationalized in the second wave of nationalizations.
A. 15 April, 1980 B. 16 April, 1980
C. 17 April, 1980 D. 14 April, 1980
E. None of these

43. .... is a Regional Rural Bank sponsored by Punjab & Sind Bank.
A. Punjab Gramin Bank B. Malwa Bank
C. Sutlej Gramin Bank D. Bihar Gramin Bank
E. None of these

44. The slogan of Punjab & Sind bank is:
A. Blending Modernity with Tradition
B. Honors Your Trust
C. Where service is a way of Life
D. Either A or B
E. None of these

45. Mission statement of bank is:
A. To provide excellent customer service through innovative products and services for different segments of customers using state of the art technology.
B. To dedicate ourselves wholeheartedly for "Sarva Jana Hitai Sarva Jana Sukhai"
C. Both of above
D. Either A or B
E. None of these

46. Bank of Baroda was founded by Maharaja Sayajirao Gaekwad on:
A. 21 July, 1908 B. 20 July, 1908
C. 19 July, 1908 D. 26 July, 1908
E. None of these

47. Bank of Baroda (BoB) founded on 20 July, 1908 under the ....
A. Companies Act of 1897
B. Companies Act of 1898
C. Companies Act of 1899
D. Either B or C
E. None of these

48. Bank of Baroda started with a paid up capital of:
A. ₹ 10 Lakh B. ₹ 5 Lakh
C. ₹ 20 Lakh D. ₹ 50 Lakh
E. None of these

49. Headquarter of BoB is located at:
A. New Delhi B. Gandhi Nagar
C. Vadodara (Baroda) D. Surat
E. None of these

50. Which among the following countries BoB has its branches?
A. Uganda B. United Arab Emirates
C. Fiji Islands D. United Kingdom
E. All of the above

51. Bank of Baroda was nationalized along with 13 other major commercial banks of India on:
A. 20 July, 1969 B. 19 July, 1969
C. 18 July, 1969 D. 1 May, 1969
E. None of these

52. Slogan of Bank of Baroda is:
A. Prosperity for all B. India's International Bank
C. Together we prosper D. Either A or C
E. None of these

53. Which among the following is incorrect about BoB's domestic associates?
A. Baroda Uttar Pradesh Gramin Bank
B. Baroda Rajasthan Gramin Bank
C. Baroda Gujarat Gramin Bank
D. Baroda Lakshadip Gramin Bank
E. None of these

54. The founder of Bank of Baroda, Maharaja Sayajirao Gaekwad belongs to:
A. Maratha Kingdom B. Sikh Kingdom
C. Rajput Kingdom D. Either A or B
E. None of these

55. Which among the following was the Bank of Baroda's first domestic acquisition?
A. New Citizen Bank of India
B. Hind Bank
C. Bank of Rajput
D. Either A or C
E. None of these

56. ICICI stands for:
A. Indian Credit and Investment Corporation of India

B. Investment Corporation In Credit
C. Industrial Credit Investment Corporation of India
D. Either A or B
E. None of these

57. Headquarter of ICICI Bank is located at:
A. Mumbai B. Hyderabad
C. Mysore D. Delhi
E. None of these

58. ICICI bank was originally promoted in .... by ICICI Limited an Indian financial institution, and was its wholly owned subsidiary.
A. 1994 B. 1995
C. 1997 D. 1998
E. None of these

59. ICICI was formed in 1955 at the initiative of:
A. World Bank
B. The Government of India
C. Representatives of Indian Industry
D. All of the above
E. None of these

60. In ...., the Bank of Rajasthan (BOR) was acquired by the ICICI bank.
A. 2010 B. 2011
C. 2012 D. 2009
E. None of these

61. Punjab National Bank was actually born on ....
A. May 21, 1894 B. May 20, 1894
C. May 19, 1894 D. May 27, 1894
E. None of these

62. The 'PNB' open its doors to the general public on:
A. 12 April, 1895 B. 14 April, 1895
C. 16 April, 1895 D. 11 April, 1895
E. None of these

63. .... was the first to open an account with the bank which was housed in the building opposite to the Arya Samaj Mandir in Anarkali in Lahore.
A. Sardar Dayal Singh Majithia
B. Lala Prabhu Dayal
C. Lala Lajpat Rai
D. Mahatma Gandhi
E. None of these

64. On ...., the (PNB) bank officials decided to leave Lahore.
A. March 31, 1947 B. April 30, 1947
C. July 31, 1947 D. May 31, 1947
E. None of these

65. On March 31, 1947 the bank officials decided to leave Lahore and transfer the registered office of the PNB to .... and permission for transfer was obtained from the Lahore High Court on June 20, 1947.
A. Delhi B. Kolkata
C. Pathankot D. Amritsar
E. None of these

66. Which among the following personalities open their accounts with PNB?
A. Jawahar Lal Nehru, Indira Gandhi
B. Gobind Ballabh Pant, Lal Bahadur Shastri
C. Rafi Ahmed Kidwai
D. All of the above
E. None of these

67. Slogan of Punjab National Bank is:
A. A friend you can bank upon
B. The Name You Can Bank Upon
C. You can always bank on us
D. Either A or C
E. None of these

68. Founder of the PNB was:
A. Prabhu Lal B. Hardyal Singh
C. Lala Lajpat Rai D. Knahiya Lal
E. None of these

69. Headquarter of PNB is located at:
A. New Delhi B. Patiala
C. Bhatinda D. Mumbai
E. None of these

70. The Government of India nationalized PNB and 13 other major commercial banks on:
A. 19 July, 1970 B. 19 July, 1971
C. 19 July, 1969 D. 19 July, 1972
E. None of these

71. United Bank of India is one of the .... major banks which were nationalized on July 19, 1969:
A. 14 B. 13
C. 15 D. 21
E. None of the above

72. United Bank of India Limited was formed in ....
A. 1950 B. 1947
C. 1951 D. 1956
E. None of the above

73. United Bank of India Limited was formed in 1950 with the amalgamation of:
A. Comilla Banking Corporation Limited (1914)
B. Begal Central Bank Limited (1918)
C. Comilla Union Bank Limited (1922)
D. Hooghly Bank Limited (1932)
E. All of the above

74. 'United Bank of India' is designated as Lead Bank in several districts and at present it is the Lead Bank in 30 districts in the states of:
A. West Bengal, Meghalaya, Nagaland and Arunachal Pradesh
B. West Bengal, Assam, Manipur and Tripura
C. West Bengal, Jharkhand, Bihar and Uttar Pradesh
D. Either A or C
E. None of the above

75. United Bank of India played a significant role in the spread of banking services in different parts of the country, more particularly in:

A. Eastern and North Eastern India
B. Eastern and Western India
C. Easter and Southern India
D. Either B or C
E. None of the above

76. UBI is also known as the ....
A. Tea Bank B. Coffee Bank
C. Candy Bank D. Either B or C
E. None of the above

77. United Bank of India is also known as the 'Tea Bank' because:
A. of its age - old association with the financing of tea gardens
B. It has been the largest lender to the tea industry
C. It provide land areas for tea plantation
D. All of the above
E. Only A and B

78. The Slogan of 'United Bank of India' is:
A. Your perfect financial banking partner
B. The name you can bank upon
C. The Bank that Begins with "U"
D. Either A or B
E. None of the above

79. Headquarter of United Bank of India is located at:
A. New Delhi B. Kolkata, West Bengal
C. Manipal, Karnataka D. Thrissur, Kerala
E. None of the above

80. Vijaya Bank was founded on ....
A. 23rd October, 1932 B. 23rd October, 1931
C. 23rd October, 1933 D. 23rd October 1930
E. None of the above

81. Vijaya Bank became a scheduled bank in:
A. 1960 B. 1958
C. 1959 D. 1957
E. None of the above

82. Vijaya Bank was nationalized on:
A. 15th April, 1980 B. 19th July, 1969
C. 21 August, 1981 D. 22 June, 1980
E. None of the above

83. Vijaya Bank has a .... tier organizational structure:
A. 4 B. 3
C. 5 D. 2
E. None of the above

84. The Slogan of Vijaya Bank is:
A. The Name You Can Bank Upon
B. A Friend You Can Bank Upon
C. You Can Always Bank on Us
D. Either A or C
E. None of the above

85. Headquarter of 'Vijaya Bank' is located at:
A. Bengaluru, Karantaka B. Mangalore, Karnataka
C. New Delhi D. Mumbai
E. None of the above

86. Expanded form of UCO Bank is:
A. United Cooperative Bank
B. Union Commercial Bank
C. United Commercial Bank
D. Either A or B
E. None of these

87. "Hum Hai Na" is a slogan of which bank?
A. ICICI Bank B. Punjab National Bank
C. Vijaya Bank D. Canara Bank
E. None of these

88. Which of the following bank is the first universal bank established in the country?
A. SBI B. PNB
C. ICICI Bank Limited D. HDFC Bank Limited
E. None of these

89. Laxmi Commercial Bank merged with:
A. Vijaya Bank B. Dena Bank
C. Canara Bank D. SBI
E. None of these

90. Oriental Bank of Commerce has taken over:
A. Kotak Mahindra Bank B. Axis Bank
C. Global Trust Bank D. Either A or C
E. None of these

91. Which was the first Indian bank to open the branch outside India at London in 1946:
A. Punjab National Bank B. SBI
C. Bank of India D. Canara Bank
E. None of these

92. First Public Sector Bank to issue capital to public is:
A. Axis Bank
B. Oriental Bank of Commerce
C. Laxmi Bank
D. Either A or C
E. None of these

93. Urban Cooperative Bank is:
A. Not a Commercial Bank
B. Not a Non-Commercial Bank
C. Listed Bank
D. Either B or C
E. None of these

94. EXIM means:
A. Export and Import Bank of India
B. Exchange in Monetary Transaction
C. Export in Monetary Transaction
D. Either B or C
E. None of these

95. The Export and Import Bank of India Act passed on:
A. 1981 B. 1984
C. 1986 D. 1987
E. None of these

96. EXIM bank offers credit and lines of credit(LOC) to:
A. Foreign Government and Banks

B. Domestic Government and Banks
C. Only Private Sector Banks
D. Either B or C
E. None of these

97. The Headquarter of Punjab National Bank is?
A. Mumbai B. Kolkata
C. New Delhi D. Hyderabad
E. None of these

98. First Bank in India to launch EMI facility on debit cards:
A. SBI B. Axis Bank
C. ICICI Bank D. HDFC Bank
E. None of these

99. The regulator of whole banking in India is:
A. Banking Planning Council
B. Banking Control Unit
C. RBI
D. SBI
E. None of these

100. Which of the following happened to be the first private bank in India to receive an inprinciple approval from RBI?
A. HDFC Bank
B. ICICI Bank
C. Yes Bank
D. United Western Bank
E. None of these

101. Public Sector Banks refers to:
A. More people visit these banks
B. RBI or Government of India or both have at least 51% shares in the Bank
C. Bank run by the government having the directors elected by the public
D. All of the above
E. None of these

102. Largest Public Sector Bank in India is:
A. Allahabad Bank B. ICICI
C. Punjab National Bank D. State Bank of India
E. None of these

103. Public Sector Banks includes:
A. 20 Nationalized Banks + 5 SBI Associates + IDBI
B. 20 Nationalized Banks + SBI + 7 Private Banks
C. 19 Nationalized Banks + SBI + Private Sector Banks + IDBI
D. 12 Nationalized Banks + SBI + IDBI
E. None of these

104. "The Bank that Begins With U" is a slogan of:
A. UCO Bank B. United Bank of India
C. Union Bank D. Canara Bank
E. None of these

105. "Honors Your Trust" is a slogan of:
A. IDBI B. UCO Bank
C. Axis Bank D. SBI
E. None of these

106. The private sector bank which launched FACEBOOK based instant fund transfer service to enable users to send money to friends on social media network is:
A. Kotak Mahindra Bank
B. Syndicate Bank
C. Laxmi Vilas Bank
D. HDFC Bank
E. None of these

107. "Bank of Rajasthan" merged with which bank"?
A. Global Trust Bank
B. ICICI Bank
C. Axis Bank
D. Yes Bank
E. None of these

108. Which bank opened a Lockless branch at Maharashtra to respecting the local customs:
A. State Bank of India
B. UCO Bank
C. Bank of Maharashtra
D. South Indian Bank
E. None of these

109. Note issuing deptt. of RBI should always possess the minimum gold stock of worth:
A. ₹ 200 Crore B. ₹ 150 Crore
C. ₹ 105 Crore D. ₹ 160 Crore
E. None of these

110. The State Bank of India was established under the State Bank of India Act on ....
A. 1935 B. 1948
C. 1955 D. 1952
E. None of these

111. HDFC bank is an example of ....
A. Private sector Indian bank
B. Private sector Foreign bank
C. Public sector bank
D. Nationalized bank
E. None of these

112. The first development financial institution in India that has got merged with a bank is
A. IDBI B. ICICI
C. IDFC D. UTI
E. None of these

113. Infrastructure Development Finance Company was established in
A. 1961 B. 1997
C. 1994 D. 1991
E. None of these

114. EXIM Bank is owned by
A. Govt. of India and RBI jointly
B. RBI and select Commercial Banks jointly
C. Fully owned by Govt. of India

D. Partly by financial institutions
E. None of these

115. Contribution towards Rural Infrastructure Development Fund is made by
A. NABARD and Commercial Banks jointly
B. State Govts. and Govt. of India
C. Only those commercial banks who fail to achieve the stipulated benchmark of agricultural advances and / or priority sector advances
D. Infrastructure Development Finance Company
E. None of these

116. The Apex Co-operative Bank is known as
A. Central Co-operative Bank
B. State Co-operative Bank
C. RRB
D. NABARD
E. None of these

117. The objective of Government to appoint Narsimhan Committee is
A. To strengthen the banking system
B. To improve customer service
C. To strengthen the credit portfolio
D. All the above
E. None of these

118. The following is not a housing finance intermediary agency
A. HDFC B. HUDCO
C. NHB D. SIDCO
E. None of these

119. Industrial Bank also known as:
A. Investment Bank B. State Bank
C. Commercial Bank D. Unit Bank
E. None of these

120. RRBs are coming under
A. Private sector
B. Public sector
C. Co-operative sector
D. Domestic sector
E. None of these

121. Largest nationalized bank of India is
A. Central Bank of India
B. State Bank of India
C. Reserve Bank of India
D. Punjab National Bank
E. None the above

122. The Central Bank of India is
A. Central Bank of India
B. Reserve bank of India
C. Federal Bank of India
D. United Bank of India
E. None the above

123. The main objective of EXIM Bank is to promote
A. Saving habit among public
B. Foreign trade
C. Small scale industries
D. Medium scale industries
E. None of these

124. Federal Reserve is Central Bank of:
A. India B. Pakistan
C. UK D. US
E. None of these

ANSWERS

1	2	3	4	5	6	7	8	9	10
C	A	B	A	C	B	A	C	C	C
11	**12**	**13**	**14**	**15**	**16**	**17**	**18**	**19**	**20**
D	C	D	C	B	B	D	B	C	B
21	**22**	**23**	**24**	**25**	**26**	**27**	**28**	**29**	**30**
A	B	B	C	C	A	E	A	B	C
31	**32**	**33**	**34**	**35**	**36**	**37**	**38**	**39**	**40**
A	A	B	B	B	A	A	B	A	D
41	**42**	**43**	**44**	**45**	**46**	**47**	**48**	**49**	**50**
A	A	C	C	C	B	A	A	C	E
51	**52**	**53**	**54**	**55**	**56**	**57**	**58**	**59**	**60**
B	B	D	A	B	C	A	A	D	A
61	**62**	**63**	**64**	**65**	**66**	**67**	**68**	**69**	**70**
C	A	C	A	A	D	B	C	A	C
71	**72**	**73**	**74**	**75**	**76**	**77**	**78**	**79**	**80**
A	A	E	B	A	A	E	C	B	B

81	82	83	84	85	86	87	88	89	90
B	A	B	B	A	C	A	C	C	C
91	**92**	**93**	**94**	**95**	**96**	**97**	**98**	**99**	**100**
C	B	A	A	A	A	C	C	C	A
101	**102**	**103**	**104**	**105**	**106**	**107**	**108**	**109**	**110**
B	D	D	B	B	A	B	B	A	C
111	**112**	**113**	**114**	**115**	**116**	**117**	**118**	**119**	**120**
A	B	B	C	C	B	A	D	A	B
121	**122**	**123**	**124**						
B	B	B	D						

3. Whether the company has an adequate capital structure and earning prospects.
4. Whether public interest will be served by grant of license to the company.
5. Other issues relating to branch expansion, unbanked area and other aspects.

In respect of foreign banks, (which are incorporated outside India), application for a license to the Reserve Bank of India to open banks/branches in India, would be considered by RBI on satisfying the following conditions apart from the conditions applicable to domestic banks:

(*a*) Whether carrying on of banking business by the company in India will be in public interest

(*b*) Whether the government or the law of the country in which the company is incorporated discriminates against banking companies registered in India

(*c*) Whether the company complies with provisions of the BR Act as applicable to foreign companies.

Section 11 of the Banking Regulation Act stipulates the minimum capital and reserve requirements of a Banking Company, the Reserve Bank of India can stipulate a higher requirement of capital for licensing a company.

As per the provisions of the Banking Regulation Act, 1949 Reserve Bank of India can cancel the licenses granted to any banking company on account of any one or more of the following reasons:

(*i*) The company ceases to carry on banking business in India.

(*ii*) The company fails to comply with any of the conditions imposed under the specific provisions of the Banking Regulation Act.

Before cancellation of a license for non-compliance with any of the conditions, the company has to be given an opportunity for taking necessary steps for complying with or fulfilling the conditions. However, in cases, where the Reserve Bank is of the opinion that delay will be prejudiced to the interests of the depositors or the public then Reserve Bank can take appropriate action. A banking company whose license is cancelled can appeal to the Central Government within 30 days from the date of the order of cancellation.

Branch Licensing

The opening of branches by banks is governed by the provisions of Section 23 of the Banking Regulation Act, 1949. In terms of these provisions, without the prior approval of the Reserve Bank of India (RBI), banks cannot.

- Open a new place of business in India or abroad.
- Cannot shift or change, except within the same city, town or village the location of the existing place of business.

As regards branch licensing, banks have to refer to the guidelines of the Reserve Bank from time to time, including change of premises, shifting of branches to other locations, etc. As regards Regional Rural Banks, the application for permission have to be routed through the National Bank for Agriculture and Rural Development and based on the comments of NABARD, RBI would act accordingly. The Branch Authorisation Policy for commercial banks as on 1st July, 2013 is as under:

Branch Authorisation Policy for Commercial Banks

(*i*) For the purpose of branch authorisation policy, a "branch" means a full-fledged branch, including a specialized branch, a satellite or mobile office, an Extension Counter, an off-site ATM (Automated Teller Machine), administrative office, controlling office, service branch (back office or processing centre) and credit card centre. A call centre will not be treated as a branch.

(*ii*) Domestic scheduled commercial banks (other than RRBs) are permitted to open branches, Administrative offices, Central Processing Centres (CPCs) and Service branches in Tier 2 to Tier 6 centres (with population up to 99,999 as per Census 2001 and in rural, semi-urban and urban centres in North Eastern States and Sikkim, and to open mobile branches in Tier 3 to Tier 6 centres (with population up to 49,999 as per Census 2001) and in rural, semi-urban and urban centres in North Eastern States and Sikkim without permission from Reserve Bank of India in each case, subject to reporting. Since the concept of mobile branches was mooted for rural areas, the general permission granted for operationalising mobile branches in Tier 3 to Tier 6 centres has not been extended to the operationalisation of mobile branches in Tier 2 centres.

(*iii*) With a view to further increasing operational flexibility of banks, domestic scheduled commercial banks (other than RRBs) are permitted to open offices exclusively performing administrative and controlling functions (Regional Offices/Zonal Offices) in Tier 1 Centres without the need to obtain prior permission in each case, subject to reporting.

(*iv*) Opening of branches/Central Processing Centres (CPCs)/Service branches by domestic scheduled commercial banks (other than RRBs) in Tier 1 centres (centres with population of 1,00,000 and above as per 2001 Census) will continue to require prior permission of the Reserve Bank of India, except in the case of North Eastern States and Sikkim, where the general permission would cover Tier-1 centres also.

(*v*) Domestic Scheduled Commercial Banks, while preparing their Annual Branch Expansion Plan (ABEP), should allocate at least 25 per cent of the total number of branches proposed to be opened during a year in unbanked rural (Tier 5 and Tier 6) centres. An unbanked rural centre would mean a rural (Tier 5 and Tier 6) centre that does not have a brick and mortar structure of any scheduled commercial bank for customer based banking transactions.

(*vi*) In view of the requirement for opening at least 25 per cent of the branches under ABEP in unbanked rural centres, it would now not be mandatory to open at least one-third of the total number of branches proposed to be opened in Tier 2 to Tier 6 centres in under-banked districts of under-banked States. However, as there is a continuing need for opening more branches in under-banked districts of under-banked States for ensuring more uniform spatial distribution, banks would be provided incentive for opening such branches. Accordingly, for each branch proposed to be opened in Tier 2 to Tier 6 centres of under-banked districts of under-banked States, excluding such of the rural branches proposed to be opened in unbanked rural centres that may be located in the under-banked districts of under-banked States in compliance with the requirement as indicated above, authorisation will be given for opening of a branch in a Tier 1 centre. This will be in addition to the authorisation given for branches in Tier 1 centres based on the considerations stated above.

(*vii*) Banks may consider front-loading (prioritizing) the opening of branches in unbanked rural centres over a 3 year cycle co-terminus with their Financial Inclusion Plan (2013-16). Credit will be given for the branches opened in unbanked rural centres in excess of the required 25 per cent of the ABEP for the year which will be carried forward for achieving the criteria in the subsequent ABEP/year of the Financial Inclusion Plan (FIP).

CONSTITUTION OF BANKS' BOARD OF DIRECTORS AND THEIR RIGHTS

As per the relevant provisions of the Banking Regulation Act, at least fifty one per cent of the total number of directors should be persons, who have special knowledge or practical experience, with respect of accountancy, agriculture and rural economy, banking, economics, finance, law, etc., The varied exposure and experience of different directors would be useful to the banking company.

The directors of the banking company should not have a substantial interest. As per the provisions of the Banking Regulation Act, the term "substantial interest" would mean that the total shareholding of the said banking company by an individual or his or his spouse or minor child (singly) should not exceed ₹ Five lakhs or ten per cent of the paid up capital of the banking company.

The directors of a banking company should not hold office for more than eight years continuously. The board of the bank is constituted as per the provisions of the BR Act.

BANKS' SHARE HOLDERS AND THEIR RIGHTS

As per the Banking Regulation Act, there is no specified limit on the number of shares to be held by a shareholder in a banking company. While there is no restriction on the holding of number of shares, as far as the voting rights is concerned, but no shareholder can exercise voting rights in respect of the shares held by him/her in excess of ten per cent of the total voting rights of all the shareholders of the banking company. However, this provision does not in any way affect the transfer of shares or the registration of such share transfers.

The Reserve Bank of India has directed banking companies that whenever they receive more than the prescribed percentage of share transfer to one shareholder/party, the Board of the bank should refer to the Reserve Bank. Without the Reserve Bank's acknowledgement/instructions, the Bank's Board cannot transfer such shares to a shareholder/party. This is to ensure that the controlling interest in a banking company is not changed without the knowledge and approval of the Reserve Bank.

Other Issues

According to the directives of the Reserve Bank of India, the details of the Bank's top executives including the CEO, Chairman and Managing Director and others needs to be furnished to the Reserve Bank of India. Also, information regarding the share holding pattern, direct or indirect holding and other relevant details should be furnished.

As regards payment of dividends to the shareholders, banks are required to be guided by the Banking Regulation Act and the directives of the Reserve Bank of India. While declaring dividends banks should consider the NPA levels and other applicable requirements as per the Reserve Bank directives.

CASH – CURRENCY MANAGEMENT

The currency (bank notes) of our country is issued by the Reserve Bank of India. The Reserve Bank has the sole right to issue and management of currency in India under Section 22 of the RBI Act. RBI may issue notes of different denominations as decided by the Central Government, based on the recommendations made by the Central Board of the bank from time to time. Such notes should be legal tender at any place in India.

The Reserve Bank handles the currency management function through its Department of Currency Management in Mumbai. The aggregate value of gold coins, bullion and foreign securities held by RBI should not be below the prescribed limit at any time. The Reserve Bank currency management is handled through two departments viz., the Issue Department and the Banking Department. The issue department should ensure that the aggregate value of the currency notes and bank notes in circulation from time to time should be equivalent to the eligible assets (gold coins, bullion and foreign securities) held by RBI.

Currency Chests

The Reserve Bank of India has made adequate arrangements for the issue of currency notes and distribution of coins and currency notes across India. One of the distribution channel used by the Reserve Bank is Currency Chests. Reserve Bank has authorized selected branches of banks to establish currency chests. In these currency chests, bank notes and coins are stocked/stored on behalf of the Reserve Bank. Currency chests which are managed by banks, store soiled and re-issuable notes and also fresh currency notes. The banks review the currency notes (which are in their view not fit for circulation and forward them to RBI for further action. After re-examining them, RBI if necessary, re-circulate them, otherwise arranges to destroy them, as per their procedures. The issue department co-ordinates with printing presses and mints for its regular supply of notes and coins. It also ensures that notes/coins are distributed through different channels such as Reserve Bank counters, banks, post offices, co-operative banks.

Currency Printing and Coin Minting

The Government of India on the advice of the Reserve Bank of India decides on the various denominations for printing the notes. The Reserve Bank coordinates with the Government in designing the bank notes. Printing of currency notes are handled by the Security Printing and Minting Corporation of India Limited (SPMCIL) and The Bharatiya Reserve Bank Note Mudran Pvt Ltd (BRBNMPL) in their different printing presses set up at Nashik, Devas, Mysore. SPMCIL has mints for coin production at Mumbai, Noida, Hyderabad. The Reserve Bank acts as agent for the Central Government for issue, distribution, withdrawing of the coins.

Reserve Bank of India's concern is on the level of forged notes penetrated into the circulation. The Reserve Bank has been regularly educating the public, banks and others through press releases and display of "Know Your Bank Note". Reserve Bank from time to time circulate information on the security features of the currency notes. Banks are advised to install the required ultra violet machines and counterfeit note detecting machines. Reserve Bank provides training to banks and government treasury offices and issues detailed guidelines on how to detect and take further necessary steps including impounding of such notes.

POWERS TO CONTROL ADVANCES

The core business of a banking company is to lend money in the form of loans and advances. Lending may be for short-term or medium-term or long-term. Lending money can be on secured or unsecured basis to different kinds of borrowers for various purposes.

RBI has to facilitate the flow of an adequate volume of bank credit to industry, agriculture and trade to meet their genuine needs. At the same time, to keep inflationary pressures under check, it has to restrain undue credit expansion and also ensure that credit is not diverted for undesirable purposes. As the central monetary authority, the Reserve Bank's chief function is to ensure the availability of credit to the extent that is appropriate to sustain the tempo of development and promote the maintenance of internal price stability. The Reserve Bank is empowered under the Banking Regulation Act to issue directions to control loans and advances by banking companies. Reserve Bank at its discretion may issue directions to all banking companies or to any particular banking company, The Reserve Bank may determine the policy in respect of banks' loans and advances and issue directions from time to time.

The instruments of credit control are of two types as under:

(*a*) General or Quantitative

(*b*) Selective or Qualitative

Quantitative/General Credit Control

Under the General Credit Control, the instruments often employed by RBI are discussed below:

1. Bank Rate Policy: The Bank rate has been defined in Section 49 of RBI Act as "the standard rate at which it (RBI) is prepared to buy or rediscount bills of exchange or other commercial paper eligible to purchase under this Act. By varying the rate, the RBI can to a certain extent regulate the commercial bank credit and the general credit situation of the country. The impact of this tool has not been very great because of the fact that RBI does not have a mechanism to control the unorganized sector.

2. Reserve Requirements: The Reserve Bank of India is vested with the powers to vary the CRR and SLR as explained above. By varying reserve requirements, the RBI restricts/frees the flow of funds by way of credit to different sectors of the economy. When SLR or CRR is increased by RBI, It reduces commercial banks' capacity to create credit and thus helps to check inflationary pressures.

3. Open Market Operations: Open market operations are a flexible instrument of credit control by means of which the Reserve Bank on its own initiative alters the liquidity position of the bank by dealing directly in the market instead of using its influence indirectly by varying the cost of credit. Open market operations can be carried out by purchases and sales, by Central Bank, of a variety of assets such as government securities (G-sec), commercial bills of exchange, Foreign exchange, gold and even company shares. In practice, however, RBI confines to the purchase and sale purchase of government securities including treasury bills. When the RBI purchases government securities from the banks, the latest deposits with it tend to increase adding to the cash reserves of banks and hence their capacity to expand credit increase. Conversely, when the RBI sells securities to the banks, their deposits with RBI would get reduced, contracting the credit base. The net result would be a contraction of credit and a reduction in money supply.

Repo Rate and Reverse Repo Rate:

Repos: The RBI introduced repurchase auctions (Repos) since December, 1992 with regards to dated Central Government securities. When banking systems experiences liquidity shortages and the rate of interest is increasing, the RBI will purchase Government securities from Banks, payment is made to banks and it improves liquidity and expands credit.

Reverse Repos : Since November, 1996 RBI introduced Reverse Repos to sell Govt. securities through auction at fixed cut-off rates of interest. It provides short-term avenues to banks to park their surplus funds, where there is considerable liquidity and call rate has a tendency to decline. These two rates are, now-a-days, commonly applied for reducing money supply or increasing it.

4. Moral Suasion: Moral Suasion indicates the advice and exhortations given by the Reserve Bank to the banks and other players in the financial system, with a view to regulate and control the flow of credit, generally, or to any one particular segment of the economy. This may be attempted through periodical discussions/communications. With a substantial share of banking business being in the public sector, this tool has proved effective.

5. Direct Action: This technique indicates the denial of the Reserve Bank to extend facilities to the banks which do not follow sound banking principles or where the Reserve Bank feels the capital structure of the bank is very weak. This is not attempted frequently but is used in rare cases involving continual and wilful violations of policies of the Reserve Bank/Govt. of India.

Selective Credit Control

Under the Selective Credit Control, the authority of the Reserve Bank is exercised by virtue of the provisions of Section 21 and 35 A of Banking Regulation Act. The Reserve Bank may give directions to banks generally or to any bank or a group of banks in particular on different aspects of granting credit, namely—

(*a*) the purposes for which advances may or may not be made

(*b*) the margins to be maintained in respect of secured advances

(*c*) the maximum amount of advances or other financial accommodation which may be made by a bank to or the maximum amount of guarantees which may be given by a bank on behalf of any one company, firm, association of persons or individuals, having regard to the bank's financial position such as paid-up capital, reserves and deposits and other relevant considerations, and

(*d*) the rate of interest and other terms of conditions subject to which advances or other financial accommodation may be granted or guarantees may be given.

While the first two instruments control the quantum of credit, the third instrument works as a leverage on the cost of credit. Selective Credit Control is imposed to manage the balance between the supply and demand of the essential commodities. The main purpose of the Selective Credit Control is to restrict the speculative hoarding of essential commodities using bank credit.

Some of the main restrictions on loans and advances are:

(*i*) As per the provisions of the Banking Regulation Act, no banking company in India can grant loans or advances against the security of its own shares

(*ii*) No banking company can hold shares in a company (*a*) as pledge or mortgage in excess of the limit of 30 per cent of the Paid up capital of that company or 30 per cent of the Bank's Paid-up capital and Reserves, whichever is less. No banking company can commit to grant or grant loans or advances to or on behalf of any of its directors

(*iii*) Further restrictions on the loans and advance to the director as a partner, guarantor of any loans and advances

(*iv*) No banking company can grant loans against (*a*) Fixed Deposits of other Banks (*b*) Certificate of Deposits. The restrictions on different types of loans and advance may be imposed from time to time by the Reserve Bank of India according to the requirement of the situation as well.

RBI AS A CONTROLLER OF FOREIGN EXCHANGE

RBI has got the powers under Foreign Exchange Management Act, 1999 (FEMA) to prohibit, restrict and regulate the following:

(*a*) Transfer or issue of any foreign security by a resident of India and by a person residing outside India

(*b*) Transfer or issue of any security or foreign security by any branch, office or agency in India owned by a person outside India

(*c*) Any borrowing or lending in foreign exchange

(*d*) Any borrowing or lending in rupees between a resident in India and a person outside India

(*e*) Deposits between residents in India and residents outside India (*f*) Export, import or holding of currency or currency notes

(*g*) Transfer of immovable property outside India other than a lease not exceeding five years by a person resident in India

(*h*) Acquisition or transfer of immovable property in India other than a lease by a person resident outside India

(*i*) Giving guarantee or surety in respect of any debt obligation or other viability incurred by person resident in India to a person outside India and vice-versa.

The Reserve Bank does not deal in foreign exchange directly with the public. It gives license to certain Scheduled Commercial Banks and other entities to deal in foreign exchange and those are known as authorized dealers (ADs) in foreign exchange.

MONETARY AND CREDIT POLICY

As a part of the Monetary Management, the Reserve Bank of India announces their policies on a regular basis, which is called as Monetary and Credit Policy.

Monetary Policy statement consists of two parts. Part A cover Monetary Policy and is divided into four sections viz.,–

1. Overview of global and domestic macroeconomic developments
2. Outlook and projections for growth, inflation and monetary aggregates
3. Stance of monetary policy and
4. Monetary measures.

Part B deals with the developmental and regulatory policies consisting five sections viz.,

(*a*) Financial Stability
(*b*) Financial Markets
(*c*) Credit Delivery and Financial Inclusion
(*d*) Regulatory and Supervisory Measures and
(*e*) Institutional Developments

The various aspects of global economy and domestic economy and the significant events which took place in the past year, are covered. Further the outlook for the future in respect of global and domestic economies are discussed. The policy also highlights the important risks like inflation risk, current account deficit and the monetary measures to manage such and other risks are covered. Added to these, the issues and policy measures relating to financial stability, financial markets, control measures through regulations and supervision are also covered. The Policy also indicates the quarterly review period. Various initiatives taken by the Reserve Bank of India as Regulator and Supervisor in the Indian Banking Scenario are also highlighted. It also includes the credit delivery and other issues relating to priority sector lending. The IT initiatives and the related issues are also discussed.

The Monetary policy outlines the various measures taken and expected to be taken by the Reserve Bank of India in their role as the Monetary Management.

AUDIT AND INSPECTION OF BANKING COMPANY

Audit

The balance sheet and the profit and loss account of a banking company have to be audited as stipulated under Section 30 of the Banking Regulation Act. Every banking company's account needs to be verified and certified by the Statutory Auditors as per the provisions of legal frame work.

The powers, functions and duties of the auditors and other terms and conditions as applicable to auditors under the provisions of the Companies Act are applicable to auditors of the banking companies as well. The audit of banking companies books of accounts calls for additional details and certificates to be provided by the auditors. They include:

Whether or not

- information and explanation, required by the auditor were found to be satisfactory
- the transaction of the company, as observed by the auditor were within the powers of the company
- profit and loss account shows a true picture of the profit or loss for the period for which the books have been audited and any other observations to be brought to the notice of the shareholders;

Special responsibility is cast on the bank auditor in certifying the bank's balance sheet and profit and loss account, since that reflects the sound financial position of the banking company.

Apart from the balance sheet audit, Reserve Bank of India is empowered by the provisions of the Banking Regulation Act to conduct/order a special audit of the accounts of any banking company. The special audit may be conducted or ordered to be conducted, in the opinion of the Reserve Bank of India that the special audit is necessary;

(*i*) in the public interest and/or

(*ii*) in the interest of the banking company and/or

(*iii*) in the interest of the depositors. The Reserve Bank of India's directions can order the bank to appoint the same auditor or another auditor to conduct the special audit. The special audit report should be submitted to the Reserve Bank of India with a copy to the banking company. The cost of the audit is to be borne by the banking company.

Inspection

As per Sec 35 of the Banking Regulation Act, the Reserve Bank of India is empowered to conduct an inspection of any banking company. After conducting the inspection of the books, accounts and records of the banking company a copy of the inspection report to be furnished to the banking company. The banking company, its directors and officials are required to produce the books, accounts and records as required by the RBI inspectors, also the required statements and/or information within the stipulated time as specified by the inspectors.

Government's Role: The Central Government may direct the Reserve Bank to conduct inspection of any banking company. In such cases, a copy of the report of inspection needs to be forwarded to the Central Government. On review of the inspection report, the Central Government can take appropriate action. In the opinion of the Central Government, if the affairs of the banking company is not being carried out in the interests of the banking company, public and or depositors, the Central Government may (*i*) prohibit the banking company to accept fresh deposits (*ii*) direct the Reserve Bank to apply for winding up of the banking company under the provisions of the Banking Regulation Act. Before taking action, the Government has to give an opportunity to the banking company to explain their stand. Based on the response, the Government can initiate appropriate action as required.

Scrutiny: Apart from inspecting the books and accounts of the company, the Reserve Bank can conduct scrutiny of the affairs and the books of accounts of any banking company. Like in the case of inspection, the Reserve Bank can handle the scrutiny as required.

SUPERVISION AND CONTROL

Board for Financial Supervision

To have better supervision and control, a separate board was constituted namely "The Board for Financial Supervision" as per the provisions of the Reserve Bank of India. The Board has the jurisdiction over the banking companies, Nationalised banks, State Bank of India and its subsidiaries. The members of the Board are: Governor of the Reserve Bank of India as the chairperson, Deputy Governors of the Reserve Bank of India, and one of the deputy governors should be nominated by the Governor as the full time vice chairman, Four directors from the Central Board of the Reserve Bank nominated by the Governor as members.

Functions and Powers: The Board performs the functions and exercises the powers of supervision and inspection under the Reserve Bank of India Act, in respect to different banking companies. The Board is assisted by the department of supervision. The Board has to report to the Central Board on half yearly basis. The Board meets on a monthly basis, with at least one meeting in a month. The Board has powers to constitute sub committees, like the executive committee. The vice chairman of the Board is the ex-officio chairman of the committee.

Apart from the above, the Governor may constitute an advisory committee to offer advice from time to time to the Board. The council will have at least five members who have special knowledge in different areas like accountancy, law, banking, economics, finance and management. The Governor presides over the meetings and the other members of the council are the vice chairman and other members.

WINDING UP – AMALGAMATION AND MERGERS OF BANKS

A banking company may be amalgamated with another banking company as per BR Act. The banking companies have to prepare a scheme of amalgamation, the draft copy of the scheme of amalgamation covering terms and conditions needs to be placed separately by the companies to their shareholders. Each shareholder needs to be given notice, The scheme of amalgamation should be approved by a resolution passed by majority of members representing two-thirds in value of the shareholders of each company present in person or by proxy. A shareholder, who votes against the scheme of amalgamation and gives necessary notice, may claim the value of his shares from the banking company, in case the scheme is sanctioned by the Reserve Bank. Once the scheme is sanctioned by the Reserve Bank then the assets and liabilities of the amalgamated company pass on to the other company with which it is to be amalgamated. The order of the sanction of amalgamation by Reserve Bank will be the conclusive proof of amalgamation.

In case the Central Government orders amalgamation of two companies, such amalgamation would take place after consultation with the Reserve Bank.

Under Sec 45 of the Banking Regulation Act the Reserve Bank can apply to the Central Government for an order of moratorium in respect of any company, on account of certain valid reasons. After considering various aspects, the Central Government may think it fit and proper to impose the moratorium. The period of moratorium can be extended from time to time for a maximum period of six months. During the period of moratorium, the banking company would not be allowed to make any payments to the depositors or discharge any liabilities or obligations to any other creditors unless otherwise directed by the Central Government in the order of moratorium or at any time thereafter.

Scheme of Amalgamation

During the period of moratorium, the Reserve Bank may prepare a scheme of reconstruction or amalgamation. Such a scheme may be prepared by the Reserve Bank due to any one or more of the following aspects: 1. In the public interest 2. In the interests of the depositors 3. To secure proper management of the banking company 4. In the interest of the banking system of the country. As per the various provisions, the scheme of amalgamation would be worked out and implemented. A copy of the draft of the scheme should be sent to the government and also to the banking company (transferee bank) and others concerned with the amalgamation. The Government may sanction with modifications as it may consider necessary, after that the scheme should come into effect from the date of the sanction.

Once the scheme is sanctioned by the Central Government, it would be binding on the banking company, transferee bank and the members, depositor and other creditors and others as per the sanction. The sanction by the Central Government is the conclusive proof that the amalgamation or reconstruction has been carried out with the accordance with the provisions of the relevant sections of the Act. Consequent to amalgamation, the transferee bank should carry on the business as required by the law.

The Central Government may order moratorium on the banking companies on the application of the Reserve Bank. The Reserve Bank may also apply to High Court for winding up of a banking company when the banking company is not able to pay its debts and also in certain other circumstances. The High Court would decide the case based on the merits of the case a moratorium order would be passed. After passing the order the court may appoint a special officer to take over the custody and control of the assets, books, etc. of the banking company in the interests of the depositors and customers. During the period of moratorium, the Reserve Bank is not satisfied with the functioning of the bank, and in its opinion the affairs of the banking company is being conducted not in the interests of the depositors and customers, Reserve Bank may apply to the High Court for winding up of the company.

Winding up by High Court

The High Court may order winding up of a banking company on account of (a) The banking company is unable to pay its debts (b) An application of winding up had been made by the Reserve Bank under the provisions of the Banking Regulation Act (Sec37 and 38).

The RBI is to make an application for winding up (under Sec 38 of BR Act) and under Sec 35 (4) if directed by the Central Government. Central Government may give such direction, based on the report of inspection or scrutiny made by the Reserve Bank, and on account of the situation that the affairs of the bank are being conducted to the detriment of the interests of the depositors. However, before giving such direction, the banking company would be given an opportunity to make a representation in connection with the inspection/scrutiny report.

In the following circumstances, the Reserve Bank of India can apply for winding up of a banking company:

- Non-compliance with the requirements of Sec 11 regarding minimum paid up capital and reserves.
- Prohibition to accept fresh deposits under Sec 35(4) of the Banking Regulation Act or Sec 42 (3A)(b) of the Reserve Bank of India Act.
- Failure to comply with the requirements of the applicable provisions of the Banking Regulation Act and the Reserve Bank of India Act.

Official Liquidator: Sec 38A of the Banking Regulation Act provides for appointment of an official liquidator attached to the High Court by the Central Government, to conduct the winding up proceedings of a banking company.

Reserve Bank as Liquidator

If Reserve Bank of India applies to the High Court, the Reserve Bank, State Bank or any other bank as notified by the Central Government or an individual may also be appointed as the official liquidator. Within the stipulated time, the liquidator is required to make a preliminary report regarding the availability of the assets to make preferential payments as per the provisions of the Companies Act and for discharging liabilities to depositors and other creditors. Within the stipulated time, the liquidator is required to give notice calling for claims for preferential payment and other claims from every secured and unsecured creditors. However, depositors need not make claims. The claims of every depositor of a banking company is deemed to have been filed for the amount as reflected in the books of the banking standing in his/her credit.

Voluntary Winding Up: Voluntary winding up would be permitted only when the Reserve Bank has certified that the banking company will not be able to pay in full all its debts as they accrue.

SUBMISSION OF RETURNS TO RBI

Each banking company has to prepare and furnish returns to the Reserve Bank under various provisions of the Banking Regulation Act and the Reserve Bank of India Act. The returns which are to be submitted to RBI are discussed below:

1. Return of Liquid Assets: Every banking company has to submit a return of its liquid assets as per the provisions of the Banking Regulation Act. The return should contain particular of assets and the demand and time liabilities as at the close of business of each alternate Friday. In case such Friday is a holiday then as at the close of business of the preceding working day. The Reserve Bank is also empowered to require a banking company to furnish returns showing particulars of assets and demand and time liabilities as at the close of each day of the month.

2. Monthly Returns: Every month, a banking company has to submit a monthly return to the Reserve Bank as per the provisions of the Banking Regulation Act, 1949. This return is prepared as on the last Friday of the previous month, and the return should be submitted before the end of the month succeeding to which it relates. Reserve Bank can call for information and statements at any time relating to the business or affairs of the banking company.

3. Accounts and Balance Sheet: The annual accounts and balance sheet have to be submitted to the Reserve Bank within three months from the end of the period for which they relate.

4. Return of Assets in India: A banking company has to submit to Reserve Bank under the Banking Regulations Act, a quarterly return regarding its assets in India. The return is to be submitted within one month of the end of the quarter.

5. Return of Unclaimed Deposits: Under Sec 26 of the Banking Regulation Act a banking company has to submit within thirty days of the close of each calendar year a return on unclaimed deposits (not operated for ten years).

6. Return of CRR of Non-Scheduled Banks: Every banking company (non-scheduled bank) has to furnish a return to the Reserve Bank of India under Sec 18 (i) of the Banking Regulation Act in respect of cash reserve.

7. Fortnightly Return in Form A (CRR): Under Section 42 (2) of the RBI Act, 1934, all SCBs are required to submit to Reserve Bank a provisional Return in Form 'A' within 7 days from the expiry of the relevant fortnight and the final report to be submitted to RBI within 20 days from expiry of the relevant fortnight. Based on the recommendation of the Working Group on Money Supply: Analytics and Methodology of Compilation, all SCBs in India are required to submit this report. Memorandum to form 'A' return giving details about paid-up capital, reserves, time deposits comprising short-term (of contractual maturity of one year or less) and long-term (of contractual maturity of more than one year), certificates of deposits, NDTL, total CRR requirement etc., Annexure A to Form 'A' return showing all foreign currency liabilities and assets and Annexure B to Form 'A' return giving details about investment in approved securities, investment in non-approved securities, memo items such as subscription to shares/debentures/bonds in primary market and subscriptions through private placement. For reporting in Form 'A' return, banks should convert their overseas foreign currency assets and bank credit in India in foreign currency in four major currencies viz., US dollar, GBP, Japanese Yen and Euro into rupees at RBI Reference Rates announced on its website from time to time.

8. Return in Form VIII (SLR):

(*i*) Banks should submit to the Reserve Bank before 20th day of every month, a return in Form VIII showing the amounts of SLR held on alternate Fridays during immediate preceding month with particulars of their DTL in India held on such Fridays or if any such Friday is a Public Holiday under the Negotiable Instruments Act, 1881, at the close of business on preceding working day.

(*ii*) Banks should also submit a statement as annexure to Form VIII return giving daily position of; (*a*) assets held for the purpose of compliance with SLR, (*b*) the excess cash balances maintained by them with RBI in the prescribed format, and (*c*) the mode of valuation of securities.

9. Report on NRE Deposits: NRD-CSR software package being used by the banks for submission of detailed monthly data on non-resident deposits to the Reserve Bank, has been replaced by *extensible Business Reporting Language (XBRL)* platform to provide validations for processing requirement in respect of existing NRD schemes, improve data quality, enhance the security-level in data submission, and enable banks to use various features of XBRL-based data submission, and tracking.

10. Priority Sector Lending—Revised Reporting System: Disbursement to be reported in the monthly and yearly reporting formats is defined as under:

(*i*) **Cash credit/over draft account and running accounts of similar nature:** Debit summation minus interest and other charges or sanctioned limit, whichever is lower for the particular period under consideration (monthly/quarterly/half yearly/yearly).

(*ii*) **Term Loans:** Debit summation minus interest and other charges for the particular period under consideration (monthly/quarterly/half yearly/yearly).

CORPORATE GOVERNANCE

Corporate Governance is an integral part of the management control system which reflects the corporate's strategy in maintaining the image and reputation of the company. In today's global competition, banks have to be careful in ensuring their integrity in dealing with the financial aspects of their clients. In this respect, a dynamic corporate governance practices are needed.

Corporate Governance means to ensure that the transparency, accountability in the interests of the stakeholders such as the shareholders, employees, clients and others. Over the years ever since the Cadbury Committee in 1992 came out with set of guidelines on the topic of Corporate Governance, many more committees have highlighted the need for a changing corporate governance practices with the changing time and business environment.

Effective Corporate Governance Practices

The objectives are:

(*i*) To promote transparent and efficient markets which are consistent with the rule of Law.

(*ii*) To protect and facilitate the exercise of shareholders' rights.

(*iii*) Timely and accurate disclosures to be made on all important issues relating to the corporation covering the financial situation, performance, ownership and governance of the company.

Corporate Governance in Banks

Over the years, the Reserve Bank of India as Supervisor of Banking companies in India has been playing significant role in ensuring the sound corporate governance practices which are followed by the banking companies. RBI's various guidelines in mergers and acquisitions, pattern of shareholding, restrictions on various issues, are some of the examples of RBI's role in the corporate governance practices of banks in India.

PREVENTION OF MONEY LAUNDERING ACT, 2002 (PMLA)

Laundering means acquiring, owning, possessing or transferring any proceeds (of money) of crime or knowingly entering into any transaction related to proceeds of the crime either directly or indirectly or concealing or aiding in the concealment of the proceeds or gains of crime, within or outside India. It is a process for conversion of money obtained illegally to appear to have originated from legitimate sources. Invariably, there are three stages through which money laundering takes place.

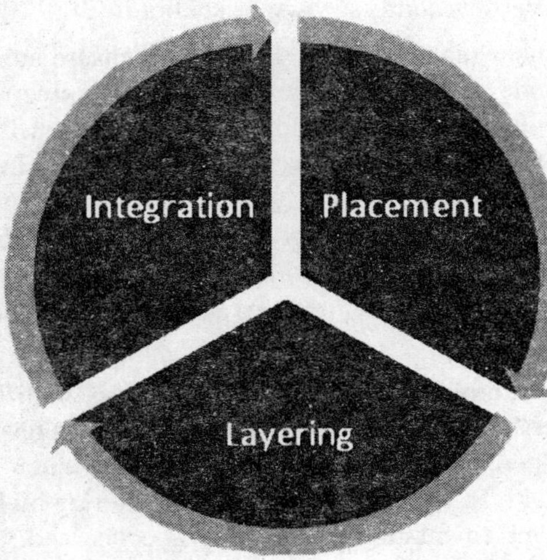

(*a*) The first step is called the placement, when the cash is deposited in the domestic banks or is used to buy goods such as precious metals, work of art, etc.

(*b*) The second step is called the layering. Once the funds are entered into the financial system (banks), the funds are converted by transfers to different destinations. This stage is called as layering. At different locations bank accounts are opened and the funds are transferred as quickly as possible (some time breaking into series of small transactions to escape from the limits set up by banks for cash transactions).

(*c*) The last stage is called the integration. In this stage, the launderer attempts to justify that the money obtained through illegal activities is legitimate. Through different methods attempts are made at this stage, like using front offices of the companies, using the tax haven and off shore units, using these funds as security for loans raised, etc.

The Prevention of Money Laundering Act, 2002 (PMLA) aimed at combating money laundering in India with three main objective to prevent and control money laundering to confiscate and seize the property obtained from laundered money, and to deal with any other issue connected with money laundering in India. The Act provides that whosoever directly or indirectly attempts to indulge or knowingly assists or knowingly is a party or is actually involved in any process or activity connected with the proceeds of crime and projective it as untainted property should be guilty offences of money laundering. For the purpose of money laundering, the PMLA identifies certain offences under the Indian Penal Code, the Narcotic Drugs and Psychotropic Substances Act, the Arms Act, the Wild Life (Protection) Act, the Immoral Traffic (Prevention) Act and the Prevention of Corruption Act, the proceeds of which would be covered under this Act.

To combat the menace of aforesaid offences of money laundering the Government is entrusting the work relating to investigation, attachment of property/proceeds of crime relating to the scheduled offences under the Act and filling of complaints etc. to the Directorate of Enforcement, which currently deals with offences under the Foreign Exchange Management Act.

Role of Banks

All banks (including RRBs and Co-operative banks) are covered under the above Act. The money launderers may open deposit accounts with banks in fake names and banks will be required to be vigilant for not becoming a party to such transactions. With a view to preventing banks from being used, intentionally or unintentionally, by criminal elements for money laundering or terrorist financing, it is clarified that whenever there is suspicion of money laundering or terrorist financing or when other factors give rise to a belief that the customer does not, in fact, pose a low risk, banks should carry out full scale customer due diligence (CDD) before opening an account.

Similarly, they have to observe the norms regarding record keeping, reporting, account opening and monitoring transactions. The Act has made various provisions regarding money laundering transactions which include maintenance of record of all transactions relating to money laundering. Records relating to such transactions should be preserved for 10 years from date of cessation of transactions between the client and the banking company.

Govt. has set up Financial Intelligence Unit (FIU-IND) to track and curb money laundering offences. Banks, financial institutions, stock brokers, etc. are to report non-cash transactions (cheques/drafts) totalling to over ₹ 1 crore a month and cash transactions of ₹ 10 lakh a month, to Financial Intelligence Unit.

Non-adherence of the provision of the Act will be an offence and these offences are cognizable/non-bailable. Punishment would be rigorous imprisonment for not less than 3 years but up to 7 years and fine as per the gravity of the offence. Enforcement Directorate has been made the designated authority to track cases of money laundering.

As per the Act, banking companies, financial institutions and intermediaries should maintain record of transactions, identity of clients etc. A director appointed by the Central Government has the right to call for records and impose penalties in case of failure on the part of the banking companies and other financial intermediaries. Central Government in consultation with the Reserve Bank has framed rules regarding the maintenance of records, retention period of records, verification of the identity of client (KYC norms) and submitting the details and information to the director when called upon to do so.

To ensure compliance under the PMLA, banking companies should strictly comply with the KYC norms without any deviation. KYC norms are applicable for both the new and existing client accounts. One of the objective of KYC norms is the clear identity of the customer. The identity does not end with obtaining the required identity proof like, verification and retaining copies of PAN card, Passport, AADHAR card, and other relevant documents as specified. Further to obtaining the required application forms, the photo identity and address proof documents, banks are required to ensure that all the relevant details like status of the customer, and relevant documentary verification to confirm the status, declaration about the multiple bank account details, source of income, source of funds, and expected income and activities in the accounts etc., are obtained and bank records are updated with these details. Banks should also accordingly set up internal control checking systems, whereby the system can identify and caution the bank officials about unusual transactions, at the time of input stage to enable the officials to take appropriate action. Banks should be very careful to avoid incidents of Money Laundering at the entry level itself. This precautionary action on the part of bank officials and the inbuilt warning system in the computers of banking companies, would go a long way to control the menace of Money Laundering. Banking companies should also ensure that as part of effective control system, that all the employees at all levels should be informed and trained to practice anti money laundering to safe-guard not only the customers funds, but also to be proactive to avoid incidents of money laundering. The internal auditors, external auditors including the Statutory Auditors and the Reserve Bank of India inspectors should include the verification of the Anti- Money Laundering procedures as part of their audit and inspection of banking companies. They should ensure that all the required guidelines and directives in respect of Anti Money Laundering including the adherence to the KYC norms, monitoring of accounts, maintenance of records, reporting of high volume transactions, suspicious transactions, filing of required returns to the authorities and proper control mechanism are adhered to. The executives should ensure monitoring and controlling of such incidents. Further the computer systems should be upgraded with the required checking and cautioning of suspicious and unauthorized transactions at the input stage.

BANKING CODES AND STANDARDS BOARD OF INDIA (BCSBI)

The Banking Codes and Standards Board of India has been registered as a separate society under the Societies Registration Act, 1860. It functions as an independent and autonomous body to monitor and assess the compliance with codes and minimum standards of service to individual customers to which the banks agree to. The Code is a voluntary initiative by a bank and is also a unilateral commitment by the bank to its individual customers to deal with them in a transparent and fair manner in its day to day operations. RBI derives supervisory comfort in case of banks which are members of the Board. Members of public can contact the BCSBI either on its website or at its postal address. Website address: www.bcsbi.org.in

The main function of the Board is to ensure adherence to the "Code of Bank's Commitment to Customers". The Code is voluntary and sets minimum standards of banking practices for banks to follow when they are dealing with individual customers in their day-to-day operations. The Code is not only meant to provide protection to the individual customers but is also expected to generate awareness in the common man about his rights as a consumer of banking services.

Banks are required to register themselves with BCSBI as members and have the Code adopted by their respective boards. Thereafter, the banks will have to enter into a covenant with BCSBI, binding them to monitoring by BCSBI as far as implementation of the code is concerned.

Any Scheduled Commercial Bank is eligible to become member of BCSBI. The Code represents each member bank's commitment to minimum standards of service to individual customers in relation to products and services offered by the bank, *e.g.*

Deposit accounts

Safe deposit lockers

Settlement of accounts of deceased account holders

Foreign exchange services

Remittances within India

Loans and advances and guarantees

Credit cards

Internet banking

In these areas the Code, inter alia, dwells upon

Interest rates

Tariff schedule

Terms and conditions governing relationship between the bank and the customer

Compensation for loss, if any, to the customer due to the acts of omission or commission on the part of the bank

Privacy and confidentiality of the information relating to the customer

Norms governing advertisements, marketing and sales by banks

Every Member bank is required to:

Have a Help desk/Helpline at the branch.

Have a Code Compliance officer at each Controlling office above the level of the branch.

Display at each branch name and contact number of Code Compliance Officer.

Display Name and address of the Banking Ombudsman.

In case, a customer is not provided services as promised in the Code, he can first approach the help desk of the branch/bank. In case the issue is not resolved, the Code Compliance Officer of the bank may be approached by the complainant. In case the issue is still not resolved to the satisfaction of the customer he should take it up with the Banking Ombudsman.

THE BANKING OMBUDSMAN SCHEME

The Banking Ombudsman Scheme enables an expeditious and inexpensive forum to bank customers for resolution of complaints relating to certain services rendered by banks. The Banking Ombudsman Scheme is introduced under Section 35 A of the Banking Regulation Act, 1949 by RBI with effect from 1995.

The Banking Ombudsman is a senior official appointed by the Reserve Bank of India to redress customer complaints against deficiency in certain banking services. As on date, fifteen Banking Ombudsmen have been appointed with their offices located mostly in state capitals. The addresses and contact details of the Banking Ombudsman offices have been provided in the annex. All Scheduled Commercial Banks, Regional Rural Banks and Scheduled Primary Co-operative Banks are covered under the Scheme.

Grounds of Complaints

The Banking Ombudsman can receive and consider any complaint relating to the following deficiency in banking services (including internet banking):

- Non-payment or inordinate delay in the payment or collection of cheques, drafts, bills etc.;
- Non-acceptance, without sufficient cause, of small denomination notes tendered for any purpose, and for charging of commission in respect thereof;
- Non-acceptance, without sufficient cause, of coins tendered and for charging of commission in respect thereof;
- Non-payment or delay in payment of inward remittances;
- Failure to issue or delay in issue of drafts, pay orders or bankers' cheques;
- Non-adherence to prescribed working hours;
- Failure to provide or delay in providing a banking facility (other than loans and advances) promised in writing by a bank or its direct selling agents;
- Delays, non-credit of proceeds to parties accounts, non-payment of deposit or non-observance of the Reserve Bank directives, if any, applicable to rate of interest on deposits in any savings, current or other account maintained with a bank;
- Complaints from Non-Resident Indians having accounts in India in relation to their remittances from abroad, deposits and other bank-related matters;
- Refusal to open deposit accounts without any valid reason for refusal;
- Levying of charges without adequate prior notice to the customer;
- Non-adherence by the bank or its subsidiaries to the instructions of Reserve Bank on ATM/Debit card operations or credit card operations;
- Non-disbursement or delay in disbursement of pension (to the extent the grievance can be attributed to the action on the part of the bank concerned, but not with regard to its employees);
- Refusal to accept or delay in accepting payment towards taxes, as required by Reserve Bank/ Government;
- Refusal to issue or delay in issuing, or failure to service or delay in servicing or redemption of Government securities;
- Forced closure of deposit accounts without due notice or without sufficient reason;
- Refusal to close or delay in closing the accounts;
- Non-adherence to the fair practices code as adopted by the bank or non-adherence to the provisions of the Code of Bank's Commitments to Customers issued by Banking Codes and Standards Board of India and as adopted by the bank;
- Non-observance of Reserve Bank guidelines on engagement of recovery agents by banks;
- Any other matter relating to the violation of the directives issued by the Reserve Bank in relation to banking or other services.

A customer can also lodge a complaint on the following grounds of deficiency in service with respect to loans and advances:

- Non-observance of Reserve Bank Directives on interest rates;
- Delays in sanction, disbursement or non-observance of prescribed time schedule for disposal of loan applications;
- Non-acceptance of application for loans without furnishing valid reasons to the applicant;

- Non-adherence to the provisions of the fair practices code for lenders as adopted by the bank or Code of Bank's Commitment to Customers, as the case may be;
- Non-observance of any other direction or instruction of the Reserve Bank as may be specified by the Reserve Bank for this purpose from time to time.
- The Banking Ombudsman may also deal with such other matter as may be specified by the Reserve Bank from time to time.

There is no cost involved in filing complaints with Banking Ombudsman. The Banking Ombudsman does not charge any fee for filing and resolving customers' complaints.

Miscellaneous Provisions

The amount, if any, to be paid by the bank to the complainant by way of compensation for any loss suffered by the complainant is limited to the amount arising directly out of the act or omission of the bank or ₹ 20 lakhs, whichever is lower.

The Banking Ombudsman may award compensation not exceeding ₹ 1 lakh to the complainant only in the case of complaints relating to credit card operations for mental agony and harassment. The Banking Ombudsman will take into account the loss of the complainants time, expenses incurred by the complainant, harassment and mental anguish suffered by the complainant while passing such award.

MULTIPLE CHOICE QUESTIONS

1. The Securitisation and Reconstruction of Financial Assets and Enforcement of Security Interest Act (SARFASIA) came into effect on............
A. Jan 2002　B. June 2002
C. May 2000　D. April 2001
E. None of these

2. Banking Ombudsman was established in..........
A. 1993　B. 1997
C. 1995　D. 1987
E. None of these

3. .... is a quasi-judicial authority appointed by the RBI to redress customer complaints against certain deficiency in banking services:
A. Banking Ombudsman
B. Consumer redressel
C. Adjudicating authority
D. Either B or C
E. None of these

4. .... in an anti money laundering measure specified in the prevention of money laundering act 2002:
A. SAA　B. FCNR
C. KYC　D. NRE
E. None of these

5. The banking ombudsman scheme is introduced under section .... of banking regulation Act:
A. 35 A　B. 35
C. 25　D. 73
E. None of these

6. The banking ombudsman scheme is introduced by:
A. RBI　B. Prime minister
C. Finance minister　D. President
E. None of these

7. The banking ombudsman scheme working is effect from
A. 1990　B. 1995
C. 2000　D. 2005
E. None of these

8. The amendment to Section 41 of Reserve Bank of India Act, 1934 was carried out of the purpose of:
A. RBI's decision to do away payment of interest on CRR balances
B. empowering NGOs involved in environmental protection
C. asking banks/financial institutions not to use coercive methods for recovery of loans
D. Other than given options
E. None of the above

9. Authority to prescribe retention period of records of banks vests with:
A. IBA　B. RBI
C. GOI　D. SEBI
E. None of these

10. Authorized Dealers for foreign exchange transactions are appointed by:
A. Reserve Bank of India
B. Government of India
C. Individual Banks
D. FEDAI
E. None of these

11. Consent of RBI is necessary before transferring funds from one chest to another; because:
A. RBI is the owner of the Chest
B. RBI arranges transit insurance
C. police protection is arranged
D. details to be kept a secret
E. None of these

12. Currency Chest is the property of:
A. State Bank of India
B. Government of India
C. Reserve Bank of India
D. Private security
E. None of these

13. For violation of FEMA, prosecution is done by:
A. RBI B. DGFT
C. FEDAI D. Enforcement Directorate
E. None of these

14. Format of cheque has been prescribed under:
A. Negotiable Instruments Act, 1881
B. Banking Transactions Act
C. Banking Regulation Act, 1949
D. Both A and C
E. None of the above

15. A bank reconciliation statement is prepared with the help of:
A. bank pass book and bank column of cash book
B. bank pass book and cash column of cash book
C. bank pass book and petty cash book
D. All of the above
E. None of these

16. The main purpose of preparing a Bank Reconciliation Statement is:
A. to know the Cash Book Balance
B. to know the Pass Book Balance
C. to compare the transactions in the Cash Book and Pass Book
D. to correct the Cash Book
E. to reconcile Balance as per Cash Book with the Pass Book Balance

17. Bank holidays under Section 25 of the Negotiable Instruments Act, 1881 are declared by:
A. State Government for the respective State
B. Banking Operations Department
C. Central Government
D. RBI
E. None of these

18. If a bank wants to introduce a new deposit scheme, the same is now approved by:
A. RBI
B. IBA
C. Respective Bank's Board
D. Both A and B
E. None of these

19. Which Act confers on banks their Right of set off:
A. Banking Regulation Act, 1949
B. Reserve Bank of India Act, 1934
C. Negotiable Instruments Act, 1881
D. Indian Contract Act, 1872
E. None of these

20. Which of the following Acts prohibits stapling of bank/currency notes:
A. Section 35A of RBI Act, 1934
B. Section 35A of BRA Act, 1949
C. Section 35A of N I Act, 1881
D. Other than given options
E. None of the above

21. Which of the following provisions empowers RBI to fix service charges on various payment or settlement services of Banks:
A. Section 12 of PMLA Act
B. Section 18 of Payment and Settlement Act, 2007
C. Section 21 of RBI Act, 1934
D. Section 22 of RBI Act, 1934
E. Section 35A, Banking Regulation Act, 1949

22. Banking Industry has been declared as public utility service for purpose of:
A. Negotiable Instruments Act, 1881
B. Reserve Bank of India Act, 1934
C. Banking Regulation Act, 1949
D. Industrial Disputes Act
E. None of these

23. Records, as per Banking Regulation Act, 1949 means:
A. Vouchers
B. Account Opening Forms
C. Ledgers/Registers
D. All of these
E. Other than given options

24. Government of India has granted greater flexibility to RBI in setting Cash Reserve Ratio (CRR) after passing the ...... Amendment Bill:
A. RBI
B. Banking Regulation Act, 1949
C. Finance
D. None of the above
E. Other than given options

25. Interest rates charged by banks are not subject to scrutiny by Courts on the ground of being excessive. It is provided for under Section ...... of Banking Regulation Act, 1949.
A. 18 B. 22
C. 23 D. 24
E. 21

26. RBI can inspect branches of banks as per the powers vested in it under:
A. Section 35 of RBI Act
B. Section 35 of BR Act
C. SEBI
D. None of these
E. Other than given options

27. Against the currency issued by the Reserve Bank of India, it has to maintain certain assets as prescribed in the Reserve Bank of India Act, 1934. Which of the following is not an eligible asset in this regard:
A. Gold
B. Foreign Exchange Reserves
C. Government Securities
D. Shares and Debentures of Joint Stock Companies
E. None of these

28. Cyber Law is:
A. that cipher is the starting point in arithmetic

B. law relating to electronic media
C. testing of atomic weapons
D. law relating to space
E. None of these

29. A commercial bank is prohibited from issuing a bank draft payable to bearer by the provisions contained in:
A. The Negotiable Instruments Act, 1881
B. The Reserve Bank of India Act, 1934
C. The Companies Act, 1956
D. The Banking Regulation Act, 1949
E. None of these

30. Matching the following:

	List-I	List-II
1.	Indian Contract Act	(*a*) 1872
2.	Companies Act	(*b*) 1956
3.	Banking Regulation Act	(*c*) 1949
4.	Indian Partnership Act	(*d*) 1932
		(*e*) 1930

Codes:

	1	2	3	4
A.	(*b*)	(*d*)	(*a*)	(*c*)
B.	(*a*)	(*c*)	(*b*)	(*d*)
C.	(*c*)	(*a*)	(*b*)	(*d*)
D.	(*a*)	(*d*)	(*c*)	(*b*)
E.	(*a*)	(*b*)	(*c*)	(*d*)

31. In India, bank is regulated by:
A. Indian Contract Act, 1872
B. Banking Regulation Act, 1949
C. Indian Companies Act, 1956
D. Banking Regulation Act, 1937
E. None of these

32. The definition of ''Customer'' is available under:
A. Negotiable Instruments Act, 1881
B. Consumer Protection Act, 1986
C. Banking Regulation Act, 1949
D. KYC Guidelines
E. None of these

33. Under provisions of which one of the following Acts, the RBI issues directives to the Banks in India?
A. RBI Act
B. Banking Regulation Act
C. Essential Commodities Act
D. Both A and B above
E. None of these

34. Bank branches need to report suspicious transactions to:
A. Controllers concerned B. RBI
C. CVC D. FIU-IND, New Delhi
E. None of these

35. The law relating to appropriation of payments is contained in:
A. The Negotiable Instruments Act, 1881
B. The Banking Regulation Act, 1949
C. The Contract Act, 1872
D. The Companies Act, 1956
E. None of these

36. Banking Code & Standards Board of India (BCSBI) has been set up for providing details of banking, and to create awareness of banking. BCSBI has been set up by:
A. SBI B. RBI
C. Ministry of Finance D. Bank of India
E. None of these

37. The law regarding negotiable instruments is contained in:
A. The Bill of Exchange Act, 1881
B. The Banking Regulation Act, 1949
C. The Cheques Act, 1881
D. The Negotiable Instruments Act, 1881
E. None of these

38. No licence from RBI is required for:
A. opening a new bank branch in India
B. opening a new bank branch outside India
C. shifting an existing branch outside the city, village or town
D. shifting an existing branch within the same city, village or town
E. None of these

39. When was the currency system in India converted into decimal system?
A. From 1st April, 1957 B. From 1st April, 1959
C. From 1st April, 1961 D. From 1st April, 1963
E. None of these

40. Statutory cash reserve ratio for scheduled banks is regulated by the Reserve Bank of India under powers conferred upon it by:
A. Reserve Bank of India Act, 1934
B. Banking Regulation Act, 1949
C. Companies Act, 1956
D. Union Ministry of Finance
E. None of these

41. Liquidity ratio is fixed by the Reserve Bank of India under the powers conferred on it by:
A. Reserve Bank of India Act, 1934
B. Companies Act, 1956
C. Banking Regulation Act, 1949
D. Special Powers given by the Union Ministry of Finance
E. None of these

42. Who decides on the value and volume of bank notes to be printed and on what basis?
A. Finance Ministry B. Planning Commission
C. RBI D. Stock Exchange
E. None of these

43. Indian Banking Regulation Act was passed in the year:
A. 1971 B. 1969
C. 1950 D. 1947
E. 1949

44. Audit adopted by banking company is:
A. Continuous Audit B. Periodical Audit
C. Internal Audit D. Balance Sheet Audit
E. None of these

45. In terms of Section 19 of the Reserve Bank of India Act, 1934, the RBI has been prohibited from:
A. making loans or advances
B. drawing or accepting bills payable otherwise than on demand
C. allowing interest on deposits or current accounts
D. All of the above
E. None of the above

46. Scheduled Banks are required to keep cash reserves with Reserve Bank of India, in terms of:
A. Section 42(i) of the RBI Act, 1934
B. Section 24 of the Banking Regulation Act, 1949
C. Section 42 of the Negotiable Instruments Act, 1881
D. All of the above
E. None of the above

47. The cash reserve requirements for Non-schedule Banks are laid down in:
A. Section 41(i) of the Reserve Bank of India Act, 1934
B. Section 41(i) of the Negotiable Instruments Act, 1881
C. Section 41 of the Banking Regulation Act, 1881
D. None of the above
E. Can't say

48. We suppose that Reserve Bank of India would like to increase the cash Reserves of the commercial banks. Which among the following would be most appropriate action of the RBI to achieve this aim?
A. RBI would release gold from its reserves
B. RBI would raise the reserve ratio
C. RBI would buy the bonds in the open market.
D. RBI will stop the transactions which involve the bills of exchange
E. None of these

49. Which among the following is a incorrect statement?
A. The Reserve Bank of India has the special powers to control and regulate the commercial banking system
B. A rise in the bank rate is a strong anti-deflationary monetary tool
C. Minimum Reserve Requirements are fixed to ensure the liquidity and solvency of individual commercial banks
D. Reserve Ratio Requirement is a quicker method than bank rate and OMO (Open Market Operations) in general credit regulations
E. None of these

50. Which one of the following measures is not adopted by Reserve Bank of India for controlling credit?
A. Capital Adequacy Ratio
B. Cash Reserve Ratio
C. Statutory Liquidity Ratio
D. Cash Liquidity Ratio
E. Cash Deposit Ratio

51. Banking companies act passed in:
A. 1950 B. 1949
C. 1943 D. 1955
E. None of these

52. Reserve Bank of India under (RBI Act) .... is solely responsible for the issuance of currency notes excluding rupee one note which issued by Finance Secretary of the Government of India:
A. Section 22 B. Section 24
C. Section 26 D. Section 28
E. None of these

53. 'ways and means' such power to lend money to government is given under section .... of RBI Act, 1934:
A. 17(4) B. 17(5)
C. 17(10) D. 17(7)
E. None of these

54. In which year Banking Commission was established:
A. 1971 B. 1972
C. 1974 D. 1975
E. None of these

55. Money Laundering is:
A. Conversion of money which is illegally obtained
B. Conversion of money which is legally obtained
C. All converted money
D. Money transferred in fake account
E. None of these

56. Under which Act, Industrial Reconstruction Bank of India was reconstituted?
A. IRBI Act, 1984 B. IRBI Act, 1986
C. IRBI Act, 1987 D. IRBI Act, 1989
E. None of these

57. One of the major challenges banking industry is facing these days is curbing deliberate efforts of some people to bring money earned through illegal activities in circulation. Which of the following act is passed to prevent this activity?
A. Payment & Settlements Act
B. Control Money Supply Act
C. Narcotics and Psychotropic Substance Act
D. Prevention of Money Laundering Act
E. None of these

58. Banking Ombudsman is appointed by:
A. Reserve Bank of India
B. Government of India
C. Concerned State Govt, where RBI office is located

D. Finance Minister
E. None of the above

59. Before approaching Ombudsman what should the complainant do?
A. Take up the matter with State Government
B. Take up the matter with concerned Bank Branch within 30 days of cause of action
C. Approach Lok Adalat
D. Can directly approach Banking Ombudsman
E. Any of the above

60. What is the maximum period within which the aggrieved customer can approach OMBUSAMAN?
A. Within 2 year
B. Within 1 year
C. Within one month
D. No such limitation period
E. None of the above

61. Who will be appointed as Banking Ombudsman?
A. CGM or GM of RBI
B. Deputy Governor of RBI
C. Governor RBI is an ex-officio Ombudsman
D. Finance Secretary
E. None of the above

62. In terms of section 5 (1)(e) of the Banking Regulation Act, 1949, a 'banking company' means any comps-which
A. transacts the business of banking in India
B. undertakes lending of money
C. accepts deposits from public and invests the same as trade and industry
D. accepts deposits from the public
E. All of the above

63. .... prepared a framework through a consultative process to secure international convergence of supervisory regulations governing the capital adequacy of international banks.
A. Basel Committee on Banking Supervision
B. Banking Committee on Banking Supervision
C. Basel Company on Banking Supervision
D. Banking Company on Banking Supervision
E. None of these

64. Section 14 of Banking Regulation Act, 1949
A. Prohibits a banking company from creating a charge upon any unpaid capital of the company
B. Contains a system of licensing of banks by the R.B.I.
C. Provides that the subscribed capital of a banking company should not be less than one-half of its authorized capital
D. Provides a Banking Ombudsman to check proper functioning of the bank
E. None of these

65. A Bank is under a statutory obligations to honour its customer's cheques vide:
A. Section 10 of the Banking Regulation Act, 1949
B. Section 3 of the R.B.I. Act, 1934
C. Section 31 of the Negotiable Instruments Act, 1881
D. Section 20 of the RBI Act, 1934
E. None of these

66. Nationalised Banks have been permitted to offer their equity shares to the public to the extent of 49% of their capital as per amendments made in 1994 in
A. Banking Regulation Act, 1949
B. Banking Companies (Acquisition & Transfer of Undertakings) Acts 1970/1980
C. Both A and B
D. Banking Regulation Act, 1967
E. None of the above

67. Section 85(1) of the Negotiable Instrument Act, 1881 provides protection to the paying banker in respect of
A. forged endorsement
B. material alterations on the face of the cheque
C. forgery of drawer's signature
D. All of these
E. None of these

68. Under Section 17 of the Banking Regulation Act, 1949, every banking company incorporated in India is required to transfer each year to a reserve fund a sum equivalent to not less than
A. 10 per cent of profit before dividends
B. 20 per cent of profit after interest tax and dividend
C. 25 per cent of profit before dividends
D. 5 per cent of gross profit
E. None of these

69. Banking ombudsman has been constituted under which act?
A. Banking Regulation Act
B. RBI Act
C. SBI Act
D. COPRA
E. None of these

70. Banking ombudsman means
A. Person appointed to recover dues from defaulting borrowers
B. A person to whom customer can approach for redress of his grievances
C. A person appointed to settle dispute between employees and management
D. A person appointed by RBI to oversee the functioning of Foreign Banks
E. None of these

71. The Securitization and Reconstruction of Financial Asset and enforce of Security Interest Act came into force from
A. 21.08.02
B. 21.06.02
C. 21.07.02
D. 21.12.02
E. None of these

72. The Banking Ombudsman Scheme is introduced under .... section of banking regulation Act.

A. 35A B. 35
C. 25 D. 73
E. None of these

73. The Banking Ombudsman Scheme working is effect from

A. 1990 B. 1995
C. 2000 D. 2005
E. None of these

ANSWERS

1	2	3	4	5	6	7	8	9	10
B	C	A	C	A	A	B	A	B	A
11	**12**	**13**	**14**	**15**	**16**	**17**	**18**	**19**	**20**
A	C	D	E	A	D	A	C	D	B
21	**22**	**23**	**24**	**25**	**26**	**27**	**28**	**29**	**30**
E	D	D	A	E	B	D	B	B	B
31	**32**	**33**	**34**	**35**	**36**	**37**	**38**	**39**	**40**
B	D	D	D	C	B	D	D	A	A
41	**42**	**43**	**44**	**45**	**46**	**47**	**48**	**49**	**50**
C	C	E	A	E	A	D	C	B	E
51	**52**	**53**	**54**	**55**	**56**	**57**	**58**	**59**	**60**
B	A	B	B	A	A	D	A	B	B
61	**62**	**63**	**64**	**65**	**66**	**67**	**68**	**69**	**70**
A	E	A	A	C	B	A	C	B	B
71	**72**	**73**							
B	A	B							

5

Customers of Banks

In the ordinary language, a person who has an account in a bank is considered as its customer. The term customer also presents some difficulty in the matter of definition. There is no statutory definition of the term either in India or in England. However, the legal decisions on the matter throw some light on the meaning of the term.

According to Dr. Hart ***"a customer is one who has an account with a banker or for whom a banker habitually undertakes to act as such."***

"Broadly speaking, a customer is a person who has the habit of resorting to the same place or person to do business. So far as banking transactions are concerned, he is a person whose money has been accepted on the footing that the banker will honour up to the amount standing to his credit, irrespective of his connection being of short or long standing." Thus, a person who has a bank account in his name and for whom the banker undertakes to provide the facilities as a banker is considered to be a customer. It is not essential that the account must have been operated upon for some time.

Thus, in order to constitute a person as a customer, he must satisfy the following conditions:

1. He must have an account with the bank *i.e.*, saving bank account, current deposit account, or fixed deposit account.
2. The transactions between the banker and the customer should be of banking nature *i.e.*, a person who approaches the banker for operating Safe Deposit Locker or purchasing travellers cheques is not a customer of the bank since such transactions do not come under the orbit of banking transactions.
3. Frequency of transactions is not quite necessary though anticipated.

SPECIAL TYPES OF CUSTOMERS

Special types of customers are those who are distinguished from other types of ordinary customers by some special features. Hence, they are called special types of customers. They are to be dealt with carefully while operating and opening the accounts. They are:

Minors

Under the Indian law, a minor is a person who has not completed 18 years of age. The period of minority is extended to 21 years in case of guardian of this person or property is appointed by a court of law before he completes the age of 18 years. According to Indian Contract Act, a minor is recognised as a highly incompetent party to enter into legal contracts and any contract entered into with a minor is not only invalid but voidable at the option of the minor. The law has specially protected a minor merely because his mental faculty has not fully developed and as such, he is likely to commit mistakes or even blunders which will affect his interests adversely. It is for this reason; the law has come to the rescue of a minor. A banker can very well open a bank account in the name of a minor. But the banker has to be careful to ensure that he does not open a current account.

If a current account is opened and stands overdrawn inadvertently, the banker has no remedy against a minor, as he cannot be taken to a court of law. It is for this reason that the banker should be careful to see that he invariably opens a savings bank account.

The conditions for opening and maintaining accounts in the names of the minors are:

1. The minor should have attained the age of discretion, *i.e.*, he must be about 14 years of age. He must be capable of understanding what he does.
2. The minor should be able to read and write.
3. The minor should be properly introduced. The account opening form should be signed by the minor in the presence of a bank officer who should be able to identify the minor. The date of birth of the minor should be recorded in the account opening form.
4. Banks usually stipulate limits up to which deposits in such accounts can be accepted.
5. Amount tendered by the minor should as far as possible be in cash.
6. In case of time deposits, the amount should be paid in cash on maturity. Prepayment cannot be allowed. Periodical payment of interest on deposits may be made to the minor.

Legal Provisions Regarding Guardianship of a Minor

According to Hindu Minority and Guardianship Act, 1956, a Guardian is one who is recognised by law to be one of the following:

***(a)* Natural Guardian:** According to Section 6 of the Hindu Minority and Guardianship Act, 1956, in case of a minor boy or an unmarried girl, his/her father and after him the mother shall be the natural guardian. In case of a married girl (minor), her husband shall be the natural guardian. The terms father or mother do not include step-father or step-mother.

***(b)* Testamentary Guardian:** A Hindu father, who is entitled to act as the natural guardian of his minor legitimate children may, by will, appoint a guardian for any of them in respect of the minor's person or property. Such guardian acts after the death of the father or the mother.

***(c)* Guardian Appointed by Court:** A guardian may be appointed by the court under the Guardians and Wards Act, 1890, but the court shall not be authorised to appoint or declare a guardian of the person of a minor, if his father is alive and is not, in the opinion of the court, unfit to be guardian of the person of the minor. Similar is the case of a minor girl, whose husband is not, in the opinion of the court, unfit to be guardian of her person. Thus, the father (or the husband in case of a married girl) is exclusively entitled to be the guardian.

Lunatics

A lunatic or an insane person is one who, on account of mental derangement, is incapable of understanding his interests and thereby, arriving at rational judgement. Since a lunatic does not understand what is right and what is wrong, it is quite likely that the public may exploit the weakness of a lunatic to their advantage and thus deprive him of his legitimate claims. On account of this, the Indian Contract Act recognises that a lunatic is incompetent to enter into any contract and any such contract, if entered into, is not only invalid but voidable at the option of the lunatic. Since a lunatic customer is an incompetent party, the banker has to be very careful in dealing with such customers. Bankers should not open an account in the name of a person of unsound mind. On coming to know of a customer's insanity, the banker should stop all operations on the account and await a court order appointing a receiver. It would be dangerous to rely on hearsay information. The bank should take sufficient care to verify the information and should not stop the account unless it is fully satisfied about the correctness of the information. In case, a person suffers from a temporary mental disorder, the banker must obtain a Certificate from two medical officers regarding his mental soundness at the time of operation on the account.

Drunkards

A drunkard is a person who on account of consumption of alcoholic drinks get himself intoxicated and thereby, loses the balance over his mental capacity and hence, is incapable of forming rational judgement. The law is quite considerable towards a person who is in drunken state. A lawful contract with such a person is invalid. This is for the simple reason that it is quite likely that the public may exploit the weakness of such a person to their advantage and thus, deprive him of his legitimate claims. A banker has to be very careful in dealing with such customers. There cannot be any objection by a banker to open an account. In case, a customer approaches the banker for encashment of his cheque especially when he is drunk, the banker should not make immediate payment. This is because the customer may afterwards argue that the banker has not made payment at all. Therefore, it is better and safer that the banker should insist upon such a customer getting a witness (who is not drunk) to countersign before making any payment against the cheque.

Married Women

An account may be opened by the bank in the name of a married woman as she has the power to draw cheques and give valid discharge. At the time of opening an account in the name of a married woman, it is advisable to obtain the name and occupation of her husband and name of her employer, if any, and record the same to enable detection if the account is misused by the husband for crediting there in cheques drawn in favour of her employer. In case of an unmarried lady, the occupation of her father and name and address of her employer, if any, may be obtained and noted in the account opening form. If a lady customer requests the bankers to change the name of her account opened in her maiden name to her married name, the banker may do so after obtaining a written request from her. A fresh specimen signature has also to be obtained for records.

While opening an account of a purdah lady (purdah nishin), the bank obtains her signature on the account opening form duly attested by a responsible person known to the bank. It is advisable to have withdrawals also similarly attested. In view of practical difficulties involved, it would be better not to open accounts in the names of purdah ladies.

Insolvents

When a person is unable to pay his debts in full, his property in certain circumstances is taken possession of by official receiver or official assignee, under orders of the court. He realises the debtor's property and rateably distributes the proceeds amongst his creditors. Such a proceeding is called 'insolvency' and the debtor is known as an 'insolvent'. If an account holder becomes insolvent, his authority to the bank to pay cheques drawn by him is revoked and the balance in the account vests in the official receiver or official assignee.

Illiterate Persons

A person is said to be illiterate when he does not know to read and write. No current account should be opened in the name of an illiterate person. However, a savings bank account may be opened in the name of such a person. On the account opening form the bank should obtain his thumb mark in the presence of two persons known to the bank and the depositor. Withdrawal from the account by the account holder should be permitted after proper identification every time. The person who identifies the drawer must be known to the bank and he should preferably not be a member of the bank's staff.

Agents

A banker may open an account in the name of a person who is acting as an agent of another person. The account should be considered as the personal account of an agent, and the banker has no authority to question his power to deal with the funds in the account unless it becomes obvious that he is being guilty of breach of trust. However, if a person is authorised to only act on behalf of the principal, the banker should see that he is properly authorised to do the acts which he claims to do. If he has been appointed by a power of attorney, the banker should carefully pursue the letter-of-attorney to confirm the powers conferred by the document on the agent. In receiving notice of the principal's death, insanity or bankruptcy, the banker must suspend all operations on the account.

Joint Stock Company

A joint stock company has been defined as an artificial person, invisible, intangible and existing only in contemplation of law. It has separate legal existence and it has a perpetual succession. The banker must satisfy himself about the following while opening an account in the name of a company:

(*a*) Memorandum of Association: Memorandum of Association is the main document of the company, which embodies its constitution and is called the charter of the company. It gives details, especially regarding objects and capital of the company's copy of this document should be insisted upon while opening an account.

(*b*) Articles of Association: The Articles of Association contain the rules and regulations of the company regarding its internal management. It contains in detail all matters which are concerned with the conduct of day-to-day business of the company. The Articles of Association is also another document that a banker insists upon. It enables the banker to know the details of company's borrowing powers quantum, persons authorised to borrow etc. This will also enable the banker to understand whether the acts of the officers are within the orbit of the Company's Memorandum and Articles.

(*c*) Certificate of Incorporation: This is another vital document the banker has to verify and insist upon receiving a copy. This document signifies that the company can commence its business activities as soon as it gets this Certificate which is not the case with a public company.

(*d*) Certificate to Commence Business: Only for public companies, the banker insists upon this document for verification. This document gives the clearance to public companies to commence their business activities. A company can borrow funds provided it has obtained this certificate.

(*e*) Application Form and Copy of the Board's Resolution: A copy of the prescribed application form duly completed in all respects has to be submitted in the beginning and that too duly signed by the company's authorised officers. Along with this, a copy of the resolution passed at the meeting of the board regarding appointment of company's bankers is quite necessary to make everything lawful. The resolution copy should be signed by the company's Chairman and Secretary in addition, a copy of the specimen signatures of the officers empowered to operate the bank account has to be furnished.

(*f*) A Written Mandate: This is also another document that a banker insists upon. It contains all the details regarding operation, overdrawing of the account and giving security to the bank by the officers of the company. This document is useful to the bank for opening as well as for operating the account of the company.

(*g*) Registration of Charges: Whenever a company borrows, it has to give certain assets by way of security and in case the banker accepts them as security, it has to be properly recorded in the company's books, register of charges and duly registered.

(*h*) Any Change in the Company's Constitution or Offices: Whenever there is any change in the constitution like Memorandum or in respect of company's offices, it has to be communicated in writing to the bank and it should not be in any way affect the earlier contracts entered into by the company with the bank. To this effect, the bankers usually take an undertaking from the company.

Clubs, Associations and Educational Institutions

Clubs, Associations and Educational Institutions are non-trading institutions interested in serving noble courses of education, sports etc. The banker should observe the following precautions in dealing with them:

(*a*) Incorporation: A sports club, an association or an educational institution must be registered or incorporated according to the Indian Companies Act, 1956, or the Co-operative Societies Acts. If it is not registered, the organisations will not have any legal existence and it has no right to contact with the outside parties.

(*b*) Rules and by-laws of the Organisation: A registered association or organisation is governed by the provisions of the Act under which it has been registered.

It may have its own Constitution, Charter or Memorandum of Association and rules and by-laws, etc., to carry on its activities. A copy of the same should be furnished by the organisation to the banker to acquaint the latter with the powers and functions of the persons managing its affairs. The banker should ensure that these rules are observed by the persons responsible for managing the organisation.

(*c*) A Copy of Resolution of Managing Committee: For opening a bank account, the managing committee of the organisation must pass a resolution—

(*i*) Appointing the bank concerned as the banker of the organisation.

(*ii*) Mentioning the name/names of the person or persons, who are authorised to operate the account.

(*iii*) Giving any other directions for the operation of the said account. A copy of the resolution must be obtained by the bank for its own record.

(*d*) An Application Form: An application form duly completed in all respects along with specimen signatures of the office bearers of the institution is quite essential for operation of the account.

(*e*) A Written Mandate: It is an important document which contains specific instructions given to the banker regarding operations, over drawing etc.

(*f*) Transfer of Funds: All funds and cheques which are in the name of the Institution should be invariably credited to the Institution account and not to the personal or private accounts of the office bearers of the institution.

(*g*) Death or Resignation: In case, the person authorised to operate the account on behalf of a organisation or association dies or resigns, the banker should stop the operations of the organisation's account till the organisation nominates another person to operate its account.

Partnership Firm

A partnership is not regarded as an entity separate from the partners. The Indian Partnership Act, 1932, defines partnership as the "relation between persons who have agreed to share the profit of the business, carried on by all or any of them acting for all." Partnership is formed or constituted on account of agreement between the partners and with the sole intention of earning and sharing profits in a particular ratio. Further, the business is carried on either by all the partners or some partners acting for all. The partners carry joint and several liabilities and the partnership does not possess any legal entity. A banker should take the following precautions while opening an account in the name of a partnership firm:

(*a*) Application Form: A prescribed application form duly completed in all respects along with specimen signatures of the partners of firm is quite essential for operation of the account.

(*b*) Partnership Deed: The banker should, very carefully examine the partnership deed, which is the charter of the firm, to acquaint himself with the constitution and business of the firm. This will help him to know his position while advancing funds to the firm.

(*c*) A Mandate: A mandate giving specific instructions to the banker regarding operations, overdrawing etc., is quite necessary. It will enable the banker to handle the accounts according to the needs of the firm.

(*d*) Transfer of Funds: The banker has to be very careful to see that the funds belonging to the firm should not be credited to the personal or private accounts of the partners.

(*e*) Sanctioning of Overdraft: While sanctioning funds by way of overdraft, the banker has to check up the partnership deed and examine the borrowing powers of the partners empowered to borrow and he can even ask for the financial statements of the previous years for information and perusal.

Joint Accounts

When two or more persons open an account jointly, it is called a joint account. The banker should take the following precautions in opening and dealing with a joint account:

(*a*) The application for opening a joint account must be signed by all the persons intending to open a joint account.

(*b*) A mandate containing name or names of persons authorised to operate an account.

(*c*) The full name of the account must be given in all the documents furnished to the banker, even if the account is to be operated upon by one or a few of the joint account holders.

(*d*) Banker must stop operating an account as soon as a notice of death, insolvency, insanity etc., of any one account holder is received.

(*e*) The joint account holder, who is authorised to operate the joint account, himself alone cannot appoint an agent or attorney to operate the account on his behalf. Such attorney or agent may be appointed with the consent of all the joint account holders.

(*f*) If all the persons are operating the account, then banker must see that any cheque drawn on him is duly signed by all.

(*g*) Banker must stop making payments as soon as letter of revocation is obtained.

(*h*) Banker must see that no loan or overdraft is granted without proper security.

Joint Hindu Family

Joint Hindu family is an undivided Hindu family which comprises of all male members descended from a common ancestor. They may be sons, grandsons and great grandsons, their wives and unmarried daughters. "A joint, Hindu family is a family which consists of more than one male member, possesses ancestral property and carries on family business." Therefore, joint Hindu family is a legal institution. It is managed and represented in its dealings and transactions with others by the Kartha who is the head of the family. Other members of the family do not have this right to manage unless a particular member is given certain rights and responsibilities with common consent of the Kartha. The banker has to exercise greater care in dealing with this account.

(*a*) He must get complete information about the joint Hindu family including the names of major and minor coparceners and get a declaration from the Kartha to this effect along with specimen signatures and signatures of all coparceners.

(*b*) The account should be opened either in the personal name of the Kartha or in the name of the family business.

(*c*) The documents should be signed by the Kartha and major coparceners.

(*d*) The account should be operated on only by the Kartha and the authorised major coparceners.

(*e*) While making advances, the banker should ascertain the purpose for which the loan is obtained and whether the loan is really needed by the joint Hindu family for business.

Trustees

According to the Indian Trusts Act, 1882, "a trust is an obligation annexed to the ownership of property and arising out of a confidence reposed in an accepted by the owner, or declared and accepted by him, for the benefit of another, or of another and the owner." As per this definition, a trustee is a person in whom the author or settler reposes confidence and entrusts the management of his property for the benefit of a person or an organisation who is called beneficiaries. A trust is usually formed by means of document called the "Trust Deed." While opening an account in the names of persons in their capacity as trustees the banker should take the following precautions:

(*a*) The banker should thoroughly examine the trust deed appointing the applicants as the trustees.

(*b*) A trust deed which states the powers and functions of trustees must be obtained by the banker.

(*c*) In case of two or more trustees, the banker should ask for clear instructions regarding the person or persons who shall operate the account.

(*d*) In case of death or retirement of one or more trustees, banker must see the provision of the trust deed.

(*e*) The banker should not allow the transfer of funds from trust account to the personal account of trustee.

(*f*) The banker should take all possible precautions to safeguard the interest of the beneficiaries of a trust, failing which he shall be liable to compensate the latter for any fraud on the part of the trustee.

(*g*) The insolvency of a trustee does not affect the trust property and the creditors of the trustee cannot recover their claims from trust property.

(*h*) A copy of the resolution passed in the meeting of trustees open the account should be obtained.

A banking institution solicits deposits of money from the members of the public. An account in a bank for this purpose may be opened by any person who (*i*) is legally capable of entering into a valid contract, (*ii*) applies to the banker in the proper manner, *i.e.*, he follows the procedure laid down by the banker and accepts the terms and conditions stipulated by the latter. The banker, however, possesses the right to reject an application for opening an account, if he is not satisfied with the identity of the applicant, *i.e.*, if the latter is deemed to be an undesirable person. Some persons like the minors, lunatics and drunkards are not competent to enter into valid contracts. Some persons who act on behalf of others have limitations on their power to contract, *e.g.*, the agents, trustees; executors etc., Institutions like schools, colleges, clubs, societies, and corporate bodies are the impersonal customers of a banker. The authority power and functions of the persons managing these institutions are embodied in their respective constitutions. The banker should, therefore, take special care and precautions to ensure that the accounts of these institutes are being conducted in accordance with the provisions of their respective charters. A banker should know the legal position of the special classes of customers and the necessary precautions to be taken while dealing with them.

MULTIPLE CHOICE QUESTIONS

1. A banker need not bother too much to open an account in the name of a person when receiving.........

A. Term deposit B. Demand deposit
C. Saving deposit D. Call deposit
E. None of these

2. Primary relationship between banker and customer is that of

A. Dealer and customer
B. Principal and agent
C. Lessor and lessee
D. Vender and buyer
E. Debtor and creditor

3. A banker has the right to disclose the account position of a customer to..........

A. Intimate friend B. Customer's wife
C. Trade reference D. Customers relatives
E. None of these

4. An account usually maintained by businessmen in a bank is
A. Current account
B. Saving bank account
C. Recurring deposit account
D. All the above
E. None of these

5. In banking sector, KYC stands for
A. Kid and young customers
B. Know youth creditors
C. Know your customers
D. Know your cash requirements.
E. None of these

6. "Either of Survivor" account in a bank is .... account.
A. Minors Account B. Joint account
C. Saving account D. Double account
E. None of these

7. Legal heirs of a deceased customer approaches the bank with a copy of the Will left by the deceased and request for payment of the deposit standing in the name of the deceased depositor. Bank should
A. obtain a probated Will and pay the amount to the legal heir
B. obtain the Will and pay the amount to the legal heir
C. both A and B
D. None of the above
E. Other than given options

8. There is a joint account in the names of A and B, to be operated by both of them jointly. There is a debit balance of ₹ 23,100 when the bank receives a notice of A's death:
A. the amount can be recovered from B only
B. the amount can be recovered from the estate of the deceased A only
C. the amount can be recovered from B and/or the estate of the deceased A
D. Other than given options
E. None of the above

9. There is a joint account in the name of Khem Singh and his wife Kartar Kaur with a mandate: "to be operated by either or survivor". Both are in dispute and each of them has instructed the bank not to honour the signature of the other in future:
A. the balance of the account will be paid to Khem Singh against a proper receipt
B. further operations on the account will be stopped, but the cheques already drawn by either of them and yet not presented will be honoured
C. further operations on the account will be stopped till a fresh mandate signed by both of them is received
D. the account will be closed and the balance remitted to them
E. None of these

10. In case of a Hindu Undivided Family, when Karta dies leaving overdraft account:
A. old account is closed and a new account opened
B. fresh HUF letter is obtained
C. all the co-parceners will operate on the account
D. None of the above
E. Other than given options

11. What are the main objectives of Consumer Protection Act, 1986?
A. To provide better protection of the interest of consumers
B. Settlement of consumer disputes
C. To deal with other connected matters
D. Both A and C
E. All of the above

12. Consumer Means:
A. Any person who buys any goods
B. Any person who hires or avails of any services
C. Any person who makes payment in full or in instalments or under Hire Purchase system
D. All of the above
E. Other than given options

13. The services under the Consumer Protection includes:
A. Banking, Financing and Insurance
B. Transport and Processing
C. Supply of electrical and other energy
D. All of the above
E. None of these

14. Which of the following is not an indicator of productivity for a bank branch?
A. Business Per Employee
B. Accounts (both deposits and advances) Per Employee
C. Net Profit Per Employee
D. Neat and clean ambience
E. None of these

15. 'Know Your Customer Guidelines' issued by RBI helps in:
A. customer identification while opening accounts
B. adopting anti-money laundering measures
C. identifying suspicious transactions
D. All of these
E. None of these

16. Customer Day in the bank is on and customers are allowed to meet the top officials of the bank on this day in every month:
A. 5th B. 10th
C. 20th D. 30th
E. 15th

17. An account should be treated as 'out of order' if:
A. the outstanding balance remains continuously in excess of the sanctioned limit/drawing power

B. there are no credits continuously for 90 days as on the date of Balance Sheet even though the outstanding balance in the account is less than the sanctioned limit/drawing power
C. credits are not enough to cover the interest debited during the same period
D. All of the above
E. None of these

18. Which of the following Acts govern a Bank Guarantee?
A. Negotiable Instruments Act, 1881
B. Indian Contract Act, 1872
C. Sale of Goods Act, 1930
D. Indian Companies Act, 1956
E. None of these

19. Out of the following who is not a customer of the bank?
A. term-deposit account holder
B. "Cash Credit on hypothecation" account holder
C. outstation party from whom the bank has received a bill of exchange for collection
D. local party from whom the bank has received a bill of exchange for collection
E. None of these

20. A customer tenders a certain amount of money into his Savings Bank Account without mentioning his account number. Bank also could not locate the same. In such a situation the amount had to be parked in the Sundry Deposits Accounts. In this case, the relationship between the bank and the customer is that of:
A. Trustee and Beneficiary
B. Bailee and Bailor
C. Bailor and Bailee
D. Lessor and Lessee
E. None of these

21. Bankers have to maintain secrecy of customers accounts as per the provisions of:
A. Banking Companies (Acquisition and Transfer of Undertaking) Act, 1970
B. Negotiable Instruments Act, 1881
C. Banking Regulation Act, 1949
D. All of the above
E. None of the above

22. The guarantor of a customer's account has the right:
A. to inspect the account in the bank's books
B. to be provided with the statement of the account
C. to be informed only about the extent of his liability
D. to be provided with all the information about the way the account is conducted
E. None of these

23. In terms of Section 59 of the Indian Contract Act, 1872, if the customer owes several distinct debts to the banker and makes payment which is not sufficient to satisfy all the debts:
A. he has the right to request the banker to apply the payment to the discharge of some particular debt
B. the banker has a right to appropriate the amount in satisfaction of any debt which is not time-barred, at his option
C. the payment will be applied in discharge of the debts in chronological order notwithstanding the instructions of the customer in this regard
D. All of the above
E. None of the above

24. For a foreigner temporarily residing in India, type of account to be opened is:
A. Resident Account B. NRO Account
C. NRE Account D. All of the above
E. None of these

25. The term "co-obligant" means:
A. a person who has guaranteed the account of another person(s)
B. a person who has executed an indemnity bond in a bank's favour
C. a person who has assumed obligations of contract jointly with other person(s)
D. a person/business undertaking opening a documentary letter of credit
E. None of these

26. When someone wants to open a new savings bank account, the bank asks him/her to bring various documents. Which of the following is one of these documents?
A. Certificate of medical fitness
B. Degree Certificate
C. Proof of Residence & Identity
D. All of the above
E. None of these

27. A student has got admission to a foreign university. From where can he/she get the foreign currency?
A. From the Bank of that country only
B. From the Ministry of Foreign Affairs
C. From office of the Consulate General of that country
D. From an authorized foreign exchange dealer
E. None of these

28. A customer wishes to purchase some US dollars in India. He/She should go to:
A. Public Debt Division of the RBI only
B. American Express Bank only
C. RBI or any branch of a bank which is authorized for such business
D. None of these
E. Other than given options

29. Which of the following products of a bank is specifically designed to provide financial help to children in their higher studies in India or in a foreign nation?
A. Personal Loan B. Corporate Loan
C. Primary Loan D. Mortgage Loan
E. Educational Loan

30. KYC Policy has been actually innovated by:
A. Fed Reserve of USA
B. Basel Committee
C. RBI
D. GOI, Ministry of Finance
E. None of these

31. Banks in our country normally publicize that additional interest rate is allowed on retail domestic term deposits of?
A. Minors B. Married Women
C. Senior citizens D. Government Employees
E. Rural residents

32. Which of the following is necessary while opening deposit accounts in banks?
A. Will B. Registration
C. Nomination D. Indemnity
E. Guarantee

33. Banking services delivered to a customer by means of a computer control system that does not directly involve banks branch is called?
A. Universal banking B. Virtual banking
C. Narrow banking D. Brick & Mortal banking
E. None of these

34. Who will settle the grievances of customers of banks?
A. Reserve Bank of India
B. State Bank of India
C. Local Courts
D. Ombuds Men
E. None of these

35. "Customer" is defined in:
A. Banking Regulation Act
B. N.I. Act
C. R.B.I. Act
D. Nowhere it is defined
E. None of these

36. Drawing power in an account means:
A. Limit sanctioned
B. Value of security
C. Value of security minus unpaid stock
D. Value of stock minus unpaid stock minus margin
E. None of these

37. Letter of Probate means:
A. A letter attached with a Will containing signatures of the witnesses
B. Confirmation of Succession Certificate
C. A certificate issued by the court containing the name of the person who has to administer the property of a deceased person
D. A certificate issued by the court containing also the name of the Executor of a will
E. None of these

38. Collection of cheques for customer is a .... function of bank.
A. agency function B. trustee function
C. planned function D. deposit function
E. None of these

39. After a customer has closed the account ....
A. the banker is no more liable to observe secrecy of his account because the contractual relationship comes to an end
B. the banker is still bound by his duty of secrecy
C. the banker's duty of secrecy comes to an end in terms of the provisions of the Negotiable Instrument Act, 1881
D. the banker is still not bound by his duty of secrecy
E. None of these

40. The relationship between a banker and its customer is basically that of
A. A debtor and a creditor
B. A trustee and the beneficiary
C. A principal and an agent
D. A trustee and an agent
E. None of these

41. When a banker accepts the securities for safe custody, the relationship between a banker and a customer is that of
A. A debtor and a creditor
B. Trustee and beneficiary
C. Principal and agent
D. Principal and creditor
E. None of these

42. A customer requests for issue of a bearer demand draft. The banker should
A. Strike off the word 'order' and should put the word 'bearer' on the draft
B. Request the customer to go to the Head Office
C. Refuse to issue the draft
D. Either A or B
E. None of these

43. A and B have jointly hired a locker under "Either or Survivor" caluse. A dies. The bank should
A. Permit B to operate the locker
B. Seal the locker and open it only in the presence of B and A is legal representative
C. Permit operation by B and legal representative of A jointly
D. Not have allowed operation
E. None of these

44. A minor can open and operate an account in his own name if he has atleast attained the age of
A. 12 years B. 16 years
C. 15 years D. 18 years
E. 20 yeear

45. The person appointed to operate the account after his death by the deceased himself before his death is called

A. Executor B. Administrator
C. Attorney D. Introducer
E. None of these

46. A joint account can be opened by the banker on receipt of application signed by
A. Majority of the joint account holders
B. All joint account holders
C. Any joint account holder
D. Either A or C
E. None of these

47. A minor cannot
A. Accept a bill
B. Draw a bill
C. Endorse a cheque
D. Either B or C
E. None of these

48. A bank maintains an account in the names of A & B payable jointly. On the death of A, the balance in the account is payable to
A. B
B. A's legal representative
C. B and A's legal representative in equal proportion
D. legal representative of A & B
E. None of these

49. The interest and principle amount of a loan not repaid by a customer in a bank, the bank consider such loan as…….. .
A. RD B. FD
C. NPA D. TOD
E. None of these

50. Minimum age to open a SB account in own name is
A. 10 B. 18
C. 21 D. 15
E. None of these

51. Replica of a bank account kept with customer is known as:
A. Book of account B. Pass Book
C. Ledger account D. Either A or C
E. None the above

ANSWERS

1	2	3	4	5	6	7	8	9	10
A	E	C	A	C	B	A	C	C	B
11	**12**	**13**	**14**	**15**	**16**	**17**	**18**	**19**	**20**
E	D	D	D	D	E	D	B	C	A
21	**22**	**23**	**24**	**25**	**26**	**27**	**28**	**29**	**30**
A	C	A	B	C	C	A	C	E	B
31	**32**	**33**	**34**	**35**	**36**	**37**	**38**	**39**	**40**
C	C	B	D	D	D	D	A	B	A
41	**42**	**43**	**44**	**45**	**46**	**47**	**48**	**49**	**50**
B	C	A	A	B	B	A	C	C	A
51									
B									

6 Reserve Bank of India (RBI)

The Reserve Bank of India is the apex financial institution of the country which is entrusted with the task of controlling, supervising, promoting, developing and planning the financial system. RBI is the queen bee of the Indian financial system which influences the commercial banks' management in more than one way. The RBI influences the management of commercial banks through its various policies, directions and regulations. Its role in banking is quite unique. In fact, the RBI performs the four basic functions of management, viz., planning, organizing, directing and controlling in laying a strong foundation for the functioning of commercial banks.

RBI possesses special status in our country. It is the authority to regulate and control monetary system of our country. It controls money market and the entire banking system of our country.

The origins of the Reserve Bank of India can be traced to 1926, when the Royal Commission on Indian Currency and Finance – also known as the Hilton-Young Commission – recommended the creation of a central bank for India to separate the control of currency and credit from the Government and to augment banking facilities throughout the country. The Reserve Bank of India Act of 1934 established the Reserve Bank and set in motion a series of actions culminating in the start of operations in 1935. Since then, the Reserve Bank's role and functions have undergone numerous changes, as the nature of the Indian economy and financial sector changed.

Origins of the Reserve Bank of India

- **1926:** The Royal Commission on Indian Currency and Finance recommended creation of a central bank for India.
- **1927:** A bill to give effect to the above recommendation was introduced in the Legislative Assembly, but was later withdrawn due to lack of agreement among various sections of people.
- **1933:** The White Paper on Indian Constitutional Reforms recommended the creation of a Reserve Bank. A fresh bill was introduced in the Legislative Assembly.
- **1934:** The Bill was passed and received the Governor General's assent.
- **1935:** The Reserve Bank commenced operations as India's central bank on April 1 as a private shareholders' bank with a paid up capital of rupees five crore (rupees fifty million).
- **1942:** The Reserve Bank ceased to be the currency issuing authority of Burma (now Myanmar).
- **1947:** The Reserve Bank stopped acting as a banker to the Government of Burma.
- **1948:** The Reserve Bank stopped rendering central banking services to Pakistan.
- **1949:** The Government of India nationalised the Reserve Bank under the Reserve Bank (Transfer of Public Ownership) Act, 1948.

Starting as a private shareholders' bank, the Reserve Bank was nationalised in 1949. It then assumed the responsibility to meet the aspirations of a newly independent country and its people. The Reserve Bank's nationalisation aimed at achieving coordination between the policies of the government and those of the central bank.

The Preamble to the Reserve Bank of India Act, 1934 (the Act), under which it was constituted, specifies its objective as "to regulate the issue of Bank notes and the keeping of reserves with a view to securing monetary stability in India and generally to operate the currency and credit system of the country to its advantage".

The objectives outlined in the Preamble hold good even after 75 years. As evident from the multifaceted functions that the Reserve Bank performs today, its role and priorities have, in the span of 75 years, changed in tandem with changing national priorities and global developments. Essentially, the Reserve Bank has demonstrated dynamism and flexibility to meet the requirements of an evolving economy.

A core function of the Reserve Bank in the last 75 years has been the formulation and implementation of monetary policy with the objectives of maintaining price stability and ensuring adequate flow of credit to productive sectors of the economy. To these was added, in more recent times, the goal of maintaining financial stability. The objective of maintaining financial stability has spanned its role from external account management to oversight of banks and non-banking financial institutions as also of money, government securities and foreign exchange markets.

The Reserve Bank designs and implements the regulatory policy framework for banking and non-banking financial institutions with the aim of providing people access to the banking system, protecting depositors' interest, and maintaining the overall health of the financial system. Its function of regulating the commercial banking sector, which emerged with the enactment of the Banking Regulation Act, 1949, has over time, expanded to cover other entities. Thus, amendments to the Banking Regulation Act, 1949 brought cooperative banks and regional rural banks under the Reserve Bank's jurisdiction, while amendments to the Reserve Bank of India Act saw development finance institutions, non-banking financial companies and primary dealers coming under its regulation, as these entities became important players in the financial system and markets.

Management

The Reserve Bank's affairs are governed by a central board of directors. The board is appointed by the Government of India in keeping with the Reserve Bank of India Act. The organization structure of RBI consists of a **Central Board** and **Local Board**.

ORGANISATION

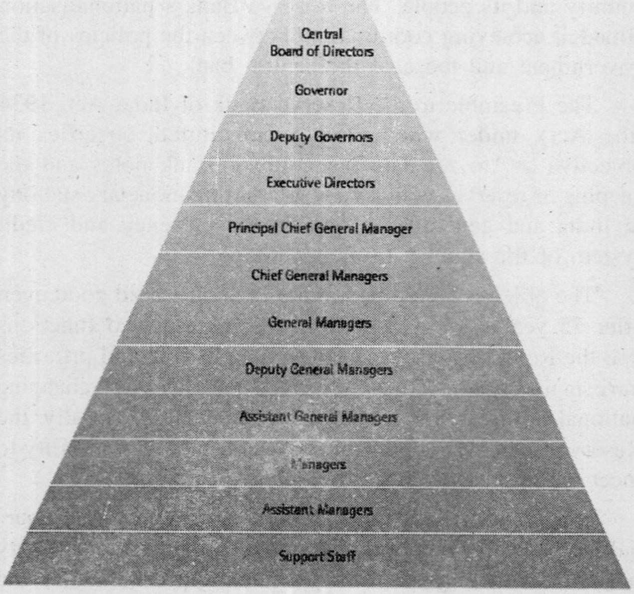

Central Board of Directors

The Central Board of Directors is at the top of the Reserve Bank's organisational structure. Appointed by the Government under the provisions of the Reserve Bank of India Act, 1934, the Central Board has the primary authority and responsibility for the oversight of the Reserve Bank. It delegates specific functions to the Local Boards and various committees.

The Governor is the Reserve Bank's chief executive. The Governor supervises and directs the affairs and business of the RBI. The management team also includes Deputy Governors and Executive Directors.

The Central Government nominates fourteen Directors on the Central Board, including one Director each from the four Local Boards. The other ten Directors represent different sectors of the economy, such as, agriculture, industry, trade, and professions. All these appointments are made for a period of four years. The Government also nominates one Government official as a Director representing the Government, who is usually the Finance Secretary to the Government of India and remains on the Board 'during the pleasure of the Central Government'. The Reserve Bank Governor and a maximum of four Deputy Governors are also ex-officio Directors on the Central Board.

Local Boards

The Reserve Bank also has four Local Boards, constituted by the Central Government under the RBI Act, one each for the Western, Eastern, Northern and Southern areas of the country, which are located in Mumbai, Kolkata, New Delhi and Chennai. Each of these Boards has five members appointed by the Central Government for a term of four years. These Boards represent territorial and economic interests of their respective areas, and advise the Central Board on matters, such as, issues relating to local cooperative and indigenous banks. They also perform other functions that the Central Board may delegate to them.

Offices and Branches

The Reserve Bank has a network of offices and branches through which it discharges its responsibilities. The units operating in the four metros — Mumbai, Kolkata, Delhi and Chennai — are known as offices, while the units located at other cities and towns are called branches. Currently, the Reserve Bank has its offices, including branches, at 27 locations in India. The offices and larger branches are headed by a senior officer in the rank of Chief General Manager, designated as Regional Director while smaller branches are headed by a senior officer in the rank of General Manager.

The Head office of the RBI, located at Mumbai is divided into several specialized departments. The main departments are:

1. **Issue Department:** It arranges for the issue and distribution of currency notes among the different centers of the country.
2. **Banking Department:** It deals with Government transactions and maintains the cash reserves of the commercial banks.
3. **Department of Banking Development:** It is concerned with the development of banking facilities in the unbanked and rural areas in the country.

4. **Department of Banking Operations:** This department supervises and controls the working of the banking institutions in the country.
5. **Non-Banking Companies Department:** It regulates the activities of non-banking financial companies existing in the country.
6. **Agricultural Credit Department:** This department studies the problems connected with the agricultural credit in the country.
7. **Industrial Finance Department:** It is concerned with the provision of finance to the industrial units in the country.
8. **Exchange Control Department:** The entire business of sale and purchase of foreign exchange is conducted by this department.
9. **Legal Department:** The main function of this department is to give legal advices to the other departments of RBI.
10. **Department of Research and Statistics:** This department is concerned with conducting research on problems relating to money, credit, finance, production etc.

Objectives of RBI

Prior to the establishment of the Reserve Bank, the Indian financial system was totally inadequate on account of the inherent weakness of the dual control of currency by the Central Government and of credit by the Imperial Bank of India.

The Preamble to the Reserve Bank of India Act, 1934 spells out the objectives of the Reserve Bank as: "to regulate the issue of Bank notes and the keeping of reserves with a view to securing monetary stability in India and generally to operate the currency and credit system of the country to its advantage."

The important objectives are:

1. **To Act as Monetary Authority:** Formulates implements and monitors the monetary policy to maintain price stability and ensuring adequate flow of credit to productive sectors.
2. **To Regulate and Supervise the Financial System of the Country:** It prescribes broad parameters of banking operations within which the country's banking and financial system functions. It helps to maintain public confidence in the system, protect depositors' interest and provide cost-effective banking services to the public.
3. **To Manage the Exchange Control:** Manages the Foreign Exchange Management Act, 1999 to facilitate external trade and payment and promote orderly development and maintenance of foreign exchange market in India.
4. **To Issue Currency:** Issues and exchanges or destroys currency and coins not fit for circulation to give the public adequate quantity of supplies of currency notes and coins and in good quality.
5. **To Undertake Developmental Role:** RBI performs a wide range of promotional functions to support national objectives.
6. **To Undertake Related Functions by Acting as:**
   - *Banker to the Government:* performs merchant banking function for the central and the state governments; also acts as their banker.
   - *Banker to banks:* maintains banking accounts of all scheduled banks.
   - Owner and operator of the depository (SGL-Subsidiary General Ledger account) and exchange (NDS).

Negotiated Dealing System is an electronic platform for facilitating dealing in Government Securities and Money Market Instruments that will facilitate electronic submission of bids/application for government bonds.

To sum up the objectives include:

1. To manage the monetary and credit system of the country.
2. To stabilizes internal and external value of rupee.
3. For balanced and systematic development of banking in the country.
4. For the development of organized money market in the country.
5. For facilitating proper arrangement of agriculture finance and be in successful for maintaining financial stability and credit in agricultural sector.
6. For proper arrangement of industrial finance.
7. For proper management of public debts.
8. To establish monetary relations with other countries of the world and international financial institutions.
9. For centralization of cash reserves of commercial banks.
10. To maintain balance between the demand and supply of currency.
11. To regulate the financial policy and develop banking facilities throughout the country.
12. To remain free from political influence while making financial decisions
13. To assist the planned process of development of the Indian economy.

Besides the traditional central banking functions, with the launching of the five-year plans in the country, the Reserve Bank of India has been moving ahead in performing a host of developmental and promotional functions, which are normally beyond the purview of a traditional Central Bank.

Functions of RBI

RBI performs various traditional banking function as well as promotional and developmental measures to meet the dynamic requirements of the country. Main functions of RBI can be broadly classified into three. These are:

I. Monetary functions or Central banking functions

II. Supervisory functions

III. Promotional and Developmental functions.

I. Monetary Functions Include

A. Issue of currency notes

B. Acting as banker to the Government

C. Serving as banker of other banks

D. Controlling credit

E. Controlling foreign exchange operations

A. Issue of Currency Notes

Under Section 22 of the Reserve Bank of India Act of 1934, the Reserve Bank of India is given the monopoly of note issue. Now, RBI is the sole authority for the issue of currency notes of all denominations except one rupee notes and coins in the country. One rupee notes and coins are issued by Ministry of Finance of GOI. The RBI has a separate department called the Issue Department for the issue of currency notes.

Since 1956, system of Note Issue changed from **Proportional Reserve System** to **Minimum Reserve System.** Under Proportional reserve system of note issue, not less than 40% of the total volume of notes issue by the RBI was to be covered by gold coins, bullion and foreign securities. But under the Minimum reserve system of note issue, RBI is required to maintain a minimum reserve of gold or foreign securities or both against the notes issued. No maximum limit is fixed on the volume of notes. RBI maintains gold and foreign exchange reserves of ₹ 200 crores of which 115 crores is in gold & balance in foreign securities, Govt. of India securities, eligible commercial bills, Pro-notes of NABARD for any loans etc.

This change from Proportional Reserve System to Minimum Reserve System is made because of two major reasons. Firstly, the planned economic development of the country called for an increased supply of money, which could not be had under the proportional reserve system. Secondly, the foreign exchange held as reserve by the Reserve bank had to be released for financing the five year plans. In short, this was to enable the expanding currency requirements of the economy.

B. Acting as Banker to Government

The Reserve Bank act as a banker to the Central and State Governments. As a banker to the—

Government RBI acts in three capacities, viz., **(*a*) as a banker, (*b*) as a financial agent, and (*c*) as a financial advisor**

(*a*) As a banker: RBI renders the following services:

1. Accepts deposits from the Central and State Government.
2. Collects money on behalf of the Government.
3. Makes payments on behalf of the Governments, in accordance with their instructions.
4. Arranges for the transfer of funds from one place to another on behalf of the Governments.
5. Makes arrangements for the supply of foreign exchange to the Central and State Governments.
6. It maintains currency chests with treasuries and other agencies in places prescribed by the Government of India. These chests are supplied with sufficient currency notes to meet the requirements for the transactions of the Government.
7. Short-term advances are granted to Central and State Governments for a period not exceeding three months. These advances are granted up to a certain limit without any collateral securities.
8. In times of emergencies like war, extraordinary loans are also granted to the Governments by the RBI.

(*b*) As a financial agent: The services given are:

1. Acts as an agent of the Central and State Governments in the matter of floatation of loans. On account of Reserve Bank's intimate knowledge of the financial markets, it is able to obtain the best possible terms for the Government in this matter. Further by coordinating the borrowing programmers of the various Governments, it is able to minimize the adverse effects of Government borrowings on the money and securities market.
2. On behalf of Central Government RBI sells treasury bills of 90 days maturity at weekly auctions and secures short-term finance for the Central Government. Apart from that RBI also sells adhoc treasury bills of 90 day's maturity to the State Governments, Semi-Government Departments and foreign central banks on behalf of the Central Government.
3. RBI manages and keeps the accounts of the public debts of the Central and State Governments. It arranges for the payment of interest and principal amount on the public debt on the due dates.
4. As an agent, RBI also represents Government of India in the International institutions like the IMF, the IBRD etc.

The Reserve Bank is an agent of Central Government and of all State Governments in India except for that of Jammu and Kashmir and Sikkim.

(*c*) As a financial adviser: Renders following services:

1. It advices the Central and State Governments on all financial and economic matters such as the floating of loans, agricultural and industrial finance etc.

2. Advice on matters of International finance is also given to Central Government.
3. It collects the recent information on current economic and financial developments in India and abroad, with the help of its Research and Statistics Department and keeps Government informed periodically.

C. Banker's Bank

RBI acts as banker to Scheduled banks. Scheduled Banks include commercial banks, foreign exchange banks, public sector banks, state co-operative banks and the regional rural banks. As a bankers' bank, it renders the following services:

1. **It holds a part of the cash balances of the commercial banks:** Every commercial bank in India is required to keep with the Reserve Bank a cash balance of not less than 6% of its demand and time liabilities. This rate can be increased up to 20%. The two main purposes of maintaining cash reserve by commercial banks are as follows. Firstly to protect the interest of the depositors, secondly to enable the Reserve Bank to accommodate the commercial banks on times of difficulties and thirdly the Reserve Bank can control the credit created by the commercial banks by varying the statutory cash reserve requirements.
2. **It acts as the clearing house:** By acting as clearing house, the Reserve bank helps the member banks in the settlement of the mutual indebtedness without physical transfer of cash.
3. It provides **cheap remittance facilities** to the commercial banks
4. **It provides financial accommodation to the commercial banks:** At times of financial crisis, the RBI is **the lender of last resort** for the commercial banks. Financial assistance is given by The Reserve bank either by rediscounting eligible bills or by granting loans against approved securities.

D. Control of Credit

RBI undertakes the responsibility of controlling credit in order to ensure internal price stability and promote sufficient credit for the economic growth of the country. Price stability is essential for economic development. To control credit, RBI makes use of both quantitative and qualitative weapons by virtue of the powers given to it by Reserve Bank of India Act of 1934 and the Indian Banking Regulation Act of 1949. These weapons are listed below.

(*a*) Quantitative Weapons

1. Bank Rate Policy: Bank rate is the lending rate of central bank. It is the official minimum rate at which central bank of a country rediscounts the eligible bills of exchange of the commercial banks and other financial institutions or grants short-term loans to them. By increasing bank rate, RBI can make bank credit costlier.

2. Open Market Operations: RBI Act authorizes the RBI to engage in the purchase of securities of central and State Government and such other securities as specified by Central Govt. But by and large, its open market operations are confined to Central Government Securities and to a very limited extend to State Government Securities. RBI uses this weapon to offset the seasonal fluctuations in money market. When there is an excessive supply of money, RBI sells the securities in the open market. In that way RBI is able to withdraw the excess money from circulation. But when there is shortage of money supply in the market, it purchases securities from the open market and as a result, more money is arrived at for circulation.

3. Variable Cash Reserve Ratio: Under the RBI Act of 1934, every scheduled and non- scheduled bank is required to maintain a fixed percentage of total time and demand liabilities as cash reserve with RBI. It is called statutory Cash Reserve Ratio (CRR). An increase in CRR reduces lending capacity of the bank and a decrease in CRR increases the lending capacity. RBI can prescribe a CRR ranging up to 15%.

4. Variable Statutory Liquidity Ratio: According to sec 24 of BRA 1949, every commercial bank is required to maintain a certain percentage of its total deposits in liquid assets such as cash in hand, excess reserve with RBI, balances with other banks, gold and approved Government and other securities. This proportion of liquid assets to total deposits is called SLR. BRA empowers RBI to fix the SLR up to 40%. The variation of the SLR is intended to reduce the lendable funds in the hands of the commercial banks and to check the expansion of bank credit. An increase in SLR will decrease the lendable funds in the hands of commercial banks and vice versa.

5. Repo Rate and Reverse Repo Rate: Repo rate is the rate at which RBI lends to commercial banks generally against government securities. Reduction in Repo rate helps the commercial banks to get money at a cheaper rate and increase in Repo rate discourages the commercial banks to get money as the rate increases and becomes expensive. Reverse Repo rate is the rate at which RBI borrows money from the commercial banks. The increase in the Repo rate will increase the cost of borrowing and lending of the banks which will discourage the public to borrow money and will encourage them to deposit. As the rates are high the availability of credit and demand decreases resulting to decrease in inflation. This increase in Repo Rate and Reverse Repo Rate is a symbol of tightening of the policy.

(*b*) Selective Credit Controls (Qualitative Weapons)

1. Credit Ceiling: In this operation, RBI issues prior information or direction that loans to the commercial banks will be given up to a certain limit. In this case commercial bank will be tight in advancing loans to the public. They will allocate loans to limited sectors. Few example of ceiling are agriculture sector advances, priority sector lending.

2. Credit Authorization Scheme: Credit Authorization Scheme was introduced in November, 1965 when P.C. Bhattacharya was the chairman of RBI. Under this instrument of credit, the commercial banks are required to obtain the RBI's prior authorization for sanctioning any fresh credit beyond the authorized limits.

3. Moral Suasion: Moral Suasion is just as a request by the RBI to the commercial banks to follow a particular line of action. RBI may request commercial banks not to give loans for unproductive purpose which does not add to economic growth but increases inflation.

4. Regulation of Margin Requirements: Margin refers to the difference between loan amount and the market value of collateral placed to raise the loan. RBI fixes a lower margin to borrowers whose need is urgent. For *e.g.*, if RBI believes that farmers should be financed urgently, RBI would direct to lower the margin requirement on agricultural commodities. RBI has used this weapon for a number of times.

5. Issuing of Directives: BRA empowers RBI to issue directives to banks and banks are bound to comply with such directives. RBI directives may relate to:

- Purpose for which advance may or may not be made
- Margins requirement
- Maximum amount of loan that can be sanctioned to any company, firm or individual
- Rate of interest and other terms and conditions on which loans may be given.

E. Control of Foreign Exchange Operations

One of the central banking functions of the RBI is the control of foreign exchange operations. For the control of foreign exchange business, the RBI has set up a separate department called the Exchange Control Department in September, 1939. This Department has been granted wide powers to regulate the foreign exchange business of the country. As the central bank of India, it is the responsibility of the RBI to maintain the external value of the Indian rupee stable. India being member of the IMF, the RBI is required to maintain stable exchange rates between the Indian rupee and the currencies of all other member countries of the I.M.F. Besides maintaining stable exchange rates, RBI also acts as the custodian of the foreign exchange reserves of the country. The foreign exchange reserves of the country held by RBI includes Euro, U.S. dollars, Japanese yen etc.

RBI also acts as the administrator of exchange control. It ensures that the foreign exchange reserves of the country are utilized only for approved purposes and the limited foreign exchange reserves of the country are conserved for the future.

II. Supervisory Functions

RBI has been given several supervisory powers over the different banking institutions in the country. The supervisory functions relate to licensing and establishment, branch expansion, liquidity of assets, amalgamation, reconstruction and liquiditation of commercial banks and cooperative banks.

III. Promotional and Developmental Functions

RBI is also performing promotional and developmental functions. These functions includes the following:

(*a*) Provision of Agricultural Credit: For the promotion of agricultural credit, RBI has set up a separate department called the Agricultural Credit Department. It has also set up two funds namely – 1. The National Agricultural Credit (Long-term operations) and 2. The National Agricultural credit (stabilization) fund for facilitating Long-term, Medium-term and Short-term finance for agricultural purposes.

(*b*) Provision for Industrial Finance: RBI has played a very significant role in the field of industrial finance by helping the setting up of a number of public sector industrial finance corporations that provide short-term, medium-term and long-term finance for industrial purpose. These industrial finance corporations include 1. Industrial finance Corporation of India (IFCI), 2. State Finance Corporations (SFC), Industrial Development Bank of India (IDBI), 3.Industrial Reconstruction Corporation of India (IRCI), 4. Refinance Corporation of India, and 5. Unit Trust of India (UTI).

Besides the above, RBI also renders the Credit Guarantee Scheme which intends to give protection to banks against possible losses in respect of their advances to small scale industrial units.

(*c*) Development of Bill Market: A bill market is a place where short-term bill of 3 month duration are generally discounted or rediscounted. RBI plays a very important role in the promotion of Bill Market as a well-developed bill market is essential for the smooth functioning of the credit system.

(*d*) Collection and Publication of Statistics on Financial and Economic Matters: These functions of RBI are extremely useful to the Government in knowing and solving the various economic problems. They are also of immense help to financial institutions, business and industry and for general public.

(*e*) Miscellaneous Functions: RBI has established training centers for staff for its own staff and other banks. Bankers' training college Mumbai, National Institute of Bank Management Mumbai, Staff Training College Madras, and College of Agricultural Banking at Pune are the institutions run by RBI.

DEVELOPMENTAL ROLE

The Reserve Bank is one of the few central banks that has taken an active and direct role in supporting developmental activities in their countries. The Reserve Bank's developmental role includes ensuring credit to productive sectors of the economy, creating institutions to build financial infrastructure, and expanding access to affordable financial services. Over the years, its developmental role has extended to institution building for facilitating the availability of diversified financial services within the country. The Reserve Bank today also plays an active role in encouraging efficient customer service throughout the banking industry, as well as extension of banking service to all, through the thrust on financial inclusion.

Towards this goal, which has evolved over many years, the Reserve Bank has taken various initiatives.

RURAL CREDIT

Given the predominantly agrarian character of the Indian economy, the Reserve Bank's role has been to ensure timely and adequate credit to the agricultural sector at affordable cost. Section 54 of the RBI Act, 1934 states that the Bank may maintain expert staff to study various aspects of rural credit and development and in particular, it may tender expert guidance and assistance to the National Bank (NABARD) and conduct special studies in such areas as it may consider necessary to do so for promoting integrated rural development.

Priority Sector Lending

The focus on priority sectors can be traced to the Reserve Bank's credit policy for the year 1967-68, and institution of a scheme of 'social control' over commercial banks in 1967 by the Government of India to remove certain deficiencies observed in the functioning of the banking system, such as, bulk of bank advances directed to large and medium-scale industries and established business houses. In order to provide access to credit to the neglected sectors, a target based priority sector lending was introduced from the year 1974, initially with public sector banks. The scheme was gradually extended to all commercial banks by 1992.

The scope and extent of priority sectors have undergone several changes since the formalisation of description of the priority sectors in 1972. The guidelines on lending to priority sector were revised with effect from April 30, 2007. The guiding principle of the revised guidelines on lending to priority sector has been to ensure adequate flow of bank credit to those sectors of the society/economy that impact large segments of the population and weaker sections, and to the sectors which are employment-intensive, such as, agriculture and small enterprises. The broad categories of advances under priority sector now include agriculture, micro and small enterprises sector, microcredit, education and housing.

Lead Bank Scheme

The Reserve Bank introduced the Lead Bank Scheme in 1969. Here, designated banks were made key instruments for local development and were entrusted with the responsibility of identifying growth centres, assessing deposit potential and credit gaps and evolving a coordinated approach for credit deployment in each district, in concert with other banks and other agencies. The Reserve Bank has assigned a Lead District Manager for each district who acts as a catalytic force for promoting financial inclusion and smooth working between government and banks.

Special Agricultural Credit Plan

With a view to augmenting the flow of credit to agriculture, Special Agricultural Credit Plan (SACP) was instituted and has been in operation for quite some time now. Under the SACP, banks are required to fix self-set targets showing an increase of about 30 per cent over previous year's disbursements on yearly basis (April – March). The public sector banks have been formulating SACP since 1994. The scheme has been extended to Private Sector banks as well from the year 2005-06.

Kisan Credit Cards

The Kisan Credit Card (KCC) Scheme was introduced in the year 1998-99 to enable the farmers to purchase agricultural inputs and draw cash for their production needs. On revision of the KCC Scheme by NABARD in 2004, the scheme now covers term credit as well as working capital for agriculture and allied activities and a reasonable component for consumption needs.

Under the scheme, the limits are fixed on the basis of operational land holding, cropping pattern and scales of finance. Seasonal sub-limits may be fixed at the discretion of the banks. Limits may be fixed taking into account the entire production credit needs along with ancillary activities relating to crop production, allied activities and also non-farm short-term credit needs (consumption needs). Limits are valid for three years subject to annual review. Security, margin and rate of interest are as per RBI guidelines issued from time to time.

Natural Calamities – Relief Measures

In order to provide relief to bank borrowers in times of natural calamities, the Reserve Bank has issued standing guidelines to banks. The relief measures include, among other things, rescheduling/conversion of short-term loans into term loans; fresh loans; relaxed security and margin norms; treatment of converted/rescheduled agriculture loans as 'current dues'; non-compounding of interest in respect of loans converted/rescheduled; and moratorium of at least one year.

MICRO, SMALL AND MEDIUM ENTERPRISES DEVELOPMENT

With the enactment of the Micro, Small and Medium Enterprises Development (MSMED) Act, 2006, the services sector has also been included in the definition of micro, small and medium enterprises, apart from extending the scope to medium enterprises. The Act sought to modify the definition of micro, small and medium enterprises engaged in manufacturing or production and providing or rendering of services.

Some of the major measures by RBI/ GOI to improve the credit flow to the MSE sector are as under:

- **Collateral Free Loans:** Reserve Bank has issued instructions/guidelines advising banks to sanction collateral free loans up to ₹ 5 lakh to the MSE borrowers. Further, banks have also been advised to lend collateral free loans up to ₹ 25 lakh, based on good track record and financial position of the units.
- **Credit Guarantee Scheme for Small Industries by SIDBI:** The main objective of the Credit Guarantee Scheme (CGS) for MSEs is to make available bank credit to first generation entrepreneurs for setting up their MSE units without the hassles of collateral/third party guarantee. The Scheme envisages that the lender availing guarantee facility would give composite credit so that the borrowers obtain both term loan and working capital facilities from a single agency. The Trust at present is providing guarantee to collateral free loans up to ₹ 1 crore under the scheme.
- **Specialised MSE Branch in every District:** Public sector banks were advised in August 2005 to operationalise at least one specialised MSE branch in every district and centre having a cluster of MSE enterprises. At the end of March 2009, 869 specialised MSE bank branches were operationalised by banks.
- **Formulation of "Banking Code for MSE Customers":** The Banking Codes and Standards Board of India (BCSBI) has formulated a voluntary Code of Bank's Commitment to Micro and Small Enterprises and has set minimum standards of banking practices for banks to follow when they are dealing with MSEs.
- **Working Group on Rehabilitation/Nursing of Potentially Viable Sick SME Units:** Detailed guidelines have been issued to banks advising them to evolve Board approved policies for the MSE sector relating to:
  - (*i*) Loan policy governing extension of credit facilities.
  - (*ii*) Restructuring/Rehabilitation policy for revival of potentially viable sick units/enterprises.
  - (*iii*) Non-discretionary one time settlement scheme for recovery of non-performing loans.

Institutions to Meet Needs of the Evolving Economy

When India embarked upon the era of planned development, the primary need was to facilitate adequate flow of credit to the industrial and other sectors according to the Plan priorities. A major task undertaken by the Reserve Bank was to put in place the necessary institutional mechanism to complement the planning efforts. This was crucial especially in the context of an underdeveloped and evolving financial system. In the absence of a well-developed capital market, the Reserve Bank played a proactive role in setting up a number of specialised financial institutions at the national and regional level to widen the facilities for term finance to industry and for institutionalisation of savings – a novel departure for a central bank. The institutions set up included:

- 1962: Deposit Insurance Corporation
- 1963: Agricultural Refinance Corporation
- 1964: Unit Trust of India
- 1964: Industrial Development Bank of India
- 1969: National Institute of Bank Management
- 1971: Credit Guarantee Corporation
- 1978: Deposit Insurance and Credit Guarantee Corporation (The DIC and CGC were merged and renamed as DICGC)
- 1982: National Bank for Agriculture and Rural Development
- 1982: Export-Import Bank of India
- 1987: Indira Gandhi Institute of Development Research
- 1988: Discount and Finance House of India
- 1988: National Housing Bank
- 1990: Small Industries Development Bank of India
- 1994: Securities Trading Corporation of India
- 1995: Bharatiya Reserve Bank Note Mudran Private Limited
- 1996: Institute for Development & Research in Banking Technology
- 2001: Clearing Corporation of India Limited
- 2008: National Payments Corporation of India

Export Credit

Recognising the important role of exports in maintaining the viability of external sector and in generating employment, the Reserve Bank had sought to ensure adequate availability of concessional bank credit to exporters. It took the lead role in setting up the Export Import Bank of India (EXIM Bank) in January 1982. In recent years, with the liberalisation of real and financial sectors of the economy, interest rates on export credit have been rationalised within the overall monetary and credit policy framework. In order to provide adequate credit to exporters on a priority basis, the Reserve Bank has also prescribed a minimum proportion of banks' adjusted net bank credit to be lent to exporters by foreign banks.

FINANCIAL INCLUSION

Post-liberalisation and deregulation of the financial sector within the country, it was observed that banking industry has shown tremendous growth in volume and range of services provided while making significant improvements in financial viability, profitability and competitiveness. However, banks had not been reaching and bringing vast segments of the population, especially the underprivileged sections of society, into the fold of basic banking services to the desired extent. This prompted the need for the RBI to develop a specific focus towards Financial Inclusion for inclusive growth.

CUSTOMER SERVICE

The Reserve Bank's approach to customer service focuses on protection of customers' rights, enhancing the quality of customer service, and strengthening the grievance redressal mechanism in banks and also in the Reserve Bank.

The Reserve Bank's initiatives in the field of customer service include the setting up of a Customer Redressal Cell, creation of a Customer Service Department and the setting up of the Banking Codes and Standards Board of India (BCSBI), an autonomous body for promoting adherence to self-imposed codes by banks. In order to strengthen the institutional mechanism for dispute resolution, the Reserve Bank in 1995 introduced the Banking Ombudsman (BO) scheme. The BO is a quasi-judicial authority for resolving disputes between a bank and its customers. At present, there are 15 Banking Ombudsman offices in the country. The scheme covers grievances of the customers against commercial banks, urban cooperative banks and regional rural banks. In 2006, the RBI introduced a revised BO scheme. Under the revised scheme, the BO and the attached staff are drawn from the serving employees of the Reserve Bank. The new scheme is fully funded by the RBI and covers grievances related to credit cards and activities of the selling agents of banks also. Under the BO scheme, both the complainant and the bank, if unsatisfied with the decision of the BO, can appeal against the decisions of the BO to the appellate authority within the Reserve Bank.

Chronology of Important Events in the History of the Reserve Bank

Year	Events
1913	The Royal Commission on Indian Finance and Currency (Chamberlain Commission) underlined the need for a central bank for India.
1926	Hilton Young Commission recommended the establishment of a central bank in India, to be named as Reserve Bank of India.
January 1927	The government introduced "The Gold Standard and Reserve Bank of India" in the legislature.
March 1927	The Bill was referred to a Joint Committee to resolve some of the controversial clauses.
January 1928	Government of India published the "New Gold Standard and Reserve Bank Bill", as amended by the Joint Committee.
February 1929	Government clarified that it did not intend to bring the Reserve Bank Bill before the legislature in the near future.
1931	Report of the Indian Central Banking Enquiry Committee released, strongly recommending the establishment of the Reserve Bank.
March 1933	Report of the India Office Committee released, recommending establishment of Reserve Bank of India as a private shareholders' bank.
July 1933	London Committee, which was set up after the India Office Committee, adopted the 1928 Reserve Bank Bill as the basis and proposed certain amendments to the Bill.
Sept. 1933	Reserve Bank of India Bill, drafted on the basis of London Committee recommendations, introduced in the Legislative Assembly.
Dec. 1933	Reserve Bank of India Bill passed by the Assembly.
February 1934	Reserve Bank of India Bill was passed by the Council of States.
March 1934	Reserve Bank of India Bill received the assent of the Governor-General.
April 1935	The Reserve Bank of India was created as a private share holders' bank. Sir Osborne Smith was appointed the first Governor of the Reserve Bank of India.
July 1937	Sir James Braid Taylor assumed office of the Governor.
March 1937	The Reserve Bank acted as banker to the Government of Burma and was also responsible for note issue in Burma as per the Burma Monetary Arrangements Order.
January 1938	The Reserve Bank issued its own bank notes.
Sept. 1939	Introduction of Exchange Controls in India under Defence of India Rules.
1939	Indian Bank Act to bring banks within the ambit of the Reserve Bank.
March 1940	The Reserve Bank's accounting year changed from January -December to July- June.
1940	The silver rupee replaced by the quaternary alloy rupee. One Rupee note reintroduced. This note had the status of a rupee coin and represented the introduction of official fiat money in India.
August 1943	Sir C. D. Deshmukh took over as Governor.

1944	The Public Debt Act passed by the Government enabled the consolidation of laws relating to Government securities and management of public debt by the Reserve Bank.
February 1945	Non-scheduled banks were allowed to open accounts with the Reserve Bank.
1945	Establishment of Department of Banking Operations and Development and Research and Statistics Department in the Reserve Bank.
January 1946	High Denomination Bank Notes of ₹ 500, ₹ 1,000 and ₹ 10,000 were demonetised to curb unaccounted money.
1946	Interim arrangements for bank supervision were put in place by an ordinance.
March 1947	The Reserve Bank ceased to function as Central Bank of Burma.
1947	Foreign Exchange Regulation Act was passed.
1948	Industrial Finance Corporation of India was established on the recommendation of the Central Board of the Reserve Bank.
June 1948	The Reserve Bank ceased to function as Central Bank of Pakistan.
January 1949	The Reserve Bank was nationalised.
March 1949	Banking Companies Act, 1949 came into force, replacing the earlier interim arrangements. This formed the statutory basis of bank regulation and supervision in India.
July 1949	Sir Benegal Rama Rau assumed office as Governor.
Sept. 1949	Devaluation of the Rupee by 30.5 per cent consequent on the identical devaluation of Pound Sterling.
April 1950	Foreign Exchange Regulation Act, 1949 came into force.
1952	The Reserve Bank launched a pioneering project of All India Rural Credit Survey.
Sept. 1954	The Reserve Bank set up Bankers' Training College at Mumbai (earlier Bombay).
May 1955	The Imperial Bank was nationalised and renamed as State Bank of India with the Reserve Bank taking a 60 per cent stake in it.
1956	Introduction of selective credit controls.
October 1956	Introduction of decimal coinage.
1956	System of note issue was changed from proportional reserve system to minimum reserve system.
January 1957	Shri K.G. Ambegoankar was appointed as Governor.
March 1957	Shri HVR Iyengar appointed as Governor.
1961	Failure of two commercial banks, namely, Palai Central Bank Ltd (Kerala) and Lakshmi Bank (Maharashtra). This led to deliberations on the need for deposit insurance in India.
1962	Deposit Insurance Corporation came into existence.
March 1962	Shri P.C. Bhattacharya appointed as Governor.
July 1963	Agricultural Refinance Corporation was set up as a subsidiary of the Reserve Bank.
1963	Reserve Bank Staff Training College (RBSC) was established.
February 1964	Unit Trust of India came into existence with 50 per cent share holding by the Reserve Bank.
June 1964	Industrial Development Bank of India came into existence with the Reserve Bank wholly contributing the capital of ₹ 10 crore.
1966	Cooperative banks brought under the ambit of regulation of the Reserve Bank.
June 1966	Indian rupee was devalued by 36.5 per cent.
March 1966	Department of Financial Companies was established.
April 1967	The size of the bank notes was reduced.
July 1967	Shri L.K. Jha appointed as Governor.
April 1968	Demonetisation of quaternary coins.
May 1968	The Bill for setting up of the Agricultural Credit Corporation passed in Parliament.
Dec. 1968	The Deposit Insurance Corporation (Amendment) Bill, 1968 came into force. All central, state and urban cooperative banks with paid-up capital of Rs 1 lakh or more were covered under the scheme.
1969	The government propounded the tenet of "Social Banking". This led to nationalisation of 14 commercial banks.
July 1969	The Banking Companies (Acquisition and Transfer of Undertakings) Ordinance 1969 promulgated.
Sept. 1969	National Institute of Bank Management (NIBM) established at Mumbai which was subsequently shifted to Pune.
Sept. 1969	Cooperative Bankers Training College was established at Pune.
May 1970	Shri B.N. Adarkar appointed as Governor.
June 1970	Shri S. Jagannathan appointed as Governor.
January 1971	Credit Guarantee Corporation of India was established.
Dec. 1972	Basic Statistical Returns (BSR) Scheme introduced to collect banking statistics.
Sept.1973	The Foreign Exchange Regulation Act, 1947 was amended.
January 1974	Foreign Exchange Regulation Act, 1973 came into force. The Cooperative Bankers' Training College was renamed as College of Agricultural Banking.
1975	Exchange rate of Rupee was linked to the basket of currencies of major trading partners.
May 1975	Shri N. C. Sengupta was appointed as Governor.
August 1975	Shri K. R. Puri was appointed as Governor.
Nov. 1975	Agricultural Refinance Corporation (ARC) was renamed as Agricultural Refinance and Development Corporation (ARDC).
February 1976	Regional Rural Banks Act, 1976 received assent of the President.
February 1976	Industrial Development Bank of India delinked from the Reserve Bank.
May 1977	Shri M. Narasimham was appointed as Governor.
Dec. 1977	Dr. I.G. Patel was appointed as Governor.
January 1978	Demonetisation of high denomination notes (₹ 1,000, ₹ 5,000 and ₹ 10,000) effected.
July 1978	Deposit Insurance Corporation and Credit Guarantee Corporation of India Ltd. were merged and renamed as Deposit Insurance and Credit Guarantee Corporation (DICGC).
April 1979	Six more Indian scheduled commercial banks were nationalised.

July 1982	National Bank for Agriculture and Rural Development (NABARD) was set up.
Sept. 1982	Dr. Manmohan Singh was appointed as Governor.
1984	MICR Clearing was introduced. Release of Sukhomoy Chakravarty Report on monetary measurement; Dr. C. Rangarajan (Deputy Governor) Committee Report on computerisation in banking system.
1985	The Reserve Bank celebrates its Golden Jubilee Year. The Honourable Prime Minister Rajiv Gandhi graced the inaugural function.
January 1985	Shri A. Ghosh was appointed as Governor.
February 1985	Shri R.N. Malhotra was appointed as Governor.
Dec. 1987	Indira Gandhi Institute of Development and Research was set up.
April 1988	Discount and Finance House of India Ltd. was set up, marking the beginning of RBI's role in financial markets.
July1988	National Housing Bank was set up under the National Housing Bank Act, 1987.
1990	Small Industries Development Bank of India was set up.
Dec. 1990	Shri S. Venkitaramanan was appointed as Governor.
1991	Paradigm shift in economic management and the Reserve Bank steps in as the facilitator. Support to economic reforms, liberalisation, privatisation, and globalisation and contributory presence in world bodies.
July 1991	The value of the rupee was adjusted downwards in two stages, on July 1 and 3, 1991. Two-step downward adjustment of the rupee in terms of the intervention currency, pound sterling, worked out to 17.38 per cent. Thereafter, the rupee exchange rate was anchored on a rupee-US dollar rate close to ₹ 26 a dollar.
August 1991	A high-powered Committee on the Financial System (CFS) was constituted by the Government of India in August 1991 to examine all aspects relating to the structure, organisation, functions and procedures of the financial system (Chairman: Shri M. Narasimham).
Nov. 1991	Committee on the Financial System submitted its report in November 1991, made wide-ranging recommendations, which formed the basis of financial sector reforms relating to banks, development financial institutions (DFIs) and the capital market in the years to come.
March 1992	A dual exchange rate system called Liberalised Exchange Rate Management System (LERMS) introduced. Forex management under deregulated regime led to a series of measures culminating in FEMA 1999.
Dec. 1992	Dr. C. Rangarajan was appointed as Governor.
1993	Unified Exchange Rate was introduced.
August 1994	Rupee made convertible on the Current Account. India attained the status of Article VIII of the Articles of Agreement of the IMF.
Sept. 1994	The Reserve Bank and the Government of India signed an agreement as per which automatic monetisation of the budget deficit through the issue of ad-hoc treasury bills would phase out over a period of three years.
Nov. 1994	Board for Financial Supervision constituted as a Committee of the Central Board of Directors.
February 1995	Bharatiya Reserve Bank Note Mudran Limited established as a fully owned subsidiary of the Reserve Bank. It commenced printing of notes on June 1 and December 11, at Mysore and Salboni, respectively.
June 1995	Banking Ombudsman scheme for redressal of customer grievance against the banking sector introduced.
1996	The Reserve Bank becomes a member of the Bank for International Settlements.
July 1996	Institute for Development and Research in Banking Technology, Hyderabad was established by the Reserve Bank as an autonomous entity.
Sept. 1996	The Reserve Bank's Web site became operational
April 1997	The Reserve Bank and the Government of India agreed to replace the system of ad-hoc Treasury Bills by Ways and Means Advances, ending automatic monetisation of fiscal deficits.
Nov. 1997	Dr. Bimal Jalan was appointed as Governor.
April 1998	The framework for further strengthening the banking sector was provided by the Committee on Banking Sector Reforms (Chairman: Shri M. Narasimham)
Dec. 1998	The Monetary Museum Web Site launched.
1999	"Clean Note Policy" introduced for better currency management.
Dec. 1999	Foreign Exchange Management Act, 1999 replaced FERA, 1973.
June 2000	FEMA became operational.
April 2001	Clearing Corporation of India was established.
March 2002	Bharatiya Reserve Bank Note Mudran became private limited company.
Sept. 2003	Dr. Y.V. Reddy was appointed as Governor.
February 2004	Market Stabilisation Scheme was launched.
Nov. 2004	The Reserve Bank Monetary Museum was set up in Mumbai.
January 2006	Revamped Banking Ombudsman Scheme came into effect.
March 2006	Banking Codes and Standards Board of India constituted.
July 2006	Customer Service Department was set up at the Reserve Bank.
2008	Payment and Settlements System Act, 2007 came into force with effect from August 12, 2008. Cheque truncation was introduced in Delhi region as a pilot project.
Sept. 2008	Dr. D. Subbarao was appointed as Governor.
Dec. 2008	Incorporation of National Payment Corporation of India.
2008/9	RBI pursued an accommodative monetary policy beginning mid-September 2008 to mitigate the adverse impact of the global financial crisis on the economy.
April 2009	The Reserve Bank enters its Platinum Jubilee year.
July 2009	The Reserve Bank establishes a new department — Financial Stability Unit.
Nov. 2009	The Reserve Bank purchased 200 mts of gold under IMF's limited gold sales programme.
2009/10	From October 2009, the RBI began the process of exit from the expansionary monetary policy.
2013	Rahuram Rajan took charge as the 23rd Governor of RBI
2018	Shaktikanta Das was appointed as 25th Governor of RBI.

RBI PUBLICATIONS

Annual

(a) Statutory

(*i*) Annual Report

(*ii*) Trend and Progress of Banking in India

(b) Others

(*i*) A Profile of Banks

(*ii*) Annual Report on Banking Ombudsman Scheme, 2007-08

(*iii*) Basic Statistical Returns of Scheduled Commercial Banks in India

(*iv*) Branch Banking Statistics

(*v*) Directory of Commercial Bank Offices in India

(*vi*) Handbook of Monetary Statistics of India

(*vii*) Handbook of Statistics on Indian Economy

(*viii*) Manual on Financial and Banking Statistics

(*ix*) Report on Currency and Finance

(*x*) State Finances : A Study of Budgets

(*xi*) Statistical Tables Relating to Banks in India

Half-Yearly

Report on Foreign Exchange Reserves

Quarterly

(*i*) Macroeconomic and Monetary Developments

(*ii*) Occasional Papers

(*iii*) Quarterly Statistics on Deposits and Credit of Scheduled Commercial Banks

(*iv*) Survey of Professional Forecasters

(*v*) Variation to Foreign Exchange Reserves in India: Sources, Arbitrage and Costs

Monthly

(*i*) Monetary and Credit Information Review

(*ii*) RBI Bulletin

Weekly

Weekly Statistical Supplement

Other Important Publications

- Book on 'External Debt Management: Issues, Lessons and Preventive Measures'
- DRG Studies
- Handbook of Instructions-Basic Statistical Returns 1 and 2
- Handbook of Statistics on State Government Finances
- India's Financial Sector an Assessment Vol. I to VI 2009
- Mint Road Milestones - RBI at 75
- Payment Systems in India
- Perspectives on Central Banking — Governors Speak (1935 to 2010)
- RBI - Note Refund Rules
- RBI - Staff Studies
- Reports on Currency and Finance - Special Edition
- Reserve Bank of India: Functions and Working
- The Banking Ombudsman Scheme, 2002
- The Banking Ombudsman Scheme, 2006
- The Reserve Bank of India History 1935 - 1981 (3 Volumes)
- 50 Years of Central Banking - Governors Speak

MULTIPLE CHOICE QUESTIONS

1. Which of the following is correct?
A. Reserve Bank of India Act, 1935
B. Reserve Bank of India Act, 1934
C. Reserve Bank of India Act, 1930
D. Reserve Bank of India Act, 1937
E. None of these

2. The Central Office of the Reserve Bank was initially established in ....
A. Indore B. Delhi
C. Calcutta D. Mumbai
E. None of these

3. The Central Office of the Reserve Bank of India is now located at:
A. Mumbai B. Hyderabad
C. New Delhi D. Goa
E. None of these

4. The Central Office of the Reserve Bank was permanently moved to Mumbai in ....
A. 1934 B. 1937
C. 1935 D. 1938
E. None of these

5. Which among the following is correct about The Central Office of RBI?
A. Where Governor Sits
B. Where only Policies are formulated
C. Both of above
D. Where Governor doesn't sit
E. None of these

6. When RBI came into existence on 1-4-1935, it was:
A. Privately Owned
B. Governmental Owned

C. Privately + Governmental Owned
D. All are correct
E. None of these

7. Reserve Bank is fully owned by the Government of India since nationalization in:
A. 1950 B. 1949
C. 1965 D. 1947
E. None of these

8. Management of RBI consists of (Regarding Governor and Deputy Governors):
A. 1 Governor + 3 Deputy Governor
B. 1 Governor + 4 Deputy Governor
C. 1 Governor + 5 Deputy Governor
D. 1 Governor + 6 Deputy Governor
E. None of these

9. BFS stands for:
A. Bureau of Financial Supervision
B. Board for Financial Supervision
C. Bi-lateral Financial System
D. All of these
E. None of these

10. The BFS was constituted in:
A. December 1994 B. November 1994
C. September, 1994 D. May 1994
E. None of these

11. Which among the following is correct about objectives of BFS?
A. To undertake cosolidated supervision of the financial sector
B. Financial Sector comprising of commercial banks, financial institutions and non-banking finance companies
C. Both of above
D. Can't Say
E. None of these

12. The BFS's board member are appointed for term of:
A. 2 years B. 3 years
C. 4 years D. 5 years
E. None of these

13. The member of BFS board is chaired by:
A. Any Deputy Governor
B. Governor
C. Deputy Governor appointed by Governor
D. Chief Minister
E. None of these

14. The Deputy Governor in charge of banking regulation and supervision, is nominated as the .... of the (BFS) board.
A. Head B. Vice-Chairman
C. President D. Vice-President
E. None of these

15. RBI does not issue:
A. One Rupee Note B. Hundred Rupee Note
C. Twenty Rupee Note D. Fifty Rupee Note
E. None of these

16. Which state government's business is not transacted by RBI?
A. Himachal Pradesh B. Jammu and Kashmir
C. Manipur D. Bihar
E. None of these

17. The regulatory authority for Regional Rural Banks is RBI and:
A. NABARD B. BhartiyaMahila Bank
C. Laxmi Bank D. Bank of India
E. None of these

18. When RBI desires to restrict expansion of credit it raises the:
A. Bank Rate
B. SLR
C. Both SLR and Bank Rate
D. Remain Constant
E. None of these

19. Sub Section 12AB of section 17 of RBI Act defines the term:
A. Repo Rate B. Reverse Repo Rate
C. SLR D. Bank Rate
E. None of these

20. Where are four regional centres of RBI located?
A. Mumbai, Kolkata, Chennai and Delhi
B. Kolkata, Chennai, Mumbai, Gujrat
C. Gurarat, Mumbai, Kolkata, Delhi
D. Either B or C
E. None of these

21. "INDIA's Central Bank" is a slogan of:
A. Reserve Bank of India
B. State Bank of India
C. IDBI
D. Bank of India
E. None of these

22. SLR stands for:
A. Special Liquidity Ratio
B. Special Lending Rate
C. Statutory Liquidity Ratio
D. Either A or B
E. None of these

23. .... is the rate of interest which is levied on long-term loans and advances taken by commercial banks from RBI.
A. Reverse Repo Rate B. Fixed Interest Rate
C. Bank Rate D. Repo Rate
E. None of these

24. Reserve Bank of India was nationalized in:
A. 1948 B. 1949
C. 1947 D. 1945
E. None of these

25. RBI is lender of last resort which reveals:
A. RBI advances money to public whenever there is any emergency
B. Commercial banks give fund to the RBI
C. RBI advances necessary credit against eligible securities to financial institutions
D. All of the above
E. None of the above

26. Reserve Bank of India was set up on the recommendations of which of the following commission/committee?
A. D.R. Mehta Commission
B. Basel Committee
C. Royal Commission on Indian Currency and Finance
D. K. Santhanam Committee
E. None of these

27. The designer of Indian Rupee Sign is:
A. Hitendra Swami
B. Udaya Kumar Dharmalingam
C. PandurangaKumarlingam
D. Either A or C
E. None of these

28. Number of different denomination notes issued by RBI:
A. 10 B. 9
C. 11 D. All of these
E. None of these

29. Financial Inclusion is:
A. Delivery of banking services at an affordable cost to weaker sections
B. Delivery of financial services at an affordable cost to weaker sections
C. Social responsibility of banking and government system
D. All of above
E. None of these

30. The higher denomination banknotes in ₹ 1,000, ₹ 5,000, ₹ 10,000 were reintroduced by RBI in the year:
A. 1950 B. 1964
C. 1954 D. 1962
E. None of these

31. The denomination of ₹ 1,000, ₹ 5,000, ₹ 10,000 were again demonetized by RBI in:
A. 1970 B. 1978
C. 1984 D. 1976
E. None of these

32. The highest denomination note of ₹ 10,000 was printed first time by RBI in:
A. 1945 B. 1938
C. 1954 D. 1952
E. None of these

33. Number of Language appearing on Bank notes are:
A. 18 B. 15
C. 19 D. 27
E. None of these

34. Which language is prominently displayed in the center where other languages are also appeared in the note?
A. Urdu B. Hindi
C. Gujarati D. Tamil
E. None of these

35. Where the RBI has no branch the bank which can act as its agent is?
A. Any commercial bank
B. Any nationalised bank
C. SBI
D. Indian bank
E. None of these

36. RBI issues currency notes on the basis of........... .
A. Minimum reserve
B. General reserve
C. Proportional reserve
D. Gold reserve
E. None of these

37. The term "Reserve" in Reserve Bank of India indicates:
A. Reserved for Govt. Business alone
B. It keeps reserves of all commercial banks
C. No special significance
D. It keeps foreign currency
E. None of these

38. The authority controlling the clearing house scheme is:
A. RBI B. SBI
C. SEBI D. Govt.
E. None of these

39. Cash Reserve Ratio of banks is insisted in RBI Act of 1934 under section:
A. 15 B. 42
C. 32 D. 18
E. None of these

40. Which of the following is quantitative measure of credit control of RBI?
A. Direct action
B. Moral suasion
C. Open market operation
D. Margin requirement
E. None of these

41. RBI started functioning on ....
A. 1-4-1935 B. 1-4-1948
C. 1-4-1882 D. 1-4-1945
E. None of these

42. The rate at which RBI lends short term funds to bank is:
A. Reverse repo rate B. Repo rate
C. Interest rate D. Liquidity repo rate
E. None of these

43. The proportion of deposits that banks have to keep with RBI is:
A. CRR B. SLR
C. PLR D. LRR
E. None of these

44. For issuing commercial papers:
A. Prior approval of RBI is not required
B. Prior approval of RBI is required
C. Prior approval of SEBI is required
D. Prior approval of SBI is required
E. None of these

45. Certificate of deposits are issued by:
A. RBI B. Commercial banks
C. SBI only D. All the above
E. None of these

46. .... control s the money supply in a country
A. RBI or Central Bank
B. SEBI
C. Government
D. All of these
E. None of these

47. .... is the rate banks receive for depositing funds with the Central Bank:
A. Reverse repo rate B. Repo rate
C. Interest rate D. All of these
E. None of these

48. .... policy is taken by RBI
A. Monetary B. Fiscal
C. Both of them D. All of these
E. None of these

49. Repo rate means
A. rate at which Govt. Borrows money
B. rate at which RBI lends to banks
C. rate at which RBI borrows money
D. rate at which SBI borrows money
E. None of these

50. Whose signature appears on Indian ₹ 100 note?
A. Finance Minister
B. RBI Governor
C. Finance Secretary
D. Chairman, Planning Commission
E. None of these

51. RBI stipulates a healthy mix of CASA in the business figures of banks. What is CASA?
A. Customer Analysis and Savings Pattern
B. Cost Appreciation and Selling Analysis
C. Current Account and Saving Account
D. Credit and Savings Aggregate
E. None of these

52. Who is the Chairman of the committee constituted by RBI to study issues and concerns in the Micro Finance Institutions (MFI) Sector?
A. YH Malegam B. Dr. KC Chakraborty
C. C. Rangrajan D. M. Damodaran
E. Usha Thorat

53. Which of the following tools is used by the RBI to control credit and monetary situations of the markets?
A. RTGS B. NEFT
C. ECS D. CRR
E. Balance of trade

54. Functions of Reserve Bank are:
A. Bankers bank
B. Banker to Government
C. Lender of last resort
D. Controlling financial requirements of banks through Repo/Reverse Repo
E. All the above

55. Reverse Repo Rate has the following characteristic:
A. Borrowing by RBI from banks
B. Borrowing with government security as collateral
C. Short Term Borrowing
D. All the above
E. None of the above

56. The following is a mechanism for injecting liquidity by RBI to the financial system:
A. Reverse Repo
B. Hike in CRR
C. Hike in interest rate
D. Repo
E. None of the above

57. Increasing Cash Reserve Ratio from time to time by Reserve Bank of India leads to:
A. Decrease in deposit
B. Increasing in deposit
C. Increase in lendable resources
D. Decrease in lendable resources
E. Any of the above

58. Who was the first governor of RBI?
A. Osborne Smith B. James Taylor
C. C. Deshmukh D. B.R. Rao
E. None of the above

59. RBI was established in 1935 pursuant to recommendation of:
A. The Hilton Young Commission
B. All India Rural Credit Survey Committee
C. Gorawala Committee
D. Talwar Committee
E. None of the above

60. One rupee note and all coins will be issued by:
A. Reserve Bank of India
B. Central Government
C. Central and State Governments collectively
D. None of the above
E. All the above

61. Who will sign One Rupee Note?
A. Governor- RBI
B. Governors of concerned state governments
C. Finance Secretary, Ministry of Finance
D. Finance Minister
E. None of the above

62. What is MSF?
A. Marginal Standing Facility
B. Micro and Small Finance
C. Medium Size Finance
D. Mid Term Sanction facility
E. None of the above

63. The term 'moral suasion' refers to:
A. The moral duty of a borrower to deal with only one bank
B. The advice given by the Reserve Bank of India to banks/financial institutions in the matter of their lending and other operations with the objective that they might implement or follow it
C. The banker's duty of secrecy as regards the affairs and accounts of his customers
D. All of the above
E. None of the above

64. When the Reserve Bank of India (RBI) is the lender of last resort, what does it mean?
A. RBI advances money to public whenever there is any emergency
B. Commercial banks give fund to the RBI
C. RBI advances necessary credit against eligible securities
D. All of the above
E. None of the above

65. In periods of depression when the Reserve Bank of India (RBI) desires to encourage the banking system to create more credit, what it does?
A. Permits the Bank Rate to be decided by market forces
B. Raises the Bank Rate
C. Reduces the Bank Rate
D. All of the above
E. None of the above

66. In periods of boom, which leads to economic instability, the Reserve Bank of India (RBI) resorts to?
A. Hike in the Bank Rate as a measure of open market operations
B. Buying of approved securities in the market as a measure of open market operations
C. Sale in the market of first class securities in its possession to reduce the supply of money as a measure of open market operations
D. All of the above
E. None of the above

67. Which of the following instruments of credit control adopted by the Reserve Bank of India (RBI) does not fall within 'general' or 'quantitative' methods of credit control?
A. Bank rate
B. Open market operations
C. Stipulation of certain minimum margin in respect of advance against specified commodities
D. Variable reserve requirements
E. None of the these

68. Which of the following extreme measures may be resorted to by the Reserve Bank of India (RBI), in order to safeguard the interest of the depositing public when the affairs of a bank are observed to be beyond redemption?
A. Refusal of a licence or cancellation of an existing licence
B. Merge the bank with any public sector bank
C. Applying to the Central Government for an order of moratorium and thereafter reconstructing or amalgamating the bank with another bank
D. All of the above
E. None of the these

69. For which of the following, the Reserve Bank of India has stipulated the maximum capital adequacy requirement?
A. Private sector banks
B. Banks that undertake insurance business
C. Local Area Banks
D. Scheduled Commercial Banks
E. None of these

70. The currency notes of which of the following denominations are not printed in India?
A. ₹ 5 B. ₹ 10
C. ₹ 50 D. ₹ 1,000
E. ₹ 2,500

71. The Reserve Bank of India was originally constituted as a share holder's Bank with a share capital of
A. ₹ 50 lakh B. ₹ 100 lakh
C. ₹ 10 crores D. ₹ 5 crores
E. None of these

72. Credit rationing is a .... method of credit control.
A. quantitative credit control
B. qualitative credit control
C. direct credit control
D. continuous credit control
E. None of these

73. Which type of securities are held by Reserve Bank of India before issuance of currency notes?
A. Gold coins and bullion
B. Foreign Securities
C. Government of India's securities
D. All of these
E. None of these

74. Introduction of rating methodology for banks was introduced by RBI on the lines of
A. CAMEL B. IRAC
C. CMA D. Either B or C
E. None of these

75. In periods of boom, which leads to economic instability, Reserve Bank resorts to:
A. sale in the market of first class securities in its possession to reduce the supply of money as a measure of open market operations
B. buying of approved securities in the market as a measure of pen market operations
C. hike in the bank rate as a measure of open market operations
D. All the above
E. None of these

76. The primary function of Central Bank is to........... of the country.
A. control the system
B. regulate the monetary system
C. plan the monetary system
D. check and balance the money flow
E. None of these

77. Every Central Bank has the monopoly right of ....
A. moral suasion B. note issue
C. direct action D. credit regulation
E. None of these

78. Open market operation is another important .... weapon of credit control?
A. qualitative B. normal
C. quantitative D. self kill
E. None of the above

79. .... is a method of credit control adopted by the modern central banks?
A. Consumer credit
B. Margin requirements
C. Variable reserve ratio
D. Rationing of credit
E. None of these

80. What is CRR?
A. Cash Reserve Ratio
B. Current Ratio Rate
C. Review Report
D. Credit Rating Record
E. None of these

81. The rate of which discounting the bills of first class banks is done by RBI is called:
A. Bank Rate B. Prime Lending Rate
C. Loan Rate D. Discounting Rate
E. None of these

82. Gilt edged securities refer to:
A. Government Securities
B. Securities issued by Municipal Corporations
C. Securities issued by first class companies
D. Both B and C
E. None of these

83. Full form of SLR:
A. Statutory Liquidity Ratio
B. State Level Recovery
C. Sundry Leverage Ratio
D. State Liquidity Reserve
E. None of these

84. Who is authorised to issue coin in India?
A. RBI B. Ministry of Finance
C. SBI D. All the above
E. None of these

85. Which one is the banker's bank?
A. RBI B. Federal Bank
C. Union Bank D. Bank of India
E. None of these

86. Which one is the custodian of foreign balances of country?
A. RBI B. Federal Bank
C. Union Bank D. Bank of India
E. None of these

87. Which one is the controller of credit?
A. RBI B. Federal Bank
C. Union Bank D. Bank of India
E. None of these

88. Treasury bills are issued by:
A. RBI B. IMF
C. IBRD D. IFCI
E. None of these

89. REPO rate was introduced in:
A. 1990 B. 1992
C. 1982 D. 1980
E. None of these

90. Reverse repo is introduced in:
A. January 1996 B. April 1996
C. November 1996 D. December 1996
E. None of these

91. CTS in India is a project undertaken by ....
A. SBT B. PNB
C. SIB D. RBI
E. None of these

92. CTS in INDIA is undertaken during:
A. 2000 B. 2005
C. 2008 D. 2010
E. None of these

93. RBI first implemented CTS at:
A. Delhi B. Kolkata
C. Mumbai D. Bangalore
E. None of these

ANSWERS

1	2	3	4	5	6	7	8	9	10
B	C	A	B	C	A	B	B	B	B
11	**12**	**13**	**14**	**15**	**16**	**17**	**18**	**19**	**20**
C	A	B	B	A	B	A	A	B	A
21	**22**	**23**	**24**	**25**	**26**	**27**	**28**	**29**	**30**
A	C	C	B	C	C	B	B	D	C
31	**32**	**33**	**34**	**35**	**36**	**37**	**38**	**39**	**40**
B	B	B	B	C	A	B	A	B	C
41	**42**	**43**	**44**	**45**	**46**	**47**	**48**	**49**	**50**
A	B	A	A	B	A	A	A	B	B
51	**52**	**53**	**54**	**55**	**56**	**57**	**58**	**59**	**60**
C	C	D	E	D	D	D	A	A	B
61	**62**	**63**	**64**	**65**	**66**	**67**	**68**	**69**	**70**
C	A	B	C	C	B	C	D	C	E
71	**72**	**73**	**74**	**75**	**76**	**77**	**78**	**79**	**80**
D	B	D	A	A	B	B	C	C	A
81	**82**	**83**	**84**	**85**	**86**	**87**	**88**	**89**	**90**
A	A	A	B	A	A	A	A	B	C
91	**92**	**93**							
D	C	A							

7

State Bank of India (SBI)

EVOLUTION OF STATE BANK OF INDIA

The origin of the State Bank of India goes back to the first decade of the nineteenth century with the establishment of the Bank of Calcutta in Calcutta on 2 June 1806. Three years later the bank received its charter and was re-designed as the Bank of Bengal (2 January 1809). A unique institution, it was the first joint-stock bank of British India sponsored by the Government of Bengal. The Bank of Bombay (15 April 1840) and the Bank of Madras (1 July 1843) followed the Bank of Bengal. These three banks remained at the apex of modern banking in India till their amalgamation as the Imperial Bank of India on 27 January 1921.

Primarily Anglo-Indian creations, the three presidency banks came into existence either as a result of the compulsions of imperial finance or by the felt needs of local European commerce and were not imposed from outside in an arbitrary manner to modernize India's economy. Their evolution was, however, shaped by ideas culled from similar developments in Europe and England, and was influenced by changes occurring in the structure of both the local trading environment and those in the relations of the Indian economy to the economy of Europe and the global economic framework.

The establishment of the Bank of Bengal marked the advent of limited liability, joint-stock banking in India. So was the associated innovation in banking, viz. the decision to allow the Bank of Bengal to issue notes, which would be accepted for payment of public revenues within a restricted geographical area. This right of note issue was very valuable not only for the Bank of Bengal but also its two siblings, the Banks of Bombay and Madras. It meant an accretion to the capital of the banks, a capital on which the proprietors did not have to pay any interest. The concept of deposit banking was also an innovation because the practice of accepting money for safekeeping (and in some cases, even investment on behalf of the clients) by the indigenous bankers had not spread as a general habit in most parts of India. But, for a long time, and especially up to the time that the three presidency banks had a right of note issue, bank notes and government balances made up the bulk of the investible resources of the banks.

The three banks were governed by royal charters, which were revised from time to time. Each charter provided for a share capital, four-fifth of which were privately subscribed and the rest owned by the provincial government. The members of the board of directors, which managed the affairs of each bank, were mostly proprietary directors representing the large European managing agency houses in India. The rest were government nominees, invariably civil servants, one of whom was elected as the president of the board.

The business of the banks was initially confined to discounting of bills of exchange or other negotiable private securities, keeping cash accounts and receiving deposits and issuing and circulating cash notes. Loans were restricted to ₹ 1 lakh and the period of accommodation confined to three months only. The security for such loans was public securities, commonly called Company's Paper, bullion, treasure, plate, jewels, or goods 'not of a perishable nature' and no interest could be charged beyond a rate of twelve per cent. Loans against goods like opium, indigo, salt woolens, cotton, cotton piece goods, mule twist and silk goods were also granted but such finance by way of cash credits gained momentum only from the third decade of the nineteenth century. All commodities, including tea, sugar and jute, which began to be financed later, were either pledged or hypothecated to the bank. Demand promissory notes were signed by the borrower in favor of the guarantor, which was in turn endorsed to the bank. Lending against shares of the banks or on the mortgage of houses, land or other real property was, however, forbidden.

Indians were the principal borrowers against deposit of Company's paper, while the business of discounts on private as well as salary bills was almost the exclusive monopoly of individuals Europeans and their partnership firms. But the main function of the three banks, as far as the government was concerned, was to help the latter raise loans from time to time and also provide a degree of stability to the prices of government securities.

A major change in the conditions of operation of the Banks of Bengal, Bombay and Madras occurred after 1860. With the passing of the Paper Currency Act of 1861, the right of note issue of the presidency banks was abolished and the Government of India assumed from 1 March 1862 the sole power of issuing paper currency within British India. The task of management and circulation of the new currency notes was conferred on the presidency banks and the Government undertook to transfer the Treasury balances to the banks at places where the banks would open branches. None of the three banks had till then any branches (except the sole attempt and that too a short-lived one by the Bank of Bengal at Mirzapore in 1839) although the charters had given them such authority. But as soon as the three presidency bands were assured of the free use of government Treasury balances at places where they would open branches, they embarked on branch expansion at a rapid pace. By 1876, the branches, agencies and sub agencies of the three presidency banks covered most of the major parts and many of the inland trade centers in India. While the Bank of Bengal had eighteen branches including its head office, seasonal branches and sub agencies, the Banks of Bombay and Madras had fifteen each.

The presidency Banks Act, which came into operation on 1 May 1876, brought the three presidency banks under a common statute with similar restrictions on business. The proprietary connection of the Government was, however, terminated, though the banks continued to hold charge of the public debt offices in the three presidency towns, and the custody of a part of the government balances. The Act also stipulated the creation of Reserve Treasuries at Calcutta, Bombay and Madras into which sums above the specified minimum balances promised to the presidency banks at only their head offices were to be lodged. The Government could lend to the presidency banks from such Reserve Treasuries but the latter could look upon them more as a favor than as a right.

The decision of the Government to keep the surplus balances in Reserve Treasuries outside the normal control of the presidency banks and the connected decision not to guarantee minimum government balances at new places where branches were to be opened effectively checked the growth of new branches after 1876. The pace of expansion witnessed in the previous decade fell sharply although, in the case of the Bank of Madras, it continued on a modest scale as the profits of that bank were mainly derived from trade dispersed among a number of port towns and inland centers of the presidency.

India witnessed rapid commercialization in the last quarter of the nineteenth century as its railway network expanded to cover all the major regions of the country. New irrigation networks in Madras, Punjab and Sind accelerated the process of conversion of subsistence crops into cash crops, a portion of which found its way into the foreign markets. Tea and coffee plantations transformed large areas of the eastern Terais, the hills of Assam and the Nilgiris into regions of estate agriculture par excellence. All these resulted in the expansion of India's international trade more than six-fold. The three presidency banks were both beneficiaries and promoters of this commercialization process as they became involved in the financing of practically every trading, manufacturing and mining activity in the sub-continent. While the Banks of Bengal and Bombay were engaged in the financing of large modern manufacturing industries, the Bank of Madras went into the financing of large modern manufacturing industries; the Bank of Madras went into the financing of small-scale industries in a way which had no parallel elsewhere. But the three banks were rigorously excluded from any business involving foreign exchange. Not only was such business considered risky for these banks, which held government deposits, it was also feared that these banks enjoying government patronage would offer unfair competition to the exchange banks which had by then arrived in India. This exclusion continued till the creation of the Reserve Bank of India in 1935.

The presidency Banks of Bengal, Bombay and Madras with their 70 branches were merged in 1921 to form the Imperial Bank of India. The triad had been transformed into a monolith and a giant among Indian commercial banks had emerged. The new bank took on the triple role of a commercial bank, a banker's bank and a banker to the government.

But this creation was preceded by years of deliberations on the need for a 'State Bank of India'. What eventually emerged was a 'half-way house' combining the functions of a commercial bank and a quasi-central bank. The establishment of the Reserve Bank of India as the central bank of the country in 1935 ended the quasi-central banking role of the Imperial Bank. The latter ceased to be bankers to the Government of India and instead became agent of the Reserve Bank for the transaction of government business at centers at which the central bank was not established. But it continued to maintain currency chests and small coin depots and operate the remittance facilities scheme for other banks and the public on terms stipulated by the Reserve Bank. It also acted as a bankers' bank by holding their surplus cash and granting them advances against authorized securities. The management of the bank clearing houses also continued with it at many places where the Reserve Bank did not have offices. The bank was also the biggest tenderer at the Treasury bill auctions conducted by the Reserve Bank on behalf of the Government. The establishment of the Reserve Bank simultaneously saw important amendments being made to the constitution of the Imperial Bank converting it into a purely commercial bank. The earlier restrictions on its business were removed and the bank was permitted to undertake foreign exchange business and executor and trustee business for the first time.

The Imperial Bank during the three and a half decades of its existence recorded an impressive growth in terms of offices, reserves, deposits, investments and advances, the increases in some cases amounting to more than six-fold. The financial status and security inherited from its forerunners no doubt provided a firm and durable platform. But the lofty traditions of banking which the Imperial Bank consistently maintained and the high standard of integrity it observed in its operations inspired confidence in its depositors that no other bank in India could perhaps then equal. All these enabled the Imperial Bank to acquire a pre-eminent position in the Indian banking industry and also secure a vital place in the country's economic life.

When India attained freedom, the Imperial Bank had a capital base (including reserves) of ₹11.85 crores, deposits and advances of ₹ 275.14 crores and ₹ 72.94 crores respectively and a network of 172 branches and more than 200 sub offices extending all over the country.

In 1951, when the First Five Year Plan was launched, the development of rural India was given the highest priority. The commercial banks of the country including the Imperial Bank of India had till then confined their operations to the urban sector and were not equipped to respond to the emergent needs of economic regeneration of the rural areas. In order, therefore, to serve the economy in general and the rural sector in particular, the All India Rural Credit Survey Committee recommended the creation of a state-partnered and state-sponsored bank by taking over the Imperial Bank of India, and integrating with it, the former state-owned or state-associate banks.

An act was accordingly passed in Parliament in May 1955 and the State Bank of India was constituted on 1 July 1955. More than a quarter of the resources of the Indian banking system thus passed under the direct control of the State. Later, the State Bank of India (Subsidiary Banks) Act was passed in 1959, enabling the State Bank of India to take over eight former State-associated banks as its subsidiaries (later named Associates).

ORGANIZATIONAL STRUCTURE

The Bank's management and organizational structure is sufficiently decentralized to provide senior managers decision making responsibility within their business units allowing them to continuously improve their management skills. In 1978, the services of the Indian institute of management, Ahmedabad were engaged and on their advice, the modular structure *i.e.* Zonal and regional offices were created under each local head office to handle growth and achieve efficient branch banking. The administrative structure was decentralized by making the controlling offices near to operating offices.

In 1994, the Bank engaged Mckinsey & co. a firm of leading international consultants to help the bank identify strategies, structures, systems etc. to face the new challenges and retain its eminent position in the Indian banking industry. The present structure of the Bank is the outcome of the comprehensive change programmes covering all aspects structure, system, process, etc. implemented by the bank based on the diagnostic and recommendations of the consultants. In order to exploit the synergies among the various SBUs having close linkages or dealings with the same or integrated groups of customers they have been grouped together under a few business groups, each being headed by a senior executive of the rank Dy. Managing Director.

Each business group has full profit and loss responsibility for the group and enjoys a high level of autonomy including control over human and capital resource in order to achieve the Group's business goals.

The organizational structure of the Bank is reviewed at periodic intervals and wherever feasible departments are merged with a view to improves efficiencies. The bank has carried out the exercise at corporate centre and is rolling it out at local, regional and Zonal office levels.

Corporate Centre

Corporate centre is at the apex level of the organizational structure. It is responsible for long term planning and policy formation. This management of the Bank consists of the following members:

Chairman: Chairman is the chief executive officer of the Bank who presides over the Banks central board of directors.

The staff functionaries are in charge of policy planning functions. The group executives have operational responsibility for the SBUs attached to their groups. All these executives are independently responsible for matters related to their group or staff area and directly report to the chairman.

Local Head Office: Chief General Manager is the top management executive heading the circle. Staff functionaries, network chiefs and the circle vigilance officer directly report to him. The circle management committee covers the following areas:

- Review of business programmes of the circle.
- Review of functioning of all departments at the local head office.
- Ensuring compliance with the corporate objectives at suitable intervals.

Zonal Office: DGM is the executive heading the module. All personal Banking branches, branches with AGM incumbency and AGMs in charge of regions in the module directly report to the DGM. The Zonal office credit committee is constituted to handle credit proposals relating to sanction of loans as well as matters related to advances such as write off, losses, bad debts, initiation, withdrawal of legal action etc.

Regional Office: Assistant general manager is the head of regional network branches with incumbency of chief manager and below in a region. The necessary planning support is provided by the sales planners.

ORGANIZATION CHART AT NATIONAL LEVEL

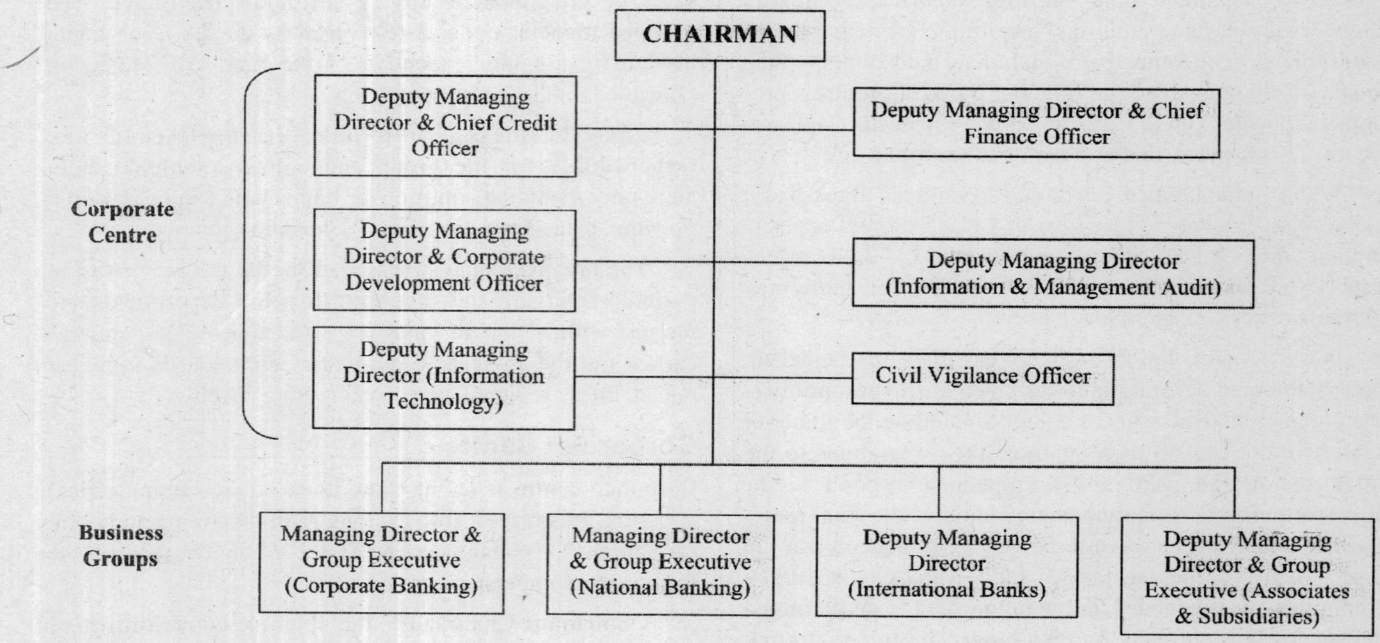

ORGANIZATION CHART AT STATE LEVEL (LOCAL HEAD OFFICE)

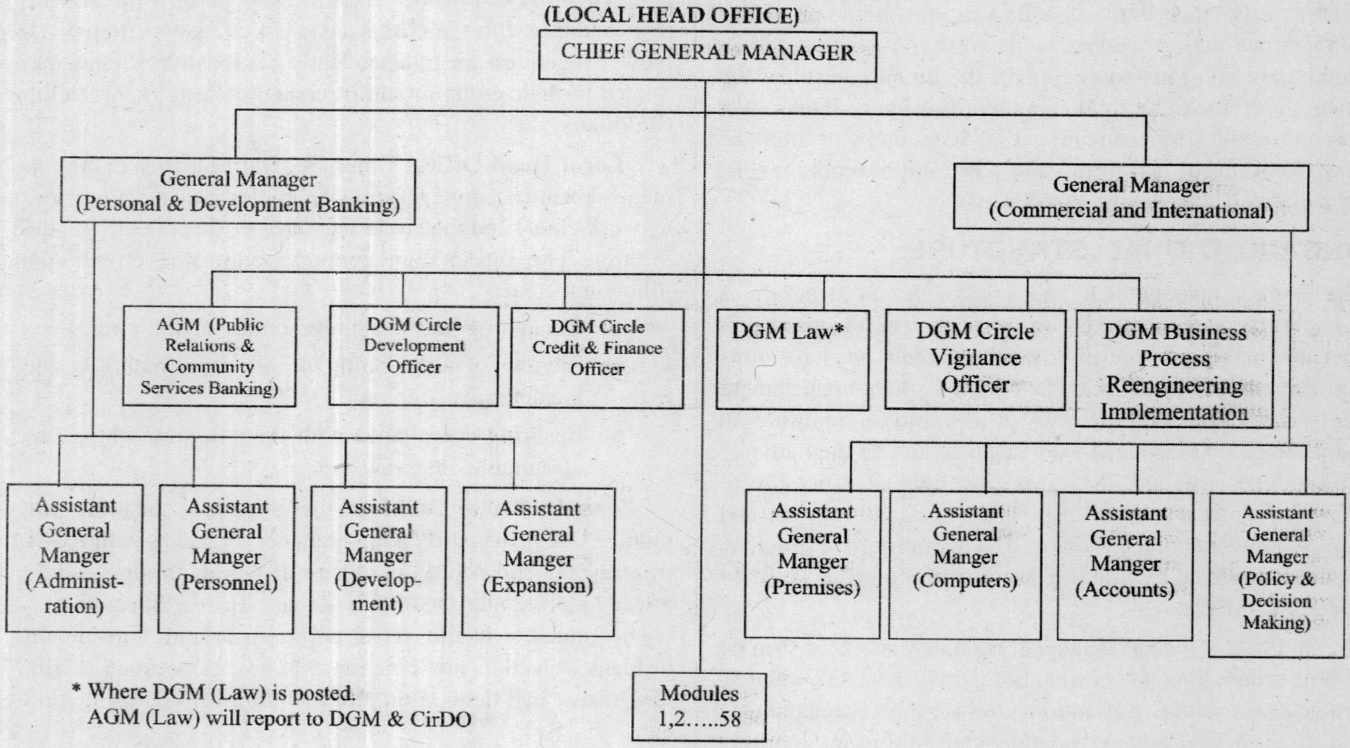

* Where DGM (Law) is posted.
AGM (Law) will report to DGM & CirDO

ORGANISATION CHART OF A REGIONAL OFFICE

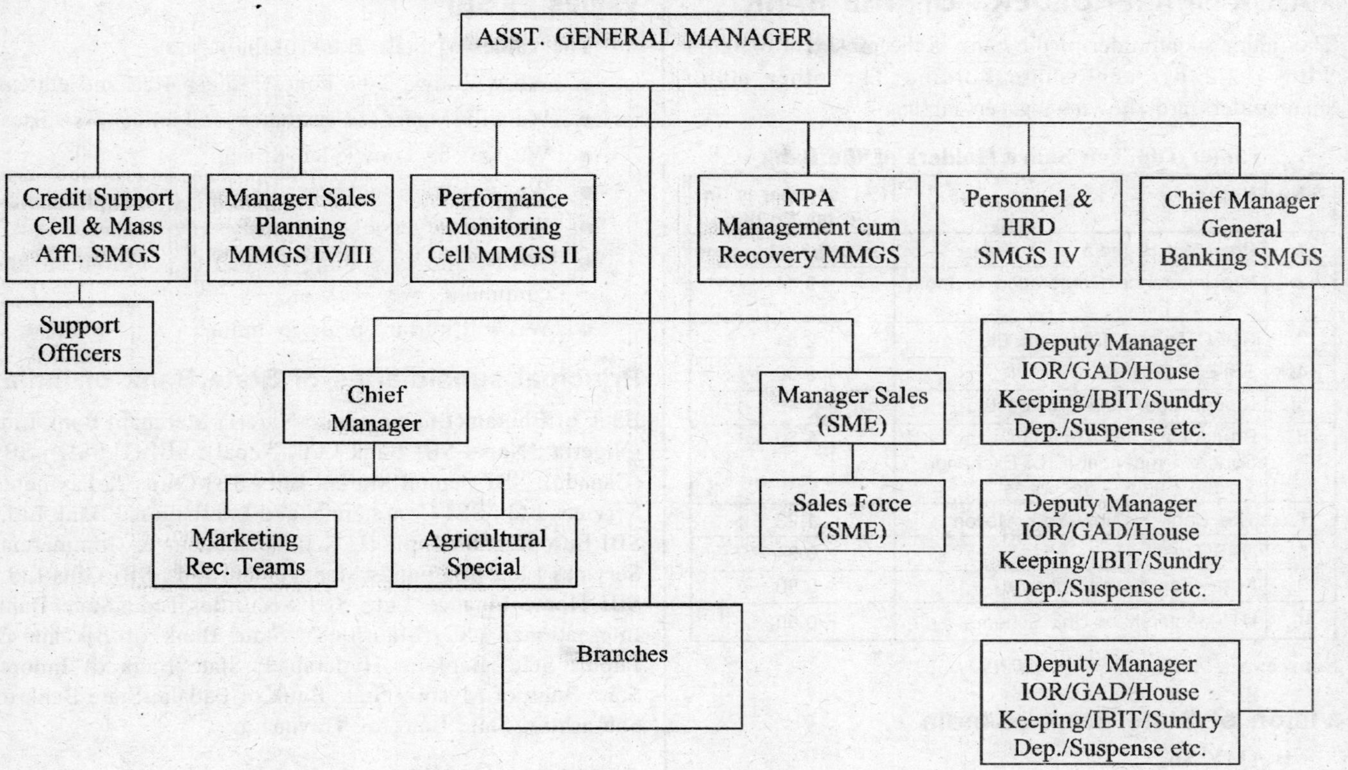

ORGANIZATION CHART OF A BRANCH

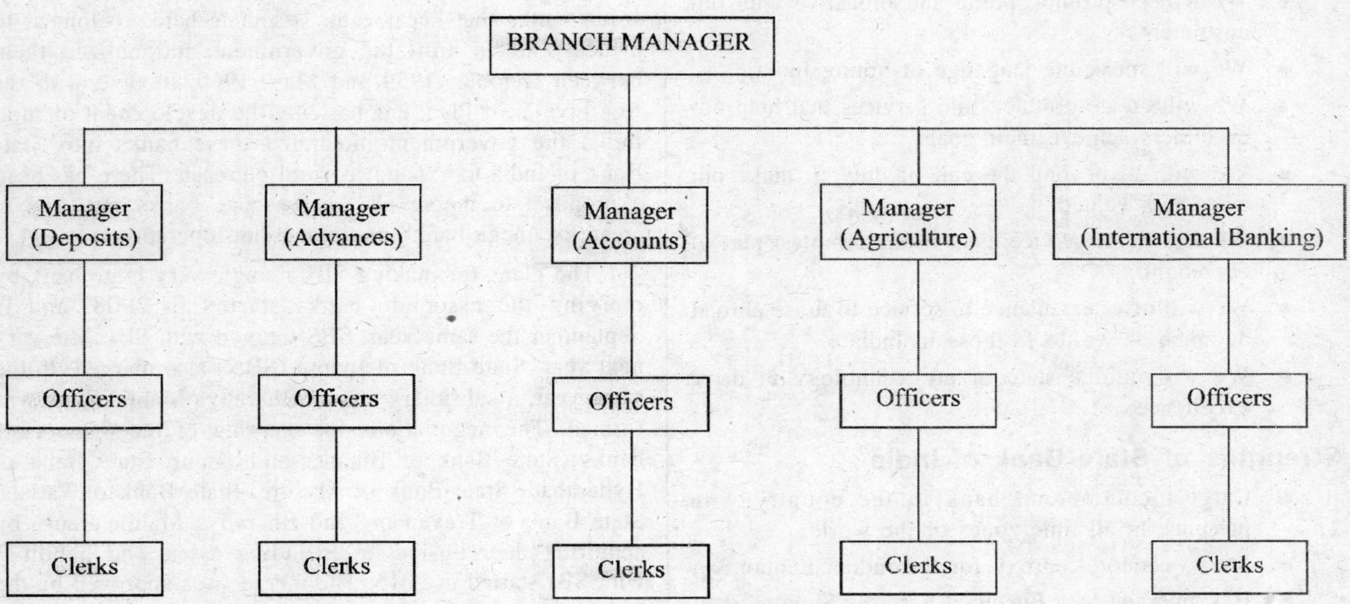

MAJOR SHAREHOLDERS OF THE BANK

The major shareholder of the bank is the president of India with 56.92 per cent share holding The other major shareholders are shown in given table:

Table: Top Ten Share Holders of the Bank

S.No.	Name	(%) of shares in Total Equity
1.	President of India	56.92
2.	Life Insurance Corporation of India P & GS Fund	9.14
3.	HDFC Trustee Company Ltd.	2.84
4.	SBI-ETF SENSEX	2.06
5.	Nippon Life India Trustee Ltd	1.46
6.	Prudential ICICI Trust Ltd - Sensex Prudential ICICI Exchange Traded Fund – Securities	1.36
7.	The Bank of New York Mellon	1.23
8.	NPS Trust	0.94
9.	Kotak Tax Saver Scheme	0.90
10.	UTI-Mastershare Unit Scheme	0.60

Source: *SBI Annual Report - 2020-21*

Vision of State Bank of India

- MY SBI.
- MY CUSTOMER FIRST.
- MY SBI: FIRST IN CUSTOMER SATISFACTION.

Mission of State Bank of India

- We will be prompt, polite and proactive with our customers.
- We will speak the language of young India.
- We will create products and services that help our customers achieve their goals.
- We will go beyond the call of duty to make our customers valued.
- We will be of service even in the remotest part of our country.
- We will offer excellence in service to those abroad as much as we do to those in India.
- We will imbibe state of art technology to drive excellence.

Strengths of State Bank of India

- Largest commercial bank in the country with presence in all time zones of the world.
- Macro economic proxy for the Indian Economy.
- Has emerged as a Financial Services Supermarket.
- Group holds more than 25 per cent market share in deposits and advances.
- Large base of skilled manpower.
- SBI Group has more than 115 million customers – Every tenth Indian is a customer.

Values of SBI

The values of State Bank of India are:

- We will always be honest, transparent and ethical.
- We will respect our customers and fellow associates.
- We will be knowledge driven.
- We will learn and we will share our learning.
- We will never take the early way out.
- We will do everything we can to contribute to the community we work in.
- We will nurture pride in India.

Principal subsidiaries of State Bank of India

Bank of Bhutan (Bhutan); Indo Nigeria Merchant Bank Ltd. (Nigeria); Nepal SBI Bank Ltd. (Nepal); SBI (U.S.A.); SBI (Canada); SBI Capital Market Ltd.; SBI Cards & Payments Services Ltd.; SBI Commercial and International Bank Ltd.; SBI European Bank plc (U.K.); SBI Factors & Commercial Services Ltd.; SBI Funds Management Ltd.; SBI Gilts Ltd.; SBI Home Finance Ltd.; SBI Securities Ltd.; State Bank International Ltd. (Mauritius); State Bank of Bikaner & Jaipur; State Bank of Hyderabad; State Bank of Indore; State Bank of Mysore; State Bank of Patiala; State Bank of Saurashtra; State Bank of Travancore.

Associate Banks

SBI has five associate banks that with SBI constitute the State Bank Group. All use the same logo of a blue keyhole and all the associates use the "State Bank of" name followed by the regional headquarters' name. Originally, the then seven banks that became the associate banks belonged to princely states until the government nationalized them between October, 1959 and May, 1960. In tune with the first Five Year Plan, emphasizing the development of rural India, the government integrated these banks into State Bank of India to expand its rural outreach. There has been a proposal to merge all the associate banks into SBI to create a "mega bank" and streamline operations.

The plans for making SBI a single very large bank by merging the associate banks started in 2008, and in September the same year, SBS merged with SBI. The very next year, State Bank of Indore (SBN) also merged. In the same year, a subsidiary named Bharatiya Mahila Bank was formed. The negotiations for merging of the 6 associate banks (State Bank of Bikaner and Jaipur, State Bank of Hyderabad, State Bank of Mysore, State Bank of Patiala, State Bank of Travancore and Bharatiya Mahila Bank) by acquiring their businesses including assets and liabilities with SBI started in 2016. The merger was approved by the Union Cabinet on 15 June 2016. The State Bank of India and all its associate banks used the same blue Keyhole logo. The State Bank of India word mark usually had one standard typeface, but also utilized other typefaces.

On 15 February 2017, the Union Cabinet approved the merger of five associate banks with SBI. What was overlooked, however, were different pension liability provisions and accounting policies for bad loans, based on regional risks.

The State Bank of Bikaner & Jaipur, State Bank of Hyderabad, State Bank of Mysore, State Bank of Patiala and State Bank of Travancore were merged with State Bank of India with effect from 1 April 2017.

Non-Banking Subsidiaries of SBI

1. SBI Capital Markets Ltd. (SBI CAP)
2. SBI Funds Management Pvt. Ltd (SBI FUNDS)
3. SBI Factors and Commercial Services Pvt. Ltd.
4. SBI DFHI (Discount & Finance House of India) Ltd.
5. SBI GILTS Ltd.
6. SBI Commercial and International Bank Ltd.
7. SBI Mutual Fund (A Trust)

Joint Ventures of SBI

1. SBI Cards and Payment Services Pvt. Ltd.
2. Gt.Capital Business Process Management Service Pvt. Ltd.
3. SBI Life Insurance Co. Ltd.
4. Credit Information Bureau (India) Ltd. (CIBIL)

Other Associates of SBI

1. Clearing Corporation of India Ltd.
2. Nepal SBI Bank Ltd.
3. Bank of Bhutan
4. UTI Asset Management Company Pvt. Ltd.

Foreign Subsidiaries

1. SBI International Mauritius Ltd, Offshore Bank
2. SBI Canada
3. SBI Lagos
4. SBI California

OBJECTIVES OF THE STATE BANK OF INDIA (SBI)

There were certain laudable objectives behind establishing the SBI by nationalising the Imperial Bank. Here, the major aims and objectives of the State Bank of India discuss below:

1. State owned Commercial Bank: The main purpose of instituting the State Bank of India has been to set up a strong public sector commercial bank with a view to providing control over the strategic section of the banking sector in the country.

2. Country Wide Spread: Its aim has been to setup a large network of branches all over the country. According to the State Bank of India Act, the bank has a statutory obligation to open 400 new branches in the rural and semi-urban areas during the first five years of its existence or such extended period as may be permitted by the government.

3. Rural Branches and Agricultural Finance: The SBI at extending banking facilities in rural areas and provide credit to the rural sector. It's main purpose was to start rural branches to fill the vacuum in those areas where other commercial banks were reluctant to move. For this purpose, the SBI created a special fund called the "Integration and Development fund', having an initial investment of ₹ 50 lakhs. The SBI shouldered the responsibility of promoting agricultural finance and overcoming the deficiencies of the system of rural finance.

The SBI also aimed at tapping and mobilising rural savings for productive purposes in the rural sector of the economy.

4. Promoting Co-operative Banking: The State Bank sought to help the growth of Co-operative movement by providing finance, training facilities, etc. To promote agricultural financing, the SBI provides financial assistance to co-operative institutions directly as well as indirectly.

5. Assistance to the Reserve Bank: The SBI also sought to help the Reserve Bank in effectively implementing its monetary and credit policies. The SBI also aims at channelising the flow of its credit in tune with the broad objectives of the monetary policy of the country.

6. Supporting General Economic Policy and Planning: The SBI is supposed to conduct its activities in conformity with the major macro-economic goals and the general economic policies and planning designed by the government.

FUNCTIONS OF THE STATE BANK OF INDIA

The functions on the business transactions of the State Rank of India are stipulated under the State Bank of India Act, 1955. Some of the major functions may be mentioned as under:

1. Agent of the Reserve Bank of India: The State Bank of India acts as an agent of the Reserve Bank of India at all places in the country where there are no Branches of the banking Department of Reserve Bank. At such places, instead of Reserve Bank, it plays receives, collects and remits money, bullion, securities on behalf of the government and also transacts other business entrusted to it by the Reserve Bank.

2. Advancing and Lending: The State Bank of India advances and lends money and open cash credit against the security of; (*a*) stock, funds, other securities (except immovable property) in which a trustee is authorized to invest trust money; (*b*) debentures or others securities issued by or on behalf of a district hoard, municipal board, other local board or committee, under the authority of law, (*c*) debentures of companies with limited liability; (*d*) bypothecation of goods to the State Bank; (*e*) Bill of exchange and pro-notes, etc.

3. Dealing in Bill of Exchange: The State Bank of India undertakes the business of drawing, accepting, discounting, buying and selling of bill of exchange and other negotiable securities.

4. Investment: The investment of the funds of the bank in any specified securities and the conversion of the same into money.

5. Remittances: The issuing of demand drafts, telegraphic transfers and other remittances.

6. Deposits: Receiving of deposits and keeping cash accounts.

7. Dealing in Gold & Silver: The buying and selling of Gold and Silver.

8. Underwriting: The underwriting of the issues of any stocks, shares, debentures, etc.

9. Agent of Co-operative Banks: Acting as agent of any registered Co-operative Bank.

10. Agent of the Government: Acting as an agent of the Central and any state government in implementing any scheme for financing the construction of dwelling houses.

11. Borrowing: The borrowing of money for the purpose of business of the State Bank.

12. Administration of Estates: The administration of estates for any purpose as an executor, trustee, or otherwise.

13. Liquidation and consolidator of banking system: The Banking Regulation Act has authorised the SBI to act as the liquidator of a banking company in the event of its winding up by acquiring its assets and liabilities, if such an application is made by the Reserve Bank of India. In this way, it helps in consolidating and strengthening the banking system.

14. Dealing in Foreign Exchange: The SBI serves as a major authorized dealer of foreign exchange in the country. It also finances the foreign trade of the country.

Above all, with the passing of the State Bank Laws (Amendment) Act 1973, the State Bank of India renders all normal banking functions on per with the other commercial banks of the country.

SPECIAL BRANCH OF STATE BANK OF INDIA (AGRI. DEV. BRANCH)

With a view to providing credit to farmers on an intensive areas basis the State Bank of India and its Associate Banks have initiated new experiment by setting up special "Agricultural Development Branches" in selected intensive centres throughout the country. As a part of the area approach, the State Bank of India has formulated the "village Adoption Approach" in 1973-74, for the financing of agricultural operations for the benefit of small farmers. Under the scheme a branch adopts a few villages for intensive and integrated financing of farmers for meeting their credit requirements. These Agricultural Development Branches have been opened in backward and underdeveloped areas.

The states of Uttar Pradesh, Haryana, Himachal Pradesh and West Bengal passed Bill to enable Commercial Banks to undertake financing of agriculture on a large scale. These Bills became Act during the year 1973-74. During the year 1974-75, three more states viz, Karnataka, Maharashtra and Rajasthan passed the necessary enactment to facilitate lending by Commercial Banks for agriculture as suggested by the Talwar Committee Report. Draft Bill have been prepared by the Government of Assam, Andhra Pradesh, Bihar, Jammu & Kashmir, Meghalaya and Odisha, also.

OBJECTIVES AND FUNCTIONS OF AGRICULTURAL DEVELOPMENT BRANCH OF SBI

One of the major strategies of the bank to increase its involvement in the development of agriculture was to open Agricultural Development Branches with adequate technical and extension support at the centres with the requisite potential for agriculture development. The State Bank of India, has been playing a pioneering role in financing agriculture and rural development through its special branches called Agricultural Development Branches in the country. This role has been multi-dimensional; and it has always given a lead to others. The scheme of Agricultural Development Branches started by State Bank of India is unparalleled in the history of rural banking not only in this country but also in the whole world.

The objectives of an Agricultural Development Branches are not only to finance agriculture but also to promote agricultural development as a whole in the area of its operations. In other words it will be the responsibility of the Agricultural Development Branch to develop the various facets up agricultural economy in its area by granting not only crop loans but also term loan including loans for special farming activities. It would render also necessary technical advice to the farmers.

The Agricultural Development Branches of the bank provide a package of assistance which, besides credit support, including technical and other facilities. For the purpose, each Agricultural Development Branches is staffed by a set of technical officers, extension officers, veterinary surgeons and agricultural assistants according to the requirements of the area. In order to guide the technical wing of the ADB's, each local head office of the bank has a separate technical cell consisting of a chief technical officer and technical officers specialising in animal husbandry, agronomy, horticulture, etc.

Functions of Agricultural Development Branch

The major functions of Agricultural Development Branches are summarised below:

1. All types of direct and indirect agricultural lendings, including grant of loans for allied agricultural activities. 2. Deposits from farmers. 3. Remittances, collections etc, on farmers' accounts alone. 4. Lending under DIR scheme (Differential Rate of Interest Scheme-1972). 5. Financing of cottage and very small agro-based industries like rice milling, oil processing units etc. 6. Financing of artisans engage in rural arts and crafts. 7. Financing of small units engaged in rural repair shops. 8. Financing of petty rural trade.

Besides the above activities, the Agricultural Development Branches will also accept deposits from farmers and grant-agricultural loans against gold ornaments and silverwares even if requests for such services are received from the villages/areas not covered by them.

The following further activities at centres where ADBs are in the only commercial bank offices.

1. Acceptances of deposits from all types of customers. 2. Extension of collection and remittance facilities to all types of customers. 3. Priority sector lendings for the borrowers established at the centres where the branches are functioning.

Area of Operation

As part of area approach to banking, the State Bank of India has formulated 'intensive centre scheme' the basic objective of the scheme is to select compact areas, where the economy in its various facets can be improved by the State Bank credit support. Preference is given to areas which are backward and where special schemes of the government are being taken up, like Gramodaya Project, Village Adoption Scheme. Farm Graduate Scheme, Small Farmers Scheme, Integrated Rural Development Programme etc. Agricultural Development Branches are setup at such intensive centres with the support of technical and other field staff to assist farmers to make gainful use of credit. The centres are selected in consulation with the state governments. The starting of Agricultural Development Branches constitutes the logical extension of village adoption. These branches are located in areas which are not only backward, but possess the potential for a reasonable quick changeover to new technology and where the small farmers can be made receptive to the new technology within a reasonably short period of time.

The Agricultural Development Branches commence work with the preparation of business plans for a period of 2-3 or 4-5 years. It is done after carrying out intensive survey of the area, identifying the credit needs and formulate bankable schemes with all the details. Each branch covers an area of one or two blocks, or a cluster of about 100-125 villages within a radius of about 40 kms and serves a population of nearly one lakh. These plans are based on the development plan prepared with reference to the potential and local resources of the area; and the progress of the plan is reviewed at regular intervals. Finance is also provided for undertaking allied agricultural activities, such as dairy and poultry, with a view to improving the incomes of small and marginal farmers and making their operations viable. Loans are also granted for construction of godowns, custom service unites, transportation and marketing of crops. The bank thus look to the area for its development in an integrated manner, covering all the important facts of its agricultural economy.

HRD PHILOSOPHY OF THE BANK

HRD in State Bank of India is a continuous movement and direction to enable every individual as a member of an effective team and the SBI community, to realize and activate his potential so as to contribute to the achievement of the Banks goals and derive satisfaction thereof. The HRM policy aims at creating a facilitating environment for overall development of people and thereby enabling them to translate their potentials into role related competencies. The Bank recognizes the value of the contribution of the individuals in achieving the corporate objectives. All HR related interventions are based on the philosophy of individual and organizational development. The interventions aim at achieving professional excellence in individual and fostering team work.

Some of the HR policies of the Bank as well as areas of concern and where the policies are being reviewed and revamped are: Recruitment Policy, Career systems-consisting of manpower planning, potential appraisal and promotions and career planning and development inclusive of placement, Work planning involving role analysis and performance appraisal systems. Performance counseling, job rotation, self renewal systems-comprising role efficiency and organizational development and cultural systems, which deal with HRD climate, value system, quality orientation, communication and empowerment.

Formal HRD structure emerged in 1979. In order to design a system, it was essential to state the values in respect of its people's area and to describe the aims and objectives of having an HRD system. The values stated were that the Bank should respect all individuals, all individuals should feel wanted and valued by the Bank and bank should create an enabling culture whereby individuals get an opportunity to grow to their full potential. The aims and the objectives fixed by the bank are:

- To create a climate of openness and trust.
- To build collaborative culture-whereby everyone is an important member of an effective team to promote human capabilities and competencies in the organization.
- To bring about integration of the individual and organizational goals.
- To improve the quality of work life.

Based on the above aims SBI adopted the following HRD policies:

Manpower Planning: Banks manpower planning is meant to improve the innovative and creative abilities of its people through promoting a conducive climate, enhancing the human touch and improving interpersonal relations. Manpower requirements are assessed at the micro level even though overall decisions are made within frame work of government guidelines and corporate perspectives. Branch activity analysis and productivity norms are the basis upon which the assessments are made. Manpower planning in the bank is subordinate to guide lines issued by the Govt. of India and RBI.

Training and Development: Training system enables the employees to take up their assignments and perform tasks with a higher level of confidence and perfection. Training system not only addresses the needs in the areas of knowledge and skills but also looks at the need for change in the attitude of employees. The Training programmes are aligned to the Bank's business, goals and objectives and endeavor to build up competencies in the staff to achieve the declared objectives of the bank. While exclusive programmes on customer service are held in the training system, all training programmes have the customer as the central theme. Eminent specialists in different fields of management, banking, finance, HRM etc. are invited for delivering guest lecturers to make the programmes more efficient. Training is a key variable in human resource development strategy of the Bank. The bank has constituted "advisory council" comprising management experts, academicians and the Bank's senior executives. The advisory council aims at improving the training effectiveness.

Quality Circles: Quality circle is a small group in which people who works in the first line work place, continually improve and maintain the quality of products, services, job and so on. This small group promotes the activity in such a way as to autonomously administer it, utilize the quality circle concept and technique, display creativity and make self development and mutual development. Quality circle was introduced in SBI in 1984 in Bhopal circle. Presently there are over 1000 Quality circles operating in full swing at branch level in different circles.

Job Rotation: Developing functional versatility among employees is a must and it is possible only through job rotation. In SBI, the process of job rotation was started from 1989. Along with job rotation, job analysis occupies a central position in the design of HRD activities in SBI. The purpose of role analysis is to reduce role ambiguity of the role-occupant for maximizing his individual contribution to the bank. The bank has well designed transfer, promotion, and placement policy. The career system in SBI includes various elements like career surveys, career information, career monitoring and several career support systems like human resource planning, potential appraisal and career planning are its inputs.

Employee Welfare: The SBI has introduced a no. of welfare schemes to improve the Quality of work life of the employees. These schemes include canteen facilities, education scholarship to children of employees, consumer cooperative stores, housing loans, SBI employees mutual welfare scheme, festival advances, conveyance loans etc.

Human Resource Information System: Different aspects of information about individual employees- biographical, cultural traits, performance records, promotions obtained, potential for higher positions, critical incidents, placements enjoyed etc. are well managed in SBI. The State Bank institute of information and communication management conducts a series of computer based human resource information system courses for various categories of employees. HRD Policies of the Bank seems to be of the ideal order to win competitive battles in globalised environment.

Functions

SBI along with its non banking subsidiaries has emerged as a financial service. Super market offering the entire range of financial services including investment banking, housing finance, factoring project finance, asset management primary dealership, securities trading credit card, gold banking etc. Internet banking facility provided by the bank is being used by more than 2, 50,000 customers. The bank is working on core banking, 1291 branches are providing this service. The Bank has introduced customized products for tourism, besides tie-up arrangements with manufacturers of dental and medical equipments, loan for renovation and modernization of clinics, offices etc. SBI's international group (Banking group) delivers the full range of cross border finance solutions through four wings viz: The domestic division, the foreign office division, the foreign department and the international services division. Besides SBI provides a wide range of schemes like Housing loan scheme, Educational loan scheme, Agricultural loans. SBI is also providing finance to artisans, doctors, milk producing societies, small business units under different schemes. A joint venture between SBI and Cardiff S.A of France was incorporated on 29th March 2001. It is registered as SBI life insurance Company limited. SBI has divided the market into four segments viz: Commercial and institutional segment (C&I), Small industrial business segment (SIB), Personal segment (Per), and Agricultural segment (Agl).

STATE BANK OF INDIA PRODUCTS AND SERVICES

State Bank of India offers a wide range of services in the Personal Banking Segment which are indexed here.

Term Deposits

SBI provide security, trust and competitive rate of interest. Flexibility in period of term deposit from 7 days to 10 years. It is affordable low minimum deposit amount with SBI for a nominal amount of ₹ 1,000 only. Customers can avail a loan/overdraft against their deposit. SBI provides loan/ overdraft up to 90 per cent of their deposit amount at nominal cost.

Recurring Deposits

Recurring Deposit provides customers the element of compulsion to save at high rates of interest applicable to Term Deposits along with liquidity to access that savings any time. Recurring Deposit is flexibility in period of deposit with maturity ranging from 12 months to 120 months. It is low minimum monthly deposit amount. The customer can start a Recurring Deposit with SBI for a monthly installment of ₹ 100 only.

SBI Home Loan

It offers interest rates concessions on Green Homes in accordance with SBI's commitment to Environment protection. The product gives the customers a onetime irrevocable option to choose one of the three customized combinations of fixed and floating interest rates and also to choose the order in which the fixed and floating rate will be availed. The minimum loan amount sanctioned is ₹ 5 lakh. Its products are again segregated into different types on the basis of their term of repayment and their loan package: SBI-Maxgain Home Loans, Realty Home Loans, Home Equity Loans, NRI Home Loans, Tribal Plus, Gram Niwas, Sahyog Niwas, Green Home Loan, Surakshit Home Loan, Yuva Home Loan, Home Loan Pal. Thus, the bank provides its customers comfortable repayment obligations – Tenure of the loans equal to the residual maturity of the original Home Loans.

SBI Car Loan

The bank provides its customers the best car loan schemes with excellent service and lower costs. A quick view by the customers of similar schemes available with other banks shows that SBI Car Loans for new and old vehicles offer for the customers.

SBI Education Loan

A term loan granted to Indian Nationals for pursuing higher education in India or abroad where admission has been secured. All courses having employment prospects are eligible for getting education loans and they are briefed below.

SBI Loan to Pensioners

The customer can avail of a loan from their branch to meet their personal expenses. They can avail a loan of up to a maximum of 12 months pension, subject to a ceiling of ₹ 1 lakh. The loan may be repaid over a 5 years and will carry a low interest rate of 11.45 per cent per annum.

SBI Loan against Shares/Debentures

The customers can avail of loans up to ₹ 20 lakh against their shares/debentures to enable them to meet contingencies, personal needs or even for subscribing to rights or new issue of shares.

SBI Agricultural Loans

Agricultural loans are provided for the purchase of assets connected with rural activities under agriculture, horticulture, plantation, sericulture, animal husbandry, fisheries etc., where the loan amount is repayable over a period of time exceeding 3 years.

Under this agricultural loan there are other kinds of benefits provided by SBI through schemes such as the Kisan Credit Card Scheme, Land Development Schemes, Minor Irrigation Schemes, Farm Mechanisation Schemes, Krishi Plus Scheme for Customised Hiring of Tractor to Rural Youth, Lead Bank Scheme etc.

SBI Industrial Loans

SBI offers working capital finance to meet the entire range of short-term fund requirements that arise within a corporate's day-to-day operational cycle. The SBI working capital loans can help company in financing inventories, managing internal cash flows, supporting supply chains, funding production and marketing operations, providing cash support to business expansion and carrying current assets. The SBI corporate term loans can support company in funding ongoing business expansion, repaying high cost debt, technology upgradation, R&D expenditure, leveraging specific cash streams that accrue into a company, implementing early retirement schemes and supplementing working capital. Hence, the Bank extends financial assistance to help agriculturists, industrialists and common man in various modes.

MULTIPLE CHOICE QUESTION

1. India's largest commercial Bank is:
A. Bank of Baroda
B. State Bank of India
C. ICICI
D. Punjab National Bank
E. Central Bank of India

2. 'You can Always Bank on Us' is the slogan of:
A. State Bank of Mysore
B. State Bank of Hyderabad
C. State Bank of Travancore
D. State Bank of Patiala
E. None of these

3. Slogan of 'State Bank of Travancore' is:
A. We understand your world
B. The name you can bank upon
C. A long tradition of trust
D. Always with you
E. None of these

4. Which bank launched 'Mobicash easy' scheme:
A. State Bank of Patiala
B. State Bank of India
C. Axis Bank
D. ICICI Bank
E. None of the above

5. Head Office of SBI is situated at:
A. Mumbai, Maharashtra
B. Kolkata, West Bengal
C. New Delhi
D. Chennai, Tamil Nadu
E. None of the above

6. Two new Savings Bank products for children namely 'PehlaKadam and PehliUdaan' introduced by
A. State Bank of India
B. United Bank of India
C. Axis Bank
D. ICICI Bank
E. None of these

7. Which Indian Bank became the first to touch a market capitalization of ₹ 1,00,000 Crore in India:
A. SBI B. Axis Bank
C. HDFC Bank D. Punjab National Bank
E. None of these

8. Original name of the State Bank of India was:
A. Bank of Calcutta B. Bank of Bengal
C. Both the Above D. Bank of Madras
E. None of these

9. State Bank of India comes in to existence in the year:
A. 1947 B. 1955
C. 1959 D. 1949
E. None of these

10. State Bank of India was formulated under:
A. SBI Act, 1957 B. SBI Act, 1959
C. SBI Act, 1955 D. SBI Act, 1949
E. None of these

11. Which is the first Bank to launch the Mutual Fund:
A. SBI B. PNB
C. RBI D. HDFC
E. None of these

12. What is tag line of SBI ?
A. With you all the way, Pure Banking Nothing Else, The Nation's banks on us
B. The name you can bank upon
C. India's International Bank
D. Badhti Ka Naam Zindagi
E. None of these

13. "Imperial Bank of India" is the former name of which of the following bank:
A. SBI B. IndusInd Bank
C. RBI D. Axis Bank
E. None of these

14. State Bank of India started the Merchant Banking division in:
A. 1970 B. 1972
C. 1974 D. 1975
E. None of These

15. Name of the first bank to receive approval for getting full bank licence in Singapore is:
A. Punjab National Bank B. Syndicate Bank
C. State Bank of India D. Axis Bank
E. None of these

ANSWERS

1	2	3	4	5	6	7	8	9	10
B	B	C	B	A	A	A	C	B	C
11	**12**	**13**	**14**	**15**					
A	A	A	B	C					

8

Commercial Banks

The Banks which perform all kinds of banking business and generally finance trade and commerce are called commercial banks. Since, their deposits are for a short period, these banks normally advance short-term loans to businessmen and traders and avoid medium and long term lending. However, recently. Commercial banks have also extended their areas of operation to medium-term and long-term finance:

- A commercial bank is a financial intermediary.
- Its central objective is commercial that is, profit making.
- It takes money from a surplus unit by paying a low rate of interest and lends the same fund to a deficit unit at a higher rate of interest and thus makes profit.
- It is said to be a dealer in credit.
- It may be organized privately or by the Government.

FUNCTIONS OF COMMERCIAL BANKS

The Commercial Banks perform a variety of functions which can be divided in the following three categories:

1. Basic Functions
2. Agency Functions
3. General Utility Functions

Basic Functions

The basic functions of bank are those functions without performing which an institution cannot be called a banking institution at all. That is why these functions are also called primary or acid test function of a bank. The basic/primary/ acid test function of a bank are:

(*a*) Accepting Deposits

(*b*) Advancing of Loans

(*c*) Credit Creation.

Accepting Deposits

The first and the most important function of a bank is to accept deposits from those people who can save and spare for the safe custody with the bankers. It serves two purposes for the customers. On one hand their money is safe with the bank without any fear of theft and on the other hand they also earn interest as per the kind of saving they have made. For this purpose, the banks have different kinds of deposit accounts to attract the people which are as under:

(*i*) Saving Deposit Account

(*ii*) Fixed Deposit Account

(*iii*) Current Deposit Account

(*iv*) Recurring Deposit Account

(*v*) Home Loan Account

(*i*) Saving Deposit Account: The Saving Bank Account is the most common bank account being utilized by the general public. The basic purpose of this account is to mobilise the small savings of the general public. Certain restrictions are imposed on the depositors regarding the number of withdrawals and amount to be withdrawn in a given period of time. Generally, the rate of interest paid by the bank on these deposits is low as compared to recurring or fixed deposit account.

Cheque facility is also provided to the depositors with certain extra restrictions on the depositors. One of the conditions is that the depositor shall have to maintain a minimum balance in the account say ₹ 1,000 in urban areas and ₹ 500 for rural areas. Some service charges are also imposed if the depositor uses the cheque facility at large levels.

(*ii*) Fixed Deposit Account: This is an account where money can be deposited for a fixed period of time say one year or two years or three years of five years and so on. Once the money is deposited for a fixed period of time, the depositor is prohibited from withdrawal of money from the bank before the expiry of the stipulated period of time. The basic advantage to be customer is that he is offered interest at the higher rate of interest and the banker is free to utilize the money for that fixed period.

But where a customer is in need of money in any contingency or emergency, the bank also has the facility to provide loan against the fixed deposit receipt at liberal terms and conditions. Even if a customer insist on the withdrawal of his money the fixed deposit receipt can also be encashed before the expiry of the stipulated period of time with the condition that the customer shall not be entitled to higher rate of interest, but the customer is allowed that rate of interest which is applicable on the saving deposit account as if the amount was deposited in the savings account.

***(iii)* Current Deposit Account:** In the savings bank account, there are restrictions on the number of withdrawals that can be made in a day or a week or a month. Therefore, it does not suit to the needs of traders and businessmen who has to make several payments daily and deposits money in a similar manner. Therefore, there is a facility for them in the shape of another account called Current Deposit Account. These accounts are generally maintained by the traders and businessmen who have to make a number of payments every day. Money from this account can be withdrawn by the account holder as many times as desired by the customer. Normally, bank does not pay any interest on these current accounts, rather some incidental charges are charged by the banker as service charges. These accounts are also called demand deposits or demand liabilities.

The facility of Over Drafts is provided to the traders through these current accounts for which the banks charge interest on the outstanding balance of the customers. A limit is fixed by the bankers for withdrawal of over drafts and the customer is not allowed to withdraw more than that limit from his O/D current account. Say if a trader has an O/D limit of ₹ 1,00,000 with a bank, he can withdraw money upto ₹ 1,00,000 from the bank without depositing any money with the bank. But he cannot withdraw more than ₹ 1,00,000. He shall have to pay interest on such withdrawals.

***(iv)* Recurring Deposit Account:** To encourage regular savings by the general public, another account is opened in the banks called Recurring Deposit Account. This account is preferred by the fixed income group, because a particular amount fixed at the time of opening the account has to be deposited in the account every month for a stipulated period of time. Say ₹ 500 per month for a period of three years. In this case the customer is bound to deposit ₹ 500 per month regularly for a period of three years. Generally the bank pays rate of interest higher than that of a saving account and just equal to the fixed deposit account on such recurring deposit accounts.

The withdrawal of money is allowed only after the stipulated period of time along with the interest. Rather the account stands closed at the end of the stipulated period of time. In this case also the bank provide a facility to withdraw the money before the stipulated period of time in the case of any emergency. The bank shall allow rate of interest which is applicable on saving bank account in case the customer want to close the account before the stipulated period of time.

***(v)* Home Loan Account:** Home loan account facility has been introduced in some scheduled commercial banks to encourage savings for the purchasing of or construction of a house to live. In this account, the customer is required to deposit a particular amount per month or half yearly or even yearly for a period of five years. After the stipulated period bank provide three to five times of the deposited amount a loan to the subscribers to purchase or construct a house. Rate of interest is also very attractive on this account nearly equal to that of the fixed deposit account. Even the rebate of Income Tax is also available on the amount contributed in this account under Section 88 of the Income Tax Act, 1961. Facility to close the account after the stipulated period of time is also allowed.

Advancing of Loans

Advancing of loans is the second acid test function of the commercial banks. After keeping certain cash reserves, the banks lend their deposits to the needy borrowers. It is one of the primary functions without which an institution can not be called a bank. The bank lends a certain percentage of the cash lying in the deposits on a higher rate of interest than it pays on such deposits. The longer the period for which the loan is required the higher is the rate of interest. Similarly, higher the amount of loan, the higher shall be the rate of interest. Before advancing the loans the bank satisfy themselves about the credit worthiness of the borrowers. This is how a bank earns profits and carries on its banking business. There are various types of loans which are provided by the banks to the borrowers. Some of the important ways of advancing loans are as under:

(i) Call Money Advances
(ii) Cash Credits
(iii) Overdrafts
(iv) Discounting Bills of Exchange
(v) Term Loans

***(i)* Call Money Advances:** The Call Money Market which is also known as inter-bank call money market deals with very short period loans called call loans. The Call Money Market is a very important constituent of the organized money market which functions as an immediate source of very short-term loans. The major suppliers of the funds in the call money market are All Commercial Banks, State Bank of India (SBI), Life Insurance Corporation of India (LIC), General Insurance Corporation (GIC), Unit Trust of India (UTI) and Industrial Development Bank of India (IDBI) and the major borrowers are the scheduled Commercial Banks. No collateral securities are required against these call money market loans.

As the participants are mostly banks, it is also called inter-bank call money market. The Scheduled Commercial Banks use their surplus funds to lend for very short period to the bill brokers. The bill brokers and dealers in the stock exchanges generally borrow money at call from the commercial banks. The bill brokers in turn use them to discount or purchase the bills. Such funds are borrowed at the call rate which varies with the volume of funds lent by the commercial banks. When the brokers are asked to pay off the loans immediately, then they borrow from SBI, LIC, GIC, and UTI etc. These loans are granted by the commercial banks for a very short period, not exceeding seven days in any case. The borrowers have to repay the loan immediately when ever the lender bank call them back.

***(ii)* Cash Credits:** This is a type of loan which is provided to the businessmen against their current assets such as shares, stocks, bonds etc. These loans are not based on credit worthiness or personal security of the customers. The bank provides this loan through opening an account in the name of the customer and allows them to withdraw borrowed amount of loan from time to time upto the limit fixed by the bank which is determined by the value of security provided by the borrowers. Interest is charge only on the amount of money actually withdrawn from the banks and not on the amount of the sanctioned amount of loan.

In some other cases, certain banks follow a different procedure for cash credits. The whole amount of loan is credited to the current account of the borrower. In case of new customer, a separate account is opened and amount of loan is transferred to it. The borrower is free to withdraw the money through cheques as and when required by the borrower. But in this case the borrower has to pay the interest on the whole amount credited in their accounts.

***(iii)* Overdrafts:** The facility of Over Drafts is provided to the traders and businessmen through current accounts for which the banks charge interest on the outstanding balance of the customers. A limit is fixed by the bankers for withdrawal of over drafts and the customer is not allowed to withdraw more than that limit from his Over Draft Current Account. This facility is required by the traders and businessmen because they issue several cheques in a day and similarly deposits. So, many cheques daily go in their current accounts. They may not be knowing at a particular day that whether there is a balance in the account or not and their issued cheques are not dishonored so they are provided with the facility of overdrafts. Say it a trader has an Over Draft limit of ₹ 2,00,000 with a bank, he can withdraw money upto ₹ 2,00,000 from the bank without depositing any money with the bank. But he cannot withdraw more than ₹ 2,00,000. He shall have to pay interest on such withdrawals.

***(iv)* Discounting Bills of Exchange:** This is another popular type of lending by the commercial banks. A holder of a bill of exchange can get it discounted with a commercial bank. Bills of Exchange are also called the Commercial Bills and the market dealing with these bills is also called commercial bill market. Bills of exchange are those bills which are issued by the businessmen or firms in exchange of goods sold or purchased. The bill of exchange is a written unconditional order signed by the drawer (seller) requiring the drawee (buyer) to pay on demand or at a fixed future date, (usually three months after date written on the bill of exchange), a definite sum of money. After the bill has been drawn by the drawer (seller), it is accepted by the drawee (buyer) by countersigning the bill. Once the buyer puts his acceptance on the bill by signing it, it becomes a legal document. They are like post dated cheques issued by the buyers of goods for the goods received. The bill holder can get this bill discounted in the bill market if he wants the amount of the bill before its actual maturity. These bills of exchange are discounted and re-discounted by the commercial banks for lending credit to the bill brokers or for borrowing from the central bank. The bill of exchange market is not properly developed in India. The Reserve Bank of India introduced the bill market scheme in 1952. Its main aim was to provide finance against bills of exchange for 90 days. The scheduled commercial banks were allowed to convert a part of their advances into promissory notes for 90 days for lodging as collateral security for advances from Reserve Bank of India.

Term Loan

Earlier the commercial banks were advancing only short-term loans. The commercial banks have also started advancing medium-term and long-term loans. Now, the maturity period of term loans is more than one year. The amount of the loan sanctioned is either paid to the borrower or it is credited to the account of the borrower in the bank. The interest is charged on the whole amount of loan sanctioned irrespective of the amount withdrawn by the borrower from his account. Repayment of the loan is accepted in lump sum or in the installments.

(c) Credit Creation

Credit Creation is one of the basic functions of a commercial bank. A bank differ from the other financial institutions because it can create credit. Like other financial institutions, the commercial banks also aim at earning profits. For this purpose, they accept deposits and advance loans by keeping a small cash in reserve for day-to-day transactions. In the layman's language when a bank advances a loan, the bank creates credit or deposit. Every bank loan creates an equivalent deposit in the bank. Therefore, the credit creation means multiple expansion of bank deposits. The word creation refers to the ability of the bank to expand deposits as a multiple of its reserves.

The credit creation refers to the unique power of the banks to multiply loans and advances, the hence deposits. With a little cash in hand, the banks can create additional purchasing power to a considerable extent. It is because of this multiple credit creation power that the commercial banks have been named the "factories of creating credit" or manufacturers of money.

CREDIT CREATION

An important function performed by the commercial banks is the creation of credit. The process of banking must be considered in terms of monetary flows, that is, continuous depositing and withdrawal of cash from the bank. It is only this activity which has enabled the bank to manufacture money. Therefore, the banks are not only the purveyors of money but manufacturers of money.

Basis of Credit Creation

The basis of credit money is the bank deposits. The bank deposits are of two kinds viz., (1) Primary deposits, and (2) Derivative deposits.

1. Primary Deposits: Primary deposits arise or formed when cash or cheque is deposited by customers. When a person deposits money or cheque, the bank will credit his account. The customer is free to withdraw the amount whenever he wants by cheques. These deposits are called "primary deposits" or "cash deposits." It is out of these primary deposits that the bank makes loans and advances to its customers. The initiative is taken by the customers themselves. In this case, the role of the bank is passive. So, these deposits are also called "passive deposits." These deposits merely convert currency money into deposit money. They do not create money. They do not make any net addition to the stock of money. In other words, there is no increase in the supply of money.

2. Derivative Deposits: Bank deposits also arise when a loan is granted or when a bank discounts a bill or purchase government securities. Deposits which arise on account of granting loan or purchase of assets by a bank are called "derivative deposits." Since the bank play an active role in the creation of such deposits, they are also known as "active deposits." When the banker sanctions a loan to a customer, a deposit account is opened in the name of the customer and the sum is credited to his account. The bank does not pay him cash. The customer is free to withdraw the amount whenever he wants by cheques. Thus, the banker lends money in the form of deposit credit. The creation of a derivative deposit does result in a net increase in the total supply of money in the economy, Hartly Withers says "every loan creates a deposit." It may also be said "loans make deposits" or "loans create deposits." It is rightly said that "deposits are the children of loans, and credit is the creation of bank clerk's pen."

Granting a loan is not the only method of creating deposit or credit. Deposits also arise when a bank discounts a bill or purchase government securities. When the bank buys government securities, it does not pay the purchase price at once in cash. It simply credits the account of the government with the purchase price. The government is free to withdraw the amount whenever it wants by cheque. Similarly, when a bank purchase a bill of exchange or discounts a bill of exchange, the proceeds of the bill of exchange is credited to the account of the seller and promises to pay the amount whenever he wants. Thus, asset acquired by a bank creates an equivalent bank deposit. It is perfectly correct to state that "bank loans create deposits." The derivate deposits are regarded as bank money or credit. Thus, the power of commercial banks to expand deposits through loans, advances and investments is known as "credit creation."

Thus, credit creation implies multiplication of bank deposits. Credit creation may be defined as "the expansion of bank deposits through the process of more loans and advances and investments."

Process of Credit Creation

An important aspect of the credit creating function of the commercial banks is the process of multiple-expansion of credit. The banking system as a whole can create credit which is several times more than the original increase in the deposits of a bank. This process is called the multiple-expansion or multiple-creation of credit. Similarly, if there is withdrawal from any one bank, it leads to the process of multiple-contraction of credit. The process of multiple credit-expansion can be illustrated by assuming:

(*a*) The existence of a number of banks, A, B, C etc., each with different sets of depositors.

(*b*) Every bank has to keep 10% of cash reserves, according to law.

(*c*) A new deposit of ₹ 1,000 has been made with bank A to start with.

Suppose, a person deposits ₹ 1,000 cash in Bank A. As a result, the deposits of bank A increase by ₹ 1,000 and cash also increases by ₹ 1,000. The balance sheet of the bank is as follows:

Balance Sheet of Bank A

Liabilities	₹	Assets	₹
New deposit	1,000	New Cash	1,000
Total	1,000		1,000

Under the double entry system, the amount of ₹ 1,000 is shown on both sides. The deposit of ₹ 1,000 is a liability for the bank and it is also an asset to the bank. Bank A has to keep only 10% cash reserve, *i.e.*, ₹ 100 against its new deposit and it has a surplus of ₹ 900 which it can profitably employ in the assets like loans. Suppose bank A gives a loan to X, who uses the amount to pay off his creditors. After the loan has been made and the amount so withdrawn by X to pay off his creditors, the balance sheet of bank A will be as follows:

Balance Sheet of Bank A

Liabilities	₹	Assets	₹
Deposit	1,000	New Cash Loan to X	100 900
Total	1,000		1,000

Suppose X purchase goods of the value of ₹ 900 from Y and pay cash. Y deposits the amount with Bank B. The deposits of Bank B now increase by ₹ 900 and its cash also increases by ₹ 900. After keeping a cash reserve of ₹ 90, Bank B is free to lend the balance of ₹ 810 to any one. Suppose bank B lends ₹ 810 to Z, who uses the amount to pay off his creditors. The balance sheet of bank B will be as follows:

Balance Sheet of Bank B

Liabilities	₹	Assets	₹
Deposit	900	Cash Loan to Z	90 810
Total	900		900

Suppose Z purchases goods of the value of ₹ 810 from S and pays the amount. S deposits the amount of ₹ 810 in bank C. Bank C now keeps 10% as reserve (₹ 81) and lends ₹ 729 to a merchant. The balance sheet of bank C will be as follows:

Balance Sheet of Bank C

Liabilities	₹	Assets	₹
Deposit	810	Cash Loan	81 729
Total	810		810

Thus, looking at the banking system as a whole, the position will be as follow:

Name of bank	Deposits ₹	Cash reserve ₹	Loan ₹
Bank A	1,000	100	900
Bank B	900	90	810
Bank C	810	81	729
Total	2,710	271	2,439

It is clear from the above that out of the initial primary deposit, bank advanced ₹ 900 as a loan. It formed the primary deposit of bank B, which in turn advanced ₹ 810 as loan. This sum again formed, the primary deposit of bank C, which in turn advanced ₹ 729 as loan. Thus, the inital primary deposit of ₹ 1,000 resulted in bank credit of ₹ 2439 in three banks. There will be many banks in the country and the above process of credit expansion will come to an end when no bank has an excess reserve to lend. In the above example, there will be 10 fold increase in credit because the cash ratio is 10%. The total volume of credit created in the banking system depends on the cash ratio. If the cash ratio is 10% there will be 10 fold increase. If it is 20%, there will be 5 fold increase. When the banking system receives an additional primary deposit, there will be multiple expansion of credit. When the banking system loses cash, there will be multiple contraction of credit.

The extent to which the banks can create credit together could be found out with the help of the credit multiplier formula. The formula is:

$$K = \frac{1}{r}$$

Where K is the credit multiplier, and r, the required reserves. If the reserve ratio is 10%, the size of credit multiplier will be:

$$K = \frac{1}{r} = \frac{1}{0.1} = 10$$

It means that the banking system can create credit together which is ten times more than the original increase in the deposits. It should be noted here that the size of credit multiplier is inversely related to the percentage of cash reserves the banks have to maintain. If the reserve ratio increases, the size of credit multiplier is reduced and if the reserve ratio is reduced, the size of credit multiplier will increase.

Leaf and Cannon Criticism

Walter Leaf and Edwin Cannon objected to the theory of credit creation. According to them, the commercial bank cannot lend anything more than what it receives as cash from deposits. But the contention of Leaf and Cannon that banks cannot create credit is wrong due to the following reasons:

(*a*) A single bank may not be able to create derivative deposits in excess of its cash reserves. But the banking system as a whole can do what a single bank cannot do.

(*b*) As Crowther points out that the total net deposits of commercial banks are for in excess of their cash reserves. It means they can create credit.

Limitation on Credit Creation

The commercial banks do not have unlimited power of credit creation. Their power to create credit is limited by the following factors:

1. Amount of Cash: The power to create credit depends on the cash received by banks. If banks receive more cash, they can create more credit. If they receive less cash they can create less credit. Cash supply is controlled by the central bank of the country.

2. Cash Reserve Ratio: All deposits cannot be used for credit creation. Banks must keep certain percentage of deposits in cash as reserve. The volume of bank credit depends also on the cash reserve ratio the banks have to keep. If the cash reserve ratio is increased, the volume of credit that the banks can create will fall. If the cash reserve ratio is lowered, the bank credit will increase. The Central Bank has the power to prescribe and change the cash reserve ratio to be kept by the commercial banks. Thus, the central bank can change the volume of credit by changing the cash reserve ratio.

3. Banking Habits of the People: The loan advanced to a customer should again come back into banks as primary deposit. Then only there can be multiple expansion. This will happen only when the banking habit among the people is well developed. They should keep their money in the banks as deposits and use cheques for the settlement of transactions.

4. Nature of Business Conditions in the Economy: Credit creation will depend upon the nature of business conditions. Credit creation will be large during a period of prosperity, while it will be smaller during a depression. During periods of prosperity, there will be more demand for loans and advances for investment purposes. Many people approach banks for loans and advances. Hence, the volume of bank credit will be high. During periods of business depression, the amount of loans and advances will be small because businessmen and industrialists may not come to borrow. Hence, the volume of bank credit will be low.

5. Leakages in Credit-Creation: There may be some leakages in the process of credit creation. The funds may not flow smoothly from one bank to another. Some people may keep a portion of their amount as idle cash.

6. Sound Securities: A bank creates credit in the process of acquiring sound and profitable assets, like bills, and government securities. If people cannot offer sound securities, a bank cannot create credit. Crowther says "a bank cannot create money out of thin air. It transmutes other forms of wealth into money."

7. Liquidity Preference: If people desire to hold more cash, the power of banks to create credit is reduced.

8. Monetary Policy of the Central Bank: The extent of credit creation will largely depend upon the monetary policy of the Central Bank of the country. The Central Bank has the power to influence the volume of money in circulation and through this it can influence the volume of credit created by the banks. The Central Bank has also certain powerful weapons, like the bank rate, open market operations with the help of which it can exercise control on the expansion and contraction of credit by the commercial bank.

Thus, the ability of the bank to create credit is subject to various limitations. Still, one should not undermine the importance of the function of credit creation of the banks. This function has far-reaching effect on the working of the economy, especially on the business activity. Bank credit is the oil which lubricates the wheels of the business machine.

Agency Functions

The commercial banks also perform certain agency functions for and on behalf of their customers. The bank acts as the agent of the customer while performing these functions. Such services of the banks are called agency services. Some of the important agency services are as under:

(*i*) Remittance of funds
(*ii*) Collection and Payment of Credit Instruments
(*iii*) Execution of Standing Orders
(*iv*) Purchase and Sale of Securities
(*v*) Collection of dividends on shares and interest on debentures
(*vi*) Trustees and Executors of wills
(*vii*) Representation and Correspondence

(*i*) Remittance of Funds: Commercial banks provide a safe remittance of funds of their customers from one place to another through cheques, bank drafts, telephone transfers etc.

(*ii*) Collection and Payment of Credit Instruments: The commercial banks used to collect and pay various negotiable instruments like cheques, bills of exchange, promissory notes, hundis, etc.

(*iii*) Execution of Standing Orders: The commercial banks also execute the standing orders and instruments of their customers for making various periodic payments like subscriptions, rents, insurance premiums and fees on behalf of the customers out of the accounts of their customers.

(*iv*) Purchase and Sale of Securities: The commercial banks also undertake the sale and purchase of securities like shares, stocks, bonds, debentures etc., on behalf of their customers performing the function as a broker agent.

(*v*) Collection of Dividends on Shares and Interest on Debentures: Commercial banks also make collection of dividends announces by the companies of which the customer of the bank is a shareholder, and also collects the interest on the debentures which becomes due on particular dates generally half yearly or annually.

(*vi*) Trustees and Executors of Wills: The commercial banks preserves the wills of their customers as their trustees execute the wills after the death of the customer as per the will as the executors.

(*vii*) Representation and Correspondence: The commercial banks also act as the representative and correspondents of their customers and get passports, traveller's tickets, book vehicles and plots for their customers on the directions of the customers.

General Utility Functions

In addition to basic functions and agency functions, the commercial banks also provide general utility services for their customers which are needed in the various walks of life and the commercial banks provide a helping hand in solving the general problems of the customers, like safety from loss or theft and so many other facilities some them are as under:

(*i*) Locker Facility
(*ii*) Traveller's Cheque Facility
(*iii*) Gift Cheque Facility
(*iv*) Letter of Credit
(*v*) Underwriting Contract
(*vi*) Provides Statistical Data
(*vii*) Foreign Exchange Facilities
(*viii*) Merchant Banking Services
(*ix*) Acting as Referee

(*i*) Locker Facility: The commercial banks provide locker facility to its customers at very reasonable charges which is not possible at the premises of the customers. The customers can avail the facility of lockers in different sizes according to the needs of the customers. The locker charges also varies with the size of the lockers. The customers can keep their valuables and important documents in these lockers for safety. Lockers can be operated in the usual business hour of the bank on all working days.

***(ii)* Traveller's Cheque Facility:** Where a customers want to visit long distant places and also need money, they need not carry the money with them which is not safe during long distant journeys and there is always a fear of loss or theft during the journey. The commercial banks provide a unique facility through traveller's cheque. The customers can get traveller's cheques from the banks and travel without the fear of theft or loss of money. Wherever they need money they can approach the branch of the bank in that city and encash the traveller's cheque according to the need.

***(iii)* Gift Cheque Facility:** Some commercial banks also provide the facility of issuing gift cheques in the denomination of different amounts according to the needs of the customers, say ₹ 11, 21, 51, 101, 501 and so on. This facility is provided for the special occasions for the customers and normally the banks do not charge any thing for issuing these gift cheques.

***(iv)* Letter of Credit:** The commercial banks also help their customers by providing another unique service by providing the letter of credit in which the bank certifies the credit worthiness of the customers. These letters of credit are used in the long distant trade and specially in foreign trade where the parties do not know each other and it is bank which provide the safety to them regarding their credit worthiness by issuing letter of credit.

***(v)* Underwriting Contract:** The commercial banks underwrite the securities issued by the public or private companies and Government securities. It is the reputation of the bank which matters in the underwriting contracts. Where the bank is a very reputed one, the investors shall not have any hesitation in investing the money in which their banker is the underwriter. In case the public do not purchase the securities, it is the underwriting bank which has to purchase the securities upto the amount of which the bank has underwritten.

***(vi)* Provides Statistical Data:** The commercial banks also help their customers by providing them important information through statistical data. Commercial banks collect statistical data in which important information relating to industry, trade, commerce, money and banking is collected and published in their journals and bulletins containing research articles on the economic and financial matters. Such statistical data may be useful for the customers in dealing with their own business, trade or commerce.

***(vii)* Foreign Exchange Facilities:** The commercial banks also deals in the business of foreign currencies. These banks provide foreign exchange and also discount the foreign bills of exchange. Some commercial banks have also opened special branches for the foreign exchange services to the non-resident Indians settled abroad.

***(viii)* Merchant Banking Services:** The commercial banks have also started providing merchant banking facilities. The Banking Commission Report, 1972 emphasised the need of creating specialised institutions to cater financial requirements of different sectors exclusively and examined the need of setting up merchant banking institutions. Commission recommended the setting up of merchant banking institution.

Consequently in 1972 itself State Bank of India started its merchant banking division. Since then a number of other commercial banks and financial institutions started their merchant banking divisions. Now, the merchant banking firms in private sector have started gearing up to meet the challenge posed by commercial banks and financial institutions in the field of merchant banking in India.

***(ix)* Acting as Referee:** The commercial banks are the best source of seeking information about the creditworthiness of the customers. Banks may be referred for seeking information regarding credit worthiness, financial position, business reputation and respectability of their customers.

Innovative Functions

The adoption of Information and Communication technology enable banks to provide many innovative services to the customers such as:

1. **ATM Services:** Automated Teller Machine (ATM) is an electronic telecommunications device that enables the clients of banks to perform financial transactions by using a plastic card. Automated Teller Machines are established by banks to enable its customers to have anytime money. It is used to withdraw money, check balance, transfer funds, get mini statement, make payments etc. It is available at 24 hours a day and 7 days a week.
2. **Debit Card and Credit Card Facility:** Debit card is an electronic card issued by a bank which allows bank clients access to their account to withdraw cash or pay for goods and services. It can be used in ATMs, Point of Sale terminals, e-commerce sites etc. Debit card removes the need for cheques as it immediately transfers money from the client's account to the business account. Credit card is a card issued by a financial institution giving the holder an option to borrow funds, usually at point of sale. Credit cards charge interest and are primarily used for short-term financing.
3. **Tele-banking:** Telephone banking is a service provided by a bank or other financial institution, that enables customers to perform financial transactions over the telephone, without the need to visit a bank branch or automated teller machine.
4. **Internet Banking:** Online banking (or Internet banking or E-banking) is a facility that allows customers of a

financial institution to conduct financial transactions on a secured website operated by the institution. To access a financial institution's online banking facility, a customer must register with the institution for the service, and set up some password for customer verification. Online banking can be used to check balances, transfer money, shop online, pay bills etc.

5. **Bancassurance:** It means the delivery of insurance products through banking channels. It can be done by making an arrangement in which a bank and an insurance company form a partnership so that the insurance company can sell its products to the bank's client base. Banks can earn additional revenue by selling the insurance products, while insurance companies are able to expand their customer base without having to expand their sales forces.
6. **Mobile Banking:** Mobile banking is a system that allows customers of a financial institution to conduct a number of financial transactions through a mobile device such as a mobile phone or personal digital assistant. It allows the customers to bank anytime anywhere through their mobile phone. Customers can access their banking information and make transactions on Savings Accounts, Demat Accounts, Loan Accounts and Credit Cards at absolutely no cost.
7. **Electronic Clearing Services:** It is a mode of electronic funds transfer from one bank account to another bank account using the services of a Clearing House. This is normally for bulk transfers from one account to many accounts or viceversa. This can be used both for making payments like distribution of dividend, interest, salary, pension, etc. by institutions or for collection of amounts for purposes such as payments to utility companies like telephone, electricity, or charges such as house tax, water tax etc.
8. **Electronic Fund Transfer/National Electronic Fund Transfer(NEFT):** National Electronic Funds Transfer (NEFT) is a nation-wide payment system facilitating one-to-one funds transfer. Under this Scheme, individuals, firms and corporate can electronically transfer funds from any bank branch to any individual, firm or corporate having an account with any other bank branch in the country participating in the Scheme. In NEFT, the funds are transferred based on a deferred net settlement in which there are 11 settlements in week days and 5 settlements in Saturdays.
9. **Real Time Gross Settlement System(RTGS):** It can be defined as the continuous (real-time) settlement of funds transfers individually on an order by order basis. 'Real Time' means the processing of instructions at the time they are received rather than at some later time. It is the fastest possible money transfer system in the country.

NEFT	RTGS
• Based on Deferred Net Settlement (DNS)	• Based on Gross Settlement
• Fastest method of money transfer	• Slower than NEFT transfer
• Complete transactions in batches	• Complete transactions individually
• There is no minimum limit of transactions	• Minimum amount to be remitted is 2 lakhs
• Settlement on hour basis. (11 settlements from 9 am to 7 pm)	• Settlement in real time (at the time the transfer order is processed)

Role of Commercial Banks in a Developing Economy

A well developed banking system is necessary pre-condition for economic development of any economy. Apart from providing resources for growth of industrialisation, banks also influence direction in which these resources are utilised. In underdeveloped and developing nations banking facilities are limited to few developed cities and their activities are focussed on trade & commerce paying little attention to industry & agriculture. Commercial banks contribute to a country's economic development in the following ways:

1. **Capital Formation:** Most important determinant of economic development is capital formation. It has 3 distinctive stages:
   - Generation of savings
   - Mobilisation of savings
   - Canalisation of saving.

   Banks promote capital formation in all these stages. They promote habit of savings by offering attractive rate of return for savers. Banks are maintaining different types of accounts to mobilise savings aiming different types of customers. They make widespread arrangements to collect savings by opening branches even in remote villages. Moreover, banks offer their resources for productive activities only.
2. **Encouragement to Entrepreneurial Innovations:** Entrepreneurs in developing economies, generally hesitate to invest & undertake innovations due to lack of fund. Bank loan facilities enable them to introduce innovative ideas and increase productive capacity of the economy.
3. **Monetisation of Economy:** Monetisation means allow money to play an active role in the economy. Banks, which are creators and distributors of money, help the monetisation in two ways;
   - They monetise debt *i.e.*, buy debts (securities) which are not as acceptable as money and convert them to demand deposits which are acceptable as money.
   - By spreading branches in rural areas they convert non-monetised sectors of the economy to monetised sectors.

4. **Influencing Economic Activity:** They can directly influence the economic activity & pace of economic development through its influence on:
   (*a*) The rate of interest (reduction in rates make investment more profitable and stimulates economic activity)
   (*b*) Availability of credit. (Through Credit creation banks helps in increasing supply of purchasing power)
5. **Implementation of Monetary Policy:** Well developed banking system is necessary for effective implementation of monetary policy. Control and regulation of credit is not possible without active co-operation of banks.
6. **Promotion of Trade and Industry:** Economic progress of industrialised countries in last 2 centuries is mainly due to expansion in trade & industrialisation which could not have been made possible without development of a good banking system. Use of cheques, drafts and BoE as a medium of exchange has revolutionalised the internal and international trade which in turn accelerated the pace of industrialisation.
7. **Encouraging Right type of Industries:** In a planned economy it is necessary that banks should formulate their loan policies in accordance with the broad objectives and strategy of industrialisation as adopted in the plan.
8. **Regional Development:** Banks can play role in achieving balanced development in different regions of the economy. They can transfer surplus funds from developed region to less developed regions, where there is shortage of funds.
9. **Development of Agricultural & Other Neglected Sectors:** Under developed economies primarily agricultural economies and majority of the population live in rural areas. So far banks were paying more attention to trade and commerce and have almost neglected agriculture and industry. Banks must diversify their activities not only to extend credit to trade, but also to provide medium and long-term loans to industry and agriculture.

MULTIPLE CHOICE QUESTIONS

1. Which card is known as 'Check Card'?
A. Debit Card B. Credit Card
C. Both of the above D. RuPay Card
E. None of the above

2. Which among the following is correct?
A. EFTPOS - Online Debit or PIN debit
B. Offline Debit - Signature Debit
C. Electronic Purse Card System - Electronic Debit Dealings
D. All of the above
E. None of the above

3. Some debit cards accepted only within a particular country or region. Which among the following pairs is correct?
A. Maestro and Solo Card – United Kingdom
B. Interac – Canada
C. Carte Bleue – France
D. EC electronic cash – Germany
E. All of the above

4. PIN stands for:
A. Portable Identification Number
B. Permanent Identification Number
C. Personal Identification Number
D. Private Identification Number
E. None of the above

5. Prepaid Debit cards are also called:
A. Reloadable Debit Cards
B. Loadable Debit Cards
C. Relational Debit Cards
D. Unloadable Debit Cards
E. None of the above

6. The primary market for prepaid cards are .... people:
A. Banked People B. Unbanked People
C. Both of the above D. Can't Say
E. None of the above

7. The prepaid bank card is also called:
A. Convenience Gift Card
B. Bank Gift Card
C. Suitable Gift Card
D. Unsuitable Gift Card
E. None of the above

8. "RuPay" debit card is similar to:
A. Singapore's NETS
B. China's Union Pay
C. Both of the above
D. Unparallel
E. None of the above

9. .... also provides a unified "Kisan Card" issued by banks across the country under Kisan Credit Card, enabling farmers to transact business on ATMs and POS terminals:
A. Maestro Card B. RuPay Card
C. Forex Card D. Visa Card
E. None of the above

10. Which term is not associated with bankir operations?
A. Equator B. Prime Le ling Rate
C. Corporate Finance D. All of th e
E. None of these

11. 'Drawer' in the bank cheques is:
A. Who receives the cheques

B. Who encash the cheques
C. Who issues the cheques
D. All of these
E. None of these

12. 'Drawee in the bank cheque is:
A. Who rejects the payment of cheques
B. Who encash the cheques
C. Always the Banker
D. Who doesn't encase the cheques
E. None of these

13. Which was the first bank to set up talking ATM in India?
A. Union Bank B. Dena Bank
C. ICICI Bank D. SBI
E. None of these

14. Which of the following is correct about ATM?
A. ATM is a computer which is dedicated to perform certain specific jobs only
B. ATM is a user friendly machine and the customer does not require any training to use it
C. ATM is totally menu driven which displays instructions to the customers step by step for operating the same
D. All of the above
E. None of these

15. "Overdrafts" covered under which of following function?
A. Accepting Deposits B. Advancing of Loans
C. Both of Above D. Rejecting Deposits
E. None of these

16. For the overdraft facility, customer have to pay:
A. Interest
B. Commission
C. Normal Charges
D. Compound Interest + Commission
E. None of these

17. The account that allows you to buy, sell as well as transact without the need of any paperwork is:
A. Simple Account B. Demat Account
C. Current Account D. Saving Account
E. None of these

18. KYC is:
A. Know Your Customer
B. Know Your Cheque
C. Keep Your Cash
D. Know Your Balance
E. None of these

19. A cheque which is payable to any person who presents it for payment at the bank counter is called:
A. Cross Cheque B. Bearer Cheque
C. Open Cheque D. Account Payee Cheque
E. None of these

20. Scheduled Commercial Banks got licence under:
A. Banking Regulation Act, 1949
B. Banking Regulation Act, 1952
C. Banking Regulation Act, 1955
D. Banking Regulation Act, 1946
E. None of these

21. When ATM machine installed in the bank is out of order, it is called:
A. Operational Risk B. Electronic Default
C. ATM Auto Default D. ATM Normal Default
E. None of these

22. When the computers are not functioning in a bank, it is called:
A. Auto Default B. Computer Risk
C. Operational Risk D. Normal Risk
E. None of these

23. When the loans are not repaid in time, it is called:
A. Loan Defaulter B. Credit Risk
C. Weak Creditworthiness D. Payment Risk
E. None of these

24. When the bank products fail to survive in the market, it is called:
A. Bank Products Failure
B. Bank Failure
C. Market Risk
D. All of these
E. None of these

25. When the banks are not able to pay the amount to the depositors, it is called:
A. Bank Insolvency B. Liquidity Risk
C. Financial Default D. Operational Risk
E. None of these

26. IFSC denotes:
A. Branch Location of any Bank
B. Branch Code of any Bank
C. District Code of any Bank
D. State Code of any Bank
E. None of these

27. IFSC consists of:
A. 11 digits B. 14 digits
C. 12 digits D. 15 digits
E. None of these

28. When a Bank returns a cheque unpaid, it is called:
A. Dishonor of the Cheque
B. Cheque Bounce
C. Both Dishonor and Bounce of the Cheque
D. All of these
E. None of these

29. Accounts in which shares of various companies are traded in electronic form are called:
A. Demat Accounts B. Revenue Accounts
C. E-Accounts D. Simple Accounts
E. None of these

30. Following is not a primary function of a Bank:
A. Facilitating Import of Goods
B. Facilitating Cash Deals
C. Providing Loans
D. All of these
E. None of these

31. The reserves which can act as liquidity buffer for commercial banks during crisis times are:
A. CRR and SLR B. Only CRR
C. Only SLR D. All of these
E. None of these

32. NEFT means:
A. National Electronic Funds Transfer
B. National Electronically Financial Transfer
C. Non-Electronic Fund Transfer
D. All of these
E. None of these

33. Interest on savings bank account now caiculated by the banks on:
A. Daily Product Basis B. Monthly Product Basis
C. Weekly Basis D. Yearly Product Basis
E. None of these

34. Scheduled Commercial Banks have paid up capital and reserves – aggregate value of not less than:
A. ₹ 5,00,000 B. ₹ 6,00,000
C. ₹ 8,00,000 D. ₹ 7,00,000
E. None of these

35. Scheduled Commercial Banks' CRR can go up to maximum of:
A. 15% B. 16%
C. 17% D. 14%
E. None of these

36. From the following which is the incorrect statement about RD (Recurring Deposit)?
A. Recurring Deposit accounts are normally allowed for maturities ranging from 6 months to 120 months
B. These accounts can be opened in single or joint names
C. Rate of Interest offered is similar to that in Fixed Deposits
D. Interest is compounded on quarterly basis in recurring deposits
E. None of these

37. Rate of interest is determined by:
A. Commercial Bank B. Public Bank
C. Private Bank D. RBI
E. None of these

38. India's first non-bank owned ATM (White Label ATMs) open in?
A. Delhi B. Bihar
C. Uttar Pradesh D. Maharashtra
E. Gujarat

39. What is White Label ATM?
A. Owned by Bank B. Owned by RBI
C. Owned by State D. Owned by Center
E. None of these

40. India's largest commercial Bank is:
A. Bank of Baroda B. State Bank of India
C. ICICI D. Punjab National Bank
E. Central Bank of India

41. A bank account which does not require any minimum balance is termed as
A. Nil balance account B. Zero balance account
C. Frill account D. No Frill account
E. None of these

42. Bank deposits that can be withdrawn without notice are called :
A. Demand Deposits
B. Fixed Deposits
C. On Demand and Time Deposits
D. Basic Savings Deposits
E. None of these

43. "DD" in banking term stands for:
A. Demand Cheque B. Doordarshan
C. Demand Draft D. Daily Delivery
E. None of these

44. In MICR cheque, first six numbers indicates:
A. Branch Code and Location
B. City Location
C. Cheque Number
D. Account Number
E. None of these

45. Which of the following Cheque is not honoured by the bank?
A. Stale Cheque B. Crossed Cheque
C. Self Cheque D. Open Cheque
E. None of these

46. Which of the following is not required for opening a bank account?
A. Identity Proof B. Domicile Certificate
C. Recent Photographs D. All of these
E. None of these

47. Which of the following is a retail banking product?
A. Home Loans
B. Working capital finance
C. Corporation term loans
D. Either B or C
E. None of these

48. Which of the following is not included in e - banking?
A. Automated teller machine
B. Credit card
C. Net banking
D. ATM card
E. None of these

49. Loan taken by the person, not telling the purpose of taking loan is called:
A. Non-Personal Loan B. Hidden Loan
C. Concealed Loan D. Personal Loan
E. None of these

50. NBFCs are an important part of the Indian financial system. What is meant by this term?
A. New Banking Financial Companies
B. Non Banking Financial Companies
C. Neo Banking Financial Confederation
D. Non banking Fiscal Companies
E. None of these

51. Banking loan against property requires the asset to be free from encumbrances. What does it mean?
A. The asset to be free from any liability
B. The asset to be properly registered
C. The property to be fully constructed
D. The asset should not have multiple owners
E. None of these

52. Electronic Clearing Service in banks can be availed only by:
A. Individuals B. Corporates
C. Senior Citizens D. All of these
E. None of these

53. Interest payable on savings bank accounts is?
A. De-regulated by RBI
B. Regulated by State Governments
C. Regulated by Central Govt.
D. Regulated by RBI
E. Regulated by Finance Minister

54. Fixed deposits and recurring deposits are:
A. Repayable after an agreed period
B. Repayable on demand
C. Not repayable
D. Repayable after death of depositors
E. Repayable on demand or after an agreed period as per bank's choice

55. Accounts are allowed to be operated by cheques in respect of?
A. Both Savings Bank Accounts and Fixed Deposit Accounts
B. Savings Bank Accounts and Current Accounts
C. Both Savings Bank Accounts and Loan Accounts
D. Both Savings bank Accounts and Cash Accounts only
E. Both Current Accounts and Fixed Deposit Accounts

56. Which of the following is correct statement?
A. No interest is paid on Current Deposit Accounts
B. Interest is paid on Current Accounts at the same rate as term deposit accounts
C. The rate of interest on Current Accounts and Savings Accounts are the same
D. No interest is paid on any deposit by the bank
E. Savings deposits are the same as current deposits

57. When a Bank returns a cheque unpaid, it is called?
A. Payment of the cheque
B. Drawing of the cheque
C. Canceling of the cheque
D. Dishonour of the cheque
E. Taking of the cheque

58. Which of the following types of accounts are known as 'Demat Accounts'?
A. Accounts which are Zero Balance
B. Accounts which are opened to facilitate repayment of a loan taken from the bank. No other business can be conducted from there
C. Accounts in which shares of various companies are traded in electronic form
D. Accounts which are operated through internet banking facility
E. None of the above

59. Interest on Savings Bank Account is now calculated by banks on:
A. Minimum balance during the month
B. Minimum balance from 7th to last day of the month
C. Minimum balance from 10th to last day of the month
D. Maximum balance during the month
E. Daily product basis

60. Largest shareholder (in percentage shareholding) of a Nationalized Bank is:
A. RBI B. NABARD
C. LIC D. Govt. of India
E. IBA

61. The KYC does not include obtaining the following:
A. Identity Proof
B. Address Proof
C. Customer Profile
D. Vehicle details of the customer
E. None of the above

62. AML Stands for:
A. Anti Monitory Limit
B. Anti Money Laundering
C. Always money laundering
D. Anytime Money Laundering
E. None of the above

63. Nomination is available for:
A. Deposit accounts B. Safe custody articles
C. Lockers D. Partnership firms
E. Only A, B, C

64. Nomination can be given only for:
A. Individuals B. Joint Individuals
C. Limited Companies D. Only A and B
E. None of the above

65. Money deposited at a bank that cannot be withdrawn for at fixed period of time is known as a ....

A. Term deposit
B. Checking Account
C. Saving Bank deposit
D. No Frills Accounts
E. Current deposit

66. With reference to a cheque which of the following is the 'drawee bank'?
A. The bank that collects cheque
B. The payee's bank
C. The endorsee's bank
D. The bank of the Drawer of the Cheque
E. None of the above

67. Base Rate is the rate below which no Bank can allow their lending to anyone. Who will fix this 'Base Rate' for Banks?
A. Individuals Banks Board
B. Ministry of Commerce
C. Ministry of Finance
D. RBI
E. Interest Rate Commission of India

68. Expand NPA:
A. No Provision Account
B. Non Performing Asset (An asset which ceases to generate income)
C. No Profit Account
D. Non-Personal Accounts
E. None of the above

69. The National Social Security Fund (NSSF) helps which of the following groups of society?
A. Bank employees
B. Central Government employees
C. Workers in the unorganized sector
D. Workers in the textile industry
E. Women employees

70. Indian commercial banks are categorised into:
A. Public Sector Banks
B. Foreign Banks
C. Private Sector Banks
D. All the above
E. None of the above

71. The Cash Reserve Ratio is to be maintained by Commercial Banks in the form of:
A. Cash in hand at branches
B. Balance with other banks
C. Balance in a special account with RBI
D. Funds in the currency chest
E. Any of the above options

72. Land Development Banks provide long-term credit for schemes of basic importance to agriculture as:
A. mechanization of agriculture *i.e.*, loans for purposes of tractors, power tillers, threshers etc.
B. land reclamation, soil conservation, plantation of fruit orchards, dairy development schemes etc. involving heavy expenditure
C. minor irrigation purposes like wells, dug-cum-bore wells, tube wells, pump sets and irrigation tanks
D. Only A and B
E. All of the above

73. The paid-up capital of Non-Schedule Bank is less than
A. ₹ 5 lakh B. ₹ 10 lakh
C. ₹ 12 lakh D. ₹ 15 lakh
E. None of the above

74. Which of the following category of banks were mooted with a view to providing an institutional mechanism for promoting rural and semi-urban savings as well as the provision of credit for viable economic activities in local areas?
A. Regional Rural Banks
B. Local Area Banks
C. Private Sector Banks
D. Land Development Banks
E. All of the above

75. Which of the following statements about Local Area Banks are correct?
A. Local Area Banks are required to observe the priority sector lending targets at 40 per cent of net bank credit as applicable to other domestic bank
B. Local Area Banks have to lend at least 25 per cent of their priority sector deployments (10 per cent of net bank credit) to weaker sections within the over all 40 per cent targets for priority sector
C. Local Area Banks are registered as a public limited company under the Companies Act, 1956
D. Only A and B
E. All of the above

76. In the context of banking business, the increasing trend in the Burden Bearing Ratio would show the following:
A. Less burden bearing capacity of the bank
B. More burden bearing capacity of the Bank
C. Gradual increase in the bad debts
D. Improvement in the business growth
E. None of these

77. Which of the following statements are correct in regard to foreign banks operating in India?
A. The parent foreign bank of a wholly owned subsidiary would continue to hold 100 per cent equity in the Indian subsidiary for a minimum prescribed period of operation
B. Foreign banks would be permitted to acquire a controlling stake in a phased manner, but only in those private sector banks which are identified by the Reserve Bank for restructuring
C. Foreign banks would be allowed to open more than the existing WTO commitment of 12 branches in a year
D. Only A and B
E. All of the above

78. In which city the Bank of International Settlements (BIS) located?
A. New York B. Basel
C. Washington D. Davos
E. Paris

79. Which of the following Acts has specially been enacted to help banks deal with bad loans?
A. Negotiable Instrument Act
B. Banking Regulation Act
C. SARFAESI Act
D. Companies Act
E. Offshore Banking Act

80. The headquarter of Bank of India is located in which of the following city?
A. Kolkata B. New Delhi
C. Mumbai D. Manipal
E. Chennai

81. Which of the following is not the name of a bank, functioning in India?
A. Central Bank of India
B. Aegon Religare
C. United Bank of India
D. Dena Bank
E. Citi Bank

82. When banks accept a fixed sum of money from an individual for a definite term and pay on maturity with interest, the deposit is known as:
A. demand deposit B. term deposit
C. bond D. mortgage
E. advance

83. Which of the following terms is NOT used in Banking/ Finance related matters?
A. Discount Rate B. Letter of Credit
C. Cheque Clearing D. General Ledger
E. Law of Motion

84. Which of the following is not the name of a bank, functioning in India?
A. Central Bank of India
B. Aegon Religare
C. United Bank of India
D. Dena Bank
E. Citi Bank

85. When banks accept a fixed sum of money from an individual for a definite term and pay on maturity with interest, the deposit is known as:
A. demand deposit B. term deposit
C. bond D. mortgage
E. advance

86. Banks recover term loan from the parties in EMIs. What the letter 'E' represents in the term?
A. Easy B. Effective
C. Equated D. Essential
E. Economical

87. Which of the following organizations/agencies is not associated with the world of banking and finance?
A. SEBI B. AMFI
C. RBI D. ECGC
E. ONGC

88. The financial results of banks and other organizations normally are expressed in quarters. What does Q-1 means?
A. Results of January - March
B. Performance during April - June
C. Profits during July - September
D. The period when the profits were highest
E. None of these

89. Who amongst the following CANNOT work as a Business Correspondent as given in the scheme launched by the banks?
A. Self Help Group B. Post Office
C. Kirana Store D. A Bank Officer
E. Cooperative Society

90. Some banks are financing projects like Construction Roads/Bridges etc. Financing such projects means banks are helping exactly in:
A. Developing Core Sector Industry
B. Project Management
C. Infrastructural Development
D. Financial Inclusion
E. All of these

91. Which of the following is NOT a Nationalized Bank in India?
A. Union Bank of India
B. Central Bank of India
C. Yes Bank
D. Syndicate Bank
E. Indian Bank

92. Sub-prime lending refers to:
A. lending to the customers who are most valued for the bank.
B. lending to the customers who come to the bank for the very first time
C. lending to the people with less than standard credit status
D. lending to the people who live a sub-standard life.
E. None of these

93. Insurance cover for bank deposits in our country is provided by:
A. SBI B. Government of India
C. DICGC D. GIC
E. None of these

94. The following contains an order to pay money:
A. Bill of Exchange B. Cheque
C. Promissory Note D. Only A and B
E. None of these

95. Factoring means:
A. Financing against bills receivables
B. Financing invoices without recourse only
C. Purchasing and/or administering the receivables of a concern
D. Collecting the receivables and remitting to the seller
E. None of these

96. Banker's lien is a type of security:
A. Hypothecated B. Mortgaged
C. Implied pledge D. Pledged
E. None of these

97. .... is a new scheme of deposit mobilization have been evolved by the Indian commercial banks.
A. Current deposit
B. Saving deposit
C. Insurance linked deposit
D. Fixed deposit
E. None of these

98. The banker's answer in case of dishonor of a cheque on an account of insufficiency of funds is generally:
A. Refer to drawer (RD)
B. No funds (NF)
C. Not arranged for (NAF)
D. Either B or C
E. None of these

99. The title of the endorsee will not be better than of the endorser in case a cheque is crossed containing the words:
A. & co B. Not negotiable
C. Account Payee D. Either A or C
E. None of these

100. Cancellation of crossing can be done by:
A. Holder of the cheque
B. Payee of the cheque
C. Drawer of the cheque
D. Bank's authority only
E. None of these

101. The period of limitation in case of deposits with bankers from the date on which:
A. Deposit was made
B. Deposit matures
C. Date of demand for payment by the customer
D. Either A or B
E. None of these

102. Pay order is issued by the banks for:
A. Local payments B. Inter-state payments
C. Foreign payments D. Bank's employee payment
E. None of these

103. The recurring deposit account combine the characteristics of .... and fixed deposit account.
A. Savings Account B. Current Account
C. Loan Account D. Either B or C
E. None of these

104. The drawee banker of a demand draft has received intimation of the loss of the draft from the purchaser. The banker should:
A. Stop the payment
B. Exercise caution
C. Refuse to accept the notice and
D. Issue a duplicate draft
E. None of these

105. .... is always drawn on a specified banker.
A. Bill of Exchange B. Promissory Note
C. Investment Receipt D. Cheque
E. None of these

106. When a banker collects a cheque for which he has already given cash, his position is that of a ....
A. collecting bank B. dealer
C. agent D. holder for value
E. None of these

107. In case of ....days of grace are allowed:
A. Withdrawal Receipt B. Bill of Exchange
C. Cheque D. Money Order
E. None of these

108. Banks create money by:
A. Liberal credit
B. Differential instrument
C. Accepting deposit
D. All or some of the above
E. None of these

109. The .... is an important function of a bank and this function distinguishes banks from the non banking institution.
A. accepting deposit B. lending money
C. creation of credit D. agency service
E. None of these

110. .... function are the core activities of banking.
A. Agency and general utility
B. Borrowing and lending
C. Accepting deposit and borrow money
D. Lending and bill discounting
E. None of these

111. Banks lend to special purpose vehicles (SPVs) in the private sector registered under .... for directly undertaking infrastructure projects.
A. Reserve Bank of India
B. State Bank of India
C. Local Courts
D. Companies Act
E. SEBI

112. Banks categorised housing loan, education loan etc. as.........
A. wholesale loan B. retail loan
C. risk loan D. personal loan
E. None of these

113. ....is automation of banks across multiple–delivery channels.
A. ANBC B. OBE
C. NABARD D. CBS
E. None of these

114. Large value payment system consist of
A. ECS B. RTGS
C. NEFT D. OBE
E. None of these

115. Banks have adopted asset-liability management and stress testing as a tool of ....
A. profit management
B. risk management
C. loss management
D. opportunity management
E. None of these

116. Which of the following NBFC converted itself into a Commercial Bank?
A. Tata Finance B. Reliance Capital Trust
C. Birla Mutual D. Kotak Mahindra
E. None of these

117. C.R.A. in banking parlance stands for:
A. Credit Rating Association
B. Credit Rating Agency
C. Credit Risk Assessment
D. Critical Risk Assessment
E. None of these

118. The powers of the Board of Directors to borrow from the bank are mentioned in:
A. Article of Association
B. Memorandum of Association
C. Special Resolution
D. A & B
E. None of these

119. Credit Risk Assessment of the borrowal units is for:
A. Assessing the repayment capacity
B. To fix the pricing of the product
C. To review the units performance
D. All of these
E. None of these

120. To be categorized as a schedule Bank the minimum capital & reserve required is:
A. ₹ 10 lacs B. ₹ 5 lacs
C. ₹ 20 lacs D. ₹ 7 lacs
E. None of these

121. The full form of RBS is:
A. Risk Based Supervision
B. Rating by System
C. Role Based Supervision
D. Rating Bank Security
E. None of these

122. Who can fix the interest rates of NRE & FCNB deposits?
A. RBI
B. Banks, as per the directive of RBI
C. Govt. of India
D. IBA
E. None of these

123. NEFT operates in .... batches:
A. hourly B. daily
C. weekly D. monthly
E. None of these

124. Which of the following Banks are not Commercial Banks?
A. Foreign Banks
B. State Cooperative Banks
C. Private Banks
D. Regional Rural Banks
E. None of these

125. The validity of a cheque is .... months from the date of cheque:
A. 3 months B. 6 months
C. 1 month D. 12 months
E. None of these

126. When a bankers name is written on a cheques instead of two parallel lines, it is a
A. General crossing
B. No crossing
C. Special crossing
D. Payable to bearer
E. None of these

127. Pledge of advance is made against
A. Gold B. Commodities
C. Coins and Notes D. All the above
E. None of these

128. The power of banks to create credit depends on
A. Deposit available with them and safe ratio
B. Safe ratio only
C. Deposit available with them only
D. All the above
E. None of these

ANSWERS

1	2	3	4	5	6	7	8	9	10
A	D	E	C	A	B	B	C	B	A
11	**12**	**13**	**14**	**15**	**16**	**17**	**18**	**19**	**20**
C	C	A	D	B	A	B	A	B	A

21	**22**	**23**	**24**	**25**	**26**	**27**	**28**	**29**	**30**
A	C	B	C	B	B	A	A	A	A
31	**32**	**33**	**34**	**35**	**36**	**37**	**38**	**39**	**40**
A	A	A	A	E	C	A	D	E	B
41	**42**	**43**	**44**	**45**	**46**	**47**	**48**	**49**	**50**
B	A	C	C	A	B	A	E	D	B
51	**52**	**53**	**54**	**55**	**56**	**57**	**58**	**59**	**60**
A	D	A	A	B	A	D	C	E	D
61	**62**	**63**	**64**	**65**	**66**	**67**	**68**	**69**	**70**
D	B	E	D	A	D	A	B	C	D
71	**72**	**73**	**74**	**75**	**76**	**77**	**78**	**79**	**80**
C	E	A	B	E	A	E	B	C	C
81	**82**	**83**	**84**	**85**	**86**	**87**	**88**	**89**	**90**
B	B	E	B	B	C	E	B	C	C
91	**92**	**93**	**94**	**95**	**96**	**97**	**98**	**99**	**100**
C	C	C	D	C	C	C	A	B	C
101	**102**	**103**	**104**	**105**	**106**	**107**	**108**	**109**	**110**
C	A	A	B	D	D	B	D	C	B
111	**112**	**113**	**114**	**115**	**116**	**117**	**118**	**119**	**120**
D	B	D	B	B	D	C	B	B	B
121	**122**	**123**	**124**	**125**	**126**	**127**	**128**		
A	B	A	B	A	C	B	A		

9

Recent Trends in Banking

Today, banking business is becoming more a cross-border game. The banking sector has experienced a process of significant structural transformations in the last few decades. With the potential to become the third largest banking industry in the world by 2025, India's banking and financial sector is expanding rapidly. Great changes have taken place in the banking industry such as deregulation of financial institutions with regard to their pricing decisions, financial innovation involving the development of new processes and financial instruments, and globalization so that most major banks operate throughout the world rather than in one country. Indian banking sector has made rapid strides in reforming itself to the new competitive business environment which changed its approach from "conventional banking to convenience banking" and "mass banking to class banking." Banking is re-defined and reengineered with the development of sophisticated instruments and innovations in market practices. The major innovations and practices in the banking industry may be listed as follows:

- Electronic Banking (E-Banking)
- Tele Banking
- Mobile Banking (M-Banking)
- Consortium Banking
- Social Banking
- Debit Cards
- Credit Cards
- Automated Teller Machine (ATM)
- E-Purse
- Electronic Fund Transfer System (EFTS)
- Real Time Gross Settlement (RTGS)
- Cheque Truncation System (CTS)
- Non Performing Assets (NPA)
- Capital Adequacy Ratio
- Banking Ombudsman
- Banking Sector Reforms in India

E-Banking

Electronic banking (E-banking) is a method of banking in which the customer conducts transactions electronically via the Internet. It is a system that allows the individuals to perform banking activities at their convenient place, via the internet. It is the automated delivery of banking products and services directly to customers through electronic, interactive communication channels. Online banking enables the customers to perform all routine transactions anytime, day or night, and can be done from anywhere. E-banking is also referred as online banking, internet banking, virtual banking etc.

To access a financial institution's online banking facility, a customer would need to register with the institution for the service, and set up some password for customer verification. The online banking facilities offered by various financial institutions have many features and capabilities in common. The common features include:

1. Bank customers can perform non-transactional tasks through online banking including: (*a*) viewing account balances, (*b*) viewing recent transactions, (*c*) ordering cheque books, and (*d*) download periodic account statements.
2. Bank customers can transact banking tasks through online banking including: (*a*) fund transfers between the customer's linked accounts, (*b*) paying third parties, including bill payments, (*c*) investment purchase or sale, (*d*) loan applications and transactions, (*e*) credit card applications, and (*f*) register utility billers and make bill payments.

Today, many banks are internet only banks. Unlike their predecessors, these internet only banks do not maintain brick and mortar bank branches. Instead, they typically differentiate themselves by offering better and more extensive online banking features. Security of customers' financial information is very important without which, online banking could not operate. The use of a secure website has become almost universally adopted to reduce the risk of unauthorised online access to a customer's records.

Tele Banking

Telephone banking (Tele banking) is a service provided by a bank or other financial institution that enables the customers to perform their financial transactions over the telephone, without the need to visit a bank branch. It refers to the use of a system to allow customers of a bank to process various banking procedures over the telephone. All the transactions can be done in the comfort of one's home using only a touch-tone telephone. The ease of access for services is one of the major advantages that telephone banking can provide for customers.

From the bank's point of view, telephone banking reduces the cost of handling transactions by reducing the need for customers to visit a bank branch for non-cash withdrawal or deposit transactions. To use a financial institution's telephone banking facility, a customer must first register with the institution for the service, and set up some password for customer verification. Most telephone banking services use an automated phone answering system with phone keypad response or voice recognition capability. To access telephone banking, the customer would call the special phone number set up by the financial institution. The service can be provided using an automated system, using speech recognition or by live customer service representatives.

The types of financial transactions which a customer may transact through telephone banking include obtaining account balances and list of latest transactions, electronic bill payments, and funds transfers between a customer's or another's accounts. Cash withdrawals and deposits require the customer to visit a bank branch or an Automated Teller Machine (ATM). Banking over a telephone system can often be more convenient than banking in person, since some functions can be accessed even when a bank is closed.

M-Banking

Mobile banking (M-banking) is a system that allows customers of a financial institution to conduct a number of financial transactions through a mobile device such as a mobile phone or tablet through specifically designed Mobile Banking Apps. It is the most convenient and easy way to stay connected with the bank. It refers to provision and availing of banking and financial services with the help of mobile telecommunication devices. The scope of offered services may include facilities to conduct bank and stock market transactions, to administer accounts and to access customised information. Mobile banking has until 2010 most often been performed via SMS, known as SMS Banking.

The typical mobile banking services may include: (1) Mini-statements and checking of account history, (2) Funds transfers between the customer's linked accounts, (3) Paying third parties, including bill payments and third party fund transfers, (4) Alerts on account activity or passing of set thresholds, (5) Cheque book and card requests, (6) Access to loan statements, (7) Access to card statements, (8) Status of requests for credit, including mortgage approval, and insurance coverage, (9) Mutual funds/equity statements, (10) Real-time stock quotes, (11) Personalised alerts and notifications on security prices, (12) Monitoring of term deposits (13) Portfolio management services, (14) ATM Location etc.

With the advent of technology and increasing use of smart phone and tablet based devices, the use of mobile banking functionality would enable customers connect across various services. The rapid growth of smart phones based on Google's Android Operating System have led to the increasing use of special client programs, called 'Apps' downloaded to the mobile devices. With further advancements in web technologies, more and more banks are launching mobile web based services. But, mobile banking is attractive and popular mainly among the younger and 'tech-savvy' customers.

Consortium Banking

Consortium is an association or group of independent members with the objective of participating in a common activity or joint venture by pooling their resources for achieving a common goal and mutual benefit. *Consortium* is a Latin word, meaning 'partnership' or 'association' where the members co-operate with one another and conduct the operations that they would not be able to do individually. Consortium banking implies the collaboration of a group of banks to make a loan. It is created to fund a specific project or to execute a specific deal. It is also known as 'loan syndication' where two or more banks come together to finance big projects requiring huge amount of money.

The consortium leverages individual banks' assets to achieve its objectives. All member banks have equal ownership shares – no one member has a controlling interest. It shares the security interest in common. After the bank's objective is met the consortium typically dissolves. Consortium lending is usually done by smaller banks to reap an opportunity to be a part of a big project financing by distributing the risks among the collaborator banks. By resorting to consortium lending, the banks not only saves their prospective customers but also builds good relations with other banks.

There is little bit difference between consortium banking and multiple banking. Under consortium banking, several banks or financial institutions finance a single borrower with common appraisal, common documentation, joint supervision and follow-up exercise. But in multiple banking, different banks provide finance and different banking facilities to a single borrower without having a common arrangement and understanding between the lenders.

Social Banking

Social banking is rightly defined by Roland Benediktar as "banking with a conscience." It calls for a move towards a more social and environmental responsibility in the financial sector beyond the principles of conventional business management. It is also known as ethical/alternative/civic/ sustainable banking. Social banking policies were made to shift the focus of commercial banks from 'selective banking' to 'mass banking.' In their financing, it deals with sustainable and socially responsible projects which have particular dimensions of environmental assumptions and notions like justice and equality. Social or ethical banks do share a common set of principles, the most prominent being transparency and social or environmental aims of the projects they finance.

Social Banking describes the provision of banking and financial services that consequently pursue, as their main objective, a positive contribution to the potential of all human beings to develop, today and in the future. In Social Banking, the focus is on satisfying existing needs in the real economy and the society whilst simultaneously taking into account their social, cultural, ecological and economic sustainability. Social banking focuses on investing in community, providing opportunities for the disadvantaged, and supporting social, environmental and ethical concerns.

Social Banking describes a process, not a steady state. It is about jointly identifying and testing creative new ways to create social and environmental screens. The kind of analysis that conventional banks generally partake is a 'single bottom line analysis' which only considers the financial performance. But, social or sustainable banks consider a 'triple bottom line analysis' that takes into account the environmental, social, and financial performance.

Debit Cards

A debit card is a plastic payment card that provides the cardholder electronic access to their bank account at a financial institution. Most cards relay a message to the cardholder's bank to withdraw funds from a payer's designated bank account. Debit cards usually allow for instant withdrawal of cash, acting as the ATM card for withdrawing cash. The card, where accepted, can be used instead of cash when making purchases. Unlike credit and charge cards, payments using a debit card are immediately transferred from the cardholder's designated bank account, instead of them paying the money back at a later date.

There are currently three ways that debit card transactions are processed, namely, (*i*) *Online debit* or *PIN debit*, (*ii*) Offline debit or *signature debit*, and (*iii*) The Electronic Purse System. One physical card can include the functions of all three types, so that it can be used in a number of different circumstances. In many countries, the use of debit cards has become so widespread that their volume has overtaken or entirely replaced cheques and, in some instances, cash transactions. Although many debit cards are of the Visa or Master Card brand, there are many other types of debit card, each accepted only within a particular country or region. The National Payments Corporation of India (NPCI) has launched a new card called RuPay.

Debit cards may also be used on the Internet. Internet purchases can be authenticated by the consumer entering their PIN. The online debit cards require electronic authorization of every transaction and the debits are reflected in the user's account immediately. The transaction may be additionally secured with the personal identification number (PIN) authentication system.

Credit Cards

A credit card is a payment card issued to users as a system of payment. It allows the cardholder to pay for goods and services based on the holder's promise to pay for them. The issuer of the card creates a revolving account and grants a line of credit to the user from which he can borrow money for payment to a merchant or as a cash advance to the user. Credit cards may be treated as 'convenient credit' that allow the consumers a continuing balance of debt, subject to interest being charged. It can be used like currency by the owner of the card. It typically involves a third-party entity that pays the seller and is reimbursed by the buyer.

Credit cards may simply serve as a form of revolving credit. The main benefit to the cardholder is convenience. Compared to debit cards and checks, a credit card allows small short-term loans to be quickly made to a cardholder who need not calculate a balance remaining before every transaction, provided the total charges do not exceed the maximum credit line for the card. A credit card issuing company, such as a bank or credit union, would enter into agreements with merchants for them to accept their credit cards. Each month, the cardholder is sent a statement indicating the purchases made with the card, any outstanding fees, and the total amount owed.

Electronic verification systems allow merchants to verify in a few seconds that the card is valid and the cardholder has sufficient credit to cover the purchase, allowing the verification to happen at time of purchase. The verification is performed using a credit card payment terminal or point-of-sale (POS) system with a communications link to the merchant's acquiring bank. Credit card issuers usually waive interest charges if the balance is paid in full each month, but typically will charge full interest on the entire outstanding balance from the date of each purchase if the total balance is not paid.

Credit Card Vs Debit Card

Credit Card	Debit Card
1. It is a "pay later product"	It is "pay now product"
2. The card holder can avail of credit for 30-45 days	Customers account is debited immediately
3. No sophisticated communication system is required for credit card operation	Sophisticated communication network/system is required for debit card operation (eg. ATM)
4. Opening bank account and maintaining required amount are not essential	Opening bank account and maintaining required amount are essential
5. Possibility of risk of fraud is high	Risk is minimised through using PIN

Credit cards are accepted in larger establishments in almost all countries, and are available with a variety of credit limits and repayment arrangements. Many credit cards offer rewards and benefits packages, such as enhanced product warranties at no cost, free loss/damage coverage on new purchases and various insurance protections. Credit cards can also offer a loyalty program, where each purchase is rewarded with points, which may be redeemed for further goods and services or cash back.

ATM

An Automated Teller Machine (ATM) is an electronic telecommunication device that enables the customers of a financial institution to perform financial transactions without the need for a human cashier, clerk or bank teller. It is also known as Automated Banking Machine (ABM). Using an ATM, customers can access their bank deposit or credit accounts in order to make a variety of transactions such as withdrawals, check balances, getting mini statements, etc. Most ATMs are connected to interbank networks, enabling people to withdraw and deposit money from machines not belonging to the bank where they have their accounts or in the countries where their accounts are held (enabling cash withdrawals in local currency).

On most modern ATMs, the customer is identified by inserting a plastic ATM card with a magnetic stripe or a plastic smart card with a chip that contains a unique card number and some security information. An ATM card is any payment card issued by a financial institution that enables a customer to access an Automated Teller Machine (ATM) in order to perform transactions such as deposits, cash withdrawals, obtaining account information, etc. It is also known as Bank Card, Money Access Card, Key Card or Cash Card. Most ATM cards today are Bank Cards such as debit or credit cards that have been ATM-enabled. Unlike an offline bank card that is signature based, an ATM card require authentication through a personal identification number (PIN).

Interbank networks allow the use of ATM cards at ATMs of financial institutions other than those of the institution that issued the cards. In some banking networks, the two functions of ATM cards and debit cards are combined into a single card called simply as a Debit Card or also commonly called as Bank Card. These are able to perform banking tasks at ATMs and also make point-of-sale transactions, with both features using a PIN. ATM cards can also be used on merchants' card terminals that deliver ATM features without any cash drawer. These terminals can also be used as cashless scrip ATMs by cashing the receipts they issue at the merchant's point of sale.

E-Purse

An electronic purse is the store of value on a card, which can be used in a manner similar to cash to pay for travel or for other small-scale transactions. Electronic purse is the secure information stored in a dedicated area or file of a smart-card. The value is placed on the card in one of three ways: (*i*) Preloaded on to the card (in the same manner as telephone cards), without the possibility to add further value. The intention is that the card is discarded when the value is expired, (*ii*) Added to the card at the time the card is issued, or when the e-purse application is added to an existing card, and (*iii*) Additional value added to an existing e-purse or top-up.

There are different concepts for electronic purse, which centre on the nature of the value. The main types are:

1. **Tokens:** The purse consists of units that have no monetary value. The units can be equivalent to individual journeys, or to money units. When the card is presented for travel, the number of units required for the applicable fare is deducted. Eventually, when all of the units have been deducted, the card is no longer usable for travel.
2. **Transport money:** The purse consists of units equivalent to money, but it can only be used for passenger transport fares. Depending on the context, this could include multiple modes, park and ride, and car parking. Although presented to the user in terms of cash equivalent, it does not have any monetary validity outside the immediate transport environment.
3. **Transport and Micro Purchases:** The purse contains units equivalent to money. The primary usage is for payment of passenger transport services. The value can also be used for small purchases at non-transport locations like kiosks and vending machines. There is likely to be a modest upper limit on the value that can be loaded to the card at any given time.
4. **E-Cash:** The purse contains electronic money, which has full monetary value, is usable at any outlet with an accepting device, and is at any time exchangeable for cash. Transport may be just one of a number of items where the e-cash can be used, and might not even be the main usage. The e-cash is subject to banking regulations, and would have to be issued and underwritten by a bank.

Though the handling requires a substantial level of technical competence, the major benefits of electronic purse are:

- Cash handling is reduced as customers migrate to prepaid tickets.
- High degree of security.
- Innovative means of adding/renewing value can be utilized.
- Electronic purse can be offered for infrequent customers when it is desired to eliminate all cash transactions.
- Third parties can become involved in issuing value.
- Incentives such as free transfers, discounts and fare-capping can be offered to the customer in a secure and consistent way.

NEFT

National Electronic Funds Transfer (NEFT) is a nation-wide payment system facilitating one-to-one funds transfer. Under this Scheme, individuals, firms and corporates can electronically transfer funds from any bank branch to any individual, firm or corporate having an account with any other bank branch in the country participating in the Scheme. NEFT is a creditpush system *i.e.*, transactions can be originated by the payer or remitter.

The NEFT system takes advantage of the core banking system in banks. Accordingly, the settlement of funds between originating and receiving banks takes places centrally at Mumbai, whereas the branches participating in NEFT can be located anywhere across the length and breadth of the country. For being part of the NEFT funds transfer network, a bank branch has to be NEFT-enabled. Indian Financial System Code (IFSC) is an alpha-numeric code that uniquely identifies a bank-branch participating in the NEFT system. This is an 11 digit code with the first 4 alpha characters representing the bank, and the last 6 characters representing the branch. The 5th character is 0 (zero). IFSC is used by the NEFT system to identify the originating/destination banks/ branches and also to route the messages appropriately to the concerned banks/branches.

Presently, NEFT operates in hourly batches – there are twelve settlements from 8 am to 7 pm on week days (Monday through Friday) and six settlements from 8 am to 1 pm on Saturdays. The beneficiary can expect to get credit for the NEFT transactions within two business hours. There is no limit – either minimum or maximum – on the amount of funds that could be transferred using NEFT. However, maximum amount per transaction is limited to ₹ 200000.

NEFT offers many advantages to the customers over the other modes of funds transfer as listed below:

- The remitter need not send the physical Cheque or Demand Draft to the beneficiary.
- The beneficiary need not visit his/her bank for depositing the paper instruments.
- The beneficiary need not be apprehensive of loss/ theft of physical instruments or the likelihood of fraudulent encashment thereof.
- Cost effective.
- Credit confirmation of the remittances sent by SMS or email.
- Remitter can initiate the remittances from his home/ place of work using the internet banking also.
- Near real time transfer of the funds to the beneficiary account in a secure manner.

Besides personal funds transfer, the NEFT system can also be used for a variety of transaction including payment of credit card dues to the card issuing banks, payment of loan EMI etc. It is necessary to quote the IFSC of the beneficiary card issuing bank to initiate the bill payment transactions using NEFT.

RTGS

Real Time Gross Settlement (RTGS) can be defined as the continuous (real-time) settlement of funds transfers individually on an order by order basis (without netting). 'Real Time' means the processing of instructions at the time they are received rather than at some later time and 'Gross Settlement' means the settlement of funds transfer instructions occurs individually (on an instruction by instruction basis). The RTGS system is primarily meant for large value transactions. The minimum amount to be remitted through RTGS is ₹ 2 lakh. There is no upper ceiling for RTGS transactions.

Under normal circumstances the beneficiary branches are expected to receive the funds in real time as soon as funds are transferred by the remitting bank. The beneficiary bank has to credit the beneficiary's account within 30 minutes of receiving the funds transfer message. The RTGS service window for customer's transactions is available to banks from 9.00 hours to 16.30 hours on week days and from 9.00 hours to 14:00 hours on Saturdays for settlement at the RBI end. However, the timings that the banks follow may vary depending on the customer timings of the bank branches.

There is a fundamental difference between NEFT and RTGS. NEFT is an electronic fund transfer system that operates on a Deferred Net Settlement (DNS) basis which settles transactions in batches. In DNS, the settlement takes place with all transactions received till the particular cut-off time. These transactions are netted (payable and receivables) in NEFT whereas in RTGS the transactions are settled individually. For example, currently, NEFT operates in hourly batches. Any transaction initiated after a designated settlement time would have to wait till the next designated settlement time. Contrary to this, in the RTGS transactions are processed continuously throughout the RTGS business hours.

Cheque Truncation System

Cheque Truncation System (CTS) or Image-based Clearing System (ICS) in India is a project undertaken by the Reserve Bank of India (RBI) in 2008 for the faster clearing of cheques. Cheque truncation means, stopping the flow of the physical cheques issued by a drawer to the drawee branch. The physical instrument is truncated at some point enroute to the drawee branch and an electronic image of the cheque is sent to the drawee branch along with the relevant information. This would eliminate the need to move the physical instruments across branches, except in exceptional circumstances. CTS is based on online image-based cheque clearing system where cheque images and Magnetic Ink Character Recognition (MICR) data are captured at the collecting bank branch and transmitted electronically.

Before CTS, to settle a cheque, it has to be presented to the drawee bank for payment. Originally this was done by taking the cheque to the drawee bank, however as cheque usage increased this became cumbersome and banks arranged

1849 (Bank Awar.)–15-II

to meet each day at a central location to exchange cheques and settle the money. This became known as central clearing. Bank customers who received cheques could deposit them at their own bank, who would arrange for the cheque to be returned to the drawee bank and the money credited to and debited from the appropriate accounts. If a cheque was dishonoured or bounced it would be physically returned to the original bank marked as such. This process would take several days, as the cheques had to be transported to the central clearing location, from where they were taken to the payee bank. If the cheque bounced, it would be sent back to the bank where the cheque was deposited. This is known as the clearing cycle. Cheques had to be examined by hand at each stage, which required a large amount of manpower.

In 1960, machine readable codes were added to the bottom of cheques in MICR format, which allowed the clearing and sorting process to be automated. This helped to speed up the clearing process; however the law in most countries still required the cheques to be delivered to the payee bank, and so physical movement of the paper continued. Starting in the mid-1990s, some countries started to change their laws to allow "truncation": cheques would be imaged and a digital representation of the cheque would be transmitted to the drawee bank, and the original cheques were destroyed. The MICR codes and cheque details are normally encoded as text in addition to the image. The bank where the cheque was deposited would typically do the truncation and this dramatically decreased the time it took to clear a cheque. In some cases large retailers that received large volumes of cheques could also do the truncation. Once the cheque has been turned into a digital document it can be processed through the banking system just like any other electronic payment.

The Reserve Bank of India first implemented CTS in National Capital Region, New Delhi from 1st February 2008. Based on the experience gained and the benefits that would accrue to the customers and banks, it was decided to operationalise CTS across the country starting 1st January 2014.

CTS have emerged as an important efficiency enhancement initiative undertaken by the Reserve Bank of India. The major benefits are:

1. Cheque truncation speeds up the process of collection of cheques resulting in better service to customers.
2. The electronic movement of images can facilitate shorter clearing cycle.
3. With the introduction of imaging and truncation, the physical movement of instruments is stopped and there is no fear of loss of instruments in transit.
4. It lowers the cost of collection of cheques, and removes the reconciliation-related and logistics-related problems.
5. It effectively eliminates the associated cost of movement of the physical cheques, reduces the time required for their collection and brings elegance to the entire activity of cheque processing.
6. It provides operational efficiency for banks and customers alike and reduces the risks associated with paper clearing.
7. Limitations of the existing clearing system in terms of geography or jurisdiction can be removed, thus enabling consolidation and integration of multiple clearing locations managed by different banks into a nation-wide standard clearing system with uniform processes and practices.

CTS bring elegance to the entire activity of Cheque processing and clearing. In addition to operational efficiency, CTS offers human resource rationalisation, cost effectiveness, business process re-engineering, adoption of latest technology and ultimately better service.

NPA

A Non-performing asset (NPA) is defined as a credit facility in respect of which the interest and/or instalment of principal has remained 'past due' for a specified period of time. NPAs refer to the loans that are in jeopardy of default. Once the borrower has failed to make interest or principal payments for 90 days, the loan is considered to be a non-performing asset. Nonperforming assets are problematic for financial institutions since they depend on interest payments for income. The account remains 'out of order' for a period of more than 90 days, in respect of an Overdraft/Cash Credit. NPAs result from defaults or the failure to meet financial obligations, say non-payment of a loan instalment.

NPAs do not just reflect badly in a bank's account books, they adversely impact the national economy. When bank do not get loan repayment or interest payments, liquidity problems may ensue. NPAs decrease profitability, reduce capital assets and lending limits, and increase the loan loss reserves. NPAs affect the credit ratings and goodwill of an organisation.

Banks classify non-performing assets further into the following three categories based on the period for which the asset has remained non-performing and the realisability of the dues:

1. **Sub-standard Assets:** A sub-standard asset is one which has been classified as NPA for a period not exceeding 12 months.
2. **Doubtful Assets:** A doubtful asset is one which has remained NPA for a period exceeding 12 months.
3. **Loss Assets:** A loss asset is one which cannot be recovered and loss has been identified by the bank. But the amount has not been written off, wholly or partly.

Capital Adequacy Ratio

For the smooth flow of credit in an economy, it is essential that banks should be financially sound so as to meet its various requirements. Banks encounter various types of risks while carrying the business of financial intermediation as it is the highly leveraged sector of an economy. Capital adequacy ratio (CAR) is one of the measures which ensure the financial soundness of banks in absorbing a reasonable amount of loss. Regulation of capital assumes significant importance so as to reduce bank failures, to promote stability, safety and soundness of the banking system, to prevent systemic disaster and to ultimately reduce losses to the bank depositors.

Capital Adequacy Ratio is the ratio which protects banks against excess leverage, insolvency and keeps them out of difficulty. It is defined as the ratio of banks capital in relation to its current liabilities and risk weighted assets. Risk weighted assets is a measure of amount of banks assets, adjusted for risks. CAR = (Bank's Capital/Risk Weighted Assets). As per RBI norms, Indian Scheduled Commercial Banks should have a CAR of 9% *i.e.*, 1% more than stipulated Basel Norms while Public Sector Banks are emphasized to keep this ratio at 12%.

Capital adequacy is an important parameter for judging the strength and soundness of the banking system. An appropriate level of capital adequacy ensures that the bank has sufficient capital to expand its business, while at the same time its net worth is enough to absorb any financial downturns without becoming insolvent. CAR is the ratio which determines banks capacity to meet the time liabilities and other risks such as credit risk, market risk, operational risk etc.

Banking Ombudsman

The Banking Ombudsman Scheme is introduced under Section 35 A of the Banking Regulation Act, 1949 by the Reserve Bank of India (RBI) with effect from 1995. The Banking Ombudsman Scheme enables an expeditious and inexpensive forum to bank customers for resolution of complaints relating to certain services rendered by banks. The Banking Ombudsman is a senior official appointed by the Reserve Bank of India to redress customer complaints against deficiency in certain banking services. All Scheduled Commercial Banks, Regional Rural Banks and Scheduled Primary Co-operative Banks are covered under the Scheme. As on date, 22 Banking Ombudsmen have been appointed with their offices located mostly in state capitals.

The major grounds of complaints that come under the purview of the Banking Ombudsman Scheme are listed below:

- Non-payment or inordinate delay in the payment or collection of cheques, drafts, bills etc.
- Non-acceptance, without sufficient cause, of small denomination notes tendered for any purpose, and for charging of commission in respect thereof.
- Non-acceptance, without sufficient cause, of coins tendered and for charging of commission in respect thereof.
- Non-payment or delay in payment of inward remittances.
- Failure to issue or delay in issue of drafts, pay orders or bankers' cheques.
- Non-adherence to prescribed working hours.
- Failure to provide or delay in providing a banking facility (other than loans and advances) promised in writing by a bank or its direct selling agents.
- Delays, non-credit of proceeds to parties accounts, non-payment of deposit or nonobservance of the Reserve Bank directives, if any, applicable to rate of interest on deposits in any savings, current or other account maintained with a bank.
- Complaints from Non-Resident Indians having accounts in India in relation to their remittances from abroad, deposits and other bank-related matters.
- Refusal to open deposit accounts without any valid reason for refusal.
- Levying of charges without adequate prior notice to the customer.
- Non-adherence by the bank or its subsidiaries to the instructions of Reserve Bank on ATM/Debit card operations or credit card operations.
- Non-disbursement or delay in disbursement of pension.
- Refusal to accept or delay in accepting payment towards taxes, as required by Reserve Bank/ Government.
- Refusal to issue or delay in issuing, or failure to service or delay in servicing or redemption of Government securities.
- Forced closure of deposit accounts without due notice or without sufficient reason.
- Refusal to close or delay in closing the accounts.
- Non-adherence to the fair practices code as adopted by the bank or non-adherence to the provisions of the Code of Bank's Commitments to Customers issued by Banking Codes and Standards Board of India and as adopted by the bank.
- Non-observance of Reserve Bank guidelines on engagement of recovery agents by banks.
- Any other matter relating to the violation of the directives issued by the Reserve Bank in relation to banking or other services.

A customer can lodge a complaint before the Banking Ombudsman if the reply is not received from the bank after one's representation, or the bank rejects the complaint, or if the complainant is not satisfied with the reply given by the bank. One may lodge the complaint at the office of the Banking Ombudsman under whose jurisdiction; the bank branch complained against is situated. The Banking Ombudsman does not charge any fee for filing and resolving customers' complaints. The amount, if any, to be paid by the bank to the complainant by way of compensation for any loss suffered by the complainant is limited to the amount arising directly out of the act or omission of the bank or ₹ 10 lakh, whichever is lower.

BANKING OMBUDSMAN

- The Banking Ombudsman Scheme was introduced under **Section 35 A of the Banking Regulation Act, 1949** by **RBI** with effect from **1995.**
- The Banking Ombudsman Scheme was **first introduced in India in 1995** and it was **revised in 2002.**
- Current Banking Ombudsman Scheme introduced in **2006.**
- **From 2002 until 2006, around 36,000 complaints** have been dealt by the Banking Ombudsmen.
- Banking Ombudsman is appointed by **Reserve Bank of India.**
- Banking Ombudsman is a senior official appointed by RBI. He handle and redress customer complaints against deficiency in certain banking services.
- The **offices** of Banking Ombudsman is mostly situated at **State Capitals.**
- **Around 22** Banking Ombudsmen have been appointed.
- **All Scheduled Commercial Banks, Regional Rural Banks and Scheduled Primary Co-operative Banks** are covered under the Banking Ombudsman Scheme.

Grounds of Complaints

One can file a Complaint on the following Grounds of Complaints:

1. Any excessive delay or non - payment of collection of cheques, drafts, bills etc.
2. Without any sufficient cause non acceptance of small denomination notes.
3. Charging any commission for acceptance of small denominations notes
4. Any delay in payment of inward remittances or non payment of inward remittances.
5. If any banking organization refuses to accept taxes or any delaying in accepting taxes (as required by RBI or Government of India).
6. Any delay in issuing government securities.
7. Refusal to issue or redemption of government securities.
8. Without any sufficient reason, forced close the deposit accounts by bankers.
9. If any banker refuse to close the accounts.
10. If any banker deliberately delaying in closing the accounts.
11. Non compliance of the provisions of Banking Codes and Standard Board of India.
12. If any banker commits non - observance of Reserve Bank of India's guidelines or instructions or any violation of the directives issued by the Reserve Bank in relation to banking or other services.
13. Without any sufficient cause, non-acceptance of coins tendered or charging of commission in respect thereof.
14. Delay or Failure in issue of drafts, pay orders or banker's cheques.
15. Performance of work is not as per prescribed working hours.
16. Delay or failure in providing any bank facility.
17. Complaints file by Non-resident Indians having accounts in India in relation to their remittance from abroad, deposits and other bank related matters.
18. Without any reason, refusal to open deposit accounts.
19. Without adequate prior notice to the customer, charges levied by the banker.
20. Any violation of guidelines or instructions of RBI on ATM/Debit Card/Credit Card operations.
21. Non-disbursement or delay in disbursement of pension.

Other Grounds

A customer can also file a complaint on the following grounds of deficiency in service with respect to loans and advances:

1. The Banking Ombudsman may also deal with such other matter as may be specified by the Reserve Bank from time to time.
2. Without any valid reason non-acceptance of application of loans.
3. Any violation of the provisions of the fair practices code for lenders as adopted by the bank or Code of Bank's Commitment to Customers, as the case may be.
4. Any type of violation of the instruction, guidelines, recommendations of the RBI.
5. If any non-observance of Reserve Bank Directives on interest rates;
6. Any delays in sanction of loan applications.

Reasons, when you can File a Complaint

1. If reply is not received from the bank within a period of one month after concerned bank has received complaint representation.
2. If bank rejects the complaint.
3. If complainant is not satisfied with bank's reply.
   - Banking Ombudsman does not charge any fee for filing and resolving customer's complaints.
   - If any loss suffered by the complainant then complainant is limited to the amount arising directly out of the act or omission of the bank or ₹ 10 Lakhs whichever is lower.

DEMAT ACCOUNT

A DeMat account is one that allows you to buy, sell as well as transact without the need of any paperwork. DeMat accounts are very safe, convenient and secure.

DeMat is nothing but a dematerialized account. If one has to save money or make cheque payments, then he/she needs to open a bank account. Similarly, one needs to open a DeMat account if he/she wants to buy or sell stocks. Thus, DeMat account is similar to a bank account wherein the actual money is being replaced by shares. In order to open a DeMat account, one needs to approach the Depository Participants [DPs].

In India, a DeMat account is a type of banking account that dematerializes paper-based physical stock shares. The DeMat account is used to avoid holding of physical shares: the shares are bought as well as sold through a stock broker. In this case, the advantage is that one does not need any physical evidence for possessing these shares. All the things are taken care of by the DPs.

This account is very popular in India. Physically only 500 shares can be traded as per the provision given by SEBI. From April 2006, it has become mandatory for any person holding a DeMat account to possess a Permanent Account Number (PAN).

KNOW YOUR CUSTOMER (KYC)

The Reserve Bank of India (RBI) has advised banks to follow "KYC guidelines", wherein certain personal information of the account-opening prospect or the customer is obtained. The objective of doing so is to enable the Bank to have positive identification of its customers. This is also in the interest of customers to safeguard their hard earned money.

The KYC guidelines of RBI mandate banks to collect three proofs from their customers. They are—

1. Photograph
2. Proof of identity
3. Proof of address

What is KYC?

Know Your Customer - KYC enables banks to know/understand their customers and their financial dealings to be able to serve them better.

Who is a Customer of the Bank?

For the purpose of KYC Policy, a Customer is defined as:

- A person or entity that maintains an account and/or has a business relationship with the Bank;
- One on whose behalf the account is maintained (*i.e.* the beneficial owner);
- Beneficiaries of transactions conducted by professional intermediaries, such as Stock Brokers, Chartered Accountants, Solicitors, etc. as permitted under the law, and
- Any person or entity connected with a financial transaction, which can pose significant reputation or other risks to the Bank, say, a wire transfer or issue of a high value demand draft as a single transaction.

Camel Rating of Banks

CAMEL model of rating was first developed in the 1970s by the 3 federal banking supervisors of the U.S (the Federal Reserve, the FDIC and the OCC) as part of the Regulators. "Uniform Financial Institutions Rating System", to provide a convenient summary of bank condition at the tirfie of its on-site examination.

C - Capital Adequacy
A - Asset Quality
M - Management Quality
E - Earnings
L - Liquidity
S - Sensitivity to Market Risk/System and control

RBI plans to change system in order to make the process more forward-looking. Indian financial sector would be evaluated under a dynamic risk-based mechanism, an aspect the present CAMELS rating system lacked. RBI proposes to replace CAMELS with INROADS (Indian Risk-Oriented and Dynamic Rating System) from the next round of annual financial inspection.

For foreign banks in INDIA the rating model is a modified version called CACS , CACS means

C - Capital Adequacy
A - Asset Quality
C - Compliance
S - System and control

CORE BANKING SOLUTION (CBS)

This word is more often used by bankers and now-a-days postal officials are also using it. CBS is an acronym of Core Banking Solutions. Again one will wonder what the meaning of core is, core is also an acronym. It stands for ***"Centralized On-line Real-time Exchange"***.

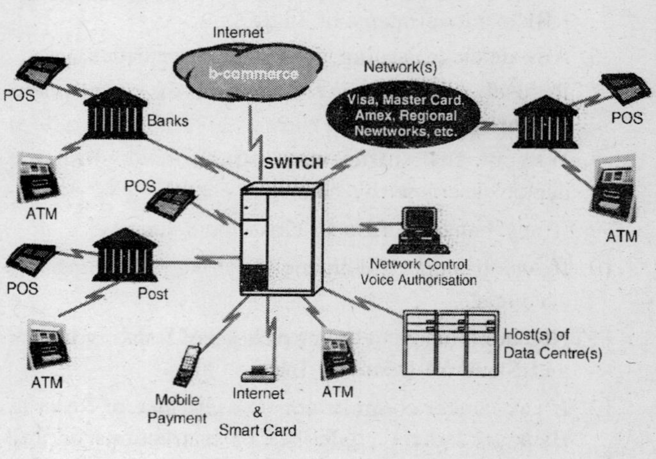

Definition

Core Banking Solution (CBS) is networking of branches, which enables Customers to operate their accounts, and avail banking services from any branch of the Bank on CBS network, regardless of where he maintains his account. The customer is no more the customer of a Branch. He becomes the Bank's Customer.

Another interesting fact regarding CBS is that all CBS branches are inter-connected with each other. Therefore, Customers of CBS branches can avail various banking facilities from any other CBS branch located anywhere in the world.

What it offers to a customer?

It offers invariably all information that a bank's customer would need if he/she visits a bank branch in person.

These are as herein follows:

1. To make enquiries about the balance or debit or credit entries in the account.
2. To obtain cash payment out of his account by tendering a cheque.
3. To deposit a cheque for credit into his account.
4. To deposit cash into the account.
5. To deposit cheques / cash into account of some other person who has account in a CBS branch.
6. To get statement of account.
7. To transfer funds from his account to some other account – his own or of third party, provided both accounts are in CBS branches.
8. To obtain Demand Drafts or Banker's Cheques from any branch on CBS – amount shall be online debited to his account.
9. Customers can continue to use ATMs and other Delivery Channels, which are also interfaced with CBS platform.

Top CBS Application Software Providers

1. Infosys Technologies Ltd. **Finnacle** is the universal banking solution from Infosys.
2. **I-flex solutions Ltd**. since late 2005 it is owned by Oracle.
3. **TCS FNS (Financial Network Services Limited)** is an Australian developer and supplier of banking application software, operating in world markets. Now owned and managed by TCS.

Thus, CBS is a step towards enhancing customer convenience through anywhere and anytime banking.

CHEQUE TRUNCATION SYSTEM

Truncation literally means stopping or cutting short. Thus, truncation of cheque means stopping the flow of the physical cheque by the presenting bank (bank where the cheque is presented/dropped off) en-route to the drawee bank's (bank on which the cheque is drawn on) branch.

Instead of the physical cheque, an *electronic image of the cheque* is transmitted to the drawee branch, along with relevant information like data on the MICR band, date of presentation, presenting bank, etc.

Cheque truncation, thus, removes the need to move the actual physical cheque from branch to branch.

BENEFITS OF CTS

(*i*) CTS speeds up the process of collection of cheques,

(*ii*) Reduces the scope for clearing-related frauds or loss of instruments in transit,

(*iii*) Lowers the cost of collection of cheques,

(*iv*) Removes reconciliation-related and logistics-related problems,

(*v*) Reduces the time of clearing cycle – that is faster processing of cheques and payment in favour of the customer,

(*vi*) Reduces scope for frauds inherent in paper instruments.

DIFFERENT TYPES OF CHEQUES

A cheque is an unconditional order addressed to a banker, signed by the person who has deposited money with a banker, requesting him to pay on demand a certain sum of money only to the order of certain person or to the bearer of the instrument.

Types of Cheques

1. Bearer Cheque: Bearer cheque are the cheques which withdrawn to the cheque's owner. These types of cheques normally used for cash transaction.

2. Order Cheque: Order cheque are the cheques which is withdrawn for the payee (the cheque withdrawn for whose person). Before withdrawn to that payee, banks cross check the identity of the payee.

3. Crossed Cheque: On that type of cheques two parallel line made on the upper part of the cheques, then that cheques formed to crossed cheques. This type of cheques payment does not formed in cash while the payment of that type of cheques transferred to the payee account and the normal person's account who recommend by the holder on the cheque.

4. Account Payee Cheque: When two parallel lines along with a crossed made on the cheque and the word 'ACCOUNT PAYEE' written between these lines, then that types of cheques are called account payee cheque. The payment of the account payee cheque takes place on the person, firm or company on which name the cheque issue.

5. Company Crossed Cheques: When two parallel lines along with a crossed made on the cheque and the word 'COMPANY' written between these lines, then that types of cheques are called company crossed cheques. Then type of withdrawn does not taken in cash while the person on which the cheque issue, transferred on its account.

Normally crossed cheque and company crossed cheque are same.

6. Stale Cheque: If any cheque issue by a holder does not get withdrawn from the bank till three months, then that type of cheques are called stale cheque.

7. Post Dated Cheque: If any cheque issue by a holder to the payee for the upcoming withdrawn date, then that type of cheques are called post dated cheque.

8. Anti Dated Cheque: If any cheque issue for the upcoming withdrawn date but it withdraw before the date printed on the cheque, then that type of cheques are called anti dated cheques.

BANDHAN BANK

Recently, there is a buzz about **BANDHAN BANK,** Lets know about it:

- **Bandhan Bank** was set up in **2001** to handle dual objective of **poverty alleviation** and **women empowerment.**
- It was previously a **Non-Banking Financial Company (NBFC)** but **Bandhan Bank** received its universal banking licence from **Reserve Bank of India.**
- The bank rolled out its services on **23rd August, 2015 (Founded).**
- The bank started with **501 branches** in all most **22 states** in India which is highest branches of any private bank on the **first day.**
- The bank will provide funds to help and develop the **Small and Medium Enterprises (SME).**
- The saving interest rates have been fixed at **4.25% below ₹ 1,00,000** and **5% above ₹ 1,00,000.**
- It is interesting to know that **Bandhan** was the only micro-finance institution that applied for a banking licence.
- **Headquarters** is located at **Kolkata, West Bengal.**
- **Slogan** of bank is **"Aapka Bhala, Sabki Bhalai".**
- Incidentally, Bandhan is the **first bank** to be **set up in eastern part of India after Independence.**

PAYMENT BANKS AND SMALL FINANCE BANKS

Payment banks can receive deposits and remittances, but cannot lend, focusing on migrant labour and low income households.

Small banks will lend to "unserved and under-served sections", including small business units, small and marginal farmers, and micro and small industries.

Payment Banks	Small Finance Banks
Objective	
Provide small savings accounts and payments /remittance services to migrant labour workforce and low-income households	Financial inclusion and supply of credit to small business units and farmers through high-technology and low-cost operations
Eligible Promoters	
Individuals or professionals with necessary experience and eligibility, existing NBFCs, corporate banking correspondents, mobile companies, supermarket chains, real estate co-ops and corporate entities	Resident individuals or professionals with 10 years of experience in banking and finance, companies and societies owned and controlled by residents, existing NBFCs, microfinance institutions and local area banks owned and controlled by residents
Scope of Activities	
Accept deposits but customer balance should not exceed ₹ 1 Lakh	Basic services of accepting deposits and lending
Cannot give loans, can issue ATM/Debit card but no credit cards	No restriction on the area of operations
Can distribute non-risk simple financial products such as mutual funds and insurance products	At least 50% of its loan portfolio should constitute loans and advances of upto ₹ 25 Lakh
NRIs will not be allowed to open accounts	
Capital Requirement and Promoter's contribution	
Minimum paid-up equity capital of ₹ 100 Crore/initially 40%, to be gradually brought down to 26% within 12 years from date of commencement	

Payment Banks

On 19 August 2015, RBI approved "in-prinicple" licenses to 6 entities to start payment banks.

These 6 entities are:

- Airtel Payments Bank Ltd.
- India Post Payments Bank Ltd.
- FINO Payments Bank Ltd.
- Paytm Payments Bank Ltd.
- Jio Payments Bank Ltd.
- NSDL Payments Bank Ltd.

MUDRA BANK

What is Mudra Bank?

- MUDRA means Micro Units Development and Refinance Agency (known as the MUDRA bank)
- Mudra bank is being set up through a statutory enactment and will be responsible for developing and refinancing through a Pradhan Mantri Mudra Yojna.
- It is first set up as a subsidiary of the **Small Industries Develpoment Bank of India (SIDBI)**. It will later be converted into full-fledged bank through an act of the parliament.
- **MUDRA** Bank is a public sector financial institution in India, It provides loan at low rates to small entrepreneurs.

OBJECTIVE

- It was launched in 8th April 2015 with the objective of regulating micro and small enterprise financing business, and supporting them particularly those members who belongs from scheduled castes and scheduled tribes.
- MUDRA Bank will also register **MFIs (Micro Finance Institutions)** and will be responsible for accreditation and rating of MFI.
- It will also make proper last mile practices to be followed by MFI to provide proper client protection and to prevent from indebtedness.

AIM

- The finance ministry said measures to be taken up by the MUDRA are targeted mainly on young, educated or skilled workers and entrepreneurs including women entrepreneurs.
- Basically small entrepreneurs and small businessman are often cut from banking system because of limited branch presence, so MUDRA bank will partner with local coordinators and provide finance to small and micro businesses.

IMPORTANT FIGURES ABOUT MUDRA BANK

- The bank will be set up with the initial corpus of ₹ 20000 cr and a credit guarantee corpus of ₹ 3000cr.
- The bank have categorized the amount of loan to be given in three different categories.
- **SHISHU:** This is the first stage and in it the loan will be given for upto ₹ 50000.
- **KISHOR:** In the second stage a loan amount will be ranging from 50,000 to ₹ 5 lakh.
- **TARUN:** This is last category which will provide upto ₹ 10 lakh.
- The bank will cater to 5.77 crore small business units that spread all across India who currently find it difficult to access credit from the regular banking system.
- According to Mr NARENDRA MODI the bank would help over 6 cr families out of which 65% of them belongs to scheduled caste and scheduled tribes.

BHARATIYA MAHILA BANK

Bharatiya Mahila Bank Ltd is the first of its kind in the Banking Industry in India formed with a vision of economic empowerment for women. Incorporated under the Companies Act 1956 on 5 August 2013, the Bank received the certificate of commencement of Business on 22 August 2013 and the Banking License from RBI on 25 September 2013. The Bank's Corporate Office is at the IFCI Towers, 9th floor, Nehru Place, New Delhi.

Launched in 2013, the Bank has carved a niche for itself as a pan India Bank with 100 branches across the country.

While the Bank focuses on the entire pyramid of Indian women, special attention is given to economically neglected, deprived, discriminated, underbanked, unbanked, rural and urban women to ensure inclusive and sustainable growth. The Bank with a team of professionals with rich experience and expertise has designed and developed new products and services to suit the needs of women of all segments including Self Help Groups, women entrepreneurs, salaried women, HNIs and Corporates.

The Savings Bank rate of interest for Rupees One lakh and above is 5% and for amount less than Rs. One lakh, the interest rate is 4.5%. The Bank has designed many women centric products keeping in mind the core strengths of women so as to enable them to unleash their hidden potentials, engage in economic activities and contribute to the economic growth of the country. Most of the products are offered with a concession in the rate of interest for women customers.

The Bank offers BMB Smartbanking – the internet banking facility with many value added features. The customers can open Recurring Deposits, Fixed Deposits etc through internet banking. When in need they can also access such Fixed Deposits to avail premature facility. The Bank's Mobile banking App can be freely downloaded from Google Play Store for Android mobiles and Apple Store for iphone. Bank is one of the pilot Banks for introduction of the new payment system UPI, launched by NPCI.

The Bank also conducts programmes on financial literacy, skill development, training for women of all segments of the society so that women in turn generate more income, more jobs and growth opportunities and contribute significantly for the economic growth of the nation.

The Bank has been allocated with an initial capital of ₹ 1000 Crores.

In April 2017 Bharatiya Mahila Bank has been merged in SBI.

Vision

Empowering Women Economically.

Mission

- To be the Bank of Best Option for all women, thereby ensuring a place of pride for Indian Women, across the globe.
- To promote Financial Literacy.
- To support women's livelihood.
- To facilitate inclusive growth.
- To constantly innovate, design and develop new products, services and facilities for women across all strata, to suit their needs right from birth throughout their entire life span and beyond.
- To provide hassle free access to all banking and financial products, services and facilities.
- To encourage women entrepreneurship.
- To eliminate lending bias against women.
- To educate and embolden women to establish their rights to asset ownership.
- To instill confidence in women to avail of banking services with a free, non-hesitant; bold mindset.
- To cater to the banking and financial needs of all including the third gender and men.
- To adopt new technologies and low cost, highly efficient delivery models and mechanisms.
- To reach out to Self-Help Groups and Joint Liability Groups.
- To perform effectively and efficiently to result in financial viability and sustainability of the Bank.
- To operate, following global best practices in the interest of all stakeholders.

MULTIPLE CHOICE QUESTION

1. Inventor of ATM was:
A. Ian Luther Steward
B. David Block
C. John Adrian Shepherd Barron (A Britisher)
D. John Benson
E. None of these

2. Inventor John Shepherd Barron installed the worlds's first automatic cash dispenser at a .... near London:
A. London Bank Branch
B. Barclays Bank Branch
C. Royal Grand Federal Bank Branch
D. Bank of Britain Branch
E. None of these

3. ATM machine was invented in the year ....
A. 1967 B. 1968
C. 1969 D. 1970
E. None of these

4. .... was the first bank to Introduce the ATM concept in India:
A. HSBC
B. SBI
C. Standard Chartered Bank
D. HDFC
E. None of these

5. HSBC introduced the ATM concept in India in:
A. 1988 B. 1987
C. 1989 D. 1990
E. None of these

6. ATM stands for:
A. Automated Teller Machine
B. Automatic Telling Machine
C. Automatic Taking Machine
D. Automated Token Machine
E. None of these

7. The first company to get RBI's permission to open White Label ATMs is:
A. Tata Communications Payment Solutions Limited (TCPSL)
B. Muthoot Finance
C. Prizm Payments
D. AGS
E. None of these

8. Which among the following is correct about Brown Label ATMs:
A. These ATMs are owned and maintained by service provider
B. Bank whose Brand name is used on ATM takes care of cash management and network connectivity
C. Both of Above
D. These ATMs are meant for NRIs only
E. None of these

9. The Banking Ombudsman Scheme was introduced under:
A. Banking Regulation Act, 1935
B. Banking Regulation Act, 1949
C. Banking Regulation Act, 1985
D. Banking Regulation Act, 1987
E. None of the above

10. The Banking Ombudsman Scheme was introduced under Section 35 A of the Banking Regulation Act, 1949 by RBI with effect from ....
A. 1992 B. 1993
C. 1995 D. 1994
E. None of the above

11. Banking Ombudsman is appointed by ....
A. Central Finance Minister
B. Reserve Bank of India
C. SEBI
D. President
E. None of the above

12. Which among the following is incorrect:
A. Banking Ombudsman is a senior official appointed by RBI.
B. The Offices of Banking Ombudsman is mostly situated at State Capitals.
C. All Scheduled Commercial Banks, Regional Rural Banks and Scheduled Primary Co-operative Banks are covered under the Banking Ombudsman Scheme
D. All of the above
E. None of the above

13. Banking Ombudsman is appointed for:
A. handling and redress banks complaints against customers' behavior
B. handling and redress customer complaints against deficiency in certain banking services
C. providing decision on important banking operations like - CRR, SLR and MSF etc.
D. Both A and B
E. None of the above

14. Which among the following is suitable ground of complaint against banks to Banking Ombudsman:
A. Charging any commission for acceptance of small denomination notes
B. Any delay in payment of inward remittances or non payment of inward remittances
C. Any excessive delay or non - payment of collection of cheques, drafts, bills etc.
D. If any banking organization refuses to accept taxes or any delaying in accepting taxes (as required by RBI or Government of India).
E. All of the above

15. A bank customer can file a complaint against banking organization if reply is not received from the bank within a period of .... after concerned bank has received complaint representation:
A. Two Months B. One Month
C. Three Months D. Fifteen days
E. None of the above

16. You can file a complaint to Banking Ombudsman:
A. If bank rejects the complaint
B. If bank show negligence for your complaint
C. Both of the above
D. If bank force you to draw back complaint
E. None of the above

17. CBS stands for:
A. Central Banking Solutions
B. Core Banking Solution
C. Code Banking Solutions
D. Cross Banking System
E. None of these

18. "EFTPOS" cards are linked with which among the following countries:
A. Australia and New Zealand
B. Monacco and Norway
C. Qatar and Kuwait
D. Australia and Norway
E. None of the above

19. Which among the following benefits is associated with RuPay:
A. International transactions lead to higher transactions costs. Such costs can be reduced by using RuPay card since processing will be done within the country. Also transactions will be faster
B. Users will get alerts for every transaction made through RuPay Card
C. Processing Fees for RuPay card compared with regular debit/credit cards will be considerably lower
D. All of the above
E. None of the above

20. The designer of Indian Rupee Sign is:
A. Hitendra Swami
B. Udaya Kumar Dharmalingam
C. Panduranga Kumarlingam
D. Both A and C
E. None of these

21. First Bank in India to launch EMI facility on debit cards:
A. SBI B. Axis Bank
C. ICICI Bank D. HDFC Bank
E. None of these

22. India's first non-bank owned ATM (White Label ATMs) open in?
A. Delhi B. Bihar
C. Uttar Pradesh D. Maharashtra
E. Gujarat

23. Obtaining cash from an ATM is similar to:
A. Writing a Cheque
B. Open any Account
C. Any banking transaction
D. Close any Account
E. None of these

24. E-Banking covers both Computer banking and ....
A. Merchant Banking B. Telephone Banking
C. Standard Banking D. Choice Banking
E. None of these

25. Which of the following features fit for E-Banking:
A. Providing Ease in banking operations
B. Stress on branch less banking
C. Time Saving
D. All of the above
E. None of these

26. The Banking Ombudsman is person appointed by the .... to redress customer complaints against certain deficiency in banking services:
A. Indian Banking Personnel Selection
B. Reserve Bank of India

C. Securities and Exchange Board of India
D. State Bank of India
E. None of these

27. Banking Ombudsman is a ....
A. Collateral Judicial Authority
B. Bi-Lateral Judicial Authority
C. Quasi Judicial Authority
D. Both A and B
E. None of these

28. Banking Ombudsman has power to summon ....
A. Bank Only B. Customer Only
C. Both of the above D. Any one
E. None of these

29. CTS stands for:
A. Cheque Transfer System
B. Cheque Truncation System
C. Cheque Truncation Standards
D. Cheque Transaction System
E. None of these

30. In order to facilitate faster collection of outstanding cheques, the Reserve Bank of India commenced a special clearing facility called ....
A. Speed Clearing B. High Clearing
C. Standard Clearing D. Ultra Clearing
E. None of these

31. Which of the following cheque is not honored by the bank:
A. Self Cheque B. Stale Cheque
C. Cross Cheque D. All of the above
E. None of these

32. The first public sector bank in India which obtained license for Internet Banking from RBI is:
A. Oriental Bank of Commerce
B. ICICI Bank
C. Punjab National Bank
D. State Bank of India
E. None of these

33. NRI deposits are called as:
A. Hot Money B. Foreign Deposits
C. NRI Funds D. Overseas Money
E. None of these

34. Social Control of the banks introduced during the year:
A. 1967 B. 1969
C. 1970 D. 1972
E. None of these

35. The credit risk to the bank is high from which of these cards:
A. Credit Card
B. Debit Card
C. Both types of Cards in ration 50:50
D. Both types of Cards in ration 60:40
E. None of these

36. Local Area Banks were established on:
A. 24.08.1996 B. 24.09.1995
C. 24.07.1992 D. 15.08.1993
E. None of these

37. Local Area Banks were registered as public limited companies under which act:
A. Companies Act, 1956
B. SEBI Act, 1885
C. Limited Liability Partnership Act
D. Both B and C
E. None of these

38. KVP (Kisan Vikas Patra) which is launched by Finance Minister Arun Jaitley, the money will double in?
A. 120 months B. 100 months
C. 180 months D. 150 months
E. None of these

39. Which country issued first purely plastic note?
A. New Zealand B. Mexico
C. Singapore D. Fiji and Canada
E. Australia

40. Mutilated Notes are?
A. Notes which are in pieces and/or of which the essential portions are missing
B. Any bank note, which is wholly or partially, obliterated, shrunk
C. Notes which are washed, altered or indecipherable
D. Notes which are wholly or partially, obliterated, shrunk, washed, altered or indecipherable
E. None of these

41. A right to keep possession of property belonging to another person until a debt owned by that person is discharged is called as:
A. Lien B. Mortgage
C. Custody D. Either B or C
E. None of these

42. Conversion of Physical form of share into electronic form is called:
A. E-Share B. DEMAT
C. Online Share Cards D. Offline Share Cards
E. None of these

43. "Microcredit" refers to:
A. Installments given by farmers against loans
B. Small credit given to poor
C. Credit given by government to improve industrialization
D. Credit given by bank to NRIs
E. None of these

44. 'Swabhiman' the financial inclusion scheme, comes under the purview of which minsitry:
A. Ministry of External Affairs
B. Ministry of Finance
C. Ministry of Home Affairs
D. Ministry of Agriculture
E. None of these

45. Credit Card is an essential component of:
- A. Electronic Commerce
- B. Internet Commerce
- C. Both of the above
- D. Either A or B
- E. None of the above

46. The concept of using a card for purchases was described in ....
- A. 1855
- B. 1887
- C. 1877
- D. 1880
- E. None of the above

47. The term credit card was first time used by:
- A. Edward Binni
- B. Edward Bellamy
- C. Edward Bamulson
- D. Edward Houston
- E. None of the above

48. Compared to debit cards and cheques, a credit card allows:
- A. small short-term loans to be quickly made to cardholder
- B. small short-term loans are made to cardholder and he need not calculate a balance remaining before every transaction
- C. total charges do not exceed the maximum credit line for the card
- D. All of the above
- E. None of the above

49. NPCI stands for:
- A. National Commission for Payment Information
- B. National Payment Corporation of India
- C. National Payment Commission of India
- D. Net Procedural Corporation of India
- E. None of the above

50. Which among the following is correct?
- A. RuPay is a combination of two words – Rupee and Payment
- B. RuPay Card is an Indian version of credit/debit card
- C. RuPay Card is very similar to international card such as Visa/Master
- D. All of the above
- E. None of the above

51. A centralized database with online connectivity to branches, internet as well as ATM-network which has been adopted by almost all major banks of our country is known as?
- A. Investment Banking
- B. Core Banking
- C. Mobile Banking
- D. National Banking
- E. Specialized Banking

52. Which of the following is an example of cash less purchase?
- A. Debit Card
- B. Credit Card
- C. ATM withdrawal
- D. All of the above
- E. None of these

53. Which one of the following is not an electronic banking delivery channel?
- A. Mobile Vans
- B. Mobile Phone Banking
- C. Internet Banking
- D. Tele Banking
- E. ATM

54. Finance Ministry advised RBI to allow common ATMs to be owned and managed by Non Banking Institutions. Such ATMs are called:
- A. NBFC ATMs
- B. Off Site ATMs
- C. Third Party ATMs
- D. White Label ATMs
- E. None of the above

55. Which of the following is a leading electronic payment technology firm? (The logo of the firm can be seen printed on credit cards/ATM centres etc.)
- A. Visa
- B. Max
- C. BSE
- D. Sensex
- E. SWAP

56. We often heard about M-Banking. What does M stands for?
- A. Money
- B. Memory
- C. Mobile
- D. Mobility
- E. None of these

57. As we know lot of new concepts are being used in the field of banking these days. Which of the following is NOT one such concept/product directly associated with banks?
- A. E-payment
- B. SMS Alert
- C. ATM/Debit Card
- D. Demat Account
- E. Number Portability

58. Which of the following cannot be a feature of a Debit card?
- A. These cards cannot be used as POS Centres
- B. Banks earn huge amount as penalties for defaulting on payment through these cards
- C. Can be used normal withdrawals
- D. Only A and B
- E. All A, B and C

59. Which one serves as a form of revolving credit?
- A. Social Bank
- B. Debit Card
- C. Credit Card
- D. E-purse
- E. None of these

ANSWERS

1	2	3	4	5	6	7	8	9	10
C	B	A	A	B	A	A	C	B	C
11	**12**	**13**	**14**	**15**	**16**	**17**	**18**	**19**	**20**
B	E	B	E	B	C	B	A	D	B
21	**22**	**23**	**24**	**25**	**26**	**27**	**28**	**29**	**30**
C	D	A	B	D	B	C	C	B	A
31	**32**	**33**	**34**	**35**	**36**	**37**	**38**	**39**	**40**
B	C	A	A	A	A	A	B	E	A
41	**42**	**43**	**44**	**45**	**46**	**47**	**48**	**49**	**50**
A	B	B	B	C	B	B	D	B	D
51	**52**	**53**	**54**	**55**	**56**	**57**	**58**	**59**	
B	D	A	D	A	C	E	D	C	

10

Regional Rural Banks (RRBs)

The Regional Rural Banks (RRBs) came into being under the 20-Point Economic Programme launched in 1975. Earlier, the Banking Commission, appointed by the Government to study the structure of banking development in India, mooted the idea of setting up RRBs in its report in 1972. The Government reviewed the recommendations of the Banking Commission, and appointed the Narasimham Study Group on July 1, 1975. It submitted the report in just 30 days and favoured the setting up of RRBs.

The Government of India promulgated the RRBs ordinance dated 26th September, 1975 which was subsequently replaced by the Regional Rural Banks Act, 1976. On October 2, 1975, five RRBs were established in four states : 2 in Uttar Pradesh, one at Moradabad by the Syndicate Bank and the other at Gorakhpur by the State Bank of India; one in Rajasthan by the United Commercial Bank; one in Bhiwani (Haryana) by the Punjab National Bank and one in Malda (West Bengal) by the United Bank of India.

Prathama Bank is the first Regional Rural Bank of India, sponsored by Syndicate Bank established on 2nd October, 1975, with its Head office at Moradabad in accordance with Regional Rural Bank Ordinance 1975 issued on 25 September 1975.

The RRBs were established with a view a developing the rural economy by providing for the purpose of development of agriculture, trade, commerce, industry and other productive activities in the rural areas, credit and other facilities, particularly to the small and marginal farmers, agricultural labourers, artisans, small entrepreneurs and for matters connected therewith and incidental thereto.

The RRBs are somewhere in between the public sector banks and the co-operative structure. They combine in themselves the characteristics of both these institutions and are expected to play a supporting role in districts where the credit gap is very large and the co-operative structure is weak. In setting up RRBs, certain norms have to be observed. These are:

- Areas should be relatively backward or tribal
- RRBs are to be set-up in areas where the co-operative banks are not active
- There should not be any commercial bank in the area
- The area should have a real potentiality for development break through with the flow of credit.

While recommending the setting up of RRBs, the Working Group on Rural Banks appointed by the Government in 1975 opined that each RRB combines in itself the "local feel and familiarity with rural problems which the co-operative possessed and the degree of business organization, ability to mobilize deposits, access to central money markets and a modernized outlook which the commercial banks have".

OBJECTIVES OF REGIONAL RURAL BANKS

The importance of the rural banking in the economic development of a country cannot be overlooked. As Gandhiji said "Real India lies in Villages," and village economy is the backbone of Indian economy. Without the upliftment of the rural economy as well as the rural people of our country, the objectives of economic planning cannot be achieved. In fact, the real growth of Indian economy lied in the freeing of rural masses from acute poverty, unemployment, and socio-economic backwardness.

Regional Rural Banks (RRBs) are oriented towards meeting the needs of the weaker sections of the rural population consisting of:

- Small and marginal farmers
- Agricultural labourers
- Artisans
- Small entrepreneurs
- Mobilise deposits from rural households.

RRBs are expected to make credit available to rural households besides inspiring carefulness. Put it simple to ensure sufficient institutional credit for agriculture and other rural sectors.

FUNCTIONS OF RRBs

A rural bank was described as "a primary banking institution set-up to serve a compact group of villages generally working as a co-operative bank, or as a subsidiary of a commercial bank", and its object would be "to provide at one place the special type of credit and banking facilities and related services needed by agriculturists and other rural producers".

The functions of RRBs are:

(*i*) To mobilize local savings.

(*ii*) To provide short-term and medium-term credit for agricultural and other purposes on its own and long-term credit as agents of the Land Development Banks.

(*iii*) To implement programmes of supervised credit tailored to the needs of individual farmers.

(*iv*) To provide various ancilliary banking services to local people.

(*v*) To set-up a medium godowns.

THE OPERATIONAL AREA OF RRB

The area of operation of RRBs is limited to the area as notified by Government of India covering one or more districts in the State.

Structure of Regional Rural Banks

In RRBs, there are three share holder namely Government of India (50% share), Sponsor Bank (35% share), and State Government (15% share).

Thus, we can say RRBs are jointly owned by Government of India, Sponsor Bank and respective State Government.

Role of RRBs/Gramin Bank

The role of RRBs can not be ignored in present day banking as these gramin banks have played a major role in implementation of central and state government sponsored various programme of poverty alleviation like SGSRY, PMRGP, Antyabasai. Payment to aganwadi, old age pension, mid-day meal, scholarship to student, Indira Awas Yojana, labour payment to NAREGA beneficiary has effectively been carried by these RRBs.

Regulatory Control

NABARD is the regulatory authority of Regional Rural Banks.

Organizational Structure

Organizational Structure for RRB's varies from branch to branch and depends upon the nature and size of business done by the branch. The Head Office of an RRB normally had three to seven departments.

The following is the decision making hierarchy of officials in a Regional Rural Bank.

- Board of Directors
- Chairman & Managing Director
- General Manager
- Chief Manager/Regional Managers
- Senior Manager
- Manager
- Officer/Assistant Manager
- Assistants.

Amalgamation of RRBs

GoI was forced to start the reform process as several RRBs suffered humongous losses and had become unviable. During a review carried out by GoI in the year 2009 it was found that the Capital Risk Weighted Assets Ratio (CRAR) of the RRBs were too low. Therefore, Dr. K.C. Chakraborty Committee suggested bringing the CRAR of RRBs to at least 9 per cent in a sustainable manner. The Committee inter-alia recommended recapitalisation support to the extent of ₹ 2,200 crore, to 40 RRBs.

As several Committees suggested for creation of viable RRBs by amalgamation of unviable RRBs, finally it was decided to amalgamate some of them on grounds of contiguity in a particular region. The process of amalgation has continued till June, 2014 and out of the originally 196 RRBs, now we have only 43 RRBs in 1 April, 2020.

MULTIPLE CHOICE QUESTIONS

1. RRB Act was enacted in the year:

A. 1974 B. 1979
C. 1975 D. 1976
E. None of these

2. Custodian of National Rural Credit Stabilisation Fund is:

A. RBI B. SBI
C. NABARD D. ARBI
E. None of these

3. Regional Rural Banks have been set up with the basic objective of:

A. Providing credit to semi-urban and urban population
B. Providing deposits facilities to farmers
C. Providing credit and deposit facilities to rural areas
D. Providing credit, deposit and other banking facilities to people in rural areas
E. None of the above

4. Regional Rural Banks are classified as:

A. subsidiaries of NABARD
B. subsidiaries of the sponsor banks
C. scheduled commercial banks
D. All of the above
E. None of the above

5. For opening a new branch, a Regional Rural Bank requires:
A. permission of NABARD
B. permission of Director, Institutional Finance
C. Approval of DRDA
D. RBI license
E. All of the above

6. Regional Rural Banks are empowered to transact the business of banking as defined under:
A. Regional Rural Banks Act, 1976
B. Negotiable Instruments Act, 1881
C. Banking Regulation Act, 1949
D. The Banking Companies (Acquisition and Transfer of Undertakings) Act, 1970
E. None of the above

7. Regional Rural Banks are managed by:
A. Reserve Bank of India
B. the State Government
C. the sponsor bank
D. a board of directors
E. All of these

8. Under which category will you classify Regional Rural Banks?
A. Scheduled Commercial Banks
B. Co-operative banks
C. Private sector banks
D. Development banks
E. None of these

9. On the current account balances maintained by the Regional Rural Banks with them, the commercial banks may:
A. pay interest up to 9 per cent
B. pay interest at such rates as may be mutually agreed to
C. pay interest as applicable to savings accounts
D. waive incidental charges
E. All of the above

10. All regional rural banks (RRBs) are required to maintain their entire statutory liquidity ratio (SLR) in:
A. current accounts with sponsor banks
B. time deposits with sponsor banks
C. government and other approved securities
D. gold holdings only
E. All of the above

11. The Regulatory Authority for Regional Rural Banks is:
A. RBI and NABARD B. Central Government
C. State Government D. Sponsor bank
E. All of the above

12. Which of the following conditions are required to be fulfilled by a Regional Rural Bank to be eligible for opening of new branches?
A. It should not have defaulted in maintenance of SLR and CRR during the last two years
B. Its net worth should show improvement and its net NPA ratio should not exceed 8 per cent
C. It should be making operational profits
D. Only A and B
E. All of the above

13. Many Regional Rural Banks were given licenses to open branches in small cities and towns. These licenses were given by:
A. Indian Banks' Association
B. NABARD
C. RBI
D. Cabinet Committee on economic affairs
E. None of these

14. The first Indian RRB that is sponsored by the Union Bank that has achieved core banking solution is:
A. Kheladi Grameen Bank
B. Riddhi Siddhi Grameen Bank
C. Rewa Siddhi Grameen Bank
D. The Rewa-Dahej Bank
E. None of these

15. Which of the following has become the first Regional Rural Bank issuing debit card in the country?
A. Punjab Gramin Bank
B. Nanital/Almora Bank
C. Kashi Gomti Sanyukta Gramin Bank
D. Baroda RRB
E. None of these

16. Grameen Bank and Micro Credit are associated with:
A. Manmohan Singh B. Bill Gates
C. Md. Yunus D. Aung San Su Ki
E. None of these

17. The issued/paid-up capital of a Regional Rural Bank should be
A. ₹ 5 lakh
B. minimum ₹ 25 lac and maximum ₹ 100 lac
C. ₹ 80 lac
D. ₹ 60 lac
E. None of the above

18. Paid-up share capital of Regional Rural Bank is contributed by
A. Central Government only
B. State Government only
C. Central Government, State Government and the sponsor commercial bank in the ratio of 50:15:35 respectively
D. NABARD, the concerned State Government and the sponsor commercial bank in the ratio of 60 : 20 : 20 respectively
E. All of the above

19 On the current account balances maintained by the Regional Rural Banks with them, the commercial banks may

A. pay interest up to 9 per cent
B. pay interest at such rates as may be mutually agreed to
C. pay interest as applicable to savings accounts
D. waive incidental charges
E. All of the above

20. Through which of the following the funds to the projects aided by the World Bank and the International Monetary Fund (IMF) are distributed?
A. Regional Branches of RBI
B. NABARD
C. Integrated Rural Development Programme
D. Agriculture Corporation Refinance and Development
E. Ministry of Finance

21. All regional rural banks (RRBs) are required to maintain their entire statutory liquidity ratio (SLR) in
A. current accounts with sponsor banks
B. time deposits with sponsor banks
C. government and other approved securities
D. gold holdings only
E. All of the above

22. The Regulatory Authority for Regional Rural Banks is
A. RBI and NABARD
B. Central Government
C. State Government
D. Sponsor bank
E. All of the above

23. Which of the following conditions are required to be fulfilled by a Regional Rural Bank to be eligible for opening of new branches?
A. It should not have defaulted in maintenance of SLR and CRR during the last two years
B. Its net worth should show improvement and its net NPA ratio should not exceed 8 per cent
C. It should be making operational profits
D. Only A and B
E. All of the above

ANSWERS

1	2	3	4	5	6	7	8	9	10
C	C	D	C	D	C	D	A	B	C
11	**12**	**13**	**14**	**15**	**16**	**17**	**18**	**19**	**20**
A	E	B	C	C	C	B	C	B	D
21	**22**	**23**							
C	A	E							

11

Co-operative Bank

CO-OPERTIVE BANKING — AN INTRODUCTION

Co-operative bank, in a nutshell, provides financial assistance to the people with small means to protect them from the debt trap of the moneylenders. It is a part of vast and powerful structure of co-operative institutions which are engaged in tasks of production, processing, marketing, distribution, servicing and banking in India. A co-operative bank is a financial entity which belongs to its members, who are at the same time the owners and the customers of their bank. Co-operative banks are often created by persons belonging to the same local or professional community or sharing a common interest. These banks generally provide their members with a wide range of banking and financial services (loans, deposits, banking accounts...). Co-operative banks differ from stockholder banks by their organizations, their goals, their values and their governance.

The Co-operative Banking System in India is characterized by a relatively comprehensive network to the grass root level. This sector mainly focuses on the local population and micro-banking among middle and low income strata of the society. These banks operate mainly for the benefit of rural areas, particularly the agricultural sector.

Co-operative banks in India came into existence with the enactment of the Agricultural Credit Co-operative Societies Act in 1904. Co-operative bank form an integral part of banking system in India. Under the Act of 1904, a number of co-operative credit societies were started. Owing to the increasing demand of co-operative credit, a new Act was passed in 1912, which was provided for establishment of co-operative central banks by a union of primary credit societies and individuals.

In 1914, the Maclagan committee envisaged a three tier structure for co-operative banking viz. Primary Agricultural Credit Societies (PACs) at the grass root level, Central Co-operative Banks at the district level and State Co-operative Banks at state level or Apex Level.

The Anyonya Co-operative Bank in India is considered to have been the first co-operative bank in Asia which was formed nearly 100 years back in Baroda. It was established in 1889 with the name **Anyonya Sahayakari Mandali Co-operative Bank Limited**, with a primary objective of providing an alternative to exploitation by moneylenders for Baroda's residents.

The concept of Urban Co-operative Bank was first spelt out by Mehta Bhansali Committee in 1939 which defined on Urban Co-operative Bank. Provisions of Section 5 (CCV) of Banking Regulation Act, 1949 (as applicable to Co-operative Societies) defined an Urban Co-operative Bank as a Primary Co-operative Bank other than a Primary Co-operative Society were made applicable in 1966.

With gradual growth and also given philip with the economic boom, urban banking sector received tremendous boost and started diversifying its credit portfolio. Besides giving traditional lending activity meeting the credit requirements of their customers they started catering to various sorts of customers viz. self-employed, small businessmen/industries, house finance, consumer finance, personal finance etc.

ROLE OF CO-OPERATIVE BANKING

Co-operative Banks are much more important in India than anywhere else in the world. The distinctive character of this bank is service at a lower cost and service without exploitation. It has gained its importance by the role assigned to them, the expectations they are supposed to fulfill, their number, and the number of offices they operate. Co-operative banks' role in rural financing continues to be important day by day, and their business in the urban areas also has increased phenomenally in recent years mainly due to the sharp increase in the number of primary co-operative banks. In rural areas, as far as the agricultural and related activities are concerned, the supply of credit was inadequate, and money lenders would exploit the poor people in rural areas providing them loans at higher rates. So, Co-operative banks mobilize deposits and purvey agricultural and rural credit with a wider outreach and provide institutional credit to the farmers. Co-operative bank have also been an important instrument for various development schemes, particularly subsidy-based programmes for poor.

The Co-operative banks in **rural areas** mainly finance agricultural based activities like:

- Farming
- Cattle
- Milk
- Hatchery
- Personal finance.

The Co-operative banks in **urban areas** finance in activities like:

- Self-employment
- Industries
- Small scale units
- Home finance
- Consumer finance
- Personal finance.

Some of the forward looking Co-operative banks have developed sufficient core competencies to such an extent that they are able to challenge state and private sector banks.

The exponential growth of Co-operative banks is attributed mainly to their much better contacts with the local people, personal interaction with customers, and their ability to catch the nerve of the local clientele. The total deposits and lendings of Co-operative banks are much more than the Old Private Sector Banks and the New Private Sector Banks.

FEATURES OF CO-OPERATIVE BANKING

1. Co-operative Banks are organized and managed on the principal of co-operation, self-help, and mutual help. They function with the rule of "one member, one vote". function on "no profit, no loss" basis. Co-operative banks, as a principle, do not pursue the goal of profit maximization.
2. Co-operative bank performs all the main banking functions of deposit mobilisation, supply of credit and provision of remittance facilities.
3. Co-operative Banks provide limited banking products and are functionally specialists in agriculture related products. However, co-operative banks now provide housing loans also.
4. Co-operative banks are perhaps the first government sponsored, government-supported, and government-subsidised financial agency in India. They get financial and other help from the Reserve Bank of India, NABARD, central government and state governments. They constitute the "most favoured" banking sector with risk of nationalisation. For commercial banks, the Reserve Bank of India is lender of last resort, but co-operative banks it is the lender of first resort which provides financial resources in the form of contribution to the initial capital (through state government), working capital, refinance.
5. Co-operative Banks belong to the money market as well as to the capital market. Primary agricultural credit societies provide short-term and medium-term loans.
6. Co-operative banks are financial intermediaries only partially.

   The sources of their funds (resources) are:

   (*a*) Central and state government

   (*b*) The Reserve Bank of India and NABARD

   (*c*) Other co-operative institutions

   (*d*) Ownership funds

   (*e*) Deposits or debenture issues.
7. Some co-operative bank are scheduled banks, while others are non-scheduled banks. Co-operative Banks are subject to CRR and liquidity requirements as other scheduled and non-scheduled banks are. However, their requirements are less than commercial banks.
8. As said earlier, co-operative banks accept current, saving, and fixed or time deposits from individuals and institutions including banks.
9. In the recent past, the RBI has introduced changes in interest rates of co-operative banks also, along with changes in interest rates of commercial banks. The interest rates structure of co-operative banks is quite complex. The rates charged by them depend upon the type of bank, the type of loans, and vary from state to state.
10. Since 1966 the lending and deposit rate of commercial banks have been directly regulated by the Reserve Bank of India. Although the Reserve Bank of India had power to regulate the rate of co-operative bank but this have been exercised only after 1979 in respect of non-agricultural advances they were free to charge any rates at their discretion. Although the main aim of the co-operative bank is to provide cheaper credit to their members and not to maximize profits, they may access the money market to improve their income so as to remain viable.
11. Co-operative banks (COBs), in short, have played a pivotal role in the development of short-term and long-term rural credit structure in India over the years. The co-operative credit effort is said to be the first ever attempt at micro-credit dispensation in India.

CLASSIFICATION OF CO-OPERATIVE BANKS

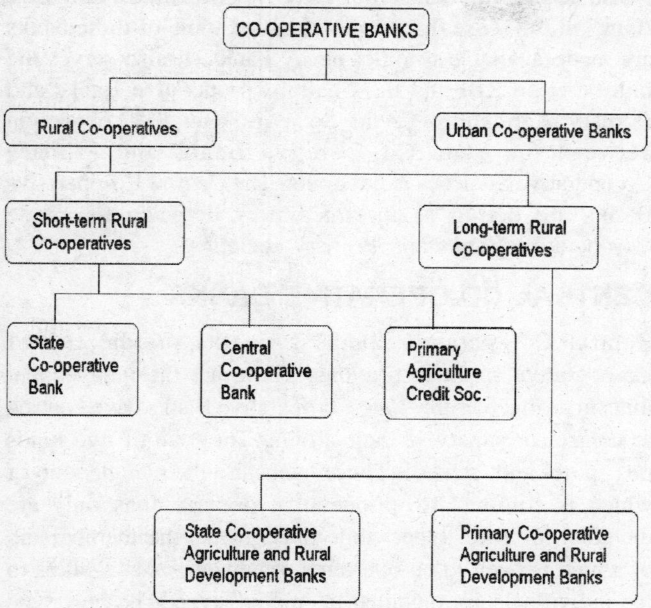

The Co-operative banking structure in India comprises of:

1. Urban Co-operative Banks
2. Rural Co-operatives

Some co-operative banks are scheduled banks, while others are non-scheduled banks. For instance, State Co-operative banks and some Urban Co-operative banks are scheduled banks but other co-operative Banks are non-scheduled banks.

Scheduled banks are those banks which have been included in the second schedule of the Reserve Bank of India act of 1934.

The banks included in this schedule list should fulfill two conditions:

1. The paid capital and collected funds of bank should not be less than ₹ 5 lac.
2. Any activity of the bank will not adversely affect the interests of depositors.

Every Scheduled bank enjoys the following facilities:

1. Such bank becomes eligible for debts/loans on bank rate from the RBI
2. Such bank automatically acquire the membership of clearing house.

Urban Co-operative Banks

Urban Co-operative Banks is also referred as Primary Co-operative banks by the Reserve Bank of India. Among the non-agricultural credit societies urban co-operative banks occupy an important place. This bank is started in India with the object of catering to the banking and credit requirements of the urban middle classes.

The RBI defines Urban Co-operative banks as "small sized co-operatively organized banking units which operate in metropolitan, urban and semi-urban centers to cater mainly to the needs of small borrowers viz., owners of small scale industrial units, retail traders, professional and salaries classes."

Urban Co-operative banks mobilize savings from the middle and lower income groups and purvey credit to small borrowers, including weaker sections of the society. These banks organize on a limited liability basis, generally extend their area of operation over a town. The main functions of these banks are to promote thrift by attracting deposits from members and non-members and to advance loans to the members. It is registered under Co-operatives Societies Act of the respective state Governments. Prior to 1966, Urban Co-operative banks were exclusively under the purview of State Government. From March 1, 1966 certain provisions of Banking Regulation Act have been made applicable to these banks. Consequently, the RBI became the regulatory an supervisory authority of Urban Co-operative Banks for their related operations. Managerial aspects of such banks continue to remain with State Governments under the respective Co-operative Societies Act. These banks with multi-presence are regulated by the Central Governments and registered under Multi-State Co-operative Societies Act. The RBI extends refinance to Urban Co-operative Banks at bank rate against their advances to tiny and cottage industrial units. These banks grants sizeable loans and advances under priority sector for lending to small business enterprises, retail trade, road and water transport operators and professional and self-employed persons. Urban Co-operative banks are mostly located in towns and cities and cater to the credit requirement of the urban clientele.

The objectives and functions of the Urban Co-operative banks:

- Primarily, to raise funds for lending money to its members.
- To attract deposits from members as well as non-members.
- To encourage thrift, self-help and mutual aid among members.
- To draw, make, accept, discount, buy, sell, collect and deal in bills of exchange, drafts, certificates and other securities.
- To provide safe-deposit vaults.

Area of Operation: The area of operation of these banks are usually restricted by its bye-laws to a municipal area or a town. In some occasions it exceeds this limit. The study group on Credit Co-operatives in Non-Agricultural Sectors has recommended that normally, it would be advisable for an urban co-operative bank to restrict its area of operation to the municipality or the taluka town where it operates.

Rural Co-operatives

Rural Co-operative Banking plays an important role in meeting the growing credit needs of rural population of India. It provides institutional credit to the agricultural and rural sector. The inadequacy of rural credit engaged the attention of RBI and Government throughout the 1950s and 1960s. One important feature of providing agriculture credit in India has been the existence of a widespread network of rural financial institutions. The rural credit structure consists of many types of financial institutions as large scale branch expansion was undertaken to create a strong institution based in rural area. It has served as an important instrument of credit delivery in rural and agricultural areas. The separate structure of rural Co-operative sector for long-term and short-term loans has enabled these institutions to develop a specialized institution for rural credit delivery. The volume of credit flowing through these institution has increased. The Rural Co-operative structure has traditionally been bifurcated into two parallel wings, *i.e.,*

I. Short-term Rural Co-operatives,

II. Long-term Rural Co-operatives.

SHORT-TERM RURAL CO-OPERATIVES

The short-term rural co-operatives provide crop and other working capital loans to farmers and rural artisans primarily for short-term purpose. These institutions have federal three-tier structure:

- At the Apex of the system is a State Co-operative bank in each state.
- At the middle (or district) level, there are Central Co-operative Banks also known as District Co-operative Banks.
- At the lowest (or village) level, are the Primary Agricultural Credit Societies.

STATE CO-OPERATIVE BANKS

State Co-operative Banks are the apex of the three-tier Co-operative structure dispensing mainly short/medium term credit. It is the principal society in a State which is registered or deemed to be registered under the Government Societies Act, 1912, or any other law for the time being in force in India relating to co-operative societies and the primary object of which is the financing of the other societies in the State which are registered or deemed to be registered. The State Co-operative Banks receive current and fixed deposits from its constituent banks as well as savings, current and fixed deposits from the general public and from local boards, other local authorities, etc. Further, they receive loans from the RBI and NABARD. NABARD is the supervisory authority for State Co-operative Banks. The state government contributes the certain portion of their working capital. The principal function of State Co-operative Banks is to assist the Central Co-operative Banks and to balance excesses and deficiencies in the resources of Central Co-operative Banks. It also acts as the "balancing centre" for Central Co-operative Banks in the sense that surplus fund of some of these banks are made available to other needy banks. It also serves the link between RBI and the Central Co-operative Banks and Primary Agriculture Credit Societies. But the connection between the State Co-operative Banks and Primary Co-operative Societies is not direct. The Central Co-operative Banks are acting as intermediaries between the State Co-operative Banks and Primary societies.

CENTRAL CO-OPERATIVE BANKS

Central Co-operative Banks form the middle tier of Co-operative credit institutions. These are the independent units in as much as the State Co-operative Banks have control, to control or supervise their affairs. They are of two kinds *i.e.*, 'pure' and 'mixed'. Those banks are the membership of which is confined to co-operative organizations only are included in 'pure' type, while those banks the membership of which is open to co-operative organizations as well as to the individuals are included in 'mixed' type. The pure type of Central Banks can be seen in Kerala, Mumbai, Odisha, etc., while the mixed type can be seen in Andhra Pradesh, Assam, Tamil Nadu, etc. The pure type of banks is based on strict co-operative principles. However, the mixed type has an advantage over the pure type in so far as they can draw their funds from the non-agricultural sector too.

The Central Co-operative Banks draw their funds from share capital, deposits, loans from the State Co-operative Banks and where State Banks do not exist from the RBI, NABARD and commercial banks. NABARD is the supervisory authority for Central Co-operative Banks. Deposits constitute the major component of sources of funds, followed by borrowings. The main function of Central Co-operative Banks is to finance the primary credit societies. In addition, they carry on Commercial banking activities like acceptance of deposits, granting of loans and advances on the security of first class guilt-edged securities, fixed deposit receipts, gold, bullion, goods and documents of title to goods, collection of bills, cheques, etc., safe custody of valuables and agency services. They are expected to attract deposits from the general public. They also act as 'balancing centres', making available access funds of one primary to another which is in need of them.

The central co-operative banks are located at the district headquarters or some prominent town of the district. These banks have a few private individuals also who provide both finance and management. The central co-operative banks have three sources of funds:

- Their own share capital and reserves
- Deposits from the public
- Loans from the state co-operative banks.

PRIMARY AGRICULTURE CREDIT SOCIETIES (PACS)

Primary Agriculture Credit Societies is the foundation of the co-operative credit system on which the super-structure of the short-term co-operative credit system rests. It deals directly with individual farmers, provide short- and medium-term credit, supply agricultural inputs, distribute consumer articles and also arrange for the marketing of products of its members through a co-operative marketing societies. These societies form the basic unit of co-operative credit system in India. These voluntary societies based on principle of one man one vote has posed challenge to exploitative practices of the village moneylenders. The farmers and other small-time borrowers come in direct contact with these societies. The success of the co-operative credit movement depends largely on the strength of these village level societies.

The major objective of Primary agricultural Credit Societies is to serve the need of weaker sections of these society. For this purpose, the people with limited means, particularly with scheduled castes and scheduled tribes, are encouraged to become members of these societies. So, they must function effectively as well-managed and multi-purpose institutions mobilizing the savings of the rural people and providing the package of services including credit, supply of agricultural inputs and implements, consumer goods, marketing services and technical guidance with focus on weaker sections. Government has promoted multi-purpose societies in tribal areas for the benefit of people living there.

LONG-TERM RURAL CO-OPERATIVES

The long-term rural co-operatives provide typically medium- and long-term loans for making investments in agriculture, rural industries and, in the recent period, housing. Generally, these co-operatives have two tiers, *i.e.,* State Co-operative Agriculture and Development Banks (SCARBDs) at the state level and Primary Co-operative Agriculture and Rural Development Banks (PCARDBs) at the taluka or tehsil level. However, some States have a unitary structure with the state level banks operating through their own branches.

State Co-operative Agriculture and Development Banks (SCARBDs)

State Co-operative Agriculture and Development Banks constitute the upper-tier of long-term co-operative credit structure. Though long-term credit co-operatives have been allowed to access public deposits under certain conditions, such deposits constitute a relatively small proportion of their total liabilities. They are mostly dependent on borrowings for on-lending.

The main objective of the Co-operative State Agriculture and Rural Development bank is to finance primary agriculture and rural development banks. The bank undertakes the following functions to achieve the above objectives:

(*a*) Floatation of Debentures

(*b*) Receiving Deposits

(*c*) Grant of loans to primary co-operative agriculture and rural development banks for purposes approved by the National Bank for Agricultural and Rural Development and Registrar of Co-operative Societies;

(*d*) To function as the agent of any co-operative bank subject to such conditions as the Registrar may specify;

(*e*) To develop, assist and co-ordinate the work of affiliated primary co-operative agriculture and rural development banks.

The bank issues long-term and medium-term loans towards agricultural and allied activities like construction of godowns, cattle shed, farm house, purchase of lands etc., and for minor irrigation purposes like construction of new wells, deepening of existing wells etc., In addition, long-term loans are also sanctioned for animal husbandry, fisheries, plantation, farm mechanization, non-farm sector and other non-minor irrigation schemes.

Primary Co-operative Agriculture and Rural Development Banks (PCARDBs)

Primary Co-operative Agriculture and Rural Development Banks are the lowest layer of long-term credit co-operatives. It is primarily dependent on the borrowings for their lending business.

They provide credit for developmental purposes like minor irrigation, cultivation of plantation crops and for diversified purposes like poultry, dairying and sericulture on schematic basis. They get requisite financial assistance from the Co-operative State Agriculture and Rural Development Bank.

In order to widen their scope of lending to compete with other financial agencies, the primary co-operative agriculture and rural development banks have been permitted to finance artisans, craftmen and small scale entrepreneurs. They have also been permitted to issue loans to small road transport operators in rural areas for purchase of goods carriers and passenger vehicles.

As a result, during 2007-08, the Primary Co-operative Agriculture and Rural Development Banks have again started lending for the Non-farm Sector including Jewel Loans.

ROLE OF NABARD IN CO-OPERATIVE CREDIT

One of the recommendations of the CRAFICARD (Committee to Review Arrangements For Institutional Credit for Agricultural and Rural Development) under the chairmanship of Sri B Sivaraman, who was appointed by the Government of India in 1979 was the establishment of National Bank for Agricultural and Rural Development (NABARD) by integrating the functions of RBI (Agricultural Credit Department-ACD) and the Agricultural Refinance and Development Corporation-(ARDC).

The National Bank for Agricultural and Rural Development (NABARD) was setup on 12th July 1982 under the National Bank for Agricultural and Rural Development Act, 1981.

NABARD is an apex institution for making policy, planning and operations in the field of credit for agriculture and other economic activities in rural areas. NABARD has paid up capital of ₹ 2000 crores, which was contributed by the Government of India and RBI in equal proportion.

Functions/Objectives of NABARD:

1. It works as an apex body, which looks after the financial needs of agriculture and rural development.
2. Provides short-term loans to state co-operatives for seasonal agricultural operations.
3. Provides medium-term loans to state co-operatives and RBBs for approved agricultural operations.
4. Provides long-term loans to state co-operatives, RBBs and commercial banks for investment in agriculture.
5. It develops policy and plans relating to agriculture and allied activities.
6. It prepares rural credit plans for all districts in the country.
7. IT maintains research and development funds for research in agriculture and rural development.
8. It inspects the central and state co-operative banks and RRBs.

NABARD and Rural Credit

1. Production Credit Refinance

   It provides Short-term credit to State Co-operative Banks, and Regional Rural Banks and other Financial Institutions approved by the Reserve Bank. This is usually for a period of 18 months for the following purposes:

   (*a*) Seasonal Agricultural operations

   (*b*) Marketing of crops

   (*c*) Marketing and distribution of fertilizers, seeds, pesticides etc.

   (*d*) Production and marketing activities of village and cottage industries, and SSI.

2. It provides Medium-term credit to State Co-operative Banks, State Land Development Banks, Regional Rural Banks, Commercial Banks and other Financial Institutions approved by RBI. This loan is extended for a period of up to 7 years for the following purposes:

   (*a*) Investment in agriculture and allied activities, *e.g.*, irrigation, land development, soil conversation, dairy, sheep, poultry, fishery, horticulture, forestry.

   (*b*) Investment activities of village and cottage industries and SSI.

3. It provides Long-term credit to State Land Development Banks, Regional Rural Banks, Commercial Banks, State Co-operative Banks and other Financial Institutions approved by RBI. This loan is extended for a period up to 25 years for the purposes like:

   (*a*) Re-finance for investment in agriculture and allied activities. (Minor irrigation, Land development, Soil conservation etc.).

   (*b*) Re-finance for Artisans/Small Scale Industries/ Tiny Industries/Village and Cottage Industries etc. (Non-farm sector)

   (*c*) Loans to State Government, for Share Capital contribution to Co-operative Institutions.

   (*d*) Investment in Share Capital/Securities of Institutions concerned with agriculture and rural development.

4. It provides re-finance to eligible institutions, normally to SCBs and RRBs for conversions and re-scheduling of loans under conditions of drought, famine or other national calamities and so on...
5. Financing Cottage/Village/Small Scale Industries, etc. located in rural areas are also eligible for re-finance from NABARD.
6. Co-operative Development Fund *i.e.*, National Agricultural Credit Stabilization Fund and National Long-term Operations Fund for the development of Co-operative Institutions.

Co-operative Development Fund

NABARD had constituted Co-operative Development Fund during 1992-93 with the objective of supporting co-operative credit institutions in undertaking various developmental activities such as Human Resource Development, building up Management Information System, Infrastructure Creation, Setting up of Business Development Department with technical, personnel, etc. The fund is augmented every year through contribution from NABARD.

MULTIPLE CHOICE QUESTIONS

1. Co-operative enterprises entered into two or more business entities, known as:
A. Mergers B. Amalgamation
C. Joint Venture D. Either A or B
E. None of these

2. The Urban Credit Co-operatives are also commonly known as ....
A. Urban Co-operative Banks
B. Co-operative Banks
C. National Banks
D. Private Banks
E. None of the above

3. The co-operative credit institutions in the country may be broadly classified into ....
A. Primary Agriculture Credit Societies and District Level Co-operative Banks
B. District Level Co-operative Banks and State Co-operative Apex Banks
C. Urban Credit Co-operatives and Rural Credit Co-operatives
D. Either A or B
E. None of the above

4. With regard to short-term credit co-operatives, at the central level .... act as a link between Primary societies and State Co-operative Apex Banks.
A. District Level Co-operative Banks
B. Primary Co-operative Agriculture and Rural Development Banks
C. State Co-operative Agriculture and Rural Development Bank
D. Either B or C
E. None of the above

5. The .... controls the co-operative banks that falls under the Banking regulation Act of 1949.
A. Reserve Bank of India
B. NABARD
C. National Co-operative Union of India
D. State Bank of India
E. None of the above

6. Under the Banking Regulation Act, 1949, which of following is not qualified to be called as banks in the co-operative sector?
A. Urban Co-operative Banks
B. Primary Agricultural Credit Societies
C. State Co-operative Banks
D. Central Co-operative Banks
E. All of the above

7. The first DCB was established at .... in 1910.
A. Mumbai in Maharashtra
B. Ahmedabad in Gujarat
C. Chennai in Tamil Nadu
D. Ajmer in Rajasthan
E. None of these

8. .... is the vertex of the pyramidal structure in a State for the provision of short- and medium-term credit to agriculturists on co-operative basis.
A. District Central Co-operative Banks
B. Primary Agricultural Credit Societies
C. State Co-operative Banks
D. All the above
E. None of these

9. A .... also acts as a balancing center and clearing house for the central co-operative banks.
A. State Co-operative Bank
B. District Central Co-operative Banks
C. Primary Agricultural Credit Societies
D. All the above
E. None of these

10. The primary function of a central co-operative bank is to:
A. to channelize the flow of funds from the State co-operative banks
B. mobilize the resources in the district for financing its members to the maximum extent possible
C. Both of these
D. Only B
E. None of the above

11. In India, the first co-operative land mortgage bank was established in 1920 at ....
A. Mumbai in Maharashtra
B. Jhang in Punjab
C. Chennai in Tamil Nadu
D. Ajmer in Rajasthan
E. None of these

12. It was from the beginning of the .... that the policies oriented towards development purposes were adopted and land mortgage banks were called "Land Development Banks".
A. First Five Year Plans
B. Second Five Year Plans
C. Third Five Year Plans
D. Fourth Five Year Plans
E. None of these

13. The .... are organized in 3 tiers namely; state, central, and primary level and they meet the long-term credit requirements of the farmers for developmental purposes.
A. Land Development Banks
B. Primary Banks

C. Urban Co-operative Banks
D. NABARD
E. None of these

14. .... are now known as Co-operative Agriculture and Rural Development Banks.
A. Land Development Banks
B. Primary Banks
C. Urban Co-operative Banks
D. NABARD
E. None of these

15. The origins of the urban co-operative banking movement in India can be traced to the close of ....
A. Eighteenth century
B. Twentieth century
C. Nineteenth century
D. Seventeenth century
E. None of these

16. Committee to Review Arrangements For Institutional Credit for Agricultural and Rural Development, under the chairmanship of Sri B Sivaraman recommended the establishment of ....
A. National Federation of State Co-operative Banks Ltd
B. National Bank for Agricultural and Rural Development
C. National Federation of Urban Co-operative Banks and Credit Societies Ltd
D. National Cooperative Agriculture & Rural Development Banks' Federation Ltd
E. None of these

17. The Registered Office of NAFCUB is at .... and the area of operation is whole of the country.
A. Mumbai B. Agra
C. Kolkata D. Delhi
E. None of these

18. The .... was set up in 1960 & is administered under the Multi-State Co-operative Societies Act, 2002.
A. National Federation of State Co-operative Banks Ltd
B. National Bank for Agricultural and Rural Development
C. National Federation of Urban Co-operative Banks and Credit Societies Ltd
D. National Co-operative Agriculture & Rural Development Banks' Federation Ltd
E. None of these

19. The National Co-operative Agriculture & Rural Development Banks' Federation was registered on .... with the main objective of promoting the interests of the Long-term Co-operative Credit Structure (LTCCS) movement in the country:
A. 6th October, 1960 B. 5th October, 1960
C. 7th October, 1960 D. 8th October, 1960
E. None of these

20. From the functional point of view the co-operative societies have been classified as:
A. Unregistered and auxiliary
B. Unregistered and registered
C. Rural and urban
D. Primary and Secondary
E. None of these

21. From the legal point of view the co-operative societies have been classified as:
A. Unregistered and Auxiliary
B. Unregistered and Registered
C. Rural and Urban
D. Primary and Secondary
E. None of these

22. The word .... literally means to work together or act together.
A. Organization B. Company
C. Co-operation D. Association
E. None of these

23. .... is based on the principle of self-interest, maximization of profits and exploitation.
A. Co-operation B. Capitalism
C. Socialism D. Trade unionism
E. None of these

24. .... is based on the principle of self-help through mutual help, abolition of profits and service above self-help.
A. Co-operation B. Capitalism
C. Socialism D. Trade unionism
E. None of these

25. In .... form of business organization profit earning is the fundamental motive.
A. co-operation B. capitalism
C. socialism D. trade unionism
E. None of these

26. In .... each works for all and all work for each.
A. co-operation B. capitalism
C. socialism D. trade unionism
E. None of these

27. The Land Improvement Loans Act was passed in ....
A. 1983 B. 1883
C. 1873 D. 1884
E. 1887

28. The Agriculturists Loan Act was passed in ....
A. 1983 B. 1883
C. 1873 D. 1884
E. 1887

29. The Madras Government sent .... for studying the co-operative movements in European countries.

A. Sir Federik Nicholson
B. Sir Edward Law
C. Dr. William King
D. Sir Maclagan
E. None of these

30. The Government of India appointed in 1901 a Committee under the Presidentship of .... to study the question of starting co-operative credit societies in India.
A. Sir Federik Nicholson
B. Sir Edward Law
C. Dr. William King
D. Sir Maclagan
E. None of these

31. The Co-operative Credit Societies Act was passed in ....
A. 1901 B. 1902
C. 1903 D. 1904
E. 1905

32. The Co-operative Societies Act was passed in ....
A. 1911 B. 1912
C. 1913 D. 1914
E. 1915

33. In the .... five year plan the Central Committee for Co-operative Training was established.
A. First B. Second
C. Third D. Fourth
E. Fifth

34. In the .... five year plan the All India Rural Credit Review Committee was set up.
A. First B. Second
C. Third D. Fourth
E. Fifth

35. In 1970, the Reserve Bank of India set up the .... for the review of rural credit system.
A. All India Rural Credit Review Committee
B. National Co-operative Development Corporation
C. Committee of Direction of the Rural Credit Survey
D. All of the above
E. None of these

36. The .... Committee constituted to Review the Arrangements for Institutional Credit for Agriculture and Rural Development in 1981, recommended the establishment of NABARD.
A. Sivaraman B. Sir Maclagan
C. Khusro D. Brahm Prakash
E. None of these

37. The Sivaraman Committee constituted to Review the Arrangements for Institutional Credit for Agriculture and Rural Development in 1981, recommended the establishment of ....
A. NABARD B. NCDC
C. NCUI D. All of the above
E. None of these

38. In India, co-operative legislation started in ....
A. 1904 B. 1912
C. 1901 D. 1882
E. 1885

39. The shortcomings in the Act of 1904 was removed by another legislation known as ....
A. Co-operative Societies Act of 1912
B. The Model Co-operative Act
C. Constitution Amendment Bill
D. The Unique Co-operative Act
E. None of these

40. The .... committee, 1945 observed that the Act of 1912 needed revision in certain respects and recommended that the provinces in which the co-operative societies Act of 1912 was in force should pass special acts keeping in view their past experience and the future needs of the movement.
A. Sivaraman B. Sir Maclagan
C. Khusro D. Saraiya
E. None of these

41. .... committee recommended that a specific provision be made in the existing Act of 1912 enabling rural societies to change their liability from unlimited to limited.
A. Sivaraman B. Sir Maclagan
C. Khusro D. Saraiya
E. None of these

42. The first co-operative bank was established by .... in 1883 in his home village known as Loreggia, Italy.
A. Dr. Leone Wollemburg
B. Robert Owen
C. Dr. William King
D. Lougi Luzzatti
E. None of these

43. The first co-operative bank was established by Wollemburg in .... in his home village known as Loreggia, Italy.
A. 1883 B. 1884
C. 1885 D. 1886
E. 1887

44. ICA is
A. International Co-operative Alliance
B. Inter-Co-operative Association
C. International co-operation for Agriculture
D. Inter-country Alliance
E. None of these

45. 'NEUE HEIMAT' and 'HOMESTEADS' in Germany are examples of ....
A. Construction Companies
B. Hotels and Resorts
C. Co-operative Housing societies

D. Old–Age Homes
E. None of these

46. NCHF stands for
A. National Co-operative Housing Federation of India
B. National Credit Housing Federation
C. National Consumer Housing Federation
D. National Co-operative Housing Finance
E. None of these

47. The Urban co-operative banks, salary earners' societies, thrift and credit societies are examples of
A. Agricultural Credit Societies
B. Non-Agricultural Credit Societies
C. Both A and B
D. Semi-Agricultural Credit Societies.
E. None of the above

48. Co-operative banks are registered under ....
A. RBI Act
B. Banking Regulation Act
C. Co-operative societies Act
D. Any of the above
E. None of these

49. Central Co-operative banks are organised at .... level.
A. Taluk
B. District
C. State
D. National
E. None of these

50. Co-operation as a form of economic activity was formally recognized in India in the year 1904 when:
A. Mahatma Gandhi inaugurated the first Indian co-operative bank
B. the first co-operative bank was established in Bombay (now Mumbai)
C. the first Co-operative Societies Act was passed
D. All of the above
E. None of the above

51. Under the Banking Regulation Act, 1949, which of the following is not qualified to be called as banks in the co-operative sector?
A. Urban Co-operative Banks
B. Primary Agricultural Credit Societies
C. State Co-operative Banks
D. Central Co-operative Banks
E. All of the above

ANSWERS

1	2	3	4	5	6	7	8	9	10
C	A	C	A	A	B	D	C	A	C
11	**12**	**13**	**14**	**15**	**16**	**17**	**18**	**19**	**20**
B	C	A	A	C	B	D	D	A	A
21	**22**	**23**	**24**	**25**	**26**	**27**	**28**	**29**	**30**
B	C	B	A	B	A	B	D	A	B
31	**32**	**33**	**34**	**35**	**36**	**37**	**38**	**39**	**40**
D	B	B	D	A	A	A	A	A	D
41	**42**	**43**	**44**	**45**	**46**	**47**	**48**	**49**	**50**
D	A	A	A	C	A	B	C	B	C
51									
B									

12 National Bank for Agriculture and Rural Development (NABARD)

NABARD is an apex development bank in India, having headquarters in Mumbai (Maharashtra) and other branches are all over the country. The committee to review arrangements for institutional credit for agriculture and rural development (CRAFICARD), set up by the Reserve Bank of India (RBI) under the chairmanship of Shri B. Sivaraman, conceived and recommended the establishment of National Bank for Agriculture and Rural Development (NABARD). It was established on 12 July 1982 by a special Act of parliament and its main focus was on upliftment of rural India by increasing the credit flow for elevation of agriculture & rural non farm sector. RBI sold its stake in NABARD to the Government of India, which now holds 99% stake. NABARD is active in developing financial inclusion policy and is a member of the Alliance for Financial Inclusion.

HISTORICAL BACKGROUND

Reserve Bank of India (RBI) established in 1934, interalia, with a mandate to setup a special Agricultural Credit Department (ACD) with expert staff. Agricultural Credit Department of RBI initiated different measures to develop a healthy rural credit structure and provided guidance to the State Government and Cooperative Credit structure.

Agricultural Refinance Corporation (ARC) was established in 1963 to support investment credit for agricultural development. Consequent to the undertaking, development and promotional functions, the ARC was renamed as Agricultural Refinance and Development Corporation (ARDC) in 1972.

Reserve Bank of India, at the instance of the Government of India (GOI), appointed a Committee to Review Arrangement for Institutional Credit for Agriculture and Rural Development (CRAFICARD) in 1979 under the Chairmanship of Shri B. Sivaraman, former member of the Planning Commission.

The Committee sought to review/examine the structure and operations of the ARDC in the light of the growing need for term loans for agricultural and allied purposes and the need for and the feasibility of integrating short-term and medium-term credit structure with long-term credit structure at the national, state, district and village levels.

CRAFICARD felt that the ARDC was not able to provide integrated credit services to its clientele on account of limitations in its statute and the Agricultural Credit Department (ACD) of RBI was not able to provide requisite attention to all the issues connected with rural credit. Further, the development role assigned to the ARDC was inadequate to take care of institution building, training and research. All these factors led to the recommendation for the establishment of NABARD, as the apex institution for integrated rural development through credit and development initiatives, to provide undivided attention, pointed focus and forceful direction to all matters and issues connected with rural credit. But the committee, however, felt that it would be necessary for the new institution to maintain organic links with the RBI so that its continued guidance in financial assistance were accessible to it.

The Committee, in its report submitted in Jan 1981, recommended favourably among other things the setting up of a National Bank for Agriculture and Rural Development. The Government of India and the Reserve Bank of India approved the proposal of CRAFICARD. The parliament approved the setting up of NABARD through the Act 61 of 1981. The NABARD Act was passed in the parliament on 1st December 1981. It came into existence on 12th July 1982 and was dedicated to the service of the nation by the then Hon'ble Prime Minister, Smt. Indira Gandhi on November 2, 1982.

NABARD was established with the major objective of, as stated in the preamble to the Act, providing credit for the promotion of agriculture, small scale industries, cottage and village industries, handicrafts and other rural crafts and other allied economic activities in rural areas with a view to promote integrated rural development and securing prosperity of rural areas and matters connected therewith or incidental thereto.

Accordingly the NABARD took over the functions of the erstwhile Agricultural Credit Department (ACD), Rural Planning and Credit Cell (RPCC) of the RBI and ARDC. After, the establishment of NABARD, the entire property, liabilities, rights, interest, privileges and other things of ARDC have been transferred to and vested with the National Bank.

Objectives

The National Bank has been set up as an apex refinance agency for institutions providing investment and production credit for promoting various development activities in the rural areas. The bank combines the developmental and financial role by undertaking the functions of agriculture and allied activities such as marketing, processing, storage and rural enterprises.

The main objectives of the National Banks are

1. To provide refinance to eligible institutions, viz., State Cooperative Agriculture and Rural Development Banks (SCARDBs), State Cooperative Banks (SCBs), Commercial Banks (CBs), Regional Rural Banks (RRBs), and Scheduled Primary Urban Cooperative Banks for supporting production and investment credit for development activities in the rural areas.
2. To take measures towards institution building for improving absorption capacity of credit delivery system including monitoring, formulation of rehabilitation schemes, restructuring of credit institutions, training of personnel, and other related matters.
3. To co-ordinate rural refinancing activities of all institutions engaged in the development work at the field level and to maintain liaison with the Central and State Governments and also the Reserve Bank of India.
4. To undertake monitoring and evaluation of projects refinanced by it.
5. To promote research in agriculture and rural development.

ROLE OF NABARD

NABARD is the apex institution in the country which looks after the development of the cottage industry, small industry and village industry, and other rural industries. NABARD also reaches out to allied economies and supports and promotes integrated development. NABARD discharge its duty by undertaking the following roles:

1. Serves as an apex financing agency for the institutions providing investment and production credit for promoting the various developmental activities in rural areas.
2. Takes measures towards institution building for improving absorptive capacity of the credit delivery system, including monitoring, formulation of rehabilitation schemes, restructuring of credit institutions, training of personnel, etc.
3. Co-ordinates the rural financing activities of all institutions engaged in developmental work at the field level and maintains liaison with Government of India, state governments, Reserve Bank of India (RBI) and other national level institutions concerned with policy formulation. Undertakes monitoring and evaluation of projects refinanced by it.
4. NABARD refinances the financial institutions which finances the rural sector.
5. NABARD partakes in development of institutions which help the rural economy.
6. NABARD also keeps a check on its client institutes.
7. It regulates the institutions which provide financial help to the rural economy.
8. It provides training facilities to the institutions working in the field of rural upliftment.
9. It regulates the cooperative banks and the RRB's, and manages talent acquisition through IBPS CWE.
10. NABARD's refinance is available to state co-operative agriculture and rural development banks (SCARDBs), state co-operative banks (SCBs), regional rural banks (RRBs), commercial banks (CBs) and other financial institutions approved by RBI. While the ultimate beneficiaries of investment credit can be individuals, partnership concerns, companies, State-owned corporations or co-operative societies, production credit is generally given to individuals. NABARD has its head office at Mumbai, India.
11. NABARD Regional Office [RO] has a Chief General Manager [CGMs] as its head, and the Head office has several top executives viz the Executive Directors [ED], Managing Directors [MD], and the Chairperson. It has 336 District Offices across the country, one special cell at Srinagar. It also has 6 training establishments.
12. NABARD is also known for its 'SHG Bank Linkage Programme' which encourages India's banks to lend to self-help groups (SHGs). Largely because SHGs are composed mainly of poor women, this has evolved into an important Indian tool for microfinance. About 1.1 crore SHGs and an estimated 13.5 crore rural households are within the fold of SHG-BLP.
13. NABARD also has a portfolio of Natural Resource Management Programmes involving diverse fields like Watershed Development, Tribal Development and Farm Innovation through dedicated funds set up for the purpose.

FUNCTIONS

The functions of NABARD can be classified into four broad categories.

1. Credit Functions
2. Promotional and Development Functions
3. Institutional Development and Supervisory Functions, and
4. Statutory and Other Functions

CREDIT FUNCTIONS

NABARD provides three types of credit namely (1) Production Credit; (2) Investment Credit and (3) Long-term loans to State Governments.

Production Credit

There are two types of production credits short-term & medium-term.

SHORT-TERM

Short-term is credit further divided into Agricultural purposes & Non-Agricultural purposes.

Agricultural Purposes

1. Seasonal Agricultural Operations (SAO)

NABARD provides short-term credit for Seasonal Agricultural Operations (SAO) by way of refinance. The State Co-operative Banks, Regional Rural Banks or any other institutions approved by the RBI are eligible to avail themselves of this refinance facility from the NABARD at concessional rates by sanction of credit limits. Refinance facilities are available for agricultural operations, marketing of crops, marketing and distribution of inputs necessary for agricultural development and any other activity for the promotion of agriculture.

2. Short-term Other Seasonal Agricultural Operations (ST-OSAO)

NABARD provides refinance support to co-operative banks for financing marketing of crops to facilitate reasonable price to farmers for their produce and recovery of crop loan by linking production with marketing. Refinance is also available to SCBs/DCCBs for financing of stocking and distribution of fertilizers and other inputs by State Marketing Federation and by Primary Agriculture/Marketing Societies.

Non-Agricultural Purposes

1. Refinance Support to Weavers and Rural Artisans

NABARD has taken steps to support the weavers and the rural artisans by providing refinance support to the Co-operative banks and the RRBs to meet working capital requirements of the handloom and handicraft sector. NABARD also sanctions credit limits to State Co-operative Banks for financing Apex societies in order to stocking and distribution of yarn to the Primary Weavers' Co-operative Societies (PWCS). NABARD provides refinance facility to the District Central Co-operative Bank (DCCB) up to 83% of ground level credit to the weavers.

2. Refinance for Pisciculture

NABARD provides refinance to the State Co-operative Banks/DCCBs for financing the pisciculture activities. It provides refinance for meeting the working requirement and off-season credit requirements of fishermen belonging to Below Poverty Line (BPL) families through the Primary Fisheries Cooperative Credit Societies (PFCS)/Primary Agricultural Credit Societies (PACS). NABARD provides 100 percent refinancing for this purposes.

3. Financing Industrial Co-operatives Labour Contract/Forest Labour Co-operative Societies and Rural artisans

NABARD extends refinance support to the SCBs on behalf of the DCCBs/District Industrial Cooperative Banks for financing the working capital requirements of industrial cooperative societies (other than weavers), labour contracts/ forest labour cooperative societies as also the artisan members of the Primary Agricultural Credit Society (PACS)/Farmers Service Society (FSS)/Large sized Adivasi Multi Purpose Society (LAMPS) to enable these banks to finance the production and marketing activities of cottage, village and small-scale primary industrial cooperative societies and marketing, manufacturing or processing activities of labour contract/forest labour cooperatives and production credit requirements of rural artisans and weaver members.

Medium-Term Loans

1. Non Schematic

NABARD provides refinance to the SCBs and the RRBs for financing farmers to enable them to buy productive assets for certain approved agricultural investment purposes.

2. Conversion of Short-term loans to Medium-Term Loans (Schematic)

In the case of loss of 50 percent or more crops due to the natural calamities, the NABARD grants medium term loans to Co-operative banks and the RRBs to enable them to extend credit related relief to the affected farmers by converting their short term loans into medium-term or allowing rescheduling of loan period to postpone the long-term loan instalments falling due. The NABARD meets out financial burden arising out of conversion of short-term loan to the extent of 60% in the case of the DCCBs and 70 percent in the case of the RRBs.

Long-term loans to State Governments

The National Bank sanctions long-term loans to the State Governments towards contribution to the share capital of the SCBs (three-tier), DCCBs/SCBs (two tier), PACS, FSS, LAMPS, SCARDBs and Primary Co-operative Agriculture and Rural Development Banks (PCARDBs) in order to strengthen the owned-funds position so as to purvey larger credit. These loans are given on soft terms with repayment period extending up to 12 years with first installment falling due at the end of the third year.

Investment Credit

The NABARD extends credit facility to banks for financing the farmers to buy productive assets. NABARD provides the refinance facility for investment credit (long-term) to the SCARDBs/SCBs/RRBs/CBs and to the Scheduled Primary Urban Cooperative Banks. The extent of refinance assistance ranges between 90 percent and 100 percent of the bank loan depending upon the category of borrowers, purposes, agencies, and regions. The repayment period is fixed between three and fifteen years depending upon the cash flow/ economic life of assets/repaying capacity.

RURAL INFRASTRUCTURE DEVELOPMENT FUND (RIDF)

Good infrastructure is essential for better productivity of capital and labour. In India where more than 60% of the population lives in rural areas and nearly two-thirds of the work force derives their livelihood from agriculture, the rural infrastructure assumes crucial importance. The direct effect of infrastructure via, technological improvement on poverty reduction relates to the increase in the demand for labour and thus wage rates. The increase in productive capacity of a labour reduces indirectly the incidence of poverty.

The Government of India announced in the Union Finance Budget for the year 1995-96, the scheme for setting up of "Rural Infrastructure Development Fund" (RIDF) in the NABARD for financing of ongoing rural infrastructure projects with a corpus of ₹ 2000 crores with the contribution from the Commercial Banks to the extent of short-fall in agricultural lending subject to a maximum of 1.5 percent of net bank credit. The cumulative corpus from RIDF I to VIII aggregated to ₹ 28,500 crores.

The eligible purposes for financing under the RIDF include rural roads and bridges, major/medium irrigation projects, soil conservation, watershed development, drainage improvement, flood protection, forest management, rural drinking water supply, systems improvement in power sector, building for primary health centres and primary and secondary schools, anganwadis, sishusiksha kendra's and other areas.

PROMOTIONAL AND DEVELOPMENT FUNCTIONS

Apart from taking up projects with a view to increase the business of providing refinance/direct finance, NABARD has also to play a developmental role to improve credit flow to the agriculture and rural sector. Accordingly many promotional and developmental initiatives have been taken up by the NABARD are briefly discussed below.

1. Kisan Credit Card Scheme

Kisan Credit Card (KCC) Scheme, which operationalised during the year 1998-99, is a landmark in the history of rural credit in India. The Scheme aims at quickening the pace and improving the quality of institutional credit delivery for agricultural purposes and was an innovating attempt at further refining the crop loan system. NABARD formulated the model KCC scheme and has been issuing operational guidelines. The credit is given to the cardholders in the form of revolving cash credit facility, which is valid for three years.

2. Watershed Development Programmes

Watershed development has proved to be a comprehensive approach to enhance productivity under rain fed agriculture. The NABARD is actively involved in participating watershed development throughout the country. The following are watershed programme implemented through NABARD.

A. Indo-German Watershed Development Project (IGWDP) (Maharashtra): It is an integrated programme for the watershed development with a participatory approach. It has been implemented since 1992 in Maharashtra through the NGOs and the village level community organizations under the bilateral aid-agreement between the German and the Indian Government. The programme has been implemented in more than one lakh hectares in the twenty-one districts of Maharashtra.

B. Watershed Development Fund (WDF): Watershed Development Fund (WDF) has been set up in the NABARD in 1999-00 with a corpus of ₹ 200 crores equally contributed by NABARD and the Government of India with an objective to spread over the watershed development throughout the country.

3. Micro-credit Innovations

NABARD had introduced, in 1992-93, a pilot project for linking the Self-Help Groups (SHGs) with the banks by providing supplementary credit to the unreached rural poor in the rural areas like the landless/marginal farmers/ agricultural labourers, rural poor women and other helpless people. SHGs are the self managed groups of poor men and women, which primarily came into existence to mobilize financial resources through their own savings, and which lent the same amongst themselves to meet the credit needs of their members. The programme made its beginning through a small pilot project in 1992 aimed at linking 500 Self-Help Groups (SHGs) across the country with banks.

4. Non-farm Sector

Non-farm sector provides employment opportunity and income generation in the rural areas. Since 1985-86, the credit package of NABARD provides financial and promotional support to different segments of rural non-farm sectors like the traditional industries (handloom, handicrafts, coir industries and others) agro-industries, small scale industries, modern industries, service and transport sector and others. NABARD implement the following project/ programme for the promotion of non-farm sector.

A. Rural Entrepreneurship Development Programmes (REDP): NABARD extents assistance to agencies that have professional competence for conducting entrepreneurship development programmes for unemployed rural youth.

B. District Rural Industries Project (DRIP): NABARD had identified five districts under the DRIP on a pilot basis during 1993-94 to generate employment opportunities by providing adequate support for rural industrialization. DRIP was extended to other nine districts during 1999-2000 and eight more districts during 2000-01, since the pilot programmes proved a successful one. The project is at present being implemented in sixty-three districts in the country.

C. Cluster Approach for Rural Industrialization: For the development of rural clusters, the NABARD identified the clusters under National Programme for Rural Industrialization (NPRI) launched by the Government of India. Thirty artisan clusters have been identified by the NABARD in the first three phases in seventeen states. The programme had been launched in twenty-two clusters.

5. Gender Development

NABARD also gives importance to the gender in the purveyance of credit and related support services. NABARD is adopting the multi-strategy to overcome the constraints that come in the way of success of women entrepreneurs. The following are gender development programme adopted by NABARD.

A. Assistance to Rural Women in Non-farm Development (ARWIND): ARWIND is a single window scheme for meeting promotional and credit needs of women. NABARD provides various assistance to agencies who fulfill the needs of the women entrepreneurship. The assistance extended by the NABARD are escort services, common facility centres/common service centres, setting up of mother units, organizing women, product design, quality control and others. NABARD provides 100 percent refinance assistance to the banks, which are extending credit facility to the women entrepreneurs under this programme.

B. Assistance for marketing of Non-farm products of Rural Women: Marketing is an important problem for women entrepreneurs. Under 'Marketing of Non- Farm Products of Rural Women (MAHIMA) scheme NABARD provides various supports to the women entrepreneurs for the promotion of marketing of products produced by women. NABARD provides 100 percent refinance to banks for assisting the women entrepreneur for the marketing of their products.

C. Development of women through Area Programme (DEWTA): NABARD has been implementing the scheme called "Development of women through area programme (DEWTAs), under which the women development cells of selected banks which are expected to identify the needs of 4000 women in respect of skill upgradation, capacity building, credit and social empowerment etc. On a pilot basis the programme has been started in four Regional Rural Banks.

D. Women Development Cells: In order to provide importance to gender development in banking and so as to give attention to the coverage of women by banks through "relationship banking", NABARD is extending support to the RRBs and the Cooperative Banks in forming Women Development Cell (WDC). NABARD has supported 100 cells in 66 RRBs, 26 CCBs, 5 SCBs and 3 SCARDBs. Through these 100 banks about five lakh women are assisted through various credit programmes.

6. Development of Weaker Section

NABARD designed various schemes for the upliftment of the weaker sections of the societies like the small and marginal farmers, scheduled castes and scheduled tribes and people who are living below poverty line. NABARD implement under mentioned special programmes for the development of the weaker section.

A. Special Lines of Credit for Tribal: NABARD makes a policy for the promotion of credit to tribal population, a separate line of credit on literal terms known as "Development of Tribal Population" (DTP) has been extended to the DCCBs and the RRBs, which are operating predominantly in tribal areas. Short-term credit limit also sanctioned to the cooperatives for financing, collection and marketing of various types of minor forest produce by the scheduled tribes.

B. SC/ST Action Plan: The National Bank makes special efforts to increase the flow of refinance to the weaker sections of the population. It also provides 100% refinance under the SC/ST plan to SC/ST population by identifying investment potential and preparing a bank plan with allocation of credit to banks.

C. Tribal Credit Specialist (TCS): Under Tribal Credit Specialist (TCS) Scheme the NABARD grants financial assistance to cooperative banks predominantly operating in tribal area for a period of 5 years in order to identify and finance those activities that could be taken up by the members of the tribal community.

D. Transfer of Technology for sustainable Development (CEC-BAIF Project): Commission of European Communities (CEC) is assisting the project and it is implemented by Bharatiya Agro Industries Foundation (BAIF) to bring major development through family oriented approach for poverty alleviation by adopting simple but appropriate technologies. The project is being implemented in 11 districts of 5 states and the major activities covered are Overhead development, Cattle Development, Sericulture and other suitable off-farm activities.

E. Maharashtra Rural Credit Project (MRCP): The project, assisted by International Fund for Agricultural Development (IFAD) and supplemented by contributions from Government of India, Government of Maharashtra and participatory banks has an objective of poverty alleviation through peoples participation, improving financial services to the rural poor, promotion of savings habit by the clients and lending to the poor.

F. Swarnjayanti Gram Swarozgar Yojana (SGSY): Government of India has launched the Swarnjayanti Gram Swarozgar Yojna (SGSY) programme with effect from 1st April 1999 by restructuring the ongoing self-employment programmes viz Training of Rural Youths for Self Employment (TRYSEM), Development of Women and Children in Rural Areas (DWCRA) etc. The aim of this programme is to uplift the families living below poverty line to above the poverty line in three years by generating income and assets through bank credit and government subsidy. NABARD provides 100 percent refinance to the banks under this scheme.

G. Comprehensive Tribal Development Programme in Gujarat and Maharashtra (WADI Programme): WADI programme has been implemented in Gujarat from 1995 and in Maharashtra from 2000 with the financial support of Kfw, Germany with a grant assistance of Deutsche Mark 26 million (₹ 550 million) DM 28 million (₹ 644 million) respectively. DHRUVA and Maharashtra Institute of Technology Transfer for Rural Areas (MITTRA) are the two implementing agencies, which are promoted by BAIF The programme in Maharashtra aims at improving the socio economic condition of 14,000 tribal families and 1,000 landless women in hilly blocks of Thane and Nasik district.

INSTITUTIONAL DEVELOPMENT AND SUPERVISORY FUNCTIONS

1. Institutional Development Functions

NABARD believes that a strong and viable rural institutional credit framework is vital for supporting the growth and development of rural sector. The following are the initiatives taken by the NABARD for strengthening institutional development

A. Development Action Plans (DAPs): The main objective of the plan is to ensure that the Cooperative Banks and the RRBs function as viable units on a sustainable basis and professionalise their operations and compete effectively with other rural financial institutions. Analysis of parameter having bearing on viability viz., financial, organizational, systems and procedure and human resource development focuses on the following points.

B. Memorandum of Understanding (MoU): Memorandum of Understanding with all the states has been made for strengthening the cooperative banks to facilitate successful completion of the DAPs and to clearly specify obligations/responsibilities of different parties to MoU in managerial, organizational and financial aspects.

C. Vikas Volunteer Vahini (VVV): Formation of farmers club called "Vikas Volunteer Vahini" (VVV) was introduced in 1982-83 as an experiment in social engineering at the grass roots levels in which borrowers have been organized at the village level to propagate the five principles of "Development through credit". NABARD provides financial support for opening and maintenance of clubs and for organizing various training programmes under the aegis of the farmers' club.

2. Supervisory Functions

Apart from the role of development banks, NABARD undertakes certain supervisory's functions

A. Inspection of Banks: The Banking Regulation Act, 1949 empowers the National Bank to undertake statutory inspection in respect of State Cooperative Banks (SCBs) and RRBs and voluntary inspection in respect of SCARDBs and Apex Non-credit Societies.

B. Board of Supervision: NABARD has constituted a Board of Supervison as internal committee to the Board of Directors of the NABARD which gives direction and guidance in respect of policies and on matters relating to supervision and inspection.

C. Statutory Functions: NABARD made recommendation to RBI for the issue of bank/branch licence, inclusion of banks in the Second Schedule to RBI Act, 1934, authorization for opening and operating NRI accounts, exemption from application of section 11(*i*) of Banking Regulation Act 1949 (as applicable to cooperative societies) and it monitoring compliance with relevant provisions of Banking Regulation Act 1949 and RBI Act 1946 by banks and bank staffs and also monitoring review of frauds in cooperative banks/RRBs. The follow up action on Inspection Reports including evaluation of compliance, internalization of findings, providing guidelines to the banks for strengthening the internal control systems and procedures in banks and liasioning with RBI/ GoI /State Governments are among the statutory functions.

D. Other Related Functions: The other related functions rendered by NABARD are recommendation to RBI on banks' request for provision of "Currency Chest" facility, Capacity building of inspecting officers through review meets/workshops, sensitization and exposure programme, Enhancing awareness of banks through literature, manuals, guidelines and others, and evaluation of ongoing refinements of norms for audit classification of banks. NABARD organises Seminars/workshops for the benefit of officials of cooperative banks, RRBs and State Government in supervision related areas, rating of supervised banks and providing policy guidelines to banks on supervision related matters and Qualitative scrutiny of inspection reports.

OTHER FUNCTIONS

A. Credit Planning and Monitoring: Credit Monitoring Arrangements (CMA) has been started from 24th April 2000. Various monitoring studies under CMA have been undertaken and major irregularities were communicated to SCBs/DCCBs to enable them to improve the quality of their appraisal of high value advances and monitory mechanism.

NABARD has opened 319 District offices throughout the country (including Union Territory of Pondicherry and 22 districts in Tamil Nadu) to strengthen the credit planning process at micro level. These district offices act as the focal points for credit planning, monitoring and co-ordination among all partners involved in Agriculture and Rural Development.

NABARD has initiated the process of preparation of Potential Linked Credit Plans (PLP) for all the districts of the country since the beginning of the VIII Five Year Plan. The plans are updated every year. The PLP also gives attention towards gaps in infrastructure impeding the progress of the development. State Focus Paper is prepared to focus on the constraints and non-credit inputs essential for exploiting the potential assessed through the PLP and drawing the attention of all partners at the state level.

B. Research and Development: NABARD pursues its Research and Development activities through in house and sponsored research. A separate Research and Development Fund has been set up for this purpose.

C. Capital Gains Bonds: In the Union budget 2000-01, the National Bank was empowered to float Capital Gains Bonds. Accordingly NABARD issues Capital Gains Bonds under Section 54 (EC) of IT Act 1961.

D. Consultancy Services: NABARD Consultancy Services (NABCONS) Cell was set up in the Bank in July 2002. Nabcons provide consultancy services to various clients in areas of micro-financing, private infrastructure and investment projects, preparation of plans for integrated development of farms, business planning for organizations, integrated area development schemes for horticulture and sericulture, technology and management of cold storages, commercial livestock, project appraisal for banks, working capital assessment, project evaluation, economic and commodity related research, marketing and value addition, organic farming, non-farm enterprise and others. The clientele include International Agencies, Banks, Planning Commission, Ministries of Government of India, State Government and private entrepreneurs.

E. Integrated Development of Backward Blocks: NABARD has taken up an action plan for the implementation of a pilot project for integrated development of backward blocks through convergence of various credit and development programmes and schemes. The project is proposed to be implemented over a period of three years for providing focused intervention by converging National Bank's programme, government schemes and initiatives of NGO's and other agencies to meet the needs of the people in the select blocks in backward areas of different states. The project is being implemented from the financial year 2003-04.

MANAGEMENT AND ORGANISATION SETUP

According to Section 5 (1) of NABARD Act, the general superintendence, direction and management of the affairs and business of the Bank vest with the Board. The Board exercises all powers and does all acts and things which may be exercised or done by the NABARD. The Board while discharging its functions acts on business principle with due regard to public interest. The Managing Director of the bank is also empowered for general superintendence, direction and management of the affairs and business of the bank.

Board of Directors

According to Section 6(1) of the NABARD Act, 1981, the Board of directors of the NABARD comprises of the following.

(*i*) A Chairman,

(*ii*) Two Directors from amongst experts in rural economics, rural development, handicrafts and other rural crafts, village and cottage industries and small-scale industries.

(*iii*) Three Directors out of whom two are with experience in the working of Co-operative banks and one with experience in the working of Commercial banks.

(*iv*) Three Directors from out of the Directors of the RBI,

(*v*) Three Directors from amongst the officials of the Central Government,

(*vi*) Two Directors from amongst the officials of the State Governments and

(*vii*) a Managing Director is assisted in his day to day work by the Chief General Managers, General Managers, Deputy General Managers and other staff who are assigned specific roles in the Head office and the Regional offices.

Chart showing Organisation setup of NABARD

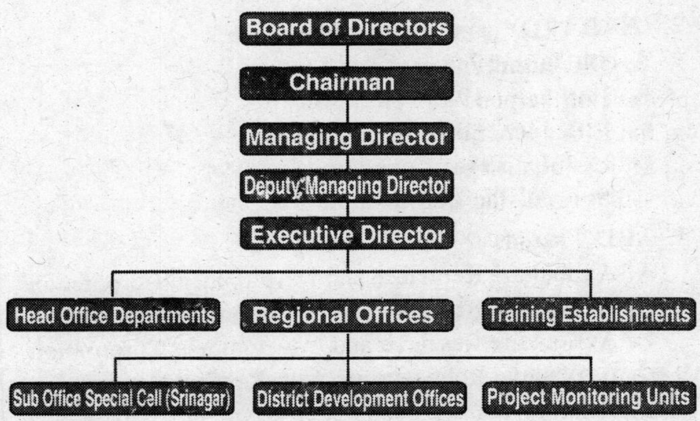

COMMITTEES OF NABARD

1. Executive Committee

The Board of National Bank has constituted an Executive Committee during 1987-88 under Section 13(1) of the NABARD Act read with Regulation 3(1) of the General Regulation 1984. The Committee may discharge such functions as may be prescribed or delegated to it by the Board. Executive Committee has the power to transact the usual business of the NABARD. The chairman may call a meeting of the Executive Committee once in two months at Mumbai.

2. Other Committees

The Board may constitute such other committees inclusive of wholly of Directors or wholly of other persons or partly of Directors and partly of other persons according to the purposes as it may decide.

3. Advisory Council

The Board shall constitute an Advisory Council consisting of such number of Directors and such other persons who have special knowledge on agriculture credit, cooperation and rural economics, small-scale industries, village and cottage industries and handicrafts and other rural crafts or have special knowledge and appreciation of the country's overall development policies and in particular overall monetary and credit policies, which is considered by the board as useful to NABARD.

VARIOUS DEPARTMENTS OF THE BANK

The various departments functioning in NABARD are Projects and Operation Department, Inspection Department, Finance and Accounts Department, Human Resource Management Department, Management Service Department, Law Department, General Administration and Premises Department, Secretary's Department, Internal Audit Department, Vikas Volunteer Vahini Department, Planning and Developmental Department, Institutional Development Department, Economic Analysis and Publications Department and Technical Services Department.

REGIONAL OFFICES/SUB-OFFICE/TRAINING ESTABLISHMENT

The Head office of the bank is located at Bandra-Kurla complex in Mumbai. NABARD had 32 Regional offices and a sub office at Port Blair, a cell at Srinagar and 414 District Development Managers' Offices.

NABARD is also maintaining Training Colleges/Centres at Bolpur, Lucknow, Hyderabad, Mangalore and Banker's Institute of Rural Development (BIRD) which is fully funded and supported by the National Bank.

MULTIPLE CHOICE QUESTIONS

1. NABARD stands for:
A. National Bank for Agriculture and Research Development
B. National Bank for Analysis of Rural Development
C. National Bank for Agriculture and Rural Development
D. National Bank for Affordable Research and Development
E. None of the above

2. 'NABARD' came into existence on:
A. 8th July, 1982
B. 19th July, 1982
C. 12th July, 1982
D. 15 July, 1984
E. None of the above

3. ARDC stands for:
A. Agriculture Refinance and Development Corporation
B. Agriculture Research and Development Commission
C. Agriculture Research and Development Corporation
D. Agriculture Refinance and Development Commission
E. None of the above

4. NABARD was set up with an initial capital of ....
A. ₹ 50 Crore B. ₹ 100 Crore
C. ₹ 200 Crore D. ₹ 500 Crore
E. None of the above

5. Headquarter of 'NABARD' is located at:
A. Mangalore, Karnataka
B. Mumbai, Maharashtra
C. New Delhi
D. Hyderabad, Andhra Pradesh
E. None of the above

6. NABARD was established on the recommendations of:
A. Shivaraman Committee
B. Malhotra Committee
C. Kumarmangalam Committee
D. Nambiar Committee
E. None of the above

7. .... is the apex institution in the country which looks after the development of the cottage industry, small industries, village industries and other rural industries:
A. NABARD B. SEBI
C. SIDBI D. RBI
E. None of the above

8. NABARD was set up essentially as a development bank for promoting:
A. Agriculture Development only
B. Rural Development only
C. Urban Development only
D. Both A and B
E. None of the above

9. The main function of NABARD is to provide refinance for rural credit disburse by the .... and other financial institutions as may be approved by the Reserve Bank of India:

A. State Co-operative Banks
B. The Regional Rural Banks
C. State Bank of India
D. State Co-operative Banks and The Regional Rural Banks
E. None of the above

10. Which among the following functions of NABARD is incorrect:

A. Providing finance and also refinance for production and marketing in the rural areas
B. Coordination and advising the operations of institutions engaged in rural credit
C. Promoting research in agriculture and rural development
D. All of the above
E. None of the above

11. CSR stands for:

A. Customer Satisfaction Responsibility
B. Corporate Social Responsibility
C. Corporate Social Reforms
D. Cooperation for Social Research
E. None of the above

12. Which among the following is considered as 100% CSR company:

A. SDB (Small Development Banks)
B. NABARD
C. RRBs (Regional Rural Banks)
D. SEBI
E. None of the above

13. Which of the following organizations/agencies is specifically set up to boost overall rural development in India?

A. RBI B. SIDBI
C. NABARD D. SEBI
E. None of these

14. Which of the following organizations maintains the Rural Infrastructure Development Fund (RIDF)?

A. RBI B. NABARD
C. SIDBI D. LIC
E. None of these

15. The National Bank for Agriculture and Rural Development (NABARD) gets some amount of its funds from which of the following organizations for its various schemes?

1. World Bank
2. Bank of America
3. IDA

A. Only 1 B. Only 2
C. Only 3 D. All of these
E. Only 1 and 3 both

16. Which of the following statement(s) is/are TRUE about the activities of the NABARD?

1. NABARD has the responsibility to inspect RRBs and Co-operative Banks.
2. NABARD maintains Research and Development Fund to promote research in agriculture and rural development.
3. NABARD is a wing of Planning Commission of India.

A. Only 1 B. Only 2
C. Both 1 and 2 only D. Only 3
E. All of these

17. Which of the following statements about the NABARD is/are TRUE?

1. NABARD has a dual role to play as it is an apex body and a refinance institution.
2. NABARD services as a refinance institution for all kinds of production and investment credit to agriculture and cottage and village industries.
3. NABARD accepts short term deposits from the public like any other bank to improve its capital base.

A. Only 1 B. Only 2
C. Only 3 D. Only 1 and 2
E. All of these

18. 'NABARD' was dedicated to which among the following Prime Ministers:

A. Gulzari Lal Nanda
B. Indira Gandhi
C. Shri Lal Bahadur Shastri
D. I.K. Gujaral
E. None of the above

19. 'NABARD was dedicated to the service of the nation by the late Prime Minister Smt. Indira Gandhi on:

A. 5 November, 1982
B. 10 November, 1982
C. 1 December, 1982
D. 2 October, 1982
E. None of the above

20. Which of the following is also known as the National Bank?

A. Reserve Bank of India
B. Asian Development Bank
C. State Bank of India
D. NABARD
E. None of these

21. Which of the following organizations/agencies works solely to monitor and arrange flow of agriculture credit in India?

A. NABARD B. SIDBI
C. RBI D. SEBI
E. None of these

22. Which of the following is NOT a scheduled Commercial Bank ?

A. HDFC Bank B. Axis Bank
C. IDBI Bank D. NABARD
E. SBI

23. NABARD is a:
A. Department of RBI
B. Wholly owned subsidiary of RBI
C. Subsidiary of SBI
D One of the above
E. None of these

24. NABARD refinance for financing Self Help Groups is to the extent of:
A. 25% B. 50%
C. 75% D. 100%
E. None of these

ANSWERS

1	2	3	4	5	6	7	8	9	10
C	C	A	B	B	A	A	D	D	E
11	**12**	**13**	**14**	**15**	**16**	**17**	**18**	**19**	**20**
B	B	C	B	E	E	D	B	A	D
21	**22**	**23**	**24**						
A	D	D	D						

13 Small Industries Development Bank of India (SIDBI)

INTRODUCTION

Banking scenario has been changed rapidly since 1990. The decade of nineties has witnessed a grass root changes in the way banking business carried out in India. Anywhere banking and anytime banking has become a reality. The financial sector now operates in a more competitive environment than before and intermediates relatively range volume of international financial flows.

On the contrary, most banks have been required to provide for the decline in the market value of their investments portfolio. Thankfully one, off setting factor has been the strong pick up in the credit take off due to buoyant demand in the economy and revival of industrial activity which have resulted in substantial increase in banks core interest income.

With a view to ensuring larger flow of financial and non-financial assistance to Small Scale Industries (S.S.I.) the Small Industries Development Bank of India (SIDBI) was set up by the Government of India under special Act passed by Parliament in October 1989 but SIDBI has been starting the work since April 2, 1990. It is the wholly-owned subsidiary of Industrial Development Bank of India (IDBI). SIDBI became operational on April 2, 1990. SIDBI has taken over the outstanding portfolio of IDBI relating to Small Scale Sector worth over ₹ 4,000 Crore. The authorized capital of SIDBI is ₹ 250 Crore which could be increased to ₹ 1,000 Crore.

SIDBI's headquarter is situated at Lucknow. It have five regional offices, 5 zones and 21 branch offices when it was started in different parts of India but now SIDBI has 82 Branches, 10 Regional Offices across the country.

After the establishment of Small Industries Development Bank of India (SIDBI), all duties related to small scale enterprises which are performed by Industrial Development Bank of India (IDBI) have been shifted to SIDBI.

DOMAIN OF SERVICE

The Small Scale Industries (SSIs) sector is a vibrant and dynamic sector of the Indian economy. The sector presently occupies an important place and its contribution in terms of generation of employment, output and exports is quite significant. The Small Scale Industries sector including tiny units comprises the domain of SIDBI's business. Besides, the projects in the services sector with total cost up to ₹ 250 million are also taken within the area of SIDBI's operations. The Bank also finances industrial infrastructure projects for the development of SSI sector. The objectives of Government policy have been to impart vitality and growth impetus to the sector by removing bottlenecks that affect the growth potential. In the liberalized era and emerging economic scenario, the sector is assured of continued support.

SIDBI and the others banks have embraced technology right from the inception of their operation and therefore they have adapted themselves to the changes into the changes in the technology easily. Whereas the public sector banks (PSBs) and the old private sector banks have not been able to keep pace with these developments.

SIDBI which is the subsidiary bank of the IDBI, has also adopted the same strategy, and SIDBI already transformed itself into a universal bank. Now, the process of progeny IDBI bank merging itself with the parent IDBI is underway and is likely to be completed soon. This trend may lead logically to promote the concept of financial super market chain and making available all types of credit and non-fund facilities under one roof or specialized subsidiaries which is under one umbrella organization. There is a need to review our regulatory framework not only in the light of the global developments that have been mentioned, but also due to domestic compulsions.

SIDBI (Small Industries Development Bank of India) is now the principal financial institution and for the purpose of promotion, financing and development of small scale industries in the country. It co-ordinates the functions of existing institution on engaged in similar activities.

According to SIDBI, it has taken over the responsibility of administering Small Industries Development Fund (SIDF) and National equity fund (NEF) which were earlier administered by IDBI.

SIDBI'S COMMITMENT

SIDBI is committed to developing a strong, vibrant and responsive small-scale sector. This commitment is to be achieved through a variety of means. Principal amongst them is finance. Alongside finance, SIDBI provides appropriate support in the form of promotional and developmental services. SIDBI has been built up as a financially sound, vibrant, forward looking and technically oriented institution and, it intends to sustain this orientation in future. SIDBI intends to provide quality services to its clients, devoid of any systemic and procedural difficulties.

OPERATIONAL EMPHASIS

SIDBI, in its operational strategy, emphasizes:

- Enhancement in the flow of financial assistance to SSIs.
- Enhancement in the capabilities of SSIs at all levels, with focus on adoption of improved and modern technology.

The small industries sector in India is dominated by a large number of small units. These micro enterprises require special nurturing. SIDBI has been operating schemes like:

- Single Window Scheme
- Composite Loan Scheme.

To ensure that financial assistance is made available to such units on easy terms and with hassle-free procedures. It has been a matter of policy in SIDBI to identify the areas of gaps in credit delivery system and fill them through devising appropriate new schemes and implementing them.

FUNCTION OF SIDBI

SIDBI has a certain function.

The important function of SIDBI are as follows:

(*i*) SIDBI re-finance loans and advances extended by the primary lending institutions to small scale industrial units and also provide sources support to them.

(*ii*) SIDBI discounts and rediscounts bills arising from sale of machinery to or manufactured by industrial units in the small scale sector,

(*iii*) SIDBI extends seeds capital/soft loan assistance under National Equity Fund, Mahila Udyam Nidhi and Mahila Vikas Nidhi and seed capital scheme through specified lending agencies.

(*iv*) SIDBI grant direct assistance as well as re-finance loan extended by primary lending Institution for financing export of products manufactured by industrial concerns in the small scale sector,

(*v*) SIDBI provides services like leasing, factoring etc. to industrial concerns in small scale sector.

(*vi*) SIDBI extends financial support to State Small Industries Development Corporation (SSIDCs) for providing source raw materials to and marketing the end products of industrial units in small scale units.

(*vii*) SIDBI provides support to National Small Industries Corporation (NSICs) for providing leasing, hire-purchase, and marketing support to industrial units in the small scale sector.

(*viii*) Re-financing of loans & advances extended by the primary lending institution to small scale industrial unit concern and also providing resources support,

(*ix*) Discounting and re-discounting of bills arising from scale of machinery to or manufactured by industrial units in the small scale sector,

(*x*) Extension of seed capital/soft loan assistance under National Equity fund. **Mahila Udyam Nidhi** and **Mahila Vikas Nidhi** and seed capital schemes through specified lending agencies,

(*xi*) Granting direct assistance as well as re-financing of loans extended by primary lending institution for financing export of products manufactured by industrial concern in the small scale sector.

(*xii*) Providing services like learning factoring etc. to industrial concerns in the small scale sector.

In setting up SIDBI, the intention of the Govt. of India was to ensure larger flow of financial assistance to small scale sector, SIDBI has already initiated step for technological upgradation and modernization of existing units. It is expanding the channels for marketing of products of SSI sector in internal and International market. It is promoting in a big way employment - oriented industries especially in semi-urban areas to credit more employment opportunities and thereby checking migration of rural population to urban and cosmopolitan areas.

Role of SIDBI

Since in inception, SIDBI has been endeavouring to meet the diverse needs of the Small and Medium Enterprises (SME) sectors through various tailor-made schemes and fulfill its vision *i.e.*, "To emerge as a single window for meeting the financial and developmental needs of the Micro Small Medium Enterprises (MSME) sector to make it strong, vibrant and globally competitive, to position SIDBI Brand as the preferred and customer-friendly institution and for enhancement of share-holder wealth and highest corporate values through modern technology platform.

While extending financial assistance to the small units all over the country SIDBI makes use of the existing banking and financial institutions, such as the commercial banks, co-operative banks and RRBs, SFCs and SIDCs which have vast network of branches all over the country. As many as 870 institutions are eligible for assistance from SIDBI.

Objectives of SIDBI

Mandatory Objectives

Four basic objectives are set out in the SIDBI Charter. They are:

1. Financing
2. Promotion
3. Development
4. Co-ordination

The Charter has provided SIDBI considerable flexibility in adopting appropriate operational strategies to meet these objectives. The activities of SIDBI, as they have evolved over the period of time, now meet almost all the requirements of small scale industries which fall into a wide spectrum constituting modem and technologically superior units at one end and traditional units at the other.

Other Objectives

- To empower the Micro, Small and Medium Enterprises (MSME) sector with a view to contributing to the process of economic growth, employment generation and balanced regional development.
- To emerge as a single window for meeting the financial and developmental needs of the MSME sector to make it strong, vibrant and globally competitive, to position SIDBI Brand as the preferred and customer-friendly institution and for enhancement of share-holder wealth and highest corporate values through modern technology platform.

SIDBI's charter includes Financing, Promotion, Development and Co-ordination for orderly growth of Small and Medium Enterprises. The Charter has provided SIDBI considerable flexibility in adopting appropriate operational strategies to meet these objectives. The activities of SIDBI, as they have evolved over the period of time, now meet almost all the requirements of SMEs which fall into a wide spectrum constituting modern and technologically superior units at one end and traditional units at the other.

SIDBI is committed to developing a strong, vibrant and responsive small scale sector. This commitment is to be achieved through a variety of means. Principal amongst them is finance. Alongside finance, SIDBI provides appropriate support in the form of promotional and developmental services. SIDBI has been built up as a financially sound, vibrant, forward looking and technically oriented institution and, it intends to sustain this orientation in future.

Features of SIDBI

Since 1992-93 SIDBI liberalized its term of assistance and amplified procedure with a view to widen its scope for large coverage of schemes. Some of salient features of SIDBI can be listed as follows.

(*a*) SIDBI has been operating **Single Window Scheme (SWS)** which is enlarged to cover units in identified area. The extent of refinance against cash credit sanctioned by banks under SWS was raised from 50 to 70 per cent.

(*b*) SIDBI provide refinance facilities under **Automatic Refinance Scheme (ARS).** The limit of term loans under ARS was initially fixed at ₹ 10 lakhs but was raised later to ₹ 50 lakh and the extent of refinance has been raised from 75 to 90 per cent.

(*c*) SIDBI has introduced equipment financing for assistance to existing well-run small-scale units for technology upgradation modernization.

(*d*) SIDBI has introduced refinance scheme for resettlement of voluntary retired worker of **National Textile Corporation (NTC)** and help them to buy up to four looms.

(*e*) SIDBI has set up a venture capital found to assist entrepreneurs within a short span of time; SIDBI has emerged as a major player in the field of finance for the small scale sector.

Problems and Issues of SIDBI

Because of their unique characteristics, SIDBI face a variety of problems. In this section, the problems are examined in connection with two stages of environmental performance improvement.

Environmental performance improvement can be divided into two major stages, namely, awareness raising and implementation. The awareness raising is significant as it relates to the establishment of a solid foundation for SIDBI to move towards environmental improvement.

Stage I: Awareness Raising

Lack of information on the cost-benefits of improving environmental performance basically, a fundamental obstacle to improving environmental performance of the SME sector is a lack of knowledge and information concerning environmental issues. SIDBI generally have a perception that the only driving force to improve environmental performance is legislative compliance. Moreover, SIDBI tend to believe that their processes have little or no impact on the environment due to their small-scale production. This perception is derived from the fact that they have limited information on the operational losses in their production processes. Hence, this mental model prevents a great number of SME's from realizing the hidden costs of inefficiencies in production. Accordingly, the SIDBI keep running their businesses as usual and resist change.

In order to motivate the SME's to improve their environmental performance critical information on cost-benefits can illustrate the benefits of environmental improvement and help to develop a positive attitude regarding environmental improvement. However, it seems that such information is not widely disseminated in the SME sector.

Weak External Pressures/Incentives

Environmental policy development in various countries began with command-and-control (CAC) measures. Accordingly, regulatory instruments were applied to force polluters to comply with regulations and standards. However, due to the large number and distribution of SME's, the command and control approach became less efficient due to resource limitations in terms of the monitoring and inspecting of personnel and budget allocation. While public pressure regarding environmental conservation and requirements by global markets on environmental standards increases, most companies are carefully watching the International Standard Organization (ISO) certification and the introduction of Environmental Management System (EMS) within their corporate and manufacturing facilities. Most industries, particularly those producing goods for export, are focusing on developing environmentally friendly products. However, most SME's, unlike large-scale industries, are not fully aware of the trend in the international market since they are often isolated from it.

In addition, voluntary approaches, such as ISO 14000, green labelling, and clean technology have become other means of management of natural resources and the environment as the market created was stimulated by consumer demand. However, compared to the SME sector, large firms are more active in taking voluntary initiatives.

Stage II: Implementation

Lack of Internal Capacity

Even though a number of SME's are moving towards better environmental performance, they are limited from taking action. The major obstacles are their weak capacity and limited resources in terms of:

Financial Resources

One of the major obstacles is the limited financial resources of SIDBI since the majority of the SME sector is pursuing a survival business strategy. They suffer from financial problems, such as late payment of bills and lack of access to loan financing, they find it difficult to adapt to the changing markets and they lack the capability to attract new financial resources. As a consequence, the adoption of full-scaled EMS, such as the ISO 14001 model, or the installation of pollution abatement technologies, seems to be too costly for SIDBI. Moreover, investment capital for major process improvement is another issue of concern since accessibility to financial resources is a major problem for a number of SME's as they tend to lack self-capacity to attract funding from local, regional and national financial institutions and also from international institutions and organizations. The problem has a supply and demand component. From the supply side, SIDBI face difficulties in obtaining loans due to the banks' perceptions of high associated risks. On the demand side, SIDBI often have inadequate financial statements and lack accounting records, business plans and the necessary knowledge to present their business case in a realistic and favourable light to financial sources. In order to address this problem, there is, therefore, a need for better information flows among the financial providers, the SME's and the concerned government agencies.

Human Resources

Lack of trained and qualified human resources is another barrier that requires improvement. Generally, human resource allocation in the SME sector is limited to essential business functions, such as technical, accountancy, sales and marketing. In most cases, there are no environmental personnel in the SIDBI to undertake related tasks effectively.

Technologies

Utilization of outdated technology, as a result of limited capital investment, makes the SIDBI less competitive. The majority of SME's is relying on outdated technologies that cause pollution and are inefficient in production. In addition, inappropriate pollution abatement technologies result in inefficiencies in pollution treatment.

R&D activities

R&D activities are limited in the SIDBI. This inhibits innovative improvement within the sector. One of the major reasons for the poor performance is technological obsolescence coupled with information deficiency and poor management practices. Thus, SIDBI lack technical capacity in these enterprises to identify access, adapt and adopt better technologies and operating practices to improve their environmental performance.

Business-as-usual Operation and Management

Normally, SIDBI functions in a business-as-usual mode. They are not fully aware of the emergence of a new business environment. For example, non-tariff barriers, new trade and technology. The nature of the SIDBI establishment is a major problem affecting environmental improvement of SIDBI in terms of infrastructure as the physical distribution of SIDBI tends to be haphazard. Many of SME's are located in concentrated commercial and residential areas, thus, they are unable to expand their sites and install pollution treatment facilities. Moreover, the scattered distribution prohibits the development of shared treatment facilities, while the stand-alone treatment system of SIDBI is not in an economy of scale to operate efficiently.

Weak Supporting Framework

Despite obstructive structures in the awareness-raising and implementation stages, the framework support of SIDBI is weak. Also, the various programmes supporting the performance of SIDBI have not helped SIDBI effectively.

Weak Institutional Arrangement of Supporting SIDBI

Linkages among agencies involved with the SIDBI development have not been strengthened. The network of institutions that is supposed to deliver supporting programmes to SIDBI development is fragmented and cannot offer the corresponding services effectively.

Lack of SIDBI Focused Programmes

Many developing countries previously pursued a strategy of accelerated industrialization based on large-scaled enterprises. Accordingly, development programmes and investment schemes were established in light of large industry promotion while there are limited focused programmes that are devoted to SIDBI development.

Gaps between international support and local implementation: Even though the environmental improvement of SIDBI has drawn the attention of international organizations, the international support for SIDBI development cannot reach local SME's effectively. The major barriers include language and the adjustment of the programmes to the local context. SIDBI have been struggling with these problems for many years and their challenge becomes more severe when they wish to improve their environmental performance.

Structure of SIDBI

SIDBI attaches a great deal of importance to the corner-stones of good corporate governance particularly the clear division of responsibility, appropriate checks and balances. The policy and strategic decisions, monitoring of performance and other important matters are dealt with by the Bank at the level of Board of Directors. As regard operational matters, the bank has decentralized the process of decision-making with adequate delegation of powers. SIDBI is operating through its head-office at Lucknow, with a network of 9 regional and seventy seven branch offices in the country. Since its inception, SIDBI is doing well in the area of financing SSIs.

Small Industries Development Bank of India Act provides for a fifteen-member board of directors. Out of these eight members or directors are appointed by the Central Government, three directors are nominated by the three largest share holding institutions, banks and insurance companies owned and controlled by Central Government, and four are elected by the public share holders.

The Bank has constituted subcommittees of the Board namely Executive Committee (EC), Audit Committee (AC) and Empowered Committee on Micro Finance (ECM). Besides, there are committees of the officials of the Bank viz. Central, Zonal Branch Credit, settlement and promotion and development proposals. Credit proposals and other operational matters are considered by the EC. The AC in addition to overseeing the functioning of the Audit Department and reviewing its major observations and also provide guidance is a matter relating to finalisation of accounts of Bank and ECM guiding the Bank in matters pertaining to micro finance.

Importance of SIDBI as a source of financing small scale industries

SIDBI provide financial assistance in the form of:

1. Direct Assistance: SIDBI has evolved itself to meet the various requirements of the Small & Medium Enterprises (SME) sector by directly offering various financial products and services. Some of the major schemes of SIDBI under direct assistance are:

A. Term Loan Assistance

Term Loans are provided for (*i*) setting up new projects and for technology upgradation, diversification, expansion, etc. of existing SMEs, (*ii*) service sector entities like hotels, tourism related activities, entertainment parks, hospitals/nursing homes, health & fitness centres, filling stations, retail chains, logistic support services, IT & IT enabled services, etc. and (*iii*) infrastructure development and upgradation.

Resource Support

The Bank provides resource support to institutions/Non-Banking Finance Companies (NBFCs) to facilitate channelising assistance to a large number of SME units and infrastructure projects having linkages to SMEs.

B. Working Capital Type Support

Working Capital Term Loan (WCTL)

The objective of the Scheme is to help SME units in starting their commercial production without difficulty and during their up scaling of operations. All the assisted units of SIDBI covered under the scheme are expected eventually to switch over to commercial banks within a reasonable time frame (say, 3-5 years) for meeting their regular working capital requirements.

Scheme for Small Enterprises Financial Centres (SEFC)

In order to meet the complete financial requirements of SME customers, particularly working capital, the Scheme for Small Enterprises Financial Centres (SEFC) Scheme has been operationalised to take up co-financing or exclusive financing of term loan requirements of SME units along with the commercial banks and the working capital requirements of these units will be met by the banks in identified clusters. The branches of SIDBI in the clusters are designated as SEFCs. Under the Scheme, SIDBI has entered into Memorandum of Understanding with 15 commercial banks for joint/co-financing of projects including working capital and non-fund based facilities for the SME sector.

C. Support against Delayed Payments

Receivable Finance Scheme (RFS)

Receivable Finance Scheme (RFS) is intended mitigate the problem of delayed payments to SME sellers/eligible service providers in respect of their sales/services rendered to large purchaser companies. Under the scheme, the Bank fixes limits to well-performing purchaser companies with sub-limits to their SME units. The bank offers bills discounting facilities to SMEs/eligible service sector units supplying components, parts, sub-assemblies, services, etc. so as to realise their sale precedes quickly. The Scheme also enables manufactures-sellers in SME/service sector to offer deferred payment terms for credit sales and realise sale proceeds by discounting bills of exchange/promissory notes arising out of such sales. The Bank also offers invoice-discounting facilities to the suppliers of large corporates.

Seller-wise Receivable Finance Scheme (SRFS)

Whereas under RFS, the facility is given only in respect of a single purchaser from the SMEs, under Seller-wise Receivable Finance Scheme (SRFS), the SME units' receivables from other purchasers are also covered to improve their cash flow and liquidity by providing them with immediate financial assistance against the goods sold and/or services rendered to purchaser companies in the public / private sector with satisfactory market standing.

D. Foreign Currency Loans

To enhance the capabilities of export oriented units, SIDBI offer prepost-shipment credit to SME units in foreign currencies like US Dollar, Euro, etc. Foreign currency assistance is also extended by way of term loans for importing plant and machinery or equipments, etc. The related schemes are briefly given below:

Pre-Shipment Credit in Foreign Currency/Rupee to enable Small and Medium Enterprises (SME) / Export Houses (EH) / Trading Houses (TH), etc. to raise finance to fulfill their export commitments.

The assistance may be availed in designated foreign currencies or in rupee.

- Post-Shipment Credit by way of negotiation/ purchase/discount of export bills of eligible entities which have been sanctioned limits by SIDBI. This facility can be availed either in foreign currency or in rupee.
- Foreign Currency Tern, Loan Scheme for setting up new projects as for expansion, diversification, technology upgradation and modernization of existing units.
- Opening of Foreign Letters of Credit (FLO) to enable small, and medium enterprises (SMEs), import capital equipment for new projects, expansion, diversion, technology upgradation and modernization. FLCs are also opened to enable import of raw materials, consumables etc. by SME units and Export/Trading Houses sourcing their requirements for export from SMEs.
- Booking of Forward Contracts to provide SIDBI, clients with the facility of hedging of foreign exchange risks related to their import, export transactions.
- Line of Credit in Foreign Currency to Commercial Banks for providing resource support to institutions / banks for extending export and domestic credit to SME units / EH / TH, etc.

MULTIPLE CHOICE QUESTIONS

1. When was 'Small Industries Development Bank of India' (SIDBI) established?
A. 1st April 1986 B. 1st April 1990
C. 1st April 1994 D. 1st April 1998
E. 1st April 1999

2. Where is the Headquarter of SIDBI?
A. New Delhi B. Mumbai
C. Kolkata D. Lucknow
E. None of these

3. What is the Authorised Capital of SIDBI?
A. ₹ 250 crore B. ₹ 500 crore
C. ₹ 1000 crore D. ₹ 1200 crore
E. None of these

4. What is the Paid-up Capital of SIDBI?
A. ₹ 250 crore B. ₹ 350 crore
C. ₹ 531.92 crore D. ₹ 550 crore
E. None of these

5. What is one of the major objectives of SIDBI?
A. Principal Financial Institution for Promotion, Financing and Development of Agriculture sector in India
B. Principal Financial Institution for Promotion, Financing and Development of MSME sector in India
C. Principal Financial Institution for Promotion, Financing and Development of Export sector in India
D. Principal Financial Institution for Promotion, Financing and Development of Housing sector in India
E. None of these

6. Which of the following statements is correct regarding SIDBI?
1. It has been separated from IDBI and is not an independent unit.
2. It has its assets base of more than ₹ 16000 crore.
3. It is one of the 10 largest Development Banks of the world.

A. 1 B. 1 and 2

C. 1 and 3 D. 1, 2 and 3
E. None of these

7. What is the maximum number of vehicles that a borrower should have so that the financing bank may get refinance from SIDBI?
A. 6 B. 10
C. 20 D. 30
E. No limit

8. What is the maximum Project Cost under National Equity Fund Scheme of SIDBI?
A. ₹ 5 lac B. ₹ 10 lac
C. ₹ 25 lac D. ₹ 50 lac
E. ₹ 75 lac

9. Which of the following has largest stake in the capital of SIDBI?
A. IDBI B. LIC
C. State Bank group D. Either A or B
E. None of these

10. SIDBI has recently tied up with .... to provide loans and other financial products to Small and Medium Enterprises?
A. Yes Bank B. Krishna Baldeo Bank
C. Dena Bank D. Punjab National Bank
E. None of these

11. What is the name of Credit Rating Agency set up by SIDBI in Sept. 2005 for aggregate rating of SMEs?
A. SME Rating Agency
B. SME Investment Rating Agency
C. SME Credit Rating Agency
D. SME Overall Rating Agency
E. None of these

12. What is the Paid up Capital of SME Rating Agency, SMERA?
A. ₹ 1 crore B. ₹ 2 crore
C. ₹ 5 crore D. ₹ 10 crore
E. ₹ 12 crore

ANSWERS

1	2	3	4	5	6	7	8	9	10
B	D	C	C	B	B	C	D	C	A
11	**12**								
A	C								

14 Merchant Banking

INTRODUCTION

Financial Service is rendered through numerous intermediaries who are known by different names. One of the prominent intermediaries is known as merchant banker. Their scope of operation differs from country to country. *Merchant banking* as it is known in present days had its origin in U.K and U.S.A in early fifties. But the roots of this service rendering industry can be traced as back as in late eighteenth century and early nineteenth century. There were merchants, who traded overseas, built reputation and later shared their goodwill with newer traders to facilitate their merchant activities especially by providing guarantees for payments. Subsequently, they entered any field which added to their business depending on the demand of time. Thus, as time changed their role changed, consequently it has never been possible to pinpoint their role. As Sir Edward Reid of Baring Brothers & Co. commented, it is (merchant banking) sometimes applied to banks which are not merchants, merchants who are not banks and sometimes to houses who are neither merchants nor banks." Report of the Committee on the Working of Monetary System (1961) observed that origin of merchant bankers is associated with a variety of financial services including accepting house. This is why merchant bankers are popular as 'issue houses' or 'accepting houses' in U.K. In U.S.A, investment bankers have been performing the task being performed by merchant bankers elsewhere. Whether these are called accepting house or investment banker or merchant bankers, their common object is to facilitate trade and industry. Meeting their diverse and dynamic needs with the change in time and complexities in business has always been a challenge for merchant banking.

CONCEPT AND NATURE OF MERCHANT BANKING

Despite the fact that merchant banking is emerging as one of the prominent segment of financial service sector, it is difficult to define what merchant banking is. The reason is very obvious as its limits have never been adequately and strictly defined and it caters to wide variety of financial activities. Dictionary of Banking and Finance explains merchant bank as an organisation that underwrites securities for corporations, advises such clients on mergers and is involved in the ownership of commercial ventures. Securities and Exchange Board of India (Merchant Bankers) Rules 1992 defines merchant bankers as "any person who is engaged in the business of issue management either by making arrangement regarding selling, buying or subscribing to securities or acting as manager, consultant, adviser or rendering corporate advisory services in relation to such issue management. The Guidelines for Merchant Bankers (issued by Ministry of Finance, Deptt. of Economic Affairs, Stock Exchange Division on 9-4-1990) instead of defining merchant banking stated that these guidelines shall apply to those presently engaged in merchant banking activity including as managers to issue and undertakes authorised activities. These activities interalia include underwriting, portfolio management etc. Thus. to define merchant bankers, a definite better approach is to include those agencies as merchant bankers which do what a merchant banker does.

To understand nature of merchant banking well, a contrast may be involved, between commercial banking and merchant banking. Although the terms 'Merchant' and 'Commercial' have similar connotations yet commercial banking and merchant banking are different. Commercial bankers are basically a financing agency where as merchant banks provide basically financial (not financing) services. Commercial bankers are comparatively retail banking activity where as merchant banking is a whole sale banking (even if it provides financing services also). A merchant banking firm does not undertake commercial banking whereas its, reverse is possible. Commercial banking involves collections of savings and putting it, to optimum use as per plans and guidelines whereas merchant banking refers to just an agency facilitating transfer capital from those who own to those who can use it without handling the amount of its own. Merchant bankers is more of an intermediary. In the same context, a merchant bank can be distinguished from a development bank since the latter is more involved in fund raising and lending. Like commercial banks, development banks may also have separate merchant banking division.

FUNCTIONS OF MERCHANT BANKER

Setting up of new industrial units, expansion, diversification and modernisation of existing units have been the central plank of the rapid industrialisation in any economy. This process besides adequate financial resources requires sound technical and managerial inputs. Though, a number of financial agencies are instituted to cater to the needs of rapid industrialisation, the task of financing has become more complicated, thus requiring a fresh look. In view of increasing specialisation in every sphere, the process of industrialisation from the primary planning stages of setting up a new unit to that of research and development including expansion, diversification or modernisation requires the services of specialists or professionals. Thus, the need for having expert advice, guidance of specialists or professionals in the field has become an absolute necessity with rapid economic growth and spectacular industrial development in India. It has also been necessitated by the plethora of regulations for industry, capital, issues, foreign investment and collaboration, amalgamations, Companies Act, SEBI, Government policy regarding backward area development, export promotion and import substitution etc. A few agencies are able to provide expert advice in the diversified areas mentioned above. But it is inconvenient to entrepreneurs industrialists to knock at the doors of several agencies in getting the guidance of specialists and professionals. Hence, it is highly essential to provide expert advice in diversified areas under a single roof to provide a comfortable cushion to entrepreneurs to accelerate industrial development. This is where merchant bankers come to picture. Although is it is very difficult to spell out all the areas where merchant bankers can interact, yet, some important areas where merchant bankers have decisive role are discussed here. These role can broadly be divided into two parts. One is **service based** another is **fund based.**

A. Service based Functions

Project Counselling

The first step to launch a business unit is selection of a viable project. Merchant bankers undertake this assignment on a very large scale since they have experts with them in diverse fields. Project counselling covers a variety of sub assignments. Illustrative list of services which can be rendered under this category is:

- Guidance in relation to project viability *i.e.*, project identification and counselling. It may be for setting up new units, expansion or improvement of existing facilities.
- Selection of consultants for preparation of project reports/market surveys etc. Sometimes merchant bankers also engage in preparation of project reports or market surveys.
- Advice on various procedural steps including obtaining of governmental approvals clearance etc. *e.g.,* for foreign collaboration.
- Proposing a suitable capital structure laying broad as well as specific features.
- Techno-economic soundness of the project and marketing aspects. Financial engineering *i.e.*, selection of right mix of financing pattern specifically for short-term requirements.
- Organisation and management set up for a strong base and efficient working of the project.

Credit Syndication

Normally, every project has to raise debt funds for different sources as per need. Substantial debt raising may be required for a new and capital intensive project. For such project merchant bankers may undertake credit syndication. Credit syndication is credit procurement service. As per the requirements, such syndication can be from national as well as international sources. Some of the important credit syndication services offered are.

- Preparing applications for financial assistance to be submitted to financial institutions and banks.
- Monitoring the sanction of funds while acting as a specialised liaison agency.
- Negotiating the term of assistance on behalf of client.
- Post-sanction formalities with these institutions and banks.
- Assistance in drawl of term loans and or bridging loans.
- Assessing working capital requirements and arranging it.

Need of syndication arises due to the fact that specially in big projects one institution may hesitate to meet the whole debt requirement of the project. They want to spread the risk. Further shortage of funds availability with one lender also requires credit syndication. The merchant banker by rendering credit syndication services saves the time of the borrower.

The modus operandi of a syndication is really quite simple. The borrower approaches several banks which might be willing to syndicate a loan, specifying the amount and the tenor for which loan is to be syndicated. On receiving a query, the syndicator scouts for banks who may be willing to participate in the syndicate. Based on an informal survey, it communicates its desire to syndicate the loan at an indicative price to the corporate borrower, all in a matter of days. After reviewing the bids from various banks, the borrower awards the mandate to the bank that offers him the best terms.

The syndicator, on his part, can underscore his willingness to syndicate the loan on a firm commitment basis or on a best-efforts basis. The former is akin to underwriting and will attract capital adequacy requirements. That may reduce the bank's flexibility. "In India, given fact that banks may not be willing to maintain capital in the interim period, most syndicates the likely to be done on a best-efforts basis."

Best-efforts, as the name suggests, limits the obligation of the syndicator, as he is not compelled to provide the loan on his own, in case he fails to arrange the loan.

However, more often than not, the syndicator would try to fulfill his commitments for the inability to do so would tarnish his reputation. Once the syndicator has been awarded a mandate, the borrower has to sign a 'clear market clause' which stops him from seeking a syndicated loan from any other bank, till such time as the documentation for the syndication is drawn up by the syndicate manager. This may take about three-four weeks.

In the interim period, the syndicate manager gets the banks to agree to syndicating the loan. It can do this on a 'broadcast' basis, by sending taxes to the concerned banks inviting participation. If the company is well known, the loan uncomplicated and the market liquid, such a method would work well. However, if the corporate tends to keep a low profile and the loan structure is complicated, the syndicate manager would have to woo the participant banks with offer documents or an information memorandum on the company. The document is similar to a prospects but less detailed. Nevertheless drawing up such a document does call for a lot of homework. The syndicate manager has to be very careful because he can be held responsible for any inaccuracy or omission of material facts.

The participants, after reviewing the prospects, decide whether or not to join the syndicate. However, given the fact that most of the participants may be smaller Indian banks, they may take weeks to give the final nod. Once the bank decides to become a member of the syndicate, it indicates the amount and the price that it is likely to charge on the loan. Based on information received from all participants, the syndicate manager prepares a common document to be signed by all the members of the syndicate and the borrowing company. The document usually lists out details of the agreement with regard to tenor, interest prepayment clause, security, covenants, warranties and agency clause.

Issue Management

Traditionally, this is one of the main functions of merchant banker. When ever an issue is made whether it is public issue or private placement and further whether it is for equity shares, preference shares or debentures, the merchant banker has a crucial role to play. Raising of funds from public has many dimensions and formalities which are not possible for the concerned. companies to comply with, where merchant banker comes to their rescue. Marketing effort to convince the prospective investor needs special attention. Here, again merchant bankers are specialists. The specific important activities related to issue management performed by merchant banks are mentioned here:

- Advise the company about the quantum and terms of raising funds.
- Advise as to what type of security may be acceptable in the market as well as to the concerned lending institutions at the time of issue.
- Advise as to whether a fresh issue to be made or right issue to be made or if both, then in what proportion, obtaining the desired consents, if any, from government or other authorities.
- Advice on the appointment of bankers, brokers to the issue.
- Advice on the selection of issue house or Registrar to the issue, printer advertising agency etc.
- Fixing the terms of the agencies engaged to facilitate making a public issue.
- Preparation of a complete action plan and budget for total expenses of the issue.
- Drafting of documents like prospectus, letter of offer and getting approval from concerned agencies.
- Assisting in advertisement campaigns, holding the press, brokers' and investors' conferences etc. for grooming the issue.
- Advise the company for the issue period and days of opening and closing the issue.
- Monitoring the collection of funds in public issue.
- Co-ordination with underwriters, brokers and bankers to the issue and stock exchange etc.
- Strict compliance of post-issue activities.

Corporate Counselling

Although the functions discussed up till now are also covered under corporate counselling but here other dimensions will be deliberated. Corporate counselling is to rejuvenate the corporate units which are otherwise having signals to low productivity, low efficiency and low profitability. The merchant bankers can play a substantial role in reviving the sick units. They make mergers and acquisition exercise smooth, They can advise on improvement in the systems operating in managing the show of a corporate unit. Some of the specific assignments for the merchant banker are:

- Rejuvenating old line and ailing/sick unit or appraising their technology and process, assessing their requirements and restructuring their capital base.
- Evolving rehabilitation programmes/packages which can be acceptable to the financial institutions and banks.
- Assisting in obtaining approvals from Board for Industrial and Financial Reconstruction (BIFR) and other authorities under the Sick Industrial Companies (special provisions) Act 1985 (SICA).
- Monitoring implementation of schemes of rehabilitation.
- Advice on financial restructuring involving redeployment of corporate assets to refocus companies line of business.
- Advice on rearranging the portfolio of business assets through acquisition etc.

- Assisting in valuing the assets and liabilities.
- Identifying potential buyers for disposal of assets if required. Identify the candidates for take over.
- Advice on tactics in approaching potential acquisition.
- Assisting in deciding the mode of acquisition whether friendly or unfriendly or hostile.
- Designing the transaction to reap the maximum tax advantages. Acting as an agent for leveraged buyout (LBO) involving heavy use of borrowed funds to purchase a company or division of a company.
- Facilitating Management Buy Outs (MBO) *i.e.,* selling a part of business to their own managers by a company.
- Clearly spelling out organisation goals.
- Evolving corporate strategies to achieve the laid down goals.
- Designing or restructuring the organisational pattern and size.
- Evolving Management Information System.

Corporate advisory services should offer real value addition to the client. Highly specialised in nature, these services should be clearly distinguished from the gamut of other financial services offered by NBFCs such as underwriting or fund-based activities of leasing and hire purchase. In India, corporate advisory has a good potential. The Indian industry is going through an unprecedented churning, bracing itself for global competition. The Indian corporate sector has been on a restructuring spree. Groups have been shedding companies. Companies in turn, have been dropping divisions as they struggle to become fit to survive in the new milieu. Free pricing of issues and the opportunity to tap the international market through the Euro-issue route has greatly enhanced the need for expert advisory services. In areas of restructuring, strategic alliances and corporate planning is now advising foreign companies in their plans for development of infrastructure in India. Merchant bankers have a great role to play.

Strategic product consolidation is another recent phenomenon. Units in which the company does not plan to become a market leader are spun off to others. A good corporate advisor is always on the alert to seize such opportunities. The process of acquisition cannot be done overnight. It requires a patient search for the right company which can be acquired, the proper evaluation of the financial impact of the acquisition, a sound strategy in blending the business acquired within the fold of the group, followed by negotiation and execution of the agreement. Occasionally, advisory services are required in cases of splits within the family group. In such cases, there is a need to split the company into different units amongst the disputing family members. At the same time, the shareholders interest is to be kept in mind by the corporate advisor.

Portfolio Management

Merchant bankers as a body of professionally qualified persons also undertake assignments of managing an individual investor's portfolio. Portfolio management is being practised as an investment management counselling in which the investor is advised to seek financial assets like government securities, commercial papers, debentures, shares, warranties etc. that would grow in value and/or provide income. The investors whether local or foreigner with substantial amount for investment in securities seek portfolio management services of authorised merchant bankers. The functioning of portfolio manager can be regulated or unregulated. Portfolio manager may use totally his discretion or may act only after getting signal from investor for each transaction of sale or purchase. A diverse range of services which may be rendered by merchant banker include:

- Advising what and when to sell and buy.
- Arranging sale or purchase of securities.
- Communicating changes in investment market to the client investor.
- Compliance of regulations of different regulating bodies for sale of purchase of portfolio.
- Collection of returns and reinvest as per directions of clients.
- Evaluating the portfolio at regular intervals or at direction of investors.
- Advising on tax matters pertaining to income from and investment in portfolio.
- Safe custody of securities.

Stock Broking and Dealership

The merchant bankers who have requisite professional knowledge and experience may also act as share broker on a stock exchange and even as dealer for Over The Counter Trading. To venture into this area, it is normally desired that the merchant banker has reasonable network. Their actions and activities are regulated by rules and regulations of the concerned stock exchange. They are at liberty to appoint sub-brokers and sub-dealers to ensure wider network of their operations. They can be broker for inland as well as foreign stock exchanges. In India, the merchant bankers who desire to act as brokers are regulated by SEBI (Stock Broker and Sub-brokers) Rules 1992.

Joint Venture Abroad

Depending on economic and political considerations many countries may permit joint ventures by local businessmen abroad. Here again merchant bankers can play a decisive role. They facilitate meeting of foreign partner, get sanctions under various provisions, make techno-economic surveys, legal documentations under local as well as foreign legal provisions etc.

Debenture Trusteeship

The merchant bankers can get themselves registered to act as trustee. These trustees are to protect the interests of debenture holders as per the terms laid down in trust deed. They are, as trustees, to undertake redressal of grievances of debenture holders. They are to ensure that refund moneys are paid and debenture certificates are dispatched in accordance with the Companies Act. Debenture trustees are expected to observe high standards of integrity and fairness in discharging their functions. They can call for periodical reports from the body corporate. They charge fee for such services.

B. Fund Based Functions

Bill Discounting

Bill discounting is a service against which merchant banker has to arrange funds against the bills which have been discounted. This service is undertaken by merchant bankers generally if bill market is big as well as mature. Otherwise bill discounting is undertaken by banks only. Depending on their credibility, they may also undertake the assignment of bill acceptance. These bills accepted and or discounted can be foreign and merchant bankers can specify what types of bills they entertain. They charge commission for these services.

Venture Capital

Venture capital is the organized financing of relatively new enterprises to achieve substantial capital gains. Such new companies are chosen because of their potential for considerable growth due to advance technology, new products or services or other valuable innovations. A high risk is implied in the term and is implicit in this type of investment. Since certain ingredients necessary for success of such projects are missing in the begging but are added later on. Merchant bankers undertake to arrange and if necessary, to provide such venture capital since traditional sources of finance like banks, financial institutions or public issue etc. may not be available. Since expected returns on projects involving venture capital is high, these are normally provided on soft terms. Such scheme is also popular as seed capital or risk capital scheme. Merchant bankers deeply study such proposals before releasing the money. At opportune time such investment can be disinvested to keep the cycle of venture capital more on.

Bought out Deals

When a promoter envisages that if public issue made to raise capital will not clinch, he may approach merchant bankers (bought out dealer or sponsor) and places the shares of company initially with him which are offered to public at a later stage, this route is known as bought out deal. Many a time a syndicate of merchant bankers jointly sponsor a bought out deal to spread the risk involved. In contrast to venture capital, there is no role to be played by non-traditional technology. Such bought shares by sponsor can be disposed off at an opportune time on 'over the counter' or other stock exchanges.

Lease Financing and Hire Purchase

Depending on the funds available, merchant bankers can also enter the field of lease or hire purchase financing. Lease is an agreement where by the lessor (merchant banker in our case) conveys to the lessee (the user), in return for rent, the right to use an asset for an agreed period of time. On the other hand in hire purchase the user at the end of the agreed period has an option to purchase the asset which he has used till date. The merchant bankers can advise the client to go in for leasing or hire purchase system of financing an asset. A comparative study may be communicated to the prospective client showing benefits of these alternatives. The client can also depend on merchant banker for acquiring the needed asset and complying with all formalities.

Factoring

Factoring is a novel financing innovation. It is a mixed service having financial as well as non-financial aspects. On one hand, it involves management and collection of books debts which arise in process of credit sale. The merchant bankers can take up this assignment and are required to perform activities like sales ledger administration, credit collection, credit protection, evolving credit policy, arranging letter of credit etc. On the other hand, there is involvement of finance. Against factored debts, the merchant banker may provide advance with a certain margin. The released funds can be used by client to manage its liquidity and working capital. Merchant bankers are entitled to service charges for factoring services. The merchant banker's role is thus to:

- maintain the books of accounts pertaining to credit sales.
- make a systematic analysis of relevant information for credit monitoring and control.
- provide full or partial protection against bad debts and accepting the risk of non-realization.
- provide financial assistance to the client.
- provide information about prospective buyers.
- provide financial counseling and assisting managing the liquidity.

Underwriting

It refers to a contract by means of which merchant banker gives an assurance to the issuing company that the former would subscribe to the securities offered in the event of non-subscription by the persons to whom it was offered. The liability of merchant banker arises if the issue is not fully subscribed and this liability is restricted to the commitment extended by him. The merchant bankers undertaking underwriting make efforts on their own to induce the prospective investors to subscribe to the concerned issue. Such assignment is accepted after evaluating viz.,

- Company's standing and its past record.
- Competence of the management.
- Purpose of the issue.
- Potentials of the project being financed.
- Offer price and terms of the issue.
- Business environment.

The financial involvement of merchant banker in underwriting arises in case of development. To get their blocked funds released, the merchant bankers have stock exchange as exit route. They get underwriting commission.

These are some of the prominent activities being undertaken by merchant bankers world over. The practices may differ from country to country depending on maturity of financial sector of their economy. The multifarious activities of the corporate sector and spectacular growth of industry gives new dimensions to merchant banking activities. In the phase of globalisation of economies merchant bankers are facing new challenges. The changing international financing environment has rather pushed merchant bankers to operate at international level creating more opportunities to serve the world business community in diverse ways.

MERCHANT BANKING REGULATIONS

SEBI (Merchant Bankers') Regulations 1992 define merchant banker as "any person who is engaged in the business of issue management either by making arrangements regarding selling, buying or subscribing to securities or acting as manager, consultant, adviser or rendering corporate advisory service in relation to such issue management." Thus, regulations are applicable only to limited activities undertaken by merchant banker. On the basis of regulations, merchant banking activities can be categorised as 'authorised' and 'not authorised' activities. The merchant bankers are required to get themselves registered under regulations only for authorized activities. The authorized activities are undertaking issue management assignment, as manager, consultant, adviser, underwriter portfolio manager.

(*a*) Merchant Banking Activities not Requiring SEBI's Registration are:

- Project Counselling
- Corporate Counselling
- Factoring
- Credit Rating
- Bill acceptance and discounting
- Loan syndication
- Merger and amalgamation.

(*b*) Merchant Banking Activities requiring SEBI's registration under different regulations but not under Merchant Banking regulations:

- Venture Capital
- Mutual Funds
- Depository
- Portfolio Management
- Trusteeship of debentures
- Share Broking
- Custodian Service
- Foreign Institution of Investor
- Share Transfer.

Another angle from which authorized activities can be identified is the activities specified for each categories of merchant banker.

Categories of Merchant Bankers

The merchant banking regulations require that any body seeking registration as merchant banker has to apply in one of the following four categories:

Category I : These merchant bankers can carry on any activity of the issue management, which will *inter-alia* consist of preparation of prospectus and other information relating to the issue, determining financial structure, tie up of financiers and final allotment and refund of subscription. They can also act as adviser, consultant, manager, underwriter, portfolio manager.

Category II : Such merchant bankers can act as adviser, consultant, co-manager, underwriter and portfolio manager. This means they can not undertake issue management of their own.

Category III : These merchant bankers can neither undertake issue management nor act as co-manager. They cannot conduct business of portfolio management. Thus, the area of their operation restricts to act as underwriter, adviser and consultant to the issue.

Category IV : Such merchant bankers do not undertake any activities requiring funds. They can act only as adviser or consultant to an issue.

Registration

Any agency to operate as merchant banker has to register it-self under SEBI Regulations. Application is to be submitted in the prescribed format. To get registration and certificate to operate as merchant banker, the agency has to fulfill two sets of criteria:

(*i*) Operational capabilities.

(*ii*) Capital adequacy.

(*i*) Operational Capabilities: As mentioned earlier, the regulations desire the merchant banker to be professional, fair and competent to serve investors. In this context, SEBI before granting 'certificate to operate as merchant banker' makes sure that concerned agency is competent on these parameters. To be more specific these are :

(*a*) It is necessary that to serve the clients and investors the merchant banker should have sufficient physical infrastructure. It is desired that the applicant has the necessary infrastructure like adequate office space, equipment and manpower to effectively discharge his activities.

(*b*) To ensure that services rendered are the best, SEBI desires the applicant to have at least two persons who have the experience to conduct the business of the merchant banker.

(*c*) In order to avoid excessive registration SEBI makes sure that a person directly or indirectly connected with the applicant has not been already granted registration. Such persons include an associate, subsidiary, interconnected or group company of the applicant.

(*d*) The applicant or his partner or director should be man of integrity. SEBI requires that applicant or its main officials should not be involved in any litigation connected with the securities market which has an adverse bearing on the business of the applicant.

- They should not at any time be convicted for any offence involving mortal turpitude or has been found guilty of any economic offence.
- The applicant is to have professional qualification from any recognized institution.
- SEBI is to make sure that such registration should be in the interest of investors.

Only those applicants who qualify on all these points are granted registration.

(*ii*) Capital Adequacy: In the categories where in fund based activities are involved, SEBI desires them to have sufficient capital. The concept of adequate capital is expressed in terms of 'net worth'. 'Net worth' means the value of capital contributed to the business plus free reserves. At the time of registration as well as subsequently following pattern of 'net worth' should be at least maintained:

Category of Merchant Banker	Minimum Networth
Category I	₹ 5,00,00,000
Category II	₹ 50,00,000
Category III	₹ 20,00,000
Category IV	NIL

Those applicants who qualify on both fronts are granted registration. The registered applicants are granted certificate of registration in 'Form B' in which SEBI specifies for which category registration has been granted. If the applicant is granted a category lower than applied for, the applicant is free to approach SEBI for higher category but within one year from date of such registration. When certificate is finally granted the registered merchant bankers are to submit required fees. Registration is granted for three years at one time. To keep the registration operative, merchant bankers are to pay registration fee. The registration fee pattern is as under:

Category	Fee for first two years	Third year
Category I	₹ 2.5 lakh per year	₹ 1 lakh
Category II	₹ 1.5 lakh per year	₹ 0.5 lakh
Category III	₹ 1 lakh per year	₹ 0.25 lakh
Category IV	₹ 5,000 per year	₹ 1,000.

Once registration granted is about to expire, merchant bankers are to get this registration renewed. Application for such renewal is again to be made. To ensure that there is no break in registration, such application has to be made within 3 months before the expiry of the certificate. Although it is termed as renewal, but application is processed as for new registration, that is why application is again made in 'Form A'. Once registration is renewed due fee is to be paid which is as under :

Category	Fee for first two years	Third year
Category I	₹ 1 lakh per year	₹ 0.2 lakh
Category II	₹ 0.75 lakh per year	₹ 0.1 lakh
Category III	₹ 0.50 lakh per year	₹ 0.05 lakh
Category IV	₹ 0.05 lakh per year	₹ 0.02 lakh

Code of Conduct

Once merchant bankers are registered to ensure that they maintain high standard of services, regulations require them to adhere to a code of conduct specified in the Schedule III of the Regulations while acting as merchant bankers. Some important provisions of code are as under:

- Maintain high standard of service.
- Exercise due diligence, ensure proper care and exercise independent professional judgement.
- Disclose to the clients, possible sources of conflicts of duties and interest while providing unbiased services.
- Conduct business observing high standard of integrity and fairness in all his dealings with clients and other merchant bankers.
- Maintain secrecy about client.
- Do not engage in unfair competition.
- Not to make misrepresentation.
- Provide true and adequate information to investors.
- Not to create false market or engage in price rigging.

Lead Manager

It is required under regulations that every issue should be managed by at least one merchant banker acting as 'lead manager'. Such lead manager is not required if:

- The issue is right issue.
- The size of issue is not exceeding rupees 50 lakh.

The merchant banker acting as lead manager must enter into an agreement with the concerned company. This agreement must state their mutual rights, liabilities and

as they become more aware and educated. Regulatory agencies go on amending their rules and regulations to discipline the merchant bankers. Such changes in regulations etc. may be more frequent till the time there is professional maturity. The fast development on technology front certainly improves the quality of services if adopted. Any one not changing as per technology is sure to lag behind. Innovations always pay in profession.

MERCHANT BANKING IN INDIA

Merchant banking in India has been given a specific direction by SEBI (Merchant Bankers) Regulation. Since their role in public issue is exhaustive and their responsibilities absolute, professional expertise is needed. Thus after SEBI, merchant bankers emerged from all segments of the economy. It was no longer a monopoly of institutional and banker merchant bankers. This is shown in the following Chart.

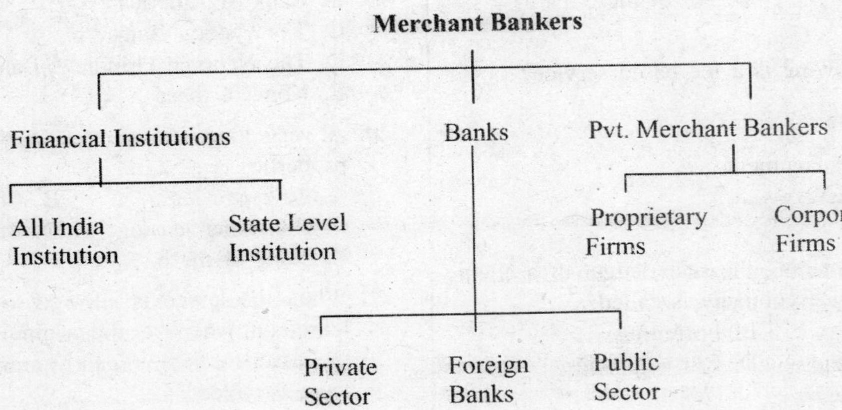

In simple terms, the merchant banking activity can be divided amongst four segments:

(*i*) Institutions like IDBI, ICICI, IFCI floated merchant banking subsidiaries or divisions.

(*ii*) Foreign banks like Grindlays, Standard Chartered, Honkong Bank, City Bank launched merchant banking divisions.

(*iii*) Nationalised banks promoted subsidiaries to carry out merchant banking activities like SBI Caps, PNB Caps, Canfina.

(*iv*) Private sector merchant bankers like JM, Kotak Mahindra, DSP, Master Trust who were either brokers or underwriters or portfolio managers.

MULTIPLE CHOICE QUESTIONS

1. The merchant banking activities in India are governed by which of the following bodies?
A. SEBI B. IRDA
C. RBI D. SBI
E. None of these

2. Merchant Banking comes into existence in India in:
A. 1971 B. 1964
C. 1965 D. 1967
E. 1968

3. Name of the bank which first time introduce the merchant banking in India is:
A. Imperial Bank of India
B. Grindlays Bank
C. United Bank
D. London Bank
E. None of these

4. Merchant Banks do not deals in:
A. providing services for mergers and acquisitions
B. regular banking services to the general public
C. long-term loans for companies
D. stock underwriting
E. None of these

5. The first foreign bank which introduced merchant bank in India is:
A. Grindlays bank B. HSBC
C. City bank D. Ceylon bank
E. None of these

6. The first Indian public sector bank which introduced its own merchant bank division in India:
A. Canara bank B. PNB
C. SBI D. Syndicate bank
E. None of these

7. Venture capital is originated in ....
A. India B. France
C. Britain D. USA
E. None of these

8. .... is considered to be the father of venture capital.
A. Dariot B. Vaghul
C. Modigliani D. Jimmy Carter
E. None of these

9. In the implementation stage of a project, venture capital firms provide .... finance.
A. Mezzanine finance B. Seed finance
C. Start up D. All of these
E. None of these

10. Which of the following is a fee based service?
A. hire purchase
B. leasing
C. capital issue management
D. underwriting
E. None of these

11. The process of managing the sales ledger of a client by a financial service company is called:
A. Factoring B. Forfeiting
C. Bill discounting D. Bill adjusting
E. None of these

12. Trade debts have to be assigned in favour of the financing company under:
A. discounting B. forfeiting
C. factoring D. all of these
E. None of these

13. Under factoring the factor acts in the capacity of:
A. an agent of his client B. a trustee
C. a holder for value D. An administrator
E. None of these

14. The first bank in India to start factoring business is:
A. Canara bank
B. SBI
C. Punjab National Bank
D. Allahabad Bank
E. None of these

15. In an option contract, if the option can be exercised only at the time of maturity, it is called ....
A. Double option B. American option
C. Put option. D. European option
E. None of these

16. The predetermined price at which an underlying asset has to be bought or sold in an option contract is called ....
A. Option price B. Exercise price
C. Spot price D. Future price
E. None of these

17. Combination of forwards by two counterparties with opposite but matching need is called:
A. Swap B. Option
C. Forward D. Future
E. None of these

18. The first Indian Bank to set up Merchant Banking division in India is ....
A. UCO Bank B. State Bank of India
C. ICICI D. Punjab National Bank
E. None of these

19. The first foreign bank which started Merchant Banking services in India is ....
A. City Bank
B. Bank of America
C. The Federal Bank
D. The National Grindlays Bank
E. None of these

20. A very long tenure lease applicable to immovable properties is ....
A. Leverage lease B. Conveyance lease
C. Consumer leasing D. Balloon lease
E. None of these

21. When the lessee is allowed to exchange equipment leased out whenever the original asset has to be sent to the lessor for some repair or maintenance, such type of lease is called ....
A. Wrap lease B. Import lease
C. Swap lease D. Leveraged lease
E. None of these

22. Refactoring charges have to be paid in the case of ....
A. Maturity factoring
B. With recourse factoring
C. Invoice factoring
D. Full service factoring
E. None of these

23. The concept of securitisation is associated with ....
A. Capital market
B. Money market
C. Debt market
D. Foreign exchange market
E. None of these

24. In the case of securitisation, the trade debts and receivables are mostly in the nature of ....
A. Short-term
B. Medium-term
C. Long-term
D. Both medium-term and long-term
E. None of these

25. Under securitisation, selected pool of assets are 'passed through', for converting them into securities, to another institution called:
A. Originator
B. Special purpose vehicle
C. Credit rating company
D. Servicing agent
E. None of these

26. Which one of the following is a short-term debt instrument?
A. Preferred stock certificate
B. Pass through certificate
C. Asset based commercial certificate
D. Principal only certificate
E. None of these

27. The asset generally not suitable for securitisation is ....
A. Receivables from government department
B. Trade receivables
C. Hire purchase finance receivables
D. Mortgage loans
E. None of these

28. .... is the venture capital assistance at the stage where the project started to fetch profit but not reached in its full efficiency.
A. Start up capital B. Mezzanine capital
C. Bridge capital D. Seed capital
E. None of these

29. In .... leasing, the risk of obsolescence is assumed by the lessee.
A. Financial lease B. Operating lease
C. Both the above D. Mortgage
E. None the above

30. .... is a tripartite lease arrangement:
A. Financial lease B. Operating lease
C. Leverage lease D. Sale and lease back
E. None of these

31. In hire purchase depreciation can be claimed by the:
A. Hirer B. Vendor
C. Financiers D. All of these
E. None of these

32. Equipment leasing is .... financial service.
A. fund based B. fee based
C. non-fund based D. any of the above
E. None of these

33. Managing the capital issue is .... financial services.
A. fund based B. fee based
C. non-fund based D. both B and C
E. None of these

34. Fee based financial services are also known as...........
A. fund based B. capital based
C. non-fund based D. cash based
E. None of these

35. .... is the design, the development and the implementation of innovative financial instruments and processes and the formulation of creative solutions to problem of finance.
A. Financial services B. Financial inclusion
C. Financial engineering D. Financial innovation
E. None of these

36. .... is more or less similar to "Consortium financing".
A. Merchant banking B. Retail banking
C. Whole sale banking D. Loan syndication
E. None of these

37. .... bonds are issued at a large discount to their nominal value.
A. Option bond
B. Index-linked guilt bond
C. Variable rate bond
D. Deep discount bond
E. None of these

38. .... is referred as both fund based and fee based financial service.
A. Hire purchase B. Leasing
C. Factoring D. Underwriting
E. None of these

39. Hire Purchase Act passed in the year:
A. 1969 B. 1982
C. 1972 D. 1976
E. None of these

40. .... supplies machinery to small scale industries under hire purchase system.
A. IDBI B. SIDMI
C. NSIC D. DIC
E. None of these

41. In India, Banks are permitted to carry on Hire purchase business:
A. Directly
B. Through its Departments
C. Through subsidiary
D. Any of the above
E. None of these

42. "Confidential invoice discounting" is another name of
A. Maturity factoring
B. Disclosed factoring
C. Undisclosed factoring
D. Notified factoring
E. None of these

43. Financial lease introduced in India by..................
A. Tata group
B. Reliance group
C. Chidambaram group
D. Murugappa group
E. None of these

44. The sale of a mortgage portfolio by setting up mortgage pass-through securities is an example of ....
A. Credit enhancement B. Securitization
C. Unbundling D. Derivatives
E. None of these

45. Merchant bankers perform the following role(s) ....
A. Market new stock and bond issues for firms.

B. Provide advice to the firms as to market conditions, price, etc.
C. Provide consultancy services for expansion etc.
D. All of the above
E. None of these

46. The means by which individuals hold their claims on real assets in a well-developed economy are ....
A. Investment assets B. Depository assets
C. Derivative assets D. Financial assets
E. None of these

47. Under "securitisation process", organisation which gives insurance and guarantee is known as:
A. SPV B. Obligor
C. Originator D. Credit enhancer
E. None of these

48. Leased asset is shown in the balance sheet of.................
A. Lessee
B. Lessor
C. Lender
D. Both lessor and lessee in 50:50 ratio
E. None of these

49. Who can claim investment allowance in relation to leased asset?
A. Lessee
B. Lessor
C. Lender
D. Both lessor and lessee in 50:50 ratio
E. None of these

50. An average lease agreement involves............
A. Two parties B. Three parties
C. Four parties D. Either B or C
E. None of these

51. .... Leasing companies are formed to promote the sale of its parent company.
A. Leverage B. Financial
C. Vendor D. Swap
E. None of these

52. .... fund generates regular income to the investors on periodical basis.
A. Balanced fund B. Income fund
C. Growth fund D. All of these
E. None of these

53. Merchant banking involves:
A. advisory services B. issue management
C. market operations D. all of these
E. None of these

54. Merchant banking functions does not include:
A. issue management
B. portfolio management services
C. market operations
D. accepting deposits and lending money
E. None of these

ANSWERS

1	2	3	4	5	6	7	8	9	10
A	D	B	B	A	C	D	A	C	C
11	**12**	**13**	**14**	**15**	**16**	**17**	**18**	**19**	**20**
A	C	C	B	D	B	A	B	D	B
21	**22**	**23**	**24**	**25**	**26**	**27**	**28**	**29**	**30**
C	B	C	D	B	A	B	B	A	C
31	**32**	**33**	**34**	**35**	**36**	**37**	**38**	**39**	**40**
A	A	D	C	C	D	D	D	C	C
41	**42**	**43**	**44**	**45**	**46**	**47**	**48**	**49**	**50**
C	C	C	B	D	D	D	B	B	A
51	**52**	**53**	**54**						
C	B	D	D						

15

Mutual Funds

INTRODUCTION

A mutual fund is a financial intermediary that pools the savings of investors for collective investment in a diversified portfolio of securities. A fund is "mutual" as all of its returns, minus its expenses, are shared by the fund's investors.

The Securities and Exchange Board of India (Mutual Funds) Regulations, 1996 defines a mutual fund as 'a fund established in the form of a trust to raise money through the sale of units to the public or a section of the public under one or more schemes for investing in securities, including money market instruments'.

According to the above definition, a mutual fund in India can raise resources through sale of units to the public. It can be set up in the form of a Trust under the Indian Trust Act. The definition has been further extended by allowing mutual funds to diversify their activities in the following areas:

- Portfolio management services
- Management of offshore funds
- Providing advice to offshore funds
- Management of pension or provident funds
- Management of venture capital funds
- Management of money market funds
- Management of real estate funds.

A mutual fund serves as a link between the investor and the securities market by mobilising savings from the investors and investing them in the securities market to generate returns. Thus, a mutual fund is akin to portfolio management services (PMS). Although, both are conceptually same, they are different from each other. Portfolio management services are offered to high net worth individuals; taking into account their risk profile, their investments are managed separately. In the case of mutual funds, savings of small investors are pooled under a scheme and the returns are distributed in the same proportion in which the investments are made by the investors/unit-holders.

Mutual fund is a collective savings scheme. Mutual funds play an important role in mobilising the savings of small investors and channelising the same for productive ventures in the Indian economy.

Benefits of Mutual Funds

An investor can invest directly in individual securities or indirectly through a financial intermediary. Globally, mutual funds have established themselves as the means of investment for the retail investor.

1. Professional management: An average investor lacks the knowledge of capital market operations and does not have large resources to reap the benefits of investment. Hence, he requires the help of an expert. It is not only expensive to 'hire the services' of an expert but also it is more difficult to identify a real expert. Mutual funds are managed by professional managers, who have the requisite skills and experience to analyse the performance and prospects of companies. They make possible an organised investment strategy, which is hardly possible for an individual investor.

2. Portfolio diversification: An investor undertakes risk if he invests all his funds in a single scrip. Mutual funds invest in a number of companies across various industries and sectors. This diversification reduces the riskiness of the investments.

3. Reduction in transaction costs: Compared to direct investing in the capital market, investing through the funds is relatively less expensive as the benefit of economies of scale is passed on to the investors.

4. Liquidity: Often, investors cannot sell the securities held easily, while in case of mutual funds, they can easily encash their investment by selling their units to the fund if it is an open-ended scheme or selling them on a stock exchange if it is a close-ended scheme.

5. Convenience: Investing in mutual fund reduces paperwork, saves time and makes investment easy.

6. Flexibility: Mutual funds offer a family of schemes, and investors have the option of transferring their holdings from one scheme to the other.

7. Tax benefits: Mutual fund investors now enjoy income-tax benefits. Dividends received from mutual funds' debt schemes are tax exempt to the overall limit of ₹ 9,000 allowed under Section 80L of the Income Tax Act.

8. Transparency: Mutual funds transparently declare their portfolio every month. Thus, an investor knows where his/her money is being deployed and in case they are not happy with the portfolio they can withdraw at a short notice.

9. Stability to the stock market: Mutual funds have a large amount of funds which provide them economies of scale by which they can absorb any losses in the stock market and continue investing in the stock market. In addition, mutual funds increase liquidity in the money and capital market.

10. Equity research: Mutual funds can afford information and data required for investments as they have large amount of funds and equity research teams available with them.

HISTORY OF MUTUAL FUNDS

The history of mutual funds, dates back to 19th century Europe, in particular, Great Britain. Robert Fleming set up in 1868 the first investment trust called Foreign and Colonial Investment Trust which promised to manage the finances of the moneyed classes of Scotland by spreading the investment over a number of different stocks. This investment trust and other investment trusts which were subsequently set up in Britain and the US, resembled today's close-ended mutual funds. The first mutual fund in the US, Massachusetts Investors' Trust, was set up in March 1924. This was the first open-ended mutual fund.

The stock market crash in 1929, the Great Depression, and the outbreak of the Second World War slackened the pace of growth of the mutual fund industry. Innovations in products and services increased the popularity of mutual funds in the 1950s and 1960s. The first international stock mutual fund was introduced in the US in 1940. In 1976, the first tax-exempt municipal bond funds emerged and in 1979, the first money market mutual funds were created. The latest additions are the international bond fund in 1986 and arm funds in 1990. This industry witnessed substantial growth in the eighties and nineties when there was a significant increase in the number of mutual funds, schemes, assets, and shareholders. In the US, the mutual fund industry registered a ten fold growth in the eighties (1980-89) only, with 25% of the household sector's investment in financial assets made through them. Fund assets increased from less than $150 billion in 1980 to over $4 trillion by the end of 1997. Since 1996, mutual fund assets have exceeded bank deposits. The mutual fund industry and the banking industry virtually rival each other in size.

GROWTH OF MUTUAL FUNDS IN INDIA

The Indian mutual fund industry has evolved over distinct stages. The growth of the mutual fund industry in India can be divided into four phases: Phase I (1964-87), Phase II (1987-92), Phase III (1992-97), and Phase IV (beyond 1997).

Phase I: The mutual fund concept was introduced in India with the setting up of UTI in 1963. The Unit Trust of India (UTI) was the first mutual fund set up under the UTI Act, 1963, a special Act of the Parliament. It became operational in 1964 with a major objective of mobilising savings through the sale of units and investing them in corporate securities for maximising yield and capital appreciation. This phase commenced with the launch of Unit Scheme 1964 (US-64) the first open-ended and the most popular scheme. UTI's investible funds, at market value (and including the book value of fixed assets) grew from ₹ 49 crore in 1965 to ₹ 219 crore in 1970-71 to ₹ 1,126 crore in 1980-81 and further to ₹ 5,068 crore by June 1987. Its investor base had also grown to about 2 million investors. It launched innovative schemes during this phase. Its fund family included five income-oriented, open-ended schemes, which were sold largely through its agent network built up over the years. Master share, the equity growth fund launched in 1986, proved to be a grand marketing success. Master share was the first real close-ended scheme floated by UTI. It launched India Fund in 1986-the first Indian offshore fund for overseas investors, which was listed on the London Stock Exchange (LSE). UTI maintained its monopoly and experienced a consistent growth till 1987.

Phase II: The second phase witnessed the entry of mutual fund companies sponsored by nationalised banks and insurance companies. In 1987, SBI Mutual Fund and Canbank Mutual Fund were set up as trusts under the Indian Trust Act, 1882. In 1988, UTI floated another offshore fund, namely, The India Growth Fund which was listed on the New York Stock Exchange (NYSB). By 1990, the two nationalised insurance giants, LIC and GIC, and nationalised banks, namely, Indian Bank, Bank of India, and Punjab National Bank had started operations of wholly-owned mutual fund subsidiaries. The assured return type of schemes floated by the mutual funds during this phase were perceived to be another banking product offered by the arms of sponsor banks. In October 1989, the first regulatory guidelines were issued by the Reserve Bank of India, but they were applicable only to the mutual funds sponsored by FIIs. Subsequently, the Government of India issued comprehensive guidelines in June 1990 covering all 'mutual funds'. These guidelines emphasised compulsory registration with SEBI and an arms length relationship be maintained between the sponsor and asset management company (AMC). With the entry of public sector funds, there was a tremendous growth in the size of the mutual fund industry with investible funds, at market value, increasing to ₹ 53,462 crore and the number of investors increasing to over 23 million. The buoyant equity markets in 1991-92 and tax benefits under equity-linked savings schemes enhanced the attractiveness of equity funds.

Phase III: The year 1993 marked a turning point in the history of mutual funds in India. The Securities and Exchange Board of India (SEBI) issued the Mutual Fund Regulations in January 1993. SEBI notified regulations bringing all mutual funds except UTI under a common regulatory framework. Private domestic and foreign players were allowed entry in the mutual fund industry. Kothari group of companies, in joint venture with Pioneer, a US fund company, set up the first private mutual fund the Kothari Pioneer Mutual Fund, in 1993. Kothari Pioneer introduced the first open-ended fund Prima in 1993. Several other private sector mutual funds were set up during this phase. UTI launched a new scheme, Master-gain, in May 1992, which was a phenomenal success with a subscription of ₹ 4,700 crore from 631akh applicants. The industry's investible funds at market value increased to ₹ 78,655 crore and the number of investor accounts increased to 50 million. However, the year 1995 was the beginning of the sluggish phase of the mutual fund industry. During 1995 and 1996, unit holders saw an erosion in the value of their investments due to a decline in the NAVs of the equity funds. Moreover, the service quality of mutual funds declined due to a rapid growth in the number of investor accounts, and the inadequacy of service infrastructure. A lack of performance of the public sector funds and miserable failure of foreign funds like Morgan Stanley eroded the confidence of investors in fund managers. Investors perception about mutual funds, gradually turned negative. Mutual funds found it increasingly difficult to raise money. The average annual sales declined from about ₹ 13,000 crore in 1991-94 to about ₹ 9,000 crore in 1995 and 1996.

Phase IV: During this phase, the flow of funds into the kitty of mutual funds sharply increased. This significant growth was aided by a more positive sentiment in the capital market, significant tax benefits, and improvement in the quality of investor service.

ORGANIZATION STRUCTURE OF MUTUAL FUNDS

Mutual funds have organization structure as per the Security Exchange Board of India guidelines, Security Exchange Board of India specified authority and responsibility of Trustee and Asset Management Companies. The objectives is to controlling, to promoted, to regulate, to protected the investors right and efficient trading of units. Operation of Mutual fund starts with investors save their money on mutual fund, than Mutual Fund manager handling the funds and strategic investment on scrip. As per the objectives of particular scheme manager selected scrips. Unit value will become high when fund manager investment policy generate the return on capital market. Unit return depends on fund return and efficient capital market. Also affects international capital market, liquidity and at last economic policy. Below the graph indicates how the process was going on to investors to earn returns. Mutual fund manager having high responsibility inside of return and how to minimize the risk. When fund provided high return with high risk, investors attract to invest more fund for same scheme.

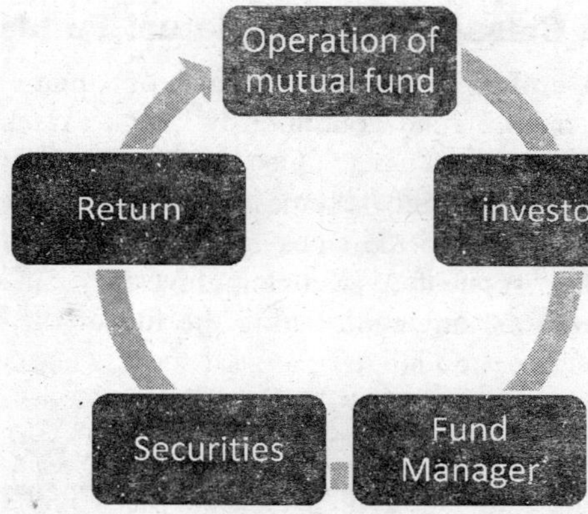

The Mutual fund organization as per the SEBI formation and necessary formation is needed for sooth activities of the companies and achieved the desire objectives. Transfer agent and custodian play role for dematerialization of the fund and unit holders hold the account statement, but custody of the unit is on particular Asset Management Company. Custodian holds all the fund units on dematerialization form. Sponsor had decided the responsibility of custodian when investor to purchase the fund and to sell the unit. Application forms, transaction slip and other requests received by transfer agent, middle men between investors and Assts Management Companies.

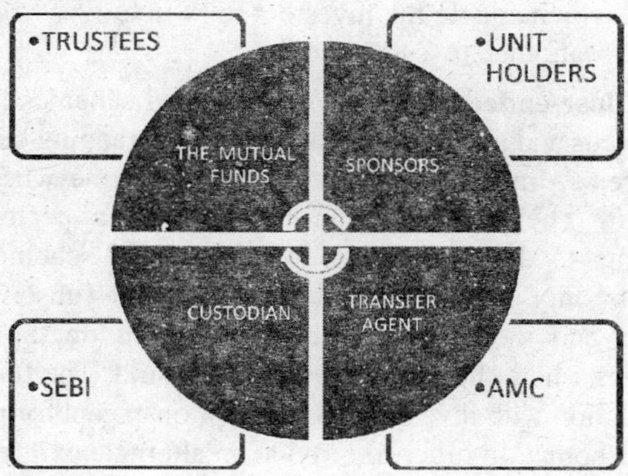

TYPES OF MUTUAL FUND SCHEMES

The objectives of mutual funds are to provide continuous liquidity and higher yields with high degree of safety to investors. Based on these objectives, different types of mutual fund schemes have evolved.

Types of Mutual Fund Schemes

Functional	*Portfolio*	*Geographical*	*Other*
Open-Ended Event	Income Funds	Domestic	Sectoral Specific
Close-Ended Scheme	Growth Funds	Off-shore	Tax Saving
Interval Scheme	Balanced Funds		ELSS
	Money Market		Special
	Mutual Funds		Gilt Funds Load Funds Index Funds
			ETFs PIE Ratio Fund

Functional Classification of Mutual Funds

1. Open-ended schemes: In case of open-ended schemes, the mutual fund continuously offers to sell and repurchase its units at net asset value (NAV) or NAV-related prices. Unlike close-ended schemes, open-ended ones do not have to be listed on the stock exchange and can also offer repurchase soon after allotment. Investors can enter and exit the scheme any time during the life of the fund. Open-ended schemes do not have a fixed corpus. The corpus of fund increases or decreases, depending on the purchase or redemption of units by investors.

There is no fixed redemption period in open-ended schemes, which can be terminated whenever the need arises. The fund offers a redemption price at which the holder can sell units to the fund and exit. Besides, an investor can enter the fund again by buying units from the fund at its offer price. Such funds announce sale and repurchase prices from time-to-time. UTI's US-64 scheme is an example of such a fund.

The key feature of open-ended funds is liquidity. They increase liquidity of the investors as the units can be continuously bought and sold. The investors can develop their income or saving plan due to free entry and exit frame of funds. Open-ended schemes usually come as a family of schemes which enable the investors to switch over from one scheme to another of same family.

2. Close-ended schemes: Close-ended schemes have a fixed corpus and a stipulated maturity period ranging between 2 to 5 years. Investors can invest in the scheme when it is launched. The scheme remains open for a period not exceeding 45 days. Investors in close-ended schemes can buy units only from the market, once initial subscriptions are over and thereafter the units are listed on the stock exchanges where they can be bought and sold. The fund has no interaction with investors till redemption except for paying dividend/bonus. In order to provide an alternate exit route to the investors, some close-ended funds give an option of selling back the units to the mutual fund through periodic repurchase at NAV related prices. If an investor sells units directly to the fund, he cannot enter the fund again, as units bought back by the fund cannot be reissued. The close-ended scheme can be converted into an open-ended one. The units can be rolled over by the passing of a resolution by a majority of the unit-holders.

3. Interval scheme: Interval scheme combines the features of open-ended and close-ended schemes. They are open for sale or redemption during pre-determined intervals at NAV related prices.

Portfolio Classification

Here, classification is on the basis of nature and types of securities and objective of investment.

1. Income funds: The aim of income funds is to provide safety of investments and regular income to investors. Such schemes invest predominantly in income-bearing instruments like bonds, debentures, government securities, and commercial paper. The return as well as the risk are lower in income funds as compared to growth funds.

2. Growth funds: The main objective of growth funds is capital appreciation over the medium-to-long- term. They invest most of the corpus in equity shares with significant growth potential and they offer higher return to investors in the long-term. They assume the risks associated with equity investments. There is no guarantee or assurance of returns. These schemes are usually close-ended and listed on stock exchanges.

3. Balanced funds: The aim of balanced scheme is to provide both capital appreciation and regular income. They divide their investment between equity shares and fixed nicebearing instruments in such a proportion that, the portfolio is balanced. The portfolio of such funds usually comprises of companies with good profit and dividend track records. Their exposure to risk is moderate and they offer a reasonable rate of return.

4. Money market mutual funds: They specialise in investing in short-term money market instruments like treasury bills, and certificate of deposits. The objective of such funds is high liquidity with low rate of return.

Geographical Classification

1. Domestic funds: Funds which mobilise resources from a particular geographical locality like a country or region are domestic funds. The market is limited and confined to the boundaries of a nation in which the fund operates. They can invest only in the securities which are issued and traded in the domestic financial markets.

2. Offshore funds: Offshore funds attract foreign capital for investment in the country of the issuing company. They facilitate cross-border fund flow which leads to an increase in foreign currency and foreign exchange reserves. Such mutual funds can invest in securities of foreign companies. They open domestic capital market to international investors. Many mutual funds in India have launched a number of offshore funds, either independently or jointly with foreign investment management companies. The first offshore fund, the India Fund, was launched by Unit Trust of India in July 1986 in collaboration with the US fund manager, Merril Lynch.

Others

1. Sectoral: These funds invest in specific core sectors like energy, telecommunications, IT, construction, transportation, and financial services. Some of these newly opened-up sectors offer good investment potential.

2. Tax-saving schemes: Tax-saving schemes are designed on the basis of tax policy with special tax incentives to investors. Mutual funds have introduced a number of tax-saving schemes. These are close-ended schemes and investments are made for ten years, although investors can avail of encashment facilities after 3 years. These schemes contain various options like income, growth or capital application. The latest scheme offered is the Systematic Withdrawal Plan (SWP) which enables investors to reduce their tax incidence on dividends from as high as 30% to as low as 3 to 4%.

3. Equity-linked savings scheme (ELSS): In order to encourage investors to invest in equity market, the government has given tax-concessions through special schemes. Investment in these schemes entitles the investor to claim an income tax rebate, but these schemes carry a lock-in period before the end of which funds cannot be withdrawn.

4. Special schemes: Mutual funds have launched special schemes to cater to the special needs of investors. UTI has launched special schemes such as Children's Gift Growth Fund, 1986, Housing Unit Scheme, 1992, and Venture Capital Funds.

5. Gilt funds: Mutual funds which deal exclusively in gilts are called gilt funds. With a view to creating a wider investor base for government securities, the Reserve Bank of India encouraged setting up of gilt funds. These funds are provided liquidity support by the Reserve Bank.

6. Load funds: Mutual funds incur certain expenses such as brokerage, marketing expenses, and communication expenses. These expenses are known as 'load' and are recovered by the fund when it sells the units to investors or repurchases the units from withholders. In other words, load is a sales charge, or commission, assessed by certain mutual funds to cover their selling costs.

Loads can be of two types—Front-end-load and back-end-load. Front-end-load, or sale load, is a charge collected at the time when an investor enters into the scheme. Back-end, or repurchase, load is a charge collected when the investor gets out of the scheme. Schemes that do not charge a load are called 'No load' schemes. In other words, if the asset management company (AMC) bears the load during the initial launch of the scheme, then these schemes are known as no-load schemes. However, these no-load schemes can have an exit load when the unit holder gets out of the scheme before a stipulated period mentioned in the initial offer. This is done to prevent short-term investments and redemptions. Some funds may also charge different amount of loads to investors depending upon the time period the investor has stayed with the funds. The longer the investor stays with the fund, less is the amount of exit load charged. This is known as contingent deferred sales' charge (CDSL). It is a back-end (exit load) fee imposed by certain funds on shares redeemed with a specific period following their purchase and is usually assessed on a sliding scale.

7. Index funds: An index fund is a mutual fund which invests in securities in the index on which it is based BSE Sensex or S&P CNX Nifty. It invests only in those shares which comprise the market index and in exactly the same proportion as the companies/weightage in the index so that the value of such index funds varies with the market index. An index fund follows a passive investment strategy as no effort is made by the fund manager to identify stocks for investment/dis-investment. The fund manager has to merely track the index on which it is based. His portfolio will need an adjustment in case there is a revision in the underlying index. In other words, the fund manager has to buy stocks which are added to the index and sell stocks which are deleted from the index.

Internationally, index funds are very popular. Around one-third of professionally run portfolios in the US are index funds. Empirical evidence points out that active fund managers have not been able to perform well. Only 20-25% of actively managed equity mutual funds out-perform benchmark indices in the long-term. These active fund managers park 80% of their money in an index and do active management on the remaining 20%. Moreover, risk averse investors like provident funds and pension funds prefer investment in passively managed funds like index funds.

8. PIE ratio fund: PIE ratio fund is another mutual fund variant that is offered by Pioneer IT! Mutual Fund. The PIE (Price-Earnings) ratio is the ratio of the price of the stock of a company to its earnings per share (EPS). The PIE ratio of the index is the weighted average price-earnings ratio of all its constituent stocks.

The PIE ratio fund invests in equities and debt instruments wherein the proportion of the investment is determined by the ongoing price-earnings multiple of the market. Broadly, around 90% of the investible funds will be invested in equity if the Nifty Index PIE ratio is 12 or below. If this ratio exceeds 28, the investment will be in debt/money markets. Between the two ends of 12 and 28 PIE ratio of the Nifty, the fund will allocate varying proportions of its investible funds to equity and debt. The objective of this scheme is to provide superior risk-adjusted returns through a balanced portfolio of equity and debt instruments.

9. Exchange traded funds: Exchange Traded Funds (ETFs) are a hybrid of open-ended mutual funds and listed individual stocks. They are listed on stock exchanges and trade like individual stocks on the stock exchange. However, trading at the stock exchanges does not affect their portfolio. ETFs do not sell their shares directly to investors for cash. The shares are offered to investors over the stock exchange. ETFs are basically passively managed funds that track a particular index such as S&P CNX Nifty.

Since they are listed on stock exchanges, it is possible to buy and sell them throughout the day and their price is determined by the demand-supply forces in the market. In practice, they trade in a small range around the value of the assets (NAV) held by them.

ETFs offer several distinct advantages.

- ETFs bring the trading and real time pricing advantages of individual stocks to mutual funds. The ability to trade intra-day at prices that are usually close to the actual intra-day NAV of the scheme makes it almost real-time trading.
- ETFs are simpler to understand and hence they can attract small investors who are deterred to trade in index futures due to requirement of minimum contract size. Small investors can buy minimum one unit of ETF, can place limit orders and trade intra-day. This, in turn, would increase liquidity of the cash market.
- ETFs can be used to arbitrate effectively between index futures and spot index.
- ETFs provide the benefits of diversified index funds. The investor can benefit from the flexibility of stocks as well as the diversification.
- ETFs being passively managed, have somewhat higher NAV against an index fund of the same portfolio. The operating expenses of ETFs are lower than even those of similar index funds as they do not have to service investors who deal in shares through stock exchanges.
- ETFs can be beneficial for financial institutions also. Financial institutions can use ETFs for utilizing idle cash, managing redemptions, modifying sector allocations, and hedging market exposure.

The first exchange traded fund-Standard and Poor's Depository Receipt (SPDR-also called Spider)-was launched in the US in 1993. ETFs have grown rapidly with around US$100 billion in assets as on December 2001. Today, about 60% of trading value on the American Stock Exchange (AMEX) is from ETFs. ETFs were launched in Europe and Asia in 2001. Currently, more than 120 ETFs are available in US, Europe, Singapore, Hongkong, Japan, and other countries. Among the popular ones are SPDRs (Spiders) based on the S&P 500 Index, QQQs (cubes) based on the Nasdaq-100 Index, i SHARES based on MSCI Indices and TRAHK (Tracks) based on the Hang Seng Index. The ETF structure has seen over $120 bn pouring into it in more than 220 funds. It has become the fastest growing fund structure. In year 2001 alone, the number of funds doubled from 100 to 200.

The first ETF to be introduced in India is Nifty Bench mark Exchange-Traded Scheme (*Nifty* BeES). It is an open-ended ETF, launched towards the end of 2001 by Benchmark Mutual Funds. The fund is listed in the capital market segment of the NSE and trades the S&P CNX Nifty Index. The Benchmark Asset Management Company has become the first company in Asia (excluding Japan) to introduce ETF.

RISKS ASSOCIATED WITH MUTUAL FUNDS

Mutual Funds are not free from risks. It is so because basically the mutual funds also invest their funds in the stock market on shares which are volatile in nature and are not risk free. Hence, the following risk are inherent in their dealings :

(*i*) **Market Risks:** In general, there are certain risks associated with every kind of investment on shares. They are called market risks. These market risks can be reduced, but cannot be completely eliminated even by a good investment management. The prices of shares are subject to wide price fluctuations depending upon market conditions over which nobody has a control. Moreover, every economy has to pass through a cycle-boom, recession, slump and recovery. The phase of the business cycle affects the market conditions to a larger extent.

(*ii*) **Scheme Risks:** There are certain risks inherent in the scheme itself. It all depends upon the nature of the scheme. For instance, in a pure growth scheme, risks are greater. It is obvious because if one expects more returns as in the case of a growth scheme, one has to take more risks.

(*iii*) **Investment Risk:** Whether the Mutual Fund makes money in shares or loses depends upon the investment expertise of the Asset Management Company (AMC). If the investment advice goes wrong, the fund has to suffer a lot. The investment expertise of various funds are different and it is reflected on the returns which they offer to investors.

(*iv*) **Business Risk:** The corpus of a mutual fund might have been invested in a company's shares. If the business of that company suffers any set back, it cannot declare any dividend. It may even go to the extent of winding up its business. Though the mutual fund can withstand such a risk, its income paying capacity is affected.

(*v*) **Political Risks:** Successive Governments bring with them fancy new economic ideologies and policies. It is often said that many economic decisions are politically motivated. Changes in Government bring in the risk of uncertainty which every player in the financial service industry has to face. So mutual funds are no exception to it.

ORGANIZATION OF THE FUND

The structure of mutual fund operations in India envisages a three tier establishment namely:

(*i*) A sponsor institution to promote the fund

(*ii*) A team of trustees to oversee the operations and to provide checks for the efficient, profitable and transparent operations of the fund, and

(*iii*) An Asset Management Company (AMC) to actually deal with the funds.

Sponsoring Institution: The company which sets up the Mutual Fund is called the sponsor. The SEBI has laid down certain criteria to be met by the sponsor. These criteria mainly deal with adequate experience, good past track record, net worth etc.

Trustees: Trustees are people with long experience and good integrity in their respective fields. They carry the crucial responsibility of safeguarding the interest of investors. For this purpose, they monitor the operations of the different schemes. They have wide ranging powers and they can even dismiss Asset Management Companies with the approval of the SEBI.

Asset Management Company (AMC): The AMC actually manages the funds of the various schemes. The AMC employs a large number of professionals to make investments, carry out research and to do agent and investor servicing. In fact, the success of any Mutual Fund depends upon the efficiency of this AMC. The AMC submits a quarterly report on the functioning of the mutual fund to the trustees who will guide and control the AMC.

OPERATION OF THE FUND

A mutual fund invites the prospective investors to join the fund by offering various schemes so as to suit to the requirements of different categories of investors. The resources of individual investors are pooled together and the investors are issued units/shares for the money invested. The amount so collected is invested in capital market instruments like shares and debentures and money market instruments like treasury bills, commercial papers, etc.

For managing this fund, a mutual fund gets an annual fee of 1.25% of funds managed at the maximum as fixed by the SEBI (MF) Regulations, 1993 and if the funds exceed ₹ 100 crores, it is only 1%. It can not take more than that. Of course regular expenses like custodial fee, cost of dividend warrants, fee for registration, the asset management fee etc. are debited to the respective scheme. These expenses cannot exceed 3% of the assets in the respective schemes each year. The remaining amount is given back to the investors in full.

FACILITIES AVAILABLE TO INVESTORS

Mutual funds provide following facilities to the investors:

***(i)* Repurchase Facilities:** The units of closed ended schemes must be compulsorily listed in recognized stock exchanges. Such units can be sold or bought at market prices. But, units of open-ended schemes are not at all listed and hence they have to be bought only from the fund. So, the fund reserves the right to buy back the units from its members. This process of buying back the units from the investors by the fund is called repurchase facility. This is available in both schemes so as to provide liquidity to investors. The price fixed for this purpose is called repurchase price.

***(ii)* Reissue Facilities:** In the case of open-ended schemes, units can be bought only from the fund and not in the open market. The units bought from the investors are again reissued to those who are interested in purchasing them. The price fixed for this purpose is called re-issue price.

***(iii)* Roll Over Facilities:** At the time of redemption, the investor is given an option to reinvest his entire investment once again for another term. An investor can overcome an adverse market condition prevailing at the time of redemption by resorting to this roll over facility. This is applicable in the case of close-ended funds.

***(iv)* Lateral Shifting Facilities:** Some mutual funds permit the investors to shift from one scheme to another on the basis of the Net Asset Value with a view to providing total flexibility in their operation. This is done without any discount on the fund and without any additional charges. This is a great privilege given to the investors. This shifting is called 'lateral shifting'.

NET ASSET VALUE

The repurchase price is always linked to the Net Asset Value (NAV). The NAV is nothing but the market price of each unit of a particular scheme in relation to all the assets of the scheme. It can otherwise be called "the intrinsic value" of each unit. This value is a true indicator of the performance of the fund. If the NAV is more than the face value of the unit, it clearly indicates that the money invested on that unit has appreciated and the fund has performed well.

INVESTORS RIGHTS

The SEBI (MF) Regulations, 1993 contains specific provisions with regard to investor servicing. Certain rights have been guaranteed to the investors as per these regulations. They are as follows:

***(i)* Unit Certificates:** An investor has a right to receive his unit certificates on allotment within a period of 10 weeks from the date of closure of subscription lists in the case of a close ended scheme and 6 weeks from the date of closure of the initial offer in the case of an open ended scheme.

***(ii)* Transfer of Units:** An investor is entitled to get the unit certificates transferred within a period of 30 days from the date of lodgement of the certificates along with the relevant transfer forms.

***(iii)* Refund of Application Money:** If a mutual fund is not able to collect the statutory minimum amount it has to return the application money as refund within a period of 6 weeks from the date of closure of subscription lists. If the refund is delayed beyond this period, each applicant is entitled to get the refund with interest at the rate of 15% p.a. for the period of delay.

***(iv)* Audited Annual Report:** Every mutual fund is under an obligation to its investors to publish the audited annual report and unaudited half yearly report through prominent newspapers in respect of each of its schemes within 6 months and 3 months respectively of the date of closure of accounts.

GENERAL GUIDELINES

For proper functioning of mutual funds and for ensuring investor protection, the following important guidelines have been framed by the Government of India:

(A) General

(*i*) Money market mutual funds would be regulated by the RBI while other mutual funds would be regulated by the Securities and Exchange Board of India (SEBI).

(*ii*) Mutual Fund shall be established in the form of Trusts under the Indian Trust Act and be authorized for business by the SEBI.

(*iii*) Mutual Funds shall be operated only by separately established Asset Management Companies (AMCs).

(*iv*) At least 50% of the Board of AMC must be independent directors who have no connections with the sponsoring organization. The directors must have professional experience of at least 10 years in the relevant fields such as portfolio management, financial administration, etc.

(*v*) The AMC should have a minimum net worth of ₹ 5 crores at all times.

(*vi*) The SEBI is given the power to withdraw the authorization given to any AMC if it is found to be not serving the best interest of investors as well as the capital market. It is not applicable to bank sponsored AMCs.

(B) Business Activities

(*i*) Both AMCs and trustees should be treated as two separate legal entitles.

(*ii*) AMCs should not be permitted to undertake any other business activity except mutual funds.

(*iii*) One AMC cannot act as the AMC for another mutual fund.

(C) Schemes

(*i*) Each scheme of a mutual fund must be compulsorily registered with the SEBI before it is floated in the market.

(*ii*) The minimum size of the fund should be ₹ 20 crores in the case of each closed-end scheme and it is ₹ 50 crores for each open-end scheme.

(*iii*) Closed-end schemes should not be kept opened for subscription for more than 45 days. For open-end scheme, the first 45 days should be considered for determining the target figure or the minimum size.

(*iv*) If the minimum amount or 60 per cent of the targeted amount, whichever is higher, is not raised, then, the entire subscription has to be refunded to the investors.

(*v*) To provide continuous liquidity, closed-end schemes should be listed on stock exchanges. In the case of open-end schemes, mutual funds shall sell and re-purchase units at pre-determined prices based on the Net Asset Value and such prices should be published at least once in a week.

(*vi*) For each scheme, there should be a separate and responsible fund manager.

(D) Investment Norms

(*i*) Mutual funds should invest only in transferable securities either in the capital market or money market or securitised debt. It cannot exceed 10 per cent in the case of growth funds and 40 per cent in the case of income funds.

(*ii*) The mutual fund should not invest more than 5% of its corpus of any scheme in any one company's shares.

(*iii*) This list of 5% can be extended to 10% if all the schemes of a mutual fund are taken together.

(*iv*) No scheme should invest if any other scheme under the same AMC.

(*v*) No mutual fund under all its schemes take together can invest more than 15 per cent of the funds in the shares and debentures of any specific industry, except in the case of those schemes which are specifically floated for investment in one or more specified industries.

(E) Expenses

(*i*) The AMC may charge the mutual fund with investment management and advisory fees. Such fees should have been disclose in the prospectus.

(*ii*) The initial issue expenses should not exceed 6% of the funds raised under each scheme.

(*iii*) Excepting the initial issue expenses, all other expenses to be charged to the fund should not exceed 3% of the weekly average net assets outstanding during the current year. It must be disclosed through advertisements, accounts etc.

(F) Income Distribution

All mutual funds must distribute a minimum of 90% of their profits in any given year.

(G) Disclosure and Reporting

(*i*) The SEBI is given wide powers to call for any information regarding the operation of mutual funds and any of its schemes from the mutual fund or any person associated with it like the AMC, Trustee, Sponsor etc.

(*ii*) Every mutual fund is required to send its copies of duly audited annual statements of accounts, six monthly unaudited accounts, quarterly statements of movements in net assets for each of its schemes to the SEBI.

(*iii*) The SEBI, can lay down the accounting policies, the format and contents of financial statements and other reports.

(*iv*) The SEBI shall also lay down a common advertising code for all mutual funds to comply with.

(H) Accounting Norm

(*i*) All mutual funds should segregate their earnings as current income, short-term capital gains and long-term capital gains.

(*ii*) Accounting for all the schemes must be done for the same year-ending.

(I) Winding Up

(*i*) Each closed-end scheme should be wound up or extended with the permission of the SEBI as soon as the predetermined period is over.

(*ii*) An open-end scheme shall be wound up, if the total number of units outstanding after repurchases at a point of time falls below 50% of the originally issued number of units.

(J) Violation of Guidelines

The SEBI can, after due investigation, impose penalties on mutual funds for violating the guidelines as may be necessary.

SELECTION OF A FUND

Mutual funds are not magic institutions which can bring treasure to the millions of their investors within a short span of time. All funds are equal to start with. But in due course of time, some excel the other. It all depends upon the efficiency with which the fund is being managed by the professionals of the fund. Hence, the investor has to be very careful in selecting a fund. He must take into account the following factors for evaluating the performance of any fund and then finally decide the one he has to choose :

(*i*) Objective of Fund: First of all, he must see the objective of the fund-whether income oriented or growth oriented. Income oriented are backed mainly by fixed interest yielding securities like debentures and bonds whereas growth oriented are backed by equities. It is obvious that growth oriented schemes are more risky than income oriented schemes, and hence, the returns from such schemes are not comparable with each other. The investor should compare the particular scheme of one fund with the same scheme of another fund and make a comparative analysis. His objective should also coincide with the objective of the scheme which he proposes to choose.

(*ii*) Consistency of Performance: A mutual fund is always intended to give steady long-term returns, and hence, the investor should measure the performance of a fund over a period of at least three years. Investors are satisfied with a fund that shows a steady and consistent performance than a fund which performs superbly in one year and then fails in the next year. Consistency in performance is a good indicator of its investment expertise.

(*iii*) Historical Background: The success of any fund depends upon the competence of the management, its integrity, periodicity and experience. The fund's integrity should be above suspicion. A good historical record could be a better horse to bet on than new funds. It is in accordance with the maxim "A known devil is better than an unknown angel."

(*iv*) Cost of Operation: Mutual Funds seek to do a better job of the investible funds at a lower cost than the individuals could do for themselves. Hence, the prospective investor should scrutinize the expense ratio of the fund and compare it with other. Higher the ratio, lower will be the actual returns to the investor.

(*v*) Capacity for Innovation: The efficiency of a fund manager can be tested by means of the innovative schemes he has introduced in the market so as to meet the diverse needs of investors. An innovator will be always a successful man. It is quite natural that an investor will look for funds which are capable of introducing innovations in the financial market.

(*vi*) Investor Servicing: The most important factor to be considered is prompt and efficient servicing. Services like quick response to investor queries, prompt dispatch of unit certificates. quick transfer of units, immediate encashment of units etc. will go a long way in creating a lasting impression in the minds of investors.

(*vii*) Market Trends: Traditionally, it has been found that the stock market index and the inflation rate tend to move in the same direction whereas the interest rates and the stock market index tend to move in the opposite direction. This sets the time for the investor to enter into fund and come out of it. A prudent investor must keep his eyes on the stock market index, interest rate and the inflation rate. Of course, there is so scientific reasoning behind it.

(*viii*) Transparency of the Fund Management: Again, the success of a mutual fund depends to a large extent on the transparency of the fund management. In these days of investor awareness, it is very vital that the fund should disclose the complete details regarding the operation of the fund. It will go a long way in creating a lasting impression in the minds of the investors to patronize the fund for ever.

In fact, the wider range of products/services offered by the different funds, have made the investor quality-conscious. He is now in a position to assess the quality of the products offered by MFs in the financial market. MFs cannot simply attract savings by mere lucrative advertisements. The cult of the equity has spread to many small investors, who have become very discerning in selecting mutual funds.

COMMERCIAL BANKS AND MUTUAL FUNDS

With a view to providing wider choice to small investors, the Government of India has permitted the banks to launch mutual funds as subsidiaries. There has been an urgent need for the banks to enter into the filed of mutual funds due to the following reasons:

(*i*) Banks are not able to provide better yields to the investing public with their savings and fixed deposit interest rates whereas many financial intermediaries, with innovative market instruments offering very attractive returns, have entered the financial market. So, banks are not able to compete with them in tapping the savings. Hence, there is a necessity to enter into the field of MFs.

(*ii*) The Gross Domestic Savings has risen from 10% in fifties to 20% in eighties, thanks to the massive branch expansion programme of banks and their growing deposit mobilization. Since the banks have branches in the rural as well as urban sectors, they can reach out to everyone in the country. Hence, a MF backed by a bank will be in a better position to tap the savings effectively and vigorously for the capital market.

(*iii*) Indian investors, particularly small and medium ones, are not very keen in investing any substantial amount directly in capital market instruments. They may also hesitate to invest in an indirect way through private financial intermediaries. On the other hand, if such intermediary has the backing of a bank, investors may have confidence and come forward to invest. Thus, banks have the advantage of public confidence which is very essential for the success of mutual funds.

(*iv*) Earlier banks were not permitted to tap the capital market for funds or to invest their funds in the market. Now, a green signal has been given to them enter into this market and reap the maximum benefits.

(*v*) Banks can provide a wider range of products/services in mutual funds by introducing innovative schemes and extend their professionalism to the mutual funds industry.

(*vi*) Banks, as merchant banks have wide experience in the capital market and hence managing a mutual fund may not be a big problem for them.

(*vii*) The entry of banks would provide much needed competition in the mutual fund industry which has been hitherto monopolized by the U.T.I. This competition will improve customer service and widen customer choice also.

(*viii*) In the Indian economy, the eighties witnessed the operation of both the process of intermediation and dis-intermediation. The dis-intermediation process can be easily harnessed by commercial banks through mutual funds. The process of dis-intermediation of time deposits into mutual funds would benefit the capital market because it would provide a sustainable domestic source of demand.

(*ix*) Above all, the investor servicing can be effectively done by banks through their network of branches spread throughout the country. Hence, the commercial banks have entered into the mutual fund market without any hesitancy.

(*x*) Moreover, the profitability of banks has been very much affected due to too many restrictions on their lending policies. They have been compelled to seek some other alternatives to increase their profits by means of diversifying their activities. Mutual Funds offer an excellent outlet for diversification.

MULTIPLE CHOICE QUESTIONS

1. Mutual Funds are regulated by:
A. Reserve Bank of India
B. Securities and Exchange Board of India
C. Mutual Funds Board of India
D. Either A or C
E. None of these

2. Mutual Fund Market regulated by:
A. Reserve Bank of India
B. Securities and Exchange Board of India
C. Unit Trust of India
D. Either A or C
E. None of these

3. The stated principal amount of a financial instrument is known as:
A. Market Value B. Book Value
C. Face Value D. Either A or B
E. None of these

4. A person who sets up a business or businesses, taking on financial risks in the hope of profit is known as:
A. Partner B. Entrepreneur
C. Owner D. Either A or C
E. None of these

5. Which of the following is a third party product often sold by banks?
A. Gift cheques B. Credit cards
C. Debit cards D. Mutual funds
E. None of these

6. Which of the following term is not related to Banking/ Finance operations?
A. Consolidation
B. Provision Coverage Ratio
C. Commodification
D. Either B or C
E. None of these

7. The securitization and Reconstruction of Financial Assets and Enforcement of Securities Interest Act (SARFAESI) meant recovery of loans which have become NPA is not applicable to:
A. Financial Institutes of Government
B. Non-Banking Financial Companies
C. Small & Cooperative Banks
D. Either A or C
E. None of these

8. .... fund invests in highly liquid securities like commercial paper.
A. Equity fund
B. Balanced fund
C. Income fund
D. Money market mutual fund
E. None of these

9. The company which sets up a mutual fund is called ....
A. Fund company B. Sponsor
C. Originator D. Obligator
E. None of these

10. The small investors' gateway to enter into big companies is ....
A. Equity shares B. Debentures
C. Preference shares D. Mutual fund
E. None of these

11. Mutual funds are very popular in:
A. USA B. UK
C. Japan D. India
E. None of these

12. In India, the company which actually deals with the corpus of the mutual fund is called:
A. sponsor company
B. trustee company
C. asset management company
D. Mutual fund company
E. None of these

13. .... variety of mutual fund is known as "Nest Eggs".
A. Balanced Funds
B. Fund of Funds
C. Money Market Mutual Fund
D. Growth Oriented Funds
E. None of these

14. Generally mutual funds are of:
A. High risk B. Risk free
C. Low risk D. Any of the above
E. None of the above

15. The corpus of funds and its duration is fixed in case of .... fund.
A. Open ended B. Balanced
C. Close ended D. Income fund
E. None of these

16. The market performance of mutual fund can be judged on the basis of:
A. Net asset value or intrinsic value
B. Capital appreciation
C. Regular/stable income
D. Any of these
E. None of these

17. The difference between open-end and closed-end mutual funds is:
A. The total number of shares under management grows and shrinks for open-end funds, but is fixed for closed-end funds
B. Open-end funds can be purchase in a variety of international markets while closed-end funds can only be purchased in their home market
C. The total number of shares under management grows and shrinks for closed-end funds, but is fixed for open-end funds
D. Open-end funds contain securities from various countries while closed-end funds contain securities from just one country
E. None of these

18. .... are examples of financial intermediaries.
A. Commercial banks
B. Insurance companies
C. Investment companies
D. All of the above
E. None of these

19. Financial intermediaries exist because small investors cannot efficiently ....
A. Diversify their portfolios
B. Gather all relevant information
C. Assess credit risk of borrowers
D. All of the above
E. None of these

20. A mutual fund in which shares are issued only when the fund is organized is called a .... fund.
A. Closed-end B. Load
C. No-load D. Open-end
E. None of these

21. The value of the mutual fund's portfolio minus the mutual fund's liabilities divided by the number of shares outstanding is called the:
A. Book value B. Outstanding balance
C. Per share value D. Net asset value
E. None of these

22. When one investment company manages a group of mutual funds, it is called a(n):
A. Family funds B. Exchange fund
C. Diversification fund D. Versatility fund
E. None of these

23. Mr. Manoj is buying shares in a mutual fund that invests in companies that are all within the same industry. What type of mutual fund has he purchased?

A. A sector fund B. A small cap fund
C. An index fund D. A growth fund
E. None of these

24. A market for existing financial securities that are currently traded between investors is called the .... market.
A. Fundamental B. Efficient
C. Secondary D. Primary
E. None of these

25. Income-cum- growth fund is also known as ....
A. Balanced fund B. Nest eggs
C. Open ended fund D. Long haul
E. None of these

26. .... fund concentrate mainly on capital appreciation.
A. Balanced fund B. Income fund
C. Growth fund D. All of these
E. None of these

27. Pure growth fund is also known as:
A. Nest eggs B. Balanced fund
C. Leverage fund D. Stop gap arrangement
E. None of these

28. Investors generally use .... as a 'parking place' or 'stop gap arrangement".
A. Balanced fund B. Income fund
C. Growth fund D. MMMF
E. None of these

29. .... mutual fund otherwise known as "intrinsic value".
A. Income B. Capital
C. Portfolio D. Net asset value
E. None of these

30. Best suited fund for a business people is..............
A. Balanced fund B. Income fund
C. Growth fund D. Taxation fund
E. None of these

31. The facility offered to the investors to shift from one scheme to another under same fund is known as:
A. Roll over facility
B. Re-purchase facility
C. Re-issue facility
D. Lateral shifting facility
E. None of these

32. .... variety of mutual fund offers tax benefits to the investors.
A. Balanced Funds
B. Fund of funds
C. Money Market Mutual fund
D. Taxation fund
E. None of these

33. Generally mutual funds are of:
A. High risk B. Risk free
C. Low risk D. Any of the above
E. None of these

34. In mutual fund, ELSS stands for:
A. Entry to Limited Subscribers Scheme
B. Equity Linked Saving Scheme
C. Entry Load for Saving Scheme
D. Entry to Linked Saving Scheme
E. None of these

35. In Mutual fund arena, SIP stands for:
A. Structural investment plan
B. Systematic investment plan
C. Stable income plan
D. Similar income plan
E. None of these

36. Secured Premium Notes (SPN) always issued with ....
A. Premium B. Discount
C. Detachable Warrant D. Coupon
E. None of these

37. .... bonds permit the bond holder to invest the interest income again in host bonds.
A. Deep discount bond B. Junk bonds
C. Bearer bond D. Bunny bonds
E. None of these

38. Gilt Edged Securities are
A. Govt. Securities B. Company's securities
C. Any of the above D. Simple Securities
E. None of these

39. Money Market mutual fund is also known as:
A. Growth fund B. Balanced fund
C. Income fund D. Cash fund
E. None of these

40. .... is the regulator of mutual funds in India.
A. RBI B. IRDA
C. SEBI D. Both SEBI and GOI
E. None of these

41. Which of the following is not a mutual fund scheme?
A. Equity schemes B. Debt schemes
C. Balanced schemes D. Mutual benefit schemes
E. None of these

42. Mutual funds invest in:
A. Stocks only
B. Bonds only
C. Stock and bonds
D. Stock, bonds and cash instruments
E. None of these

43. Name the institution which introduced mutual funds in India.
A. LIC B. RBI
C. UTI D. SBI
E. None of these

44. This fund is one that is available for subscription all through the year:
A. Open ended fund B. closed ended fund

C. growth fund D. income fund
E. None of these

45. This fund is open for subscription only during a specified period:
A. open ended fund B. closed ended fund
C. growth fund D. income fund
E. None of these

46. These funds are stocks funds that invest in stocks with the potential for long-term capital appreciation:
A. open ended fund B. closed ended fund
C. growth fund D. income fund
E. None of these

47. The aim of this fund is to provide regular and steady income to investor:
A. open ended fund B. closed ended fund
C. growth fund D. income fund
E. None of these

48. Stock mutual funds also sometimes called:
A. open ended fund B. closed ended fund
C. growth fund D. equity fund
E. None of these

49. Mutual funds are:
A. open ended fund B. closed ended fund
C. both A and B D. Open-closed fund
E. None of the above

50. uti-64 is a
A. Open ended fund B. closed ended fund
C. both A and B D. Can't say
E. None of the above

51. Mutual fund can make investment:
A. in any company listed or unlisted
B. in privately placed securities of associated company
C. up to 40% of the listed or unlisted securities of group of companies
D. Should not exceed 10% of the funds in securities of a single company
E. None of these

52. Which of the following scheme is not meant for investment purposes?
A. National saving certificate
B. Infrastructure bonds
C. Mutual funds
D. Letter of credit
E. None of these

53. Systematic investment Plans relates to:
A. Mutual Funds
B. Life Insurance Companies
C. Commercial Banks
D. Post office savings schemes
E. None of these

54. While discussing investments there is a mention of short-term government security. What is this investment?
A. Debenture B. Mutual funds
C. Treasury bill D. Share
E. None of these

55. Now-a-days Banks are selling third party products. Example of third party product is:
A. Mutual funds B. Term deposits
C. Credit cards D. All of these
E. None of these

56. Retail investors means which of the following types of stock market investors?
A. Mutual funds
B. Corporate bodies
C. Promoters of companies
D. Individuals
E. FIIs

57. Which of the following is NOT a part of India's Money Market?
A. Bill Market B. Call Money Market
C. Banks D. Mutual Funds
E. Indian Gold Council

ANSWERS

1	2	3	4	5	6	7	8	9	10
B	B	C	B	D	A	B	D	B	D
11	**12**	**13**	**14**	**15**	**16**	**17**	**18**	**19**	**20**
A	C	D	C	C	C	C	D	D	A
21	**22**	**23**	**24**	**25**	**26**	**27**	**28**	**29**	**30**
D	A	A	C	A	C	A	D	C	C
31	**32**	**33**	**34**	**35**	**36**	**37**	**38**	**39**	**40**
D	D	C	B	B	C	D	A	C	D
41	**42**	**43**	**44**	**45**	**46**	**47**	**48**	**49**	**50**
D	D	C	A	B	C	D	D	C	A
51	**52**	**53**	**54**	**55**	**56**	**57**			
D	D	A	C	A	D	E			

16

Credit Rating

INTRODUCTION

Credit Rating is a symbolic indicator of the current objective assessment by a rating agency of the relative capability and willingness of an issuer of a debt programmes to service the debt obligations as per the terms of the contract. It may be referred as current opinion of a borrower's credit quality in terms of business and financial risk. On the basis of such evaluation, the investors get some idea about the degree of certainty of timely repayment of the principal amount of the debt instrument besides regular payment of returns on it *i.e.*, interest. So, credit rating is neither a general purpose evaluation of a corporate entity nor an overall assessment of the credit risk associated with the instruments issued or to be issued by the concerned business house. It only indicates a representatives characters of the particular security which does not amount to any recommendation to purchase, sell or hold that security.

CONCEPT OF CREDIT RATING

To understand the concept of credit rating it is worth to have an idea of different credit rating agencies what they consider credit rating as:

Investment Information and Credit Rating Agency of India Ltd. (ICRA)

Rating is a symbolic indicator of the current opinion of the relative capability of timely servicing of debt and obligations by the corporate entity with reference to the instrument rated.

Credit Rating Information Services of India Ltd. (CRISIL)

Rating is current opinion as to the relative safety of timely payment of interest and principal on a debenture, structured obligation, preference shares, fixed deposits programme or short-term instruments.

Credit Analysis and Research Ltd. (CARE)

Credit rating is an opinion on the relative ability and willingness of an issuer to make timely payment on specific debt or related obligations over the life of the instrument.

Australian Ratings

Rating provides lender with a simple system of gradation by which the relative capacities of companies to make timely repayment of interest and principal on a particular type of debt can be noted.

Standard & Poors

Rating is current assessment of the credit worthiness of an obligor with respect to specific obligation.

From the above definitions, it is understood that:

(*i*) Credit rating is an assessment of the capacity of an issuer of debt security, by an independent agency, to pay interest and repay the principal as per the terms of issue of debt. A rating agency collects the qualitative as well as quantitative data from a company which has to be rated and assesses the relative strength and capacity of company to honour its obligations contained in the debt instrument through out the duration of the instrument. The rating given is based on an objective judgement of a team of experts from the rating agency.

(*ii*) The ratings are expressed in code number which can be easily comprehended even by the lay investors. The ratings are the quickest way of understanding a company's financial standing without going into the complicated financial reports. Credit rating is only a guidance to the investors and not a recommendation to a particular debt instrument. The important element for investment decision making in debt security are (i) yield to maturity (ii) risk tolerance to investor and (iii) credit risk of the security. Clearly the focus of credit rating is on any one of these three elements viz., credit risk of the security and hence it can not by itself be a basis for investment decision making. It is only a current opinion on the relative capacity of firms to repay debt in time.

(*iii*) Credit rating, as it exists in India, is done for a specific debt security and not for a company as a whole. No rating agency tells that it is an indicator of the financial status of the company. All that a rating agency claims is that the rating symbols indicate the capacity of the company to honour the terms of contract of a debt instrument.

(*iv*) A debt rating is not a one time evaluation of credit risk, which can be regarded as valid for the entire life of the security. It is an ongoing appraisal. Changes in dynamic world of business may imply a change in the risk characteristics of the security. Hence, debt rating agencies monitor the business and financial conditions of the issuer to determine whether modification in rating is warranted.

(*v*) A credit rating does not create a fiduciary relationship between the rating agency and the users of rating since there is no legal basis for such relationships.

FUNCTIONS OF CREDIT RATINGS

The credit rating firms are supposed to do the following functions:

1. Superior Information: Rating by an independent and professional firm offers a superior and more reliable source of information on credit risk for three inter related risks:

(*a*) It provides unbiased opinion.

(*b*) Due to professional resources, a rating firm has greater ability to assess risks.

(*c*) It has access to lot of information which may not be publicly available.

2. Low Cost Information: A rating firm which gathers, analyses, interprets and summarizes complex information in a simple and readily understood format for wide public consumption represents a cost effective arrangement.

3. Basis for a Proper Risk-Return Trade Off: If debt securities are rated professionally and if such ratings enjoy widespread investor acceptance and confidence, a more rational risk return trade off would be established in the capital market.

4. Healthy Discipline on Corporate Borrowers: Public exposure has healthy influence over the management of issuer because of its desire to have a clear image.

5. Formulation of Public Policy Guidelines on Institutional Investment: The public policy on the kinds of securities that are eligible for inclusion in different kinds of institutional portfolios can be developed with great confidence if securities are rated professionally by independent agencies.

ORIGIN OF CREDIT RATING

The credit rating concept originated in the USA. In 1860, Henry Vannum started publishing financial statistics of railroad companies in 1909, Mood's Investors Agencies started rating Railroad giving more thrust to the concept. Since then the importance has grown extensively in the global market. System of ratings got institutionalized following the Great Depression. In 1933, the US Controller of Currency enacted a rule that banks could purchase securities rated only BBB/Baa or above. In 1970, Penn Central, then largest Railroad company in the world went bankrupt with just under $100 million in outstanding commercial paper. This forced the investors to ask for rating for commercial paper volume and 99% of the corporate bond volume are rated in the U.S.A.

CREDIT RATING IN INDIA

The environment that prevailed in America when first ratings were assigned, prevails in many developing countries today. The Indian capital market has witnessed a tremendous growth in the past few years. Companies are relying on capital markets for financing existing operations as well as for new projects rather than on institutions. In this process, the average size of debenture issued by companies, the number of companies issuing debentures and the number of investors have grown substantially.

As the number of companies borrowings directly from capital market increases, investors find that the company's size or name is no longer a sufficient assurance of the timely payment of interest and principal. Default by large and well known companies recently in payment of interest on fixed deposits or debentures has reinforced this belief among investors. They felt the need for an independent and credible agency which judges the quality of debt obligations of different companies' and assists individual and institutional investors in making investment decisions.

In this context, the Credit Rating Information Services of India Limited was set up in 1987. Following this, Investment Information and Credit Rating Agency of India was promoted in 1991 and Credit Analysis and Research Limited was floated in 1993. All the three credit rating agencies have been approved by the Reserve Bank of India.

BENEFITS OF CREDIT RATING

The following are the benefits of credit rating:

1. Low Cost Information: Credit rating is a source of low cost information to investors. The collection, processing and analysis of relevant information is done by a specialised agency which a group of investors can trust.

2. Quick Investment Decision: In the present day, complex world ratings enable investors to take the quickest possible decisions based on associated ratings.

3. Sources of Additional Certification: Credit rating agency provides additional certification to the issue of debt/financial instrument. A highly rated firm can enter the market with great confidence. Indian experience shows that individual companies that use credit rating, benefit a great deal by getting larger amount of money from a wider audience at a lower cost.

4. Increase the Investors Population: A sound credit rating system gives an alternative method to name recognition as a determining factor in making investment and helps to increase the population of those investing in debt obligations of the company.

5. Forewarns Risks: Credit rating acts as a guide to companies which get a lower rating. It forewarns the management of the perception of risk in the market and prompts to take steps on their operating and marketing risks and thereby changes the perception in the market.

6. Encourages Financial Discipline: Rating also encourage discipline among corporate borrowers to improve their financial structure and performance to obtain better rating for their debt obligations.

7. Merchant Bankers Job Made Easy: Merchant bankers and brokers will be relieved of the responsibility of guiding investors as to the risk of a particular investment. Merchant bankers and brokers, in the absence of objective information, go on the basis of name recognition in guiding their clients. With the advent of credit rating, what they would be required to do is to bring to the attention of their clients the ratings of debt obligations.

8. Investors Protection: Hiring of credit agency implies that the management of the company is ready to show its operations for independent scrutiny. So, the investors who are not provided with confidential information can have overall assessment based on ratings. A credible and objective rating agency can provide increased disclosure, better accounting standard and improved investor protection.

9. Foreign Collaborations Made Easy: The foreign collaborators always ask for credit rating while negotiating with an Indian company. Credit rating enables to identify instantly the relative credit standing of the company. The importance of credit rating is being increasingly recognized in the Euro-markets.

10. Benefits the Industry as a Whole: Relatively small and unknown companies use ratings to instill confidence in investors. Higher rate companies get larger amount of money at a lower cost. Thus, the industry as a whole can benefit from ratings by direct mobilization of savings from individuals rather than from intermediary lending institutions.

RATING PROCESS

Any rating agency assigns a rating only when there is adequate information available to form a credible opinion and only after extensive quantitative, qualitative and if appropriate legal analyses are performed. The process of rating is broadly three tier system:

(*a*) Information

When the issuer approaches the credit rating agency, it is to provide relevant information to them. The information required by the rating agency is such which gives the real picture of the issuer. The nature and source of information required is presented in the given Chart. The credit rating agency besides depending on the information provided by the issuer collects additional information from its own sources. The information required about the issuer is not only of the past but also about its future prospects.

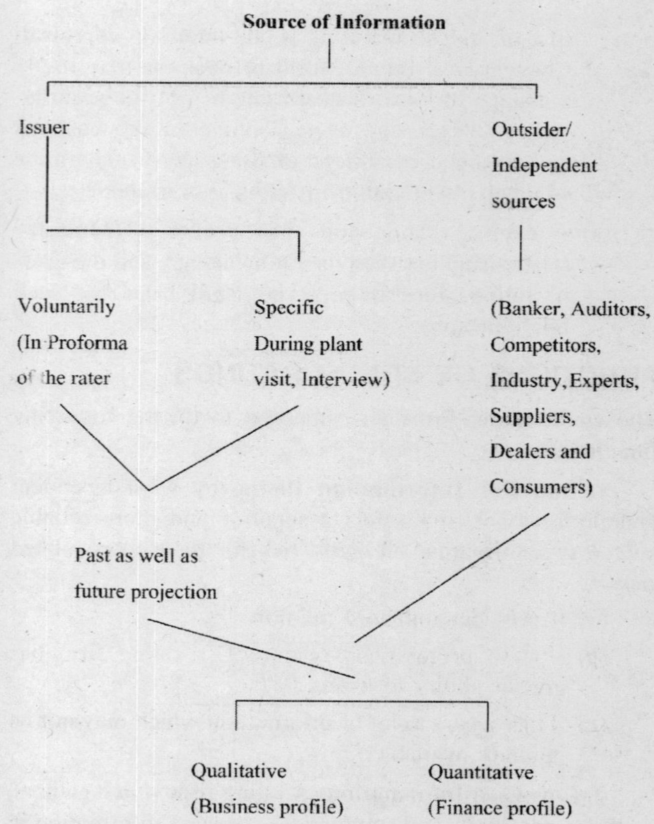

(*b*) Analysis of Information

The rating process of rating agencies is almost similar since the basic parameters to be observed to assess risks associated are same. Rating is a search for long-term fundamentals and the probabilities for changes in the fundamentals. Rating fundamentals analyse not only financial profile of the concerned issuer in context of the instrument to be rated but also evaluate its business or competitive strengths or weaknesses. These fundamentals are discussed below one by one before taking up rating process:

A. Financial Profile

Financial profile for which an in-depth study is made for issuer, covers liquidity position, capital structure, financial flexibility, cash flow adequacy, profitability, leverage, interest coverage etc. The historical facts and future projections both are extensively used for these parameters. Besides considering these, the rating agency also critically evaluates accounting policies and practices with particular reference to practices of providing for depreciation, income recognition, stock valuation, valuation of fixed assets, off balance sheet claims and liabilities etc. Extensive use is made of ratio analysis techniques. The major ratios computed are:

(*i*) Coverage Ratio: The main determinant of the quality rating of debt obligation is its coverage ratio. Coverage ratio is a measure of how many times the issuing company earned income could pay the interest changes and other cost related to the debt issue. This ratio hints at probability of default in interest payment. The trend analysis of this ratio is also of immense use. An upward trend indicates better time ahead.

***(ii)* Financial Leverage Ratios:** It is a set of ratios used to assess broadly what is the mix of fund sources. A leverage is added if a dose of debt fund is used in total funds. Higher the proportion of owned funds, lesser is the leverage and consequently more solvent the company is. A highly leveraged company's debt instruments are ranked more risky. Prime ratio used here is debt-equity ratio.

Another ratios used can be long-term debt to total capitalization (long-term debts + short-term debts + net worth) and long-term debts to equity. Rating analysts are also to consider all off balance sheet liabilities and commitments of the company to have actual idea about solvency.

***(iii)* Liquidity Ratios:** To know the firms ability to pay debts currently coming due, liquidity ratios are calculated. Most common ratios in this category, also known as short-term solvency ratios, are current ratio and quick ratio. Besides these ratios some analysts also compute and consider ratios like inventory turnover ratio, receivable turnover ratio and collection period in days. This set of ratios reflect the efficient or otherwise use of liquid resources by the issuer.

***(iv)* Cash Flow Ratios:** If cash flow of a company is sufficient in relation to interest payment liability and total long-term debts, the debt instrument of the company may get higher rating. Cash flow is normal operating income before interest, tax and depreciation. If cash flow to total long-term debt ratio is less than the firms' interest rate on debts, there is a possibility that firm may default in making payments.

***(v)* Profitability Ratios:** Another significant set of ratios is profitability ratios which indicate profit earning capacity of a company. Earnings are viewed in relation to burden of fixed changes. This set of ratios indicate the real financial health of the company. A company with higher ratios will certainly be better off in times to come. The ratios to be calculated are operating profit ratio, net profit ratio and return on investment ratio. The trend of these ratios can assist projection of financial health in future which is very relevant for rating of debt instruments.

B. Business Profile

The rating process, as mentioned earlier, is not limited to the evaluation of financial profile. Quality of debt instruments is influenced by many other variables which are not covered in examination of financial profile. Say in a rating agency financial evaluation of M/s ABC is presented which is very sound on profitability as well as liquidity front. The agency proposes to give it highest safety symbol. But say one of the analyst says that despite all these facts I don't agree to award highest safety symbol. He reveals that the product in which M/s ABC is dealing a better one and cheaper product has been recently patented. M/s ABC will no longer have the same segment of market as it use to have earlier. It is a very logical point which needs to be considered since it will influence over all earning of the firm. There can be so many other factors which are not considered in financial analysis. All such factors for convenience are grouped under the head business profile. The main factors considered here are discussed one by one.

***(i)* Issuer's Industry:** The nature of industry to which issues belong has an impact on rating of the instrument. The following questions need to be answered:

(*a*) Is the company in a capital goods industry, consumer durable goods industry, or consumer non-durable goods industry?

(*b*) Is the industry in a growth, stable or declining phase?

(*c*) What is the nature and intensity of the competition in the industry? Is it on a regional, national or international basis? Is it based on price, quality of product, marketing strategy?

(*d*) What is the labour situation in the industry? Is the industry unionized? If so, are the labour contracts negotiated on industry level?

(*e*) What is the status and history of supply factor of key raw material?

(*f*) How fast have been the technological upgradation? What have been the recent developments and possibility of future developments not only in the country but abroad also?

(*g*) Is the industry subject to some controls like in case of price control in cement, sugar, steel etc.?

(*h*) Is the company participating in more than one business? What are the potentials of all important business lines?

Answer to these questions enables the analyst to cause the industry risk which can be introduced in his model of rating. The industries with steady demand, growth and ability to maintain margins without impairing future prospect are regarded favorably while rating obviously a change in outlook for industry will lead to change in the rating for the companies in that industry.

***(ii)* Issuer's Competitors:** After general evaluation of industry, specific evaluation of issuer's position in the industry needs to be studied. The main question for it are:

(*a*) Does the company have a large enough portion of the market share to influence industry dynamics significantly?

(*b*) Does the company has a full range of products or have proprietary products or a special rich in the market?

(*c*) Is the company a relatively low cost producer?

(*d*) Are the technical facilities with the company newer or more advanced than the average competitors?

(*e*) Does the company face more onerous labour situation than its competitors?

(*f*) Does the company has competitive advance through marketing and distribution strength?

(*g*) What is the financial strength of the company in context of the competitors?

The response to above mentioned questions give a valuable clue to put a company in most suitable category of risk ranking.

***(iii)* Issuer's Management:** Operating efficiency to a large extent is dependent on the management of the issuer company. It is the management's track record which also influences determining risk tolerance. Management is tested on the related points important of which are as under :

(*a*) What is the background and history of issuer?

(*b*) What is the extent of reliance on Chief Executive Officer specially who may be close to retirement?

(*c*) To what extent is the management professional?

(*d*) How effective is the control mechanism in the company?

(*e*) What is the report of past and present creditors of the company?

(*f*) What is the relationship between organizational structure and management strategy?

(*g*) How is management able to maintain strategies and policies or retain credit worthiness in the times of stress?

(*h*) How competent is the management to cope with short-term charges?

***(iv)* Issuer's Instrument:** Debt instrument to be rated spells out certain rights of the owners. The various protective provisions contained in the terms and conditions/prospectus of debt instrument also raises the quality rating for the instrument. Such protections can be creating security against the instrument to make it secured fully or partly. The issuer can subordinates other legal claims on its assets or income. The issuer may create redemption reserve or sinking fund to pay off bonds even if the issuer defaults on its other debts. Trustees may be appointed to protect the interest of investors. Many of such provision are obligatory in Indian context.

These are the main indicative parameters examined by every rating agency. Thus, methodology used is almost similar. Almost similar information is sought by all agencies for rating purposes. The rating methodology, thus, involves coverage of a vide spectrum of the company's activities and is extremely exhaustive. An issuer, therefore, is scrutinized thoroughly on all the areas mentioned.

(c) Granting Rating Symbol

The process starts with the request of the prospective issuer's formal request for rating. The issuer is generally asked to submit required information in a set proforma of essential items. This is not an exhaustive list.

The issuer should feel free to provide additional information on any relevant aspect. The issuer company is also to provide its financial profile for last 4-5 years along with audit reports. The rating agency assigns an analytical team for the issue. The analyst take up the assignment of additional data, which they consider to be relevant. They give chance to issuer to make his presentation. The questions are raised and answers are sought.

The team may visit the premises to gather first hand information especially about qualitative aspects. They may have assess to books of record. They can interact with the executives and other concerned officials. To review in detail the borrower's key operating and financial plans, management policies and credit factors can also be analysed. The data base of the rating agency about industry concerned is also extensively used.

Following this review and discussion, a recommendations is made by the primary analyst and a rating committee meeting is convened. The committee discusses the recommendations and the pertinent facts supporting the rating. Finally, the committee votes on the recommendations.

The borrower is subsequently notified of the rating and the major supporting considerations. A borrow can appeal against a rating decision prior to its publication. If new or meaningful additional information is presented by the borrower, it will be considered by the rating committee. However, rating agencies may not guarantee that this new information will alter the rating committee's decision.

Once a final rating is assigned, it will disseminated to agency's subscriber clientele and publicly through the news media if the issuer accepts the rating. If rating is not acceptable, agency may not make public that rating. Rating agency otherwise also ensures strict confidentiality of all information collected during the rating process. Once the rated company decides to use the rating, the agency monitors the rating till the redemption/repayment of the debt obligation.

At regular intervals company is supposed to submit the updated data and communicate major changes in policy matters, if any. This surveillance system continues till the life of the concerned instrument. Under this system, a formal review is conducted annually; new developments, industry trends and financial performance releases are reviewed regularly. As a result rating may be changed or withdrawn. Rating agencies have right to disclose such changes in rating to public.

While this general framework applies to all rating exercises, there are some areas where additional specific information is needed to make the rating decisions for a specific instrument.

TYPES OF RATING

The rating methodology and process discussed earlier is primarily for debt instruments like debentures, fixed deposits, bonds etc. This type of rating constitutes the major business of a rating company. But with the passage of time these agencies have started providing other types of rating such as:

(a) Equity Rating: Rating of equity shares issued in capital market is termed as equity rating. In such exercises the opinion on the earnings prospects and risk associated with such earnings can be arrived at through comprehensive information on acquisition, interaction with the management of the corporate, critical analysis and collective judgmental process. This exercise is also known as 'equity grading' which is initiated on the initiative of the issuer of equity before making a public issue. Grading examines very closely the level, quality, growth and substantiality of earnings in the medium term on the expanded equity base resulting from the present offer and other known future equity expansion. Like credit rating, equity grading can also be communicated both as a symbolic grade and a detailed rational. Surveillance such grading will make it relevant for secondary market of the issued share. The key parameter in the whole exercise is the prospective return on net worth. Rating agencies may also make equity assessment at the request of institutional investors with the consent of the corporate house whose equity is sought to be assessed.

(b) Mutual Fund Rating: Mutual Funds which are popular world over are evaluated by rating agencies and it is known as mutual fund rating. It facilitates selection of right fund from the available funds. Given the nature of mutual funds, the analysis of performance has to rely to a large extent, on past performance. Therefore, evaluation is primarily based on the two indicators 'risk and return'. Expense ratio, turnover ratio, composition of portfolio, accounting practices, fund management qualities, NAV in past are some of the main parameters to evaluate mutual funds.

(c) Individual Credit Rating: Consumer finance is gaining popularity in developing countries. The success of consumer finance depends on the credit worthiness of the consumer. Rating agencies may take up rating of such individuals. Individual credit rating is own objective assessment of the risk attached to a financial transaction with respect to an individual at a given point of time based on qualification of parameters influencing credit risk. Every aspect of credit seeker's history; age, qualification, occupation, stability at work, residence, marital status, assets, repaying capacity, savings and earnings potentials are used to assess creditworthiness of an individual. Agencies broadly rate individuals on social status, economic status and financial status.

(d) Rating of Banks and Financial Companies: Banks and financing companies are also issuers of debts like banks issue certificates of deposits (CD). The issuer's internal affair is scanned by evaluation of their background and history. Their relation with government and central bank are studied. The issuer's innovations and competitive ability to attract cheaper funds is analysed. Maturity pattern between the source and deployment of fund is studied. Its competitive position and market share is also studied. The rating exercise could include a case by case review of major non-performing assets to determine the prospect of reliability. The quality of assets is judged. Profitability is also gazed. The quality of management is judged by the profile of operating executives, human resources policies and organizational structure. In case of financial companies, support of group companies could be important in determining their success. Accounting figures are considered after adjusting for non-standard accounting policies.

(e) Sovereign Rating: It is primarily rating of a country as to its credit worthiness and probability to risk etc. In this process economic parameters and economic policies of the country are under constant observation. Such rating influences the availability of foreign aids from agencies like World Bank. All rating agencies may not take up such assignment because of lack of infrastructure and specialists.

(f) Rating Structured Obligation: Structured obligation is a negotiable instrument or security which is backed by some asset. The main role of a credit rating agency in analyzing an asset backed security or a structured obligation is to assess the risk of default in meeting the contractual obligations to the investors. As in the rating of conventional debt instruments, the rating assesses the default risk rating to other debt instruments available to the investor. The main thrust in the evaluation of an asset backed transaction is to ensure that the cash flows from the assets and the envisaged structure are capable of meeting the committed payments to the investors even in a "worst case" scenario. A key point to kept in mind is that in the rating of a structured obligation it is not rating the issuer but is assessing the risk associated with the transaction. More specially, a AAA rating on a particular structured obligation of a particular originator does not necessarily mean that all other issues by the entity would also get a AAA.

CREDIT RATING AGENCIES IN INDIA

Currently there are four credit rating agencies in India.

1. Credit Rating Information Service Ltd. (CRISIL)
2. Information and Credit Rating Agency of India (ICRA)
3. Credit Analysis and Research (CARE)
4. Duff Phelps Credit Rating Pvt. Ltd. (DCR India)

Credit Rating Information Service Ltd. (CRISIL)

On January 1, 1988 the Industrial Credit and Investment Corporation of India (ICICI) and Unit Trust of India (UTI) joined hands to float CRISIL, first rating agency in India with an equity base of ₹ 4.00 crores. Each of them holds 18 per cent of the stock. The other promoters are : The Asian Development Bank (15 per cent) ; the LIC, the GIC and its subsidiaries and the State Bank of India (each 5 per cent); the Housing Development Finance Corporation (6.2 per cent); 9 nationalized Banks owning 19.5 per cent, the remaining equity is distributed among 10 foreign banks *i.e.*, Standard Chartered Bank, Banque Indo Suez, Mitsui Bank, Bank of Tokyo, Hongkong and Shanghai Banking Corporation, Citi Bank, Grindlays Bank, Deutsche Bank, Societe General, Banque Nationals de Peris. CRISIL became a public limited company in November 1993 and is presently a quoted company on the Bombay Stock Exchange.

Objective: The main objective of CRISIL has been to rate debt obligation of Indian companies. Its rating provides a guide to the investors as to the risk of timely payment of interest and principal on a particular debt instrument. Its ratings create awareness of the concept of credit rating amongst corporations, merchant bankers brokers, regulatory authorities and helps in creating environment that facilitates the debt rating.

At the time when CRISIL commenced its operations it was contemplated that it would undertake credit rating for a company at its specific request and subsequently it might cover all companies on its own initiative with the basic idea to provide information about creditworthiness of all companies whether they approach CRISIL or not so that investors know about the company offering securities to the public. It had also envisaged to cover under credit rating all securities viz. equity shares as well as preference shares, debentures, secured, unsecured convertible and non-convertible and fixed deposits. To achieve the objectives and contribute towards stable and healthy growth of the Indian Capital market, the thrust of the CRISIL operations was planned towards:

(*i*) Shifting the primary responsibility of established corporate credit quality from the merchant bankers/brokers/underwriters/financial advisor to CRISIL and making available widely acceptable standard and uniform rating for the investors;

(*ii*) Providing for increased disclosure, better accounting standards improved financial information to the users *i.e.*, individual investors, financial institutions, stock exchange and corporate research bodies;

(*iii*) Reducing the cost of issue by helping direct mobilization of finance without depending on intermediary agencies; and

(*iv*) Protecting the interest of investors by constant monitoring of the results of rated companies and altering the grading to reflect the true and fair state of affairs of the financial position of companies.

Credit Rating Symbols: CRISIL uses the conventional rating symbols used in the USA and widely accepted in many other countries. The following table shows the investment wise rating symbols assigned by CRISIL and the meaning of each rating from the angle of safety to the investors.

CRISIL Debenture Rating Symbols

High Investment Grades		
AAA (Triple A)	:	Highest Safety
AA (Double A)	:	High Safety
Investment Grades		
A	:	Adequate Safety
BBB (Triple B)	:	Moderate Safety
Speculative Grades		
BB (Double B)	:	Inadequate Safety
B	:	High Risk
C	:	Substantial Risk
D	:	Default

Notes: (1) CRISIL may apply '+' (plus) or '–' (minus) sign for ratings from AA to C to reflect comparative standing within the category.

(2) The contents within parenthesis are a guide to the pronunciation of the rating symbols.

(3) Preference shares rating symbols are identical to debenture rating symbols except that the letters 'pf' are prefixed to the rating symbols, *e.g.*, pf AAA ("pf Triple A").

CRISIL Fixed Deposit Rating Symbols

Investment Grades		
FAAA (F-Triple A)	:	Highest Safety
FAA (F-Double A)	:	High Safety
FA	:	Adequate Safety
Speculative Grades		
FB	:	Inadequate Safety
FB	:	High Risk
FC	:	Substantial Risk
FD	:	Default

Notes : (1) CRISIL may apply '+' (plus) or '–' (minus) sign for ratings from FAAA to FC to indicate the relative position within the category.

(2) The contents within parenthesis are a guide to the pronunciation of the rating symbols.

Credit Rating for Short-Term Instruments

Rating Symbol	Indication (Each rating indicates that the degree of safety regarding timely payment on the instrument is shown against the symbol)
P-1	Very Strong
P-2	Strong
P-3	Adequate
P-4	Minimal
P-5	Expected to be in default on maturity or in default

Note: CRISIL may apply "+" signs for ratings from P-1 to P-3 to reflect a comparatively higher standing within the category.

CRISIL monitors the ratings it assigns constantly. The ratings may be upgraded, downgraded or withdrawn depending upon new information or developments concerning the company whose debt obligation is rated. It has the right to widely disseminate the ratings through the media, through its own publications or through any other methods.

ICRA Ltd

The ICRA Ltd. has been promoted by the IFCI Ltd. as the main promoter to meet the requirements of the companies based in the northern parts of the country. Apart from the main promoter, which holds 26 per cent of the share capital, the other shareholders are the Unit Trust of India, banks, LIC, GIC, Exim Bank, HDFC Ltd. and ILFS Ltd. It started operations in 1991. In order to bring international experience and practices to the Indian capital markets, the ICRA has entered into a MoU with Moody's Investors Service to provide, through its company Financial Programmes Inc (FPI), credit education, risk management software, credit research and consulting services to banks, financial/investment institutions, financial services companies and mutual funds in India. As in the case of the CRISIL, the main objectives of the ICRA are:

- To assist investors, both individual and institutional, in making well informed decisions.
- To assist issuers in raising funds, from a wider investor base, in large amounts and at a lower cost for highly rated entities.
- To enable banks, investment bankers, brokers in placing debt with investors by providing them with a marketing tool.
- To provide regulators with market driven systems to encourage the healthy growth of the capital markets in a disciplined manner, without additional burden on the Government.

Over the years, the ICRA has diversified the range of its services. It currently provides three types of services; (1) rating services; (2) information services (3) advisory services.

ICRA Rating Scale

Long-Term including Debentures Bonds and Preference Shares

LAAA	:	Highest Safety
LAA	:	High Safety
LA	:	Adequate Safety
LBBB	:	Moderate Safety
LBB	:	Inadequate Safety
LB	:	Risk Prone
LC	:	Substantial Risk
LD	:	Default, Extremely Speculative

Medium-Term including Deposits Fixed

MAAA	:	Highest Safety
MAA	:	High Safety
MA	:	Adequate Safety
MB	:	Inadequate Safety
MC	:	Risk Prone
MD	:	Default

Short-Term Including Commercial Paper

A-1	Highest Safety
A-2	High Safety
A-3	Adequate Safety
A-4	Risk Prone
A-5	Default

Note: (*i*) The rating symbols group together similar (but not necessarily identical) concerns in terms of their relative capability of timely servicing of a debts/obligations, as per terms of contracts *i.e.*, the relative degree of safety/risk.

(*ii*) The sign (+) or (–) may be used after the rating symbol to indicate the comparative position of the company within the group covered by the symbol.

(*iii*) The letter 'P' in parenthesis after the rating symbol indicates that the debt instrument is being used to raise resources by a new company for financing a new project and the rating assumes successful completion of the project.

(*iv*) The rating symbols for different instruments of the same company need not necessarily by the same.

CARE Ltd.

The CARE Ltd. is a credit rating and information services company promoted by the Industrial Development Bank of India (IDBI) jointly with financial institutions, public/private sector banks and private finance companies. It commenced its credit rating operations in October 1993 and offers a wide range of products and services in the field of credit information and equity research. Unlike the CRISIL and the ICRA, the CARE is very cautious in entering new areas of business. Currently, it offers the following services:

(*a*) **Credit Rating:** The CARE undertake credit rating of all types of debt instruments, both short-term and long-term.

(*b*) **Advisory Services:** The CARE provides advisory services in the areas of:

- Securitisation transactions
- Structuring financial instruments
- Financing of infrastructure projects
- Municipal finances.

PRACTICAL PROBLEMS OF CREDIT RATING

1. The absence of widespread branch network of the rating agency may limit its skills in rating.
2. Inexperienced, unskilled or overloaded staff may not do justice to their job and the resulting ratings may not be perfect.
3. Since rating exercise involves a number of factors, a rigid mathematical formula can not be applied to finalize rating and some element of subjectivity creeps in, thereby giving scope for bias.
4. The time factor greatly affects rating and gives misleading conclusions. A company which experiences adverse conditions temporarily will be given a low rating judged on the basis of temporary phenomenon.
5. Since the rating agencies receive a sizable fee from the companies for awarding ratings, a tendency to inflate the ratings may develop.
6. The rating is not permanent but subject to changes and moreover the agencies can not give any guarantee for the investors.
7. Investment which have the same rating may not have identical investment quality because the number of rating categories is limited and hence can not reflect small but meaningful differences in the degree of risk.
8. Borrowing entities give misleading advertisements about the rating symbols of their instruments. For example, 'X' Co. Ltd. which has got AAX for its debenture may mobilize fixed deposits instead of revealing the low rating for fixed deposits. Such kind of window dressing should be curtailed.

MULTIPLE CHOICE QUESTIONS

1. Investment Information and Credit Rating Agency of India (IICRA) is a:
A. Private company
B. Public company
C. Govt. Company
D. Statutory company
E. None of these

2. Dunham Greenberg Formula is used for............... .
A. Individual credit rating
B. Institutional credit rating
C. Both of these
D. Social credit rating
E. None of these

3. Which of these is not a credit rating agency?
A. Moody
B. Standard & Poors
C. Price water house
D. CRISIL
E. None of these

4. Credit rating indicates .... of a company:
A. Financial status
B. Overall efficiency
C. Management efficiency
D. All the above
E. None of these

5. Credit rating is only a/an............. .
A. Opinion B. Recommendation
C. Suggestion D. Advice
E. None of these

6. Which of the following is not a credit rating agency?
A. CRISIL B. ICRA
C. DCR India D. Either A or C
E. None of these

7. CRISIL was established in:
A. 1987 B. 1991
C. 1994 D. 1996
E. None of these

8. AAA rating stands for:
A. Highest safety B. High safety
C. Moderate safety D. All the above
E. None of these

9. BBB rating indicates
A. Adequate safety
B. Reasonable safety
C. Moderate safety
D. Either A or B
E. None of these

10. Credit rating is mandatory:
A. equity shares
B. preference shares
C. debentures
D. All of the above
E. None of these

11. Systematic risk is also known as:
A. unavoidable risk
B. unique risk
C. avoidable risk
D. financial risk
E. None of these

12. Unsystematic risk is also known as:
A. unavoidable risk B. unique risk
C. avoidable risk D. Both B and C
E. None of these

13. The risk in portfolio is measured through the:
A. Weighted average of standard deviations
B. Weighted average of variance
C. Variance co-variance matrix
D. Correlation
E. None of these

14. The highest credit risk rating that can be awarded to any company by CRISIL is.....
A. ++A
B. AAA
C. +AA
D. B+
E. None of the above

ANSWERS

1	2	3	4	5	6	7	8	9	10
B	A	C	A	A	E	A	A	C	C
11	**12**	**13**	**14**						
A	D	C	B						

17

Banking Abbreviation

ADRs	: American Depository Receipts
AFS	: Available for Sale
ALM	: Asset Liability Management
ANBC	: Adjusted Net Bank Credit
ARC	: Asset Reconstruction Companies
ARC	: Agricultural Refinance Corporation
ARDC	: Agricultural Refinance and Development Corporation
ARF	: Asset Reconstruction Fund
ASBA	: Account Supported by Blocked Amount
ASBA	: Applications Supported Bank Accounts
ATM	: Automated Teller Machine
BC	: Business Correspondent
BCBS	: Basel Committee on Banking Supervision
BCSBI	: Banking Codes & Standard Board of India
BF	: Business Facilitator
BFS	: Board for Financial Supervision
BIFR	: Board for Industrial and Financial Reconstruction
BIS	: Bank for International Settlements
BO	: Banking Ombudsman
BOE	: Bill of Exchange
BOP	: Balance of Payments
BOT	: Balance of Trade
BPLR	: Benchmark Prime Lending Rate
BPSS	: Board for Regulation and Supervision of Payment and Settlement Systems
BRBNMPL	: Bharatiya Reserve Bank Note Mudran Private Limited
BSE	: Bombay Stock Exchange
BSR	: Basic Statistical Returns
CAC	: Current Account Convertibility
CAC	: Capital Account Convertibility
CAMELS	: Capital Adequacy, Asset Quality, Management, Earnings, Liquidity, Systems and Controls
CARE	: Credit Analysis and Research Limited
CAS	: Central Accounts Section
CASA	: Current and savings accounts
CBLO	: Collateralised Bank Lending Obligations
CBLO	: Collateralised Borrowing & Lending Obligation
CBS	: Core Banking Solution
CCIL	: Clearing Corporation of India Limited
CCP	: Central Counter Party
CDSL	: Central Depository Services Ltd
CE of OBE	: Credit Equivalent of Off-Balance Sheet Exposures
CFMS	: Centralised Funds Management System
CFSP	: Committee on Financial Sector Plan
CIBIL	: Credit Information Bureau of India Limited
CMB	: Cash Management Bill
CPI	: Consumer Price Index
CPPAPS	: Committee on Procedures and Performance Audit on Public Services
CRAR	: Capital to Risk Assets Ratio
CRAR	: Capital to Risk-Weighted Assets Ratio
CRISIL	: Credit Rating Information Services of India Limited
CRM	: Customer Relationship Management
CRR	: Cash Reserve Ratio
CSD	: Customer Service Department
CSF	: Consolidated Sinking Fund
CTS	: Cheque Truncation System
CTT	: Commodities Transaction Tax
DAD	: Deposit Accounts Department
DBOD	: Department of Banking Operations and Development
DBS	: Department of Banking Supervision
DCC	: District Consultative Committee
DCCB	: District Central Cooperative Bank
DEAP	: Department of Economic Analysis and Policy

DICGC : Deposit Insurance and Credit Guarantee Corporation
DNBS : Department of Non-Banking Supervision
DPG : Deferred Payment Guarantee
DPN : Demand Promissory Note
DPSS : Department of Payment and Settlement Systems
DRAT : Debt Recovery Appellate Tribunal
DRI : Differential Rate of Interest
DRT : Debt Recovery Tribunals.
DSCR : Debt Service Coverage Ratio
DSIM : Department of Statistics and Information Management
EBT : Electronic Benefit Transfer
ECBs : External Commercial Borrowings
ECS : Electronic Clearing Service
EDI : Electronic Data Interchange
EEFC : Exchange Earners' Foreign Currency
EFT : Electronic Funds Transfer
EMI : Equated Monthly Instalments
EPS : Earnings Per Share
ESOP : Employee Stock Options
Exim Bank : Export Import Bank of India
FCAC : Fuller Capital Account Convertibility
FCAs : Foreign Currency Assets
FCCB : Foreign Currency Convertible Bond
FCEB : Foreign Currency Exchangeable Bond
FCNR(B) : Foreign Currency Non-Resident (Banks)
FDI : Foreign Direct Investment
FEDAI : Foreign Exchange Dealers Association of India
FEMA : Foreign Exchange Management Act
FERA : Foreign Exchange Regulation Act
FFMC : Full Fledged Money Changers
FIIs : Foreign Institutional Investors
FIMMDA : Fixed Income Money Market and Derivatives Association of India
FINO : Financial Inclusion Network Operation
FLCCs : Financial Literacy and Credit Counselling Centres
FMC : Financial Markets Committee
FOB : Free on Board
FRAs : Forward Rate Agreements
FRBM : Fiscal Responsibility and Budget Management
FSDC : Financial Stability and Development Council
FSLRC : Financial Sector Legislative Reforms Commission
GDRs : Global Depository Receipts
GoI : Government of India
GRF : Guarantee Redemption Fund
G-Sec : Government Securities
HFT : Held for Trading
HPC on UCBs: High Power Committee on Urban Cooperative Banks
HSRS : High Speed Reader Sorter
HTM : Held-to-Maturity
HVC : High Value Clearing
IBA : Indian Banks' Association
ICICI : Industrial Credit and Investment Corporation of India
ICRA : Investment Information and Credit Rating Agency of India Limited
ICT : Information and Communication Technology
IDBI : Industrial Development Bank of India
IDMD : Internal Debt Management Department
IDR : Indian Depository Receipt
IDRBT : Institute for Development and Research in Banking Technology
IFSC : Indian Financial System Code
IGIDR : Indira Gandhi Institute of Development Research
IMF : International Monetary Fund
IPDIs : Innovative Perpetual Debt Instruments
IRDA : Insurance Regulatory Development Authority
IRS : Interest Rate Swap
JV : Joint Venture
KCC : Kisan Credit Card
KVIC : Khadi and Village Industries Corporation
KYC : Know Your Customer
LAB : Local Area Banks
LAF : Liquidity Adjustment Facility
LAMPS : Large Sized Adivasi Multipurpose Societies
LERMS : Liberalised Exchange Rate Management System
LIBOR : London Inter Bank Operations Rate
LIC : Life Insurance Corporation of India
LTCCI : Long Term Rural Cooperative Credit Institution
MCA : Ministry of Company affairs

MCX : Multi Commodity Exchange
MCX-SX : MCX Stock Exchange
MIBOR : Mumbai Inter Bank Operations Rate
MICR : Magnetic Ink Character Recognition
MIS : Management Information System
MoU : Memorandum of Understanding
MPD : Monetary Policy Department
MSE : Micro and Small Enterprise
MSF : Marginal Standing Facility
MSMED : Micro, Small and Medium Enterprises Development
MSS : Market Stabilisation Scheme
NABARD : National Bank for Agriculture and Rural Development
NBFC-D : Deposit taking NBFC
NBFC-ND : Non-deposit taking NBFC
NBFCs : Non-Banking Financial Companies
NDS : Negotiated Dealing System
NDS-OM : Negotiated Dealing System – Order Matching
NDTL : Net Demand and Time Liability
NECS : National Electronic Clearing System
NEFT : National Electronic Funds Transfer
NER : North Eastern Region
NGO : Non-Government Organisation
NI Act : Negotiable Instruments Act
NIBM : National Institute of Bank Management
NoF : Net owned Funds
NPAs : Non-Performing Assets
NPCI : National Payments Corporation of India
NPV : Net Present Value
NR(E)RA : Non-Resident (External) Rupee Account
NRE : Non-Resident External account
NREGS : National Rural Employment Guarantee Scheme
NRI : Non-Resident Indian
NRO : Non-Resident Ordinary Account
NSDL : National Securities Depository Limited
NSE : National Stock Exchange
OCB : Overseas Corporate Bodies
OLTAS : Online Tax Accounting System
OMO : Open Market Operation
OSMOS : Off-Site Monitoring and Surveillance
OSS : Off-Site Surveillance
OTC : Over-the-Counter
OTCEI : Over the Counter Exchange of India
PACS : Primary Agricultural Credit Societies
PAD : Public Accounts Department
PAN : Permanent Account Number
PCARDBs : Primary Cooperative Agriculture and Rural Development Banks
PDAI : Primary Dealers Association of India
PDO : Public Debt Office
PDO-NDS : Public Debt Office - Negotiated Dealing System
PDs : Primary Dealers
PIN : Personal Identification Number
PIO : Person of Indian Origin
POA : Power of Attorney
POS : Point of Sale
PSS Act : Payment and Settlement Systems Act
QD : Quarterly Discussion
QIB : Qualified Institutional Buyers
RBI : Reserve Bank of India
RBS : Risk Based Supervision
RBSC : Reserve Bank Staff College
RDBMS : Relational Database Management System
REC : Rural Electrification Corporation
REPO : Repurchase Option
RFC : Resident Foreign Currency Account
RFC(D) : Resident Foreign Currency (Domestic) Account
RIDF : Rural Infrastructure Development Fund
RKBY : Rashtriya Krishi Bima Yojana
RRB : Regional Rural Bank
RTGS : Real Time Gross Settlement
RWA : Risk Weighted Assets
SACPs : Special Agricultural Credit Plans
SBI : State Bank of India
SCARDBs : State Cooperative Agriculture and Rural Development Banks
SCB : Scheduled Commercial Bank
SDDS : Special Data Dissemination Standards
SDR : Special Drawing Rights
SEBI : Securities and Exchange Board of India
SFMS : Structured Financial Messaging Services
SGL : Subsidiary General Ledger
SHGs : Self-Help Groups
SIDBI : Small Industries Development Bank of India
SIDC : State Industrial Development Corporation

SIPS : Systemically Important Payment System
SJSRY : Swarna Jayanti Shahari Rozgar Yojana
SLBC : State Level Bankers' Committee
SLR : Statutory Liquidity Ratio
SLRS : Scheme for Liberation and Rehabilitation of Scavangers
SME : Small and Medium Industries
SMERA : SME rating agency of India Limited
SMEs : Small and Medium Enterprises
SPMCIL : Security Printing and Minting Corporation of India Ltd.
SPV : Special Purpose Vehicle
SSI : Small Scale Industries
SSSBE : Small Scale Service and Business Enterprises
StCB : State Co-operative Bank
SWIFT : Society for Worldwide Interbank Financial Telecommunication
TAC : Technical Advisory Committee
TAFCUBs : Task Force for Urban Co-operative Banks
TBs : Treasury Bills
UCBs : Urban Cooperative Banks
USD : United States Dollar
UTI : Unit Trust of India
WI : When Issued
WMA : Ways and Means Advances
WOS : Wholly Owned Subsidiary
WPI : Wholesale Price Index
YTM : Yield to maturity
ZTC : Zonal Training Centre

MULTIPLE CHOICE QUESTIONS

1. Expanded form of AML is:
A. Anti-Monetary Laundering
B. Asia-Money Laundering
C. Anti-Money Laundering
D. Authentic Money Lending
E. None of these

2. Expand CTS :
A. Cheque Truncation System
B. Cheque Transaction System
C. Cash Transaction System
D. Cash Truncation System
E. None of these

3. What is the full form of MICR?
A. Magnetic ink code recognition
B. Memory information code recognition
C. Magnetic information character recognition
D. Memory ink character recognition
E. Magnetic ink character recognition

4. What is the full form of NECS?
A. National E-Commerce Service
B. National Electronic Commerce Service
C. New Electronic and Clearning Service
D. National Electronic and Clearing Service
E. New E-commerce Service

5. Which of the following is the correct full form of ECS often used in banking?
A. Electronic Clash System
B. Electronic Cash Service
C. Electronic Clearing Service
D. Electronic Charging System
E. None of these

6. The abbreviation 'EPOS' stands for ....
A. Electronic Payment of Sale
B. Electronic Point of Sale
C. Electronic Purchase of Sale
D. Electronic Price of Sale
E. Electronic Platform of Sale

7. Which of the following is the full form of PURA?
A. Provision of Urban Amenities in Rural Areas
B. Programme on Urban Rural Association
C. Preferential and Uniform Re-enforcement Act
D. Perfect Urban Rural Association
E. Other than those given as options

8. IFSC has how many digits?
A. 7 B. 15
C. 11 D. 9
E. 10

9. Real Time Gross Settlement (RTGS) mechanism is primarily meant for:
A. Large value transactions
B. Foreign exchange transactions
C. Transaction between SBI and Public Sector Banks only
D. Element of clearing transactions only
E. Correct benefits transfer payments

10. The alphabet 'S' in the 'NSDL' stands for:
A. Subsidiary B. Statistics
C. Survey D. Securities
E. Settlement

11. The alphabet 'E' in the acronym 'ELSS' stands for:
A. Exchange B. Economic

C. Equity D. Employment
E. Earnings

12. The 'CDR' is a framework to ensure timely and transparent mechanism for:
A. Provision of credit to the corporate
B. Recovery of corporate debt
C. Disposal of securities of defaulting corporate
D. Restructuring of corporate debt
E. Recovery from wilful defaulters

13. The National Payment Corporation of India (NPCI) has launched a mobile based payment facility. This facility is known as:
A. NEFT B. RTGS
C. IMPS D. USSD
E. INSTAPAY

14. What is the full form of SIDBI?
A. Small Industries Development Bank of India
B. Service Infrastructure Developmental Bank of India
C. Small Scale Industrial Development Bank of India
D. Securities & Investment Derivatives Bank of India.
E. Steel Industries Developmental Bank of India

15. POSCO is in the process of establishing its plants in India. What does the letter 'P' denote in the name POSCO?
A. Popular B. Pallin
C. Pohang D. Paradeep
E. Petersburg

16. Expand the term BCBS.
A. Bank's Committee on Banking Supervision
B. Basel Committee on Banking Supervision
C. Bank's Commission on Banking Supervision
D. Basel Commission on Banking Supervision
E. None of these

17. EBT stands for
A. Electronic Beginning Transaction
B. Electronic Benefit Transfer
C. Electric Belated Transfer
D. Essential Beneficiary Transaction
E. None of these

18. IMF stands for
A. International Money Fund
B. International Monetary Fund
C. Indian Mutual Fund
D. Industrial Monetary Fund
E. None of these

19. IRDA stands for:
A. International Reconstruction and Development Association
B. Insurance Regulatory and Development Authority
C. Indian Road Development Agency
D. Industrial Re-Development Authority
E. None of these

20. NHB is:
A. Hyderabad Bank for Nation
B. National Housing Bank
C. Non - Housing Bank in India
D. National Housing Board
E. None of these

21. NDTL stands for:
A. Net Demand and Time Liabilities
B. Non Demat Terrific Liabilities
C. National Demand for True Liabilities
D. No Demand for True Liabilities
E None of these

22. LAB means:
A. Legislatively Assembled Banks
B. Lawfully Authorized Banks
C. Local Area Banks
D. Locally Associated Banks
E. None of these

23. Full form of FINO:
A. Financial Information Network and Operation Limited
B. Finance Information Network Organization
C. Finance in Network Organization
D. Financial Inclusion in Network Operation
E. None of these

24. Full form of TPA
A. Third Party Administrator
B. Total Performing Assets
C. Third Party Association
D. Transparent Performing Assets
E. None of these

25. Full Form of TRAI is?
A. Transport Regulatory Authority of India
B. Telecom Regulatory Agency of India
C. Telecom Regulatory Authority of India
D. Transport Regulatory Agency of India
E. None of these

ANSWERS

1	2	3	4	5	6	7	8	9	10
C	A	E	D	C	B	A	C	A	D
11	**12**	**13**	**14**	**15**	**16**	**17**	**18**	**19**	**20**
C	D	C	A	C	B	B	B	B	B
21	**22**	**23**	**24**	**25**					
A	C	A	A	C					

18 Glossary of Banking Terms

AAA: A type of grade that is used to rate a particular bond. It is the highest rated bond that gives maximum returns at the time of maturity.

ABO: Accumulated Benefit Obligation, ABO is a measure of liability of pension plan of an organisation and is calculated when the pension plan is terminated.

ABS: Asset-Backed Securities. It means a type of security that is backed by a pool of bank loans, leases, and other assets.

Absorption: A term related to real estate, it is a process of renting a real estate property which is newly built or recently approved.

Accrued Interest: Interest that already earned, but not yet paid is known as Accrued Interest.

Acid Test Ratio: Acid test ratio is also known as Quick ratio. It is a Liquidity ratio. Acid test ratio measures the ability of an organization to pay its current liabilities. In Quick Asset we take cash, cash equivalents, short-term investment or marketable securities or current account receivables as a Quick assets. Formula of acid test ratio = Quick Assets/Current Liabilities.

Acquisition: Purchase of controlling interest in a firm, generally through tender offer for the target shares.

Actuary: Insurance company official, responsible for estimating future claims and disbursement and for calculating necessary fund and premium levels.

ADS: Authorized Dealers

Advising Bank: A Bank usually located in the country of residence of an Exporter, used by an Importer's bank to authenticate a Letter of Credit before it is passed on to the Exporter.

AEZs: Agricultural Export Zones

Affidavit: A written statement, sworn to be true by the person signing it, before someone authorized by court of law.

Agent Bank: A participating bank in a syndicated loan that handles all the operations and deals with the borrower on behalf of the members of the syndicate.

AGM: Annual General Meeting, it is the year meeting held by every registered company. Agenda is to explain the performance during the year, presentation of annual financial statements, voting on important financial decisions. Any shareholder can participate in AGM.

AIDB: All India Development Bank

ALM: Asset/liability management involves a set of techniques to create value and manage risks in a bank.

Amalgamation: Amalgamation means merger. When two companies merged by their mutual agreement for making a large organization is known as amalgamation.

American Depository Receipt (ADR): American Depository Receipt is a certificate Which is issued by US Bank to a Non-US Company For their (Non-US Company) shares. ADRs can be traded in the US Stock market. It is a negotiable instrument and holder of ADRs get the benefit like a stock holder.

American Option: An option that can be exercised on or any time before the date of expiry.

AMFI: Association of Mutual Funds of India. AMFI is an apex body of all Asset Management Companies (AMCs) which have been registered with SEBI. (Note: AMFI is not a mutual funds regulator).

Amortization: It is an accounting technique by which intangible assets are written off over a period of time. For example, provision for doubtful debts or preliminary expenses are written off over a certain period of time.

Amount at Risk: Balance of the sum payable not covered by reserves, potentially falling on the net worth (net assets) of the company.

ANBC: Adjusted Net Bank Credit is Net Bank Credit added to investments made by banks in non-SLR bonds.

Annuity: Annuity is a type of payment at fixed intervals for a certain period or lifetime to a person who deposits some money in installments or lump sum. The amount which is paid back includes principal and interest.

APEDA: Agricultural and Processed Food Products Exports Development Authority.

Appreciation: Increase in the value of something (stocks, goods etc.) is term as Appreciation. It is due to Increase in the demand, scarcity of the goods or increase in earnings. Appreciation is opposite condition as to depreciation.

APR: It stands for Annual Percentage Rate. APR is a percentage that is calculated on the basis of the amount financed, the finance charges, and the term of the loan.

Arbitrage: Simultaneous purchase and sale of identical or equivalent financial instruments or commodity futures so as to benefit from difference in their price relationship.

Arbitration: When there is dispute between two parties, Arbitrator come to resolve the dispute. Parties have to accept the decision taken by the arbitrator. It is for the settlement of the labour dispute between employer and employees by the third party *i.e.* arbitrator.

ARM: Adjustable Rate Mortgage is basically a type of loan where the rate of index is calculated on the basis of the previously selected index rate.

Asset Management Company (AMC): These companies are specialize to the recovery of the assets on the behalf of banks or other financial institutions. The non-performing assets can be assigned to AMC for the recovery purpose by the banks.

Asset Turnover Ratio: This ratio can be explained as Net assets/Total turnover or sales. This ratio measures the operational efficiency of business assets. In simple terms, this measures how many time total assets turned in a year and how efficiently the assets are used in a business.

Asset/Liability Risk: A risk that current obligations/ liabilities cannot be met with current assets. A fundamental risk in all organizations, which should manage the risk and maintain liquidity or become insolvent.

Asset: An economic resource owned or controlled by a company and expected to generate future benefit for that company. Like land, building, machinery etc.

Assignment: Receipt of an exercise notice by an option writer (seller) that obligates him to sell (in the case of a call) or purchase (in the case of a put) the underlying security at the specified strike price.

Audit Risk: The risk of giving an incorrect audit opinion.

Audit: Financial statement and physical stock is checked annually by professional auditor (Chartered Accountant affiliated by ICAI in India).

Automated Banking Machines (ABMs): Terminals that allow bank customers to perform many everyday banking tasks, *e.g.*, deposits, withdrawals, bill payments and transfers between accounts.

Automated Teller Machines (ATMs): A computerized machine used for banking transactions, *e.g.* depositing or withdrawing money, making balance/transaction inquiries and transfers; operated through magnetic plastic cards with the help of personal identification numbers (PINs).

Available Balance: The portion of a customer's account balance having no restrictions from the bank and available for immediate withdrawals.

Average Life: Weighted average of the maturities of various loans or bonds after taking into account agreed amortization's.

Back-end Value: Amount paid to the remaining shareholders in the second stage of a two-tier or partial tender offer.

Balance of Payment (BOP): Balance of payments is statement of economic transactions of a country with rest of the world. The balance of payment classifies these transaction in two accounts – the current account and capital account.

Balance of Trade: The difference between the value of exports and imports of a country is known as Balance of payment. If difference between exports and imports are positive then it is favourable balance of trade and vice versa.

Balance Sheet: Balance Sheet is a statement a company showing the assets and liabilities of the business on a particular date. Balance Sheet is helpful to determining the financial position of the business.

Balloon Payment: Is a specific type of mortgage payment, and is named "balloon payment" because of the structure of the payment schedule. For balloon payments, the first several years of payments are smaller and are used to reduce the total debt remaining in the loan. Once the small payment term has passed (which can vary, but is commonly 5 years), the remainder of the debt is due - this final payment is the one known as the "balloon" payment, because it is larger than all of the previous payments.

Bancassurance: Selling of the different types of the insurance products (Life policies, non-life policies, car insurance, medical policies etc.) as corporate agents by the banks through their branches is known as bancaassurance.

Bank Credit: Includes Term Loans, Cash Credit, Overdrafts, Bills purchased & discounted, Bank Guarantees, Letters of Guarantee, Letters of credit.

Bank Debits: The sum of the value of all cheques and other instruments charged against the deposited funds of a bank's customer.

Bank Ombudsman: Bank ombudsman is the authority to solve the complaint of the customers against any banks. This scheme covers all scheduled banks, co-operative and the RRBs. If customer is not satisfied with the decision of the bank ombudsman then they can forward their complain to the Deputy Governor of RBI.

Bank Rate: It is a rate at which RBI lends money to commercial banks without any security. It is used for long-term Borrowing. Bank rate is not the main tool to control money supply. Repo Rate is the main tool to control Money Supply. Penal rates are linked with Bank rate.

Bank Statement: A periodic record of a customer's account that is issued at regular intervals, showing all transactions recorded for the period in question.

Banker's Acceptance: Negotiable time drafts, or bills of exchange, that have been accepted by a bank which, by accepting, assumes the obligation to pay the holder of the draft the face value of the instrument on the specified maturity date. Bankers' Acceptances are generally used to finance export, import, shipment, or storage of goods.

Bankruptcy: A condition in which a firm (or individual) is unable to meet its (his) obligations and, hence, its (his) assets are surrendered to a court for administration.

Basis Point: One-hundredth of one percentage point (*i.e.* 0.01%), normally used for indicating spreads or cost of finance.

BCBS: Basel Committee on Banking Supervision is an institution created by the Central Bank governors of the Group of Ten nations.

Bear Market: A situation when price of securities in the stock market are generally declining is known as bear market.

Beneficiary: A beneficiary can be a person or entity who is entitled to take the benefits on the behalf of some other person or entity.

Bid/Bond Guarantee: A guarantee issued by a bank on behalf of a seller to a buyer to support the sellers' bid or tender for a contract. If the sellers' bid is accepted, the buyer can claim compensation under the guarantee.

Bill Discounting: Receiving payment on a bill of exchange prior to the bill's maturity by surrendering the bill for the face value less applicable interest for the time remaining up to maturity.

Bill of Exchange: An order written by the seller of goods instructing the purchaser to pay the seller (or bearer of the bill) a specified amount on a specified future date.

Bill of Lading: A document which represents ownership of goods in transit.

Black Money: The money which is concealed from tax authorities and illegally obtained is known as black money. It is uncounted money.

Blue Chips: Shares in leading quoted companies that can be easily bought and sold without influencing their price (liquidity) and are regarded as low-risk investments.

Bonds: An instrument in which a person lends money to a corporate for a definite period of time at a fixed interest rate. Bonds are used by corporates or government to raise money.

Book Value: The cost price of an asset less accumulated depreciation.

Book-keeping: Recording of financial transactions in books of account.

Bought Financing: Short-term financing arranged by a bank for offering continuing source of funds pending receipt of loan/bond issue proceeds.

Bouncing of a Cheque: When there is not sufficient balance in the account of the customer who issued the cheque is return by the bank to the customer address. This is termed as Bouncing of cheque.

Brand Name Capital: A firm's reputation; the result of non-salvageable investment which provides customers with an implicit guarantee of product quality for which they are willing to pay a premium.

Break-even Point: Refers to the price at which a transaction produces neither a gain nor a loss.

Bridge Loan: Temporary finance provided to a project until long-term arrangements are made.

Bull Market: Bull market is a situation of market where speculators buy shares by hoping of the rise of price in near future and then resale those share to earn profit.

Bull: One who expects prices to rise.

Bullet Redemption: Repayment of a debt in one lump sum at the end of the maturity period. A common practice in Euro markets in respect of bond issues.

Bundling: Provision of more than one product or service to a customer at an inclusive price *e.g.* 'free' life insurance with a loan.

Bust-up Takeover: An acquisition followed by divestment of some or all of the operating units of the acquired firm which are presumably worth more in pieces than as a going concern.

Buy-back: A public company, which buys its own shares, by tender offer, in open market, or in a negotiated buy-back from a large block holder.

CAC: Capital Account Convertibility. It is the freedom to convert local financial assets into foreign financial assets and vice versa. This means that capital account convertibility allows anyone to freely move from local currency into foreign currency and back, or in other words, transfer of money from current account to capital account.

Call Date: Date on which a bond may be redeemed before maturity at an option of the issuer.

Call Money: Loaned funds that are repayable upon the request of either party.

Call Option: An option that gives its holder the right to buy an asset at a fixed price during a certain period.

Call Provision: A feature of a bond that entitles the issuer to retire the bond before maturity.

Cap: A ceilling on the interest rate on a floating-rate note.

Capital Adequacy Ratio (CAR): A ratio of total capital divided by risk-weighted assets and risk-weighted off-balance sheet items. A bank is expected to meet a minimum capital ratio specifically prescribed by the Regulator.

Capital Budget: The list of planned capital expenditures prepared usually annually.

Capital Gain: Gain by selling a capital asset in which a person is not doing business. Income by selling a house by a bank employee is a capital gain whereas when a builder do the same thing it is income from business and professional.

Capital investments: Money used to purchase permanent fixed assets for a business, such as machinery, land or buildings as opposed to day-to-day operating expenses.

Capital Market: Market in which financial instruments are bought and sold.

Capital Reserves: This is also known as undistributed reserve. It is a part of the company profit which is not paid out as dividends to the shareholders.

Capital Structure: The composition of a firm's long-term financing consisting of equity, preference shares, and long-term debt.

Capital: Capital is money or wealth needed to produce goods and used to generate income by investing them in some other source. Business capital comes mainly from two sources – Debt and equity. Capital = Assets – Liabilities

CAR: Capital Adequacy Ratio. It's a measure of a bank's capital. Also known as "Capital to Risk Weighted Assets Ratio (CRAR)", this ratio is used to protect depositors and promote the stability and efficiency of financial systems around the world. It is decided by the RBI.

Cash Cows: Business segments, having a high market share in low growth product markets, which generate more cash flow than needed for reinvestment.

Cash Credit (CC): An arrangement whereby the bank gives a short-term loan against the self-liquidating security.

Cash Discount: A discount given to buyers for cash rather than credit purchase.

Cash Flow Forecast: An estimate of when and how much money will be received and paid out of a business. It usually records cash flow on a month-by-month basis.

Cash Flow: Movement of cash (cash equivalents) or incoming or outgoing of cash from different operations in an organization is called as cash flow. **Cash flow** is the difference in amount of **cash** available at the beginning of a period (opening balance) and the amount at the end of that period (closing balance).

Cash Reserve Ratio (CRR): CRR is a monetary policy instrument used by RBI to control the supply of money. Banks have to keep some percentage of NDTL (Net Demand and Time Liability) with RBI this is known as CRR. The RBI have Authority to change the CRR Rate.

Certificate of Deposits: Certificate of deposits is a money market negotiable instrument. It is generally issued for 7 days to 1 year. Minimum deposit amount in certificate deposits is rupees 1 Lakh.

CHAPS: Clearing House Automated Payment System. It's a type of electronic bank-to-bank payment system that guarantees same-day payment.

Cheque Truncation: Cheque truncation is system to stopping the physical moment of the cheque. In this system, scan copy (electronic image) of cheque is used for the clearing purpose of cheque.

Cheque: Cheque is a bill of exchange. Cheque is an order to bank to pay stated amount in the cheque from the drawer account. Cheque is always payable on demand.

CIBIL: Credit Information Bureau of India Limited. CIBIL is India's first credit information bureau. Whenever a person applies for new loans or credit card(s) to a financial institution, they generate the CIBIL report of the said person or concern to judge the credit worthiness of the person and also to verify their existing track record. CIBIL actually maintains the borrower's history.

CLB: Company Law Board.

Clean-up Merger: Also called Take-out merger. The consolidation of the acquired firm into the acquiring firm after the acquirer has obtained control.

Collateral: Property (real, personal or otherwise) pledged as security for a loan. Also, any supplementary promise of payment, such as a guarantee.

Collusion: A secret agreement between two or more persons to defraud another person of his or her right in order to achieve an unlawful objective.

Commercial Credit Risk: The risk of loss from providing credit to corporate counter-parties. Extension of credit can take the form of direct loans and contingencies/ guarantees.

Commercial Paper (CP): Issue of short-term notes, without any underwriting, representing a promise to repay the amount at a specified future date.

Commitment Fee: A fee charged by a bank in respect of an unused balance of a line of credit or sanction of loan designed to offset the bank's cost of keeping the funds available.

Compound Interest: Interest payable (receivable) on interest.

Conglomerate: A combination of unrelated firms; any combination that is not vertical or horizontal.

Consumer Price Index (CPI): An index that measure movements in the average price of products and services.

Convertible Bond: A bond that is convertible into common stock.

Convertible Security: Bond or preferred stock which is convertible into equity shares generally at the option of the holder.

Core Banking Solutions (CBS): Centralized Online real Time Exchange (`CORE) is system where banks and their branches are interconnected for fast communication.

Corporate Banking: Banking services for large firms.

Corporate Governance: A system by which organizations are directed and controlled. Board of directors are responsible for the governance of their organizations.

Corporate Tax: A tax on the profits of firms, as distinct from taxation of the incomes of their owners.

Coupon Rate: The stated interest rate on a bond.

Covenant: A definite provision in a loan contract.

CPI: Consumer price index is measure to find price of a bundle of commodities. CPI is used to measure the inflation in a country.

Credit Crunch: Refers to a situation where supply of credit falls even though there is sufficient demand for it.

Credit History: A record of how a person or company has borrowed and repaid debts.

Credit Rating: A ranking applied to an individual, business or a nation based upon its credit history and current financial position. There are various credit rating companies in India such as Crisil.

Credit Risk: The risk of loss from failure of the counterparty to perform as agreed (contracted).

Credit Scoring System: A statistical system used to determine whether or not to grant credit by assigning numerical scores to various characteristics relating to creditworthiness.

Credit Worthiness: A creditor's measure of a consumer's or company's past and future ability and willingness to repay debts.

CRISIL: Credit Rating Information Services of India Limited. Crisil is a global analytical company providing ratings, research, and risk and policy advisory services.

Cross Default: Two loan agreements connected by a clause that allows one lender to recall the loan if the borrower defaults with another, and vice versa.

Cumulative Dividends: A feature of preferred stock that requires all past dividends on preferred stock to be paid before any equity dividends are paid.

Currency Basket: Arrangements whereby two or more currencies are clubbed together with defined weights, and whose exchange rate/interest rate is determined by computing weighted average market rates.

Currency Market Risk: The risk of loss from having positions in any of the currency markets. The risk can be from outright positions. It can also reside in the balance sheet or in the income flows of a company.

Current Account: Current account is only open for the business purpose. There is no limit of numbers of withdrawals from this type of account. No interest is given in this account.

Current Assets: Short-term assets, constantly changing in value, such as stocks, debtors and bank balances.

Current Liabilities: Short-term liabilities, due to be paid in less than one year, such as bank overdrafts, money owed to suppliers and employees.

Current Yield: The yield on a security resulting from dividing the interest payment or dividend on it by its current market price.

D/A (documents against acceptance): Refer to shipping documents presented to a bank on a collection basis to be passed to the buyer when he or she accepts a bill of exchange. The bank holds the bill of exchange until it ends (maturity) when they ask the buyer to pay the seller.

D/P (documents against payment): Refer to shipping documents presented to a bank on a collection basis to be passed to the buyer (drawee) when payment is made.

Debentures: Debentures is a long-term debt instrument issued by corporate to borrow money. A debentures holder gets fixed amount of interest.

Debit Card: Debit card is a plastic card issued by banks to customers to withdraw money electronically from their account without visiting the branch. Many bank issued Debit-Cum-Atm card.

Debt Consolidation: Debt consolidation is a process by which various loans and converted into a single loan to reduce interest rate and instalment value.

Debt/Equity Ratio: A comparative ratio of debt and equity used to measure the gearing/health of a business.

Debtor: A person or party who buys goods on credit is termed as debtor. Debtor is current assets of the business.

Default Risk Premium: The component of a required interest rate that is based on the lenders' perceived risk of default.

Default Risk: The risk that a borrower may not repay principal and/or interest as originally agreed.

Default: Generally, failure to satisfy an obligation when due, or the occurrence of one of the defined events of default agreed to by the parties under a contract.

Demat Account: Converting shares into electronic form and an electronic place where they are keep is known as demat account. Investor can buy or sell their shares by the help of demat account.

Depreciation: Depreciation is reduction in value of an asset due wear and tear over a period of time. For example a company purchased a machine in 2005 and planned to charge 20% depreciation. In 2010, the machine will be written off from the books of account.

Direct Financing: Provision of funds for investment to the ultimate user of funds.

Direct Tax: The impact and incidence of direct tax falls on the same person. Shifting of direct tax is not possible. Income Tax is an example of direct tax. Taxes which affect the consumer directly, such as income tax, corporate tax, capital gains tax etc.

Dishonour of Cheque: When a cheque is not paid by the paying banker due to some reason stated memo on the cheque is termed as dishonor of cheque.

Dividend Payout Ratio: It is the ratio of dividend paid per share and EPS (Earning per share)

Dividend: Dividend is the amount per share paid by a company to its shareholders. Dividend value is based upon company's profitability.

Documentary Credit: Written undertaking by a bank on behalf of an importer authorizing an exporter to draw drafts on the bank up to a specified amount under specific terms and conditions. They are used to facilitate international trade. Also called Letter of Credit (LC).

Double Entry Book-keeping: It is a method of book-keeping in which every transaction is recorded two accounts. Once in debit side and once in credit side.

DSCR: Debt Service Coverage Ratio, DSCR is a financial ratio that measures the company's ability to pay their debts.

Due Diligence: While finalizing documentation, the lead manager and the legal counsel conduct a thorough review of the borrowing entity with reference to the financials, legality, and all such matters relevant in a public offering of securities.

Earning per Share: Earnings made by a company in a financial year divided by number of issued shares.

Earning Yield: The ratio of earning per share to market price of the share.

E-Banking: Electronic Banking is facility of banking through electronic signals. ATMs, Credit Card, Debit cards transaction are the type of E Banking. Fund transfer Facilities like SWIFT, RTGS, NEFT belong to this category. Internet-banking is also example of E-Banking.

ECGC: Export Credit Guarantee Corporation of India. This organisation provides risk as well as insurance cover to the Indian exporters.

ECS: Electronic Clearing Facility is a type of direct debit. Tobin tax: Suggested by Nobel Laureate economist James Tobin, was originally defined as a tax on all spot conversions of one currency into another. Z score is a term widely used in the banking field.

Effective Rate of Interest: The percentage rate of return on an annual basis, reflecting the effect of intra-year compounding.

Electronic Fund Transfer (EFT): Transfer Funds in electronic form is termed as EFT (Electronic Fund Transfer). EFT gives facility to banks to exchange information between them. Even one branch of bank can transfer information to branch of another bank by using EFT.

Endorsement: When backside of a negotiable instrument contains signed by the holder or an order to transfer the title to some other person, this is called as endorsement.

Entrepreneur: A person who conceives, starts and manages a business.

EPS: Earnings per Share means the amount of annual earnings available to common stockholders as stated on a per share basis.

Equitable Mortgage: A type of mortgage under which one still owns the property which is security for the mortgage. The owner can occupy or live in the property.

Equity: The value of a business after all debts and other claims are settled. Also, the amount of cash a business owner invests in a business and/or the difference between the price for which a property could be sold and the total debts registered against it.

Escheat: Acquiring of the properties of person after his death by the government, in case there is no legal heir or nominee of that person then this type of property is termed as Escheat.

Escrow Account: An account for which a bank acts as an uninterested third party (custodian/depository) to ensure compliance with the terms of the deal between two parties only upon the fulfillment of some stated conditions. The account becomes operative on the occurrence of the stated event. Banks hold such accounts in which funds accumulate to pay taxes, insurance on mortgage property, etc.

Exchange Rate Risk: The risk that changes in currency exchange rates may have an unfavourable impact on costs or revenues of economic units.

Exchange Rate: The expression of a unit of foreign currency in relation to domestic country is known as exchange rate. Exchange rate can float move up or down.

Excise Duties: Duties levied on items manufactured within the country and paid by the manufacturer.

Ex-divided: Ex-dividend means without dividend. When a seller makes an ex-dividend sales contract then he is entitled to get dividend or interest payment.

Exports: Products and services sold to other countries.

Face Value: Face value also known as Nominal value is the original value of a share written or print on the share certificate.

Factoring: Sale of receivables to a financial institution usually on a 'non-recourse' basis.

FCCB: Foreign Currency Convertible Bond. A type of convertible bond issued in a currency different from the issuer's domestic currency.

FCNR Accounts: Foreign Currency Non-Resident accounts are the ones that are maintained by NRIs in foreign currencies like USD, DM, and GBP.

Fiat Money: Fiat money is a legal tender for settling debts. It is a paper money that is not convertible and is declared by government to be legal tender for the settlement of all debts.

Financial Year: A period of 12 months from 1st April to 31st March.

Fiscal Policy: Fiscal policy refers to the changing tax rates and levels of government spending to influence aggregate demand in the economy by government.

Fixed Assets: Assets such as land, buildings, machinery or property used in operating a business that will not be consumed or converted into cash during the current accounting period.

Fixed Rate: A pre-determined rate of interest applied to the principal of a loan or credit agreement.

Flat Rate: Rate of interest in a contract which remains same irrespective of market rate in future.

Floating Rate: Rate of interest which changes with change in market rate.

Foreign Exchange Rate: The value of a nation's currency in terms of another nation's currency.

Foreign Trade: The exchange of goods between two nations.

Forfaiting: A form of export finance in which the forfaiter accepts, at a discount from the exporter, a bill of exchange or promissory note (note) from the exporter's customer; the forfaiter in due course collects payment of the debt. Such notes are normally guaranteed by the customer's bank. Maturities are normally up to three years.

Forgery: When any type of alteration is made on a document or in negotiable instrument with intention to fraud is known as forgery.

Forward Contract: A contract in which one party agrees to buy, and the other to sell, a specified product at a specified price on a specified date in the future.

Forward Cover: Forward purchase or sale of foreign currency to offset an anticipated future cash flow.

FPO: Follow on Public Offerings: An issuing of shares to investors by a public-company that is already listed on an exchange. An FPO is essentially a stock issue of supplementary shares made by a company that is already publicly listed and has gone through the IPO process.

FSDC: Financial Stability and Development Council, India's apex body of the financial sector.

Fund Flow: Fund Flow is statement of change in a company net working capital during a fixed period of time.

Fund Manager: A person who manages a mutual fund and tries to maximize fund's returns while sticking to fund's objectives.

Fundamental Analysis: Analysis of a company based upon financial and operational performance.

Funded Debt: Generally, a short-term debt that has been converted into long-term debt funding.

Futures: Contracts to buy something in the future at a price agreed upon in advance. First developed in the agriculture commodity markets but often involve foreign exchange, and Government bonds.

GDR: Global Depository receipt (GDR) is a certificate issued by one country bank against a certain number of shares held in its custody but traded on the stock market of another country.

Gearing: It is the ratio of debt to equity.

Going-concern Value: The value of the firm as a whole over and above the sum of the values of each of its parts; the value of an organization's learning and reputation.

Gold Monetisation Scheme: The gold monetisation scheme was launched on November 5, 2015 by Prime Minister Narendra Modi, to reduce bullion imports and mobilise 22,000 tonnes of idle gold in the country. The amount of interest rate to be given is proposed to be left to the banks to decide. Both principal and interest to be paid to the depositors of gold, will be 'valued' in gold. For example, if a customer deposits 100 gms of gold and gets 2 per cent interest, then, on maturity he has a credit of 102 gms.

Gold Standard: A monetary system in which a country's government allows its currency unit to be freely converted into fixed amounts of gold and vice versa.

Goodwill: Intangible assets that defines firm's reputation in monetary terms.

GST: Good and Services tax is indirect tax levy on manufacture, sale and consumption of goods and services at a national level. The GST regime is expected to be functional from 1st April, 2017.

Haircut: The difference between the market value of a security and its value when used as collateral. The haircut is intended to protect a collateral taker from losses due to declines in collateral values.

HDI: HDI is Human Development index. Three Dimensions are used in HDI – 1. healthy life 2. Knowledge 3. Standard of living.

Hedge funds: Mutual funds which invests in derivatives

Hedge: One investment purchased against another investment in order to counter any loss made by either.

Hedging: Hedging is a technique used by investors to protect themselves from adverse price movements. Derivatives are used for hedging in which hedgers takes the risk of price fluctuations.

Holder in due Course: A person who receives a Document for value, before it was due and in good faith, without notice of any defect in it, he is called holder in due course.

Holder: Holder means any person who is entitled to receive or recover the amount due on the cheque, bill of exchange or promissory notes from the parties.

Holding Company: A company which controls another company, usually by owing more than half of its shares.

House Hold Income: Combined income of all members of a household is house hold income. It includes every form of income *i.e.*, salaries, wages, pensions, income from other sources.

IFSC: Indian Financial System Code (IFSC) which is an eleven alpha numeric character code. Its code is used by electronic payment system applications such as RTGS, National Electronic Fund Transfer (NEFT). The code is of 11 characters. The first part is the first 4 alphabet characters representing the Bank. Next character is 0(zero), this is reserved for future use and last six digit represents branch code.

Imports: Goods and services that a country buys from other countries.

IMPS: Inter-bank Mobile Payment Service. It is an instant interbank electronic fund transfer service through mobile phones. Both the customers must have MMID (Mobile Money Identifier Number). For this service, we don't need any GPS-enabled cell phones.

Income Statement: A statement that represents both income and expenditure of a business during a specific period of time.

Indemnity: A legal contract under which one party promises to pay another for any loses incurred to them by their acts.

Indirect Financing: The process by which deficit spending units obtain funds from financial intermediaries who, in turn, them from ultimate surplus spending units.

Indirect Taxes: Taxes, which are charged on goods produced, imported or exported: Excise and Customs duties.

Inflation Premium: A premium for anticipated inflation that investors require in addition to the pure rate of interest.

Initial Public Offering (IPO): The first offering to the public of common stock, *e.g.* of a former privately held firm, or a portion of the common stock of a hitherto wholly-owned subsidiary.

Insolvent: Insolvent is a person or organization who is unable to pay his debts, as his liabilities are more than the assets. Courts declare such persons insolvent. Banks do not open accounts of insolvent persons as they cannot enter into contract as per law.

Intangible Assets: Assets that cannot be touched. Examples are goodwill and patent rights.

Interest Rate Risk: Risk that value of financial assets will deteriorate because of fall in interest rate. For example, value of bonds decreases with decrease in interest rate.

Interest Rate: Interest rate is the price of borrowing money. As the "renting" of money creates credit, interest is the price of credit. The price of money is the cost of commodity or service bought with money.

Internal Rate of Return (IRR): The rate of discount at which the net present value of an investment is zero.

International Banking. Banking involves more than two countries. If an Indian Bank has branches in different countries like Bank of India, it is said International Banking.

Internet Banking: Online is a form of electronic banking which enables customers of banks to do banking transactions on the web. E-Banking, Virtual Banking is also similar to the internet Banking.

IPO: Initial Public Offerings is defined as the event where the company sells its shares to the public for the first time. (or the first sale of stock by a private company to the public.)

Joint Account: When two or more person jointly open account with bank, this is known as Joint Account.

Junk Bonds: Junk bonds are issued generally by smaller or relatively less well-known firms to finance their operations, or by large and well-known firms to fund leveraged buyouts. These bonds are frequently unsecured or partially secured, and they pay higher interest rates: 3 to 4 percentage points higher than the interest rate on blue chip corporate bonds of comparable maturity period.

Junk Fund: A fund which invests investor's money in junk investments means high risk investments which high returns.

Karta: Manager of a Hindu Undivided Family (HUF) who handles the family business is known as Karta. He is usually the eldest male member of the Hindu Undivided Family.

Kiosk Banking: KIOSK Banking is a facility provided by banks where customers have no need to go to the branch to make different transactions. The branch itself comes to the customer's village/place where the customer can make the transactions.

KYC Norms: KYC means "Know Your Customer". It is a process by which banks obtain personal information of the customer. The objective of doing so is to enable the Bank to have positive identification of its customers. Mainly three proofs include in KYC. They are (1) Proof of identity (2) Proof of Address (3) Photograph.

Lease Financing: Financing for the business of renting houses for a fixed period of time is known as Lease Financing. Leasing of a machinery for a specific period at specific price is an example of Lease Financing.

Lease: A contractual arrangement whereby one party (the lessor) grants the other party (the lessee) the right to use an asset in return for periodic rental payments.

Lessee: One who takes property on lease.

Lessor: A person, Corporation, or other legal entity that leases property to a lessee.

Letter of Credit: A letter from a bank guaranteeing that a buyer's payment to a seller will be received on time is known as letter of credit. If the buyer is unable to make payment on the purchase, the bank will be required to cover the full or remaining amount of the purchase to the party.

LGD: Loss Given Default. Institutions such as banks will determine their credit losses through an analysis of the actual loan defaults.

LIBID: London Interbank Bid Rate. The average interest rate at which major London banks borrow Euro currency deposits from other banks.

LIBOR: London Inter Bank Offered Rate. An interest rate at which banks can borrow funds, in marketable size, from other banks in the London interbank market.

Lien: A lender's claim on assets offered as security for a loan.

Limited Liability: Liability of an individual or a business up to the value of investment made in a business.

Line of Credit: A pre-approved credit facility (usually for one year) enabling a bank customer to borrow up to the specified maximum amount at any time during the relevant period of time.

Liquid Assets: Assets which can be readily converted into cash.

Liquidation: Divestment of all the assets of a firm so that the firm ceases to exist.

Liquidity: Ability of a business to pay off its short-term debts with current assets. Currently NISL is facing liquidity crunch.

Loan Document: A business contract by which a borrower and lender enter into an agreement. Loans are classified according to the lender or borrower involved, whether or not collateral is required, the time of maturity, conditions of repayment, and other variables.

Loan Risk: This is the risk of loss from loaning money and having the borrower fail to repay, either due to genuine reasons or willfully.

Long-term Debt: Long-term debt is obligations of the organization which are due after 1 year. It could be in the form of Bank loan, bonds, debentures etc.

Long-term Liabilities: Money that one owes over a period longer than 12 months, such as mortgages, bank loans and other obligations.

Margin Call: Margin call is a term used in two situations. **First** - Whenever a lender gives a secured loan and loan value is a fixed percentage of loan then whenever the value of security decrease below the decided ratio then lender given a margin call to borrower to bring loan to security ratio to decided level. **Secondly** in stock exchanges traders trades in various securities by paying 20-30% of the value of securities. Whenever the value of security goes below that margin, broker gives margin call to trader to bring the margin to desired level.

Market Capitalization: The total value, at market prices, of the securities at issue for a company or a stock market or sector of the stock market. Calculated by multiplying the number of shares issued by the market price per shares.

Market Value: The current value of an asset or any financial instrument in the market is called as market value.

Mark-to-market: As explained above while defining margin call, value of assets in case of securities is measured on daily basis. If the trader's asset value increased, increased value is transferred to his account. In case, the value of assets decreased margin call is made to adjust the margin.

Maturity: Maturity is the time when a bond, insurance policy or security matures and customer is eligible to get the realizable value from that instrument.

Merchant Banking: When a bank provides to a customer various types of financial services like accepting bills arising out of trade, providing advice, information or assistance on starting new business, acquisitions, mergers and foreign exchange that is known as merchant Banking.

Micro Finance: Micro Finance aims to assist poverty and empowerment of weaker sections in India. In micro finance, very small amounts are given as credit to poor in rural, semi-urban and urban areas to enable them to raise their income levels and improve living standards.

Mixed Economy: An economic system which have the characteristics of both Private and Government Enterprises. India is a mixed economy country.

Mobile Banking: M-Banking or mobile banking helps the customer to check his bank balance, order a demand draft, stop payment of a cheque, request for a cheque book and have information about latest interest rates.

Monetary Policy: Set of actions by Central bank of a country (RBI in case of India) to control the supply of money. These actions included increase in interest rate, open market purchases, changing commercial bank's reserve funds ratio (SLR) etc.

Money Laundering: When a customer uses banking channels to cover up his unlawful financial activities, it is called money laundering.

Money Market: Market dealing in short-term lending and borrowing of funds. Also know as Cash market.

Monopoly: Monopoly is a condition where only one seller in the market who controls the entire market supply and no substitute of the product is available in the market. Indian railway is an example of monopoly.

Mortgage: A mortgage is an agreement that allows a lender to seize property when a borrower fails to pay.

MSME and SME: Micro Small and Medium Enterprises (MSME), and SME stands for Small and Medium Enterprises. This is an initiative of the government to drive and encourage small manufacturers to enjoy facilities from banks at confessional rates.

Multinational Company (MNC): MNCs are a large scale company which has its production base in several countries and the bulk of the production is produced in outside nations. This company produces more overseas production than they do in its parent country.

Nationalization: When Government takes control of a business, this is known as nationalization.

NBFCs: A Non-Banking Financial Company (NBFC) is a company registered under the Companies Act, 1956 engaged in the business of loans and advances, acquisition of shares/debentures etc. NBFCs can not accept demand deposits.

NEFT: National Electronic Funds Transfer (NEFT) is a nation-wide electronic payment system. By NEFT one can transfer funds from a bank branch to any individual or corporate having a bank account with any bank branch within India. There is no limit – either minimum or maximum – on the amount of funds that could be transferred using NEFT. However, maximum amount per transaction is limited to ₹ 50,000 for cash-based remittances within India and also for remittances to Nepal.

Negotiation: Negotiation means an act of transferring of a money instrument from one person to another person in the course of business.

Net Income: If the total income in a period of a organization is deducted from all expenses during the same period is known as Net income of the Organization.

Net Present Value: Capital budgeting criterion, which compares the present value of cash inflows of a project discounted at the risk-adjusted cost of capital to the present value of investment outlays discounted at the risk-adjusted cost of capital.

Net Profit: Net profit is Gross profit minus indirect cost.

Net Worth: Book value of a company's common stock, surplus, and retained earnings.

Non-Resident: A person who is not considered as a resident of a country for tax purposes is called as Non-Resident. A person who is not a resident of India is a non-resident.

Non-Performing Assets (NPA): A Non-Performing asset shall be a loan or an advance where: (*a*) Interest or instalment of principal remain overdue for a period of more than 90 days in respect of a term loan. (*b*) The account remains out of order for a period of more than 90 days, in respect of an Overdraft/Cash Credit (*c*) The bill remains overdue for a period of more than 90 days in the case of bills purchased (*d*) Any amount to be received remains overdue for a period of more than 90 days in respect of other accounts.

Non-Recourse Discounting: Purchase from the seller of accepted term Bills of Exchange at a discount to allow for funding of the advance from the discount date until the maturity date of the bills. When the discount is provided on a non-recourse basis the financing bank has no recourse to the seller in the event of non-payment by the buyer or the buyers' bank.

NPA Account: If bank dues are not paid in any loan account within specified time period, then this type of account is treated as NPA Account and this amount is being treated as Non-Performing Assets.

NPV: Net Present Value is aggregate of future cash flows from a project minus total costs. NPV is a capital budgeting technique used to check feasibility of projects.

Obligation: The responsibility to perform some act or pay a sum of money when due.

Off-Balance Sheet: Includes all banking transactions that do not appear on the balance sheet of a bank as an asset or as a debt. Includes all commitments for which a cash flow arises conditional on a specific event. For instance, a loan guarantee will create an obligation only if there is a default. Derivatives are a form of off-balance sheet transactions.

Oligopoly: An **oligopoly** is an economic market whereby a small number of companies generate and control the entire supply of a good or service.

OMO: Open Market Operations. The buying and selling of government securities in the open market in order to expand or contract the amount of money in the banking system. Open market operations are the principal tools of monetary policy. RBI uses this tool in order to regulate the liquidity in economy.

Online Banking: Online Banking allows the customers of the banks to conduct banking transactions on the Website of the bank. Virtual Banking is also known as Online Banking.

Open-End Credit: Commonly referred to as a Line of Credit. May be used repeatedly up to a certain limit; also called a Charge Account or Revolving Credit.

Open-End Lease: Often, referred to as a finance lease. A lease that may involve a balloon payment based on the value of the property when it is returned.

Operating Cycle: The length of time taken by a firm to produce its final product, sell it to customers, and collect proceeds of the sale in cash.

Operating Lease: Short-term, cancelable lease.

Operating Synergy: Combining two or more entities results in gains in revenues or cost reductions because of complementaries or economies of scale or scope.

Operational Risk: Includes all risks not included in market risks and credit risks, such as losses arising from fraud, failure in computer systems and data entry errors.

Opportunity Cost: The rate of return that can be earned on the best alternative investment. In general, the gain or return on the next best investment opportunity or the next best use of resources, which is forgone by putting the resources to a given use.

Option Contract: A contract that gives the buyer the right, but not the obligation, to buy or sell an underlying asset by (or on) a specific date for a specific price. For this right, the purchaser pays a premium.

Option: A formal contract which grants the holder of the option the right to buy or sell a certain quantity of an underlying interest or asset at a stipulated price within a specific period of time.

OTP: One Time Password (OTP) is an additional security measure for authentication for all credit and debit card payment transactions made on IVR (interactive voice response) systems *i.e.,* transactions on mobile.

Overdraft: Facility given by a bank which allows its customers to withdraw more money than account balance. Overdraft generally have high rate of interest as borrower can demand and return the loan anytime.

Par Value: The value of a security when it is issued. For bonds and preferred stock, par value is equivalent to face value.

Partial Shipment: A load sent in more than one consignment. In a Letter of Credit, the buyer can say whether this is allowed or not allowed.

Partnerships: Shared ownership among two or more individuals, some of whom may, but do not necessarily, have limited liability with respect to obligations of the group. There is a written agreement among partners detailing the terms and conditions of participation in a business ownership arrangement.

Pass Through Certificates: Debt instruments backed by a portfolio of assets.

Payback Period: Length of time required for an asset to generate cash flows just enough to cover the initial outlay.

Payee: Payee is the person whom money is paid.

Payer: The person whose name is written on the document who has to pay to the holder is known as payer.

Personal Identification Number (PIN): Personal Identification Number is a number which an ATM card holder has to used in before he is authorized to do any banking transaction. PIN is used for security purpose.

Plain Vanilla Transactions: The most common and generally the simplest types of derivatives transaction. Transactions that have unusual or less common features are often called exotic or structured.

Plastic Money: Debit Cards, Credit Cards, ATM Cards (Visa, Master Cards etc.) are known as plastic money. These cards are like money enable us to get goods and services.

Pledge: A bailment of goods for security purpose for payment of a debt. For example, pledge of stock by a borrower to a banker for a credit limit. Pledge can be made in movable goods only.

PLR: Prime lending rate is the minimum rate of interest that is to be charged by a bank. Each bank decides its own PLR.

Ponzi schemes: It is a kind of fraud scheme which use Network marketing as a tool. Investors are paid out of new investments. These schemes end when new investments stop coming and large number of investors wants to withdraw their money. Latest Ponzi scheme in India was "Speak Asia".

POS: Point of Sale, also known as Point of Purchase, a place where sales are made and also sales and payment information are collected electronically, including the amount of the sale, the date and place of the transaction, and the consumer's account number.

Power of Attorney: A power of attorney is a document, which gives power to the person appointed by it to act for the person who signed the document.

PPF: Public Provident Fund (PPF) scheme is a popular long-term investment. PPF offers attractive interest rates.

Preference Shares: A type of shares having no voting rights and have higher rate of dividend.

Prepayment: Payment of the principal amount of a loan ahead of the scheduled date.

Present Value: The discounted value of a payment or stream of payments to be received in future, taking into consideration a specific interest or discount rate. Present Value represents a series of future cash flows expressed in today's value.

Prime Lending Rate (PLR): The rate of interest at which bank lends to their special customers is known as Prime Lending Rate. Generally, PLR is less than the normal rate of interest.

Principal: Amount of debt that must be repaid. Also means a person who deals in securities on his own account and not as a broker.

Priority Sector Lending: Some areas or fields in a country depending on its economic condition or government interest are prioritised and are called priority sectors *i.e.,* industry, agriculture.

Product Differentiation: Development of a variety of product configurations to appeal to a variety of consumer tastes.

Promissory Note: A signed, written and unconditional promise by one party to another party that commits the maker to pay a specified amount on a fixed or a determinable date. Promissory notes are negotiable instruments.

Public Sector Bank: A bank in which Government acquired fully or partly share is called as Public Sector Banks.

Purchasing Power Parity: The concept that homogeneous goods cannot have more than one price measured in any one currency. If the price increases domestically, the domestic currency will depreciate so that the price denominated in foreign currency remains the same.

Pure Conglomerate Merger: A combination of firms in non-related business activities that is neither a product-extension nor a geographic-extension merger.

Rating: Refers to the credit quality of a counterparty. External ratings are given by rating agencies (ranging from AAA very safe asset to C). Internal ratings are granted by the bank itself.

Ratio: Comparison of two figures used to evaluate business performances, such as debt/equity ratio return on investment, etc.

Recession: An economic situation of negative growth.

Reconciliation: Checking all bank account papers to make sure that the bank's records and customer's records are in sync.

Recourse: In the context of a sale of a loan by a bank to investors, they have the right to call the guarantee from the bank should the borrower be unable to meet its obligations.

Recurring Deposits (R.D.): Recurring Deposit is a special type of deposit account which enables a customer to save by paying into the account an agreed fixed sum of money monthly over a stipulated period. The deposits in this type of account earn compound interest.

Redemption: Redemption means paying off all the money borrowed under an agreement.

Repo Rate: Repo rate is the interest rate which is charged by RBI when RBI lends money to commercial bank for short period of time.

Resolution: A formal document expressing the intention of a board of directors of a corporation.

Return on capital: Return on capital is a profitability ratio. Return on capital indicates how effective a company is at turning capital into profits.

Returns: In economy, a profit from investment is termed as returns.

Reverse Repo Rate: Rate at which commercial banks lends to Central Bank

Revolving Letter of Credit: A Letter of Credit in which the value of the Letter of Credit is automatically reinstated upon utilization. A Letter of Credit may revolve by value, time or both.

Right Issue: Issue of shares in which existing shareholders gets right to buy shares in proportion of their existing holding.

Risk Assessment: A process used to identify and evaluate risks and their potential effect.

Risk Free Return: Rate of return, normally it is 90 days bills issued by a national government.

ROI: Rate on investment is return divided by value of investment.

RTGS: Real Time Gross Settlement system is a funds transfer system where transfer of money or securities takes place from one bank to another on a "real time". ('Real time' means within a fraction of seconds.) The minimum amount to be transferred through RTGS is ₹ 2 lakh. Processing charges/Service charges for RTGS transactions vary from bank to bank.

Safe Custody: When Customers keep their articles (like jewellery, boxes, wills, debentures, shares etc.) with bank for keeping them safe is called safe custody. Bank charges some amount for safe custody.

Sale: Transfer of ownership of some type of property from one person to another, for some consideration.

Salvage: The attempt to get repayment of some portion of a loan obligation which has already been written off the bank's books.

Sarfaesi Act: The Securitisation and Reconstruction of Financial Assets and Enforcement of Security Interest Act, 2002 (Sarfaesi Act) allows banks to auction properties when borrowers fail to repay their loans. It enables banks to reduce their non-performing assets.

Saving Bank Account: Saving account is used for personal purpose. It is not for Business purpose. In Saving Account, Account holders get nominal interest. In India, all bank have facility to open a saving account.

Scale Economies: The reduction in per-unit costs achievable by spreading fixed costs over a higher level of production.

Securitization: The process of transformation of a bank loan into tradable securities. It often involves the creation of a separate corporate entity, the Special Purpose Vehicle (SPV), which buys the loans financing itself with securities that are sold to investors.

Security: These are the financing and investing instrument of the organization. Securities can be bought and sold in the stock market. Shares, debentures, bonds, warrants are the types of securities.

Selective Credit Control (SCC): Control of credit flow to borrowers dealing in some essential commodities to discourage hoarding and black-marketing.

Self Help Group (SHG): SHG is a committee 10-20 people usually in village area mainly for the purpose of deposits their savings into bank by their mutual agreement. Small loan are given to members of SHG for fulfilling their business needs if they want to start a small business.

Senior Debt: Debt which, in the event of bankruptcy, must be repaid before subordinated debt receives any payment.

Series Bond: Bond which may be issued in several series under the same indenture.

Service Charge: A fee paid for using a service.

Service Provider: The organization which provides the outsourced service.

Shorting: Selling securities which an investors don't have in expectation of price drop.

Short-term Loan: Loan to a business for less than one year, usually for operating needs.

Sinking Fund: A fund to which a firm makes a periodic contribution to facilitate retirement of debt.

Smart Cards: Smart card is a plastic card with embedded microprocessor. Smarts cards are used to perform various types of financial transactions.

Sovereign Gold Bond: Sovereign Gold Bond is a Government security issued by Reserve Bank of India on the behalf of Government of India. SCBs are substitutes for holding physical gold. Investors gets market value of gold at the time of maturity and periodical interest.

Special Purpose Vehicle: A legal corporate entity created to buy loans from banks. It finances itself with securities issued to investors.

Stagnation: An economic situation of slow economic growth high rate unemployment and inflation.

Stakeholder: Any individual or group who has an interest in a firm; in addition to shareholders and bondholders, includes labour, consumers, suppliers, the local community, and so on...

Standby Letter of Credit: A guarantee issued by a bank, on behalf of a buyer that protects the seller against non-payment for goods shipped to the buyer. The buyer pays the seller directly for the goods and only if the buyer fails to pay does the seller claim under the Standby Letter of Credit.

Statement: All transactions in a bank account for a period of time. Statements are usually given once a month.

Statutory Audit: By law, certain companies need to have their accounts audited by suitably qualified accountants. This is called a statutory audit.

Stocks: Traded on a stock exchange, these are shares in a company. Essentially, one purchases shares in an exchange for owning a part of a company.

STRIPS: Separate Trading for Registered Interest & Principal Seeurities.

Swap: An agreement for an exchange of payments between two counterparties at some point(s) in the future and according to a specified formula.

SWIFT: Society for Worldwide Interbank Financial Telecommunication. It operates a worldwide financial messaging network which exchanges messages between banks and other financial institutions.

SWOT: Acronym for Strengths, Weakness, Opportunities and Threats; an approach to formulating firm strategy via assessment of a firm's capabilities in relation to the business environment.

Syndicate: Group of banks and financial institutions, which together contribute the necessary financing for a transaction.

Syndicated Loans: Loans to a company backed by a group of banks in order to share the risk in a large transaction among several financial institutions. There is usually a lead bank and several participating banks.

Systematic Risk: The risk that the failure of one participant in a payment or settlement system, or in financial markets generally to meet its required obligations when due will cause other participants or financial institutions to be unable to meet their obligations (including settlement obligations in a payment and settlement system) when due.

Take-out Merger: The second-step transaction which merges the acquired firm into the acquirer and thus takes out the remaining target shares which were not purchased in the initial (partial) tender offer.

Tangible Assets: Physical assets such as plant, machinery, factories and offices.

Tax Avoidance: Lawful agreement or re-arrangement of the affairs of an individual or company intended to avoid liability to tax.

Tax Evasion: Fraudulent or illegal arrangements made with the intention of evading tax, *e.g.* by failure to make full disclosure to the revenue authorities.

Tax Haven: An international banking and financial centre providing privacy and tax benefits.

Tax Incentives: Tax benefits. Most tax incentive measures fall into one or more of the following categories: tax exemption (tax holiday); deduction from the taxable base; reduction in the rate of tax; tax deferment, etc.

Teller: Teller is a bank employee, who provides several types of banking services to the customers of the bank.

Term Loan: A loan intended for medium-term or long-term financing to supply cash to purchase fixed assets such as machinery, land or buildings or to renovate business premises.

Time Deposits (Fixed Deposits): Time Deposit is a deposit in the bank which is not allowed to withdraw before a fixed period. If account holder wants to withdraw deposit before the fixed time then banks may charge some amount of penalty on it.

Title Deeds: Documents which prove who owns a property and under what terms.

Trade Creditors: Organisations, which are owed money for goods and services supplied.

Trade Debtors: Organisations, which owe money for goods and services supplied.

Trade Deficit: The amount by which merchandise imports exceed merchandise exports.

Transaction: Action in a bank account. Could be a deposit, withdrawal, debit card payment, service charge or interest payment.

TREASURY BILLS: TREASURY BILLS is a negotiable instrument. It is short-term instrument of borrowing. RBI issue T-Bills on discount on the behalf of government and redeem at face value. Presently, treasury bills of 91 days and 364 days are sold by RBI.

Trust Deed (Settlement Deed, Declaration of Trust or Trust Instrument): Document that lays down the foundations of how the trustees are to administer and manage the trust assets and how they are to distribute and dispose of trust assets during the lifetime of the trust.

Trust: An entity created for the purpose of protecting and conserving assets for the benefit of a third party, the beneficiary— A contract affecting three parties, the settlor, the trustee and the beneficiary.

Trustee: Trustees have a fiduciary duty to act in accordance with a trust deed and for the benefit of the beneficiary (ies).

UCPDC: 'Uniform Customs and Practice for Documentary Credit' developed by the International Chamber of Commerce as the rules that govern the operation of Letter of Credit transactions worldwide. ICC publication No. 500 contains details of the rules currently in use.

Umbrella Fund: A type of collective investment scheme. A collective fund containing several sub-funds, each of which invests in a different market or country.

Undervaluation: When a firm's securities sell for less than their intrinsic, or potential, or long-run value for one or more reasons.

Underwriters: In case of an IPO, new companies makes contracts with underwriter where underwriters promises to purchase unsubscribe shares.

Underwriting: Underwriting is an agreement by the underwriter to buy shares or debentures on a fixed date. Underwriter gets commission for this agreement.

Universal Banking: In Universal Banking, Banks are allowed to do all types of activities related to banking like acceptance of deposits, giving loans, issue of debit and credit cards, selling of insurance products etc.

Value Creation: The difference between the value of an investment and the amount of money invested by shareholders.

Variable Expenses: Costs of doing business that vary with the volume of business, such as advertising costs, manufacturing costs and bad debts.

Variable Rate: A variable rate loan or credit agreement, calls for an interest rate that may fluctuate over the life of the loan. The rate is often tied to an index that reflects changes in market rates of interest. A fluctuation in the rate causes changes in either the payments or the length of the term.

Venture Capital: Commonly refers to funds that are invested by a third party in a business either as equity or as a form of secondary debt.

Vertical Merger: A combination of firms, which operate at different levels or stages of the same industry manufacturer mergers with a type company (backward integration).

Virtual Banking: Virtual banking is also called internet banking. In virtual Banking services are accessed via internet's worldwide web. It is called virtual banking because an internet bank has no boundaries of brick and it exists only on the internet.

Warrants: A document which gives right to holder to get shares at stated price.

Wholesale Banking: Wholesale banking is different from common banking. In wholesale banking main focus is on providing financial assistance to the industries and other sectors.

Winding Up: Winding up of a company is done by paying the company's creditors, and then distributing moneys left (if any) among the members.

Working Capital: Working capital is that capital of the organization which is used to fulfill the day to day expenses of the business. Working Capital = Current assets – Current Liabilities.

Yield: (1) A measure of the income generated by a bond. The amount of interest paid on a bond divided by the price. (2) The rate of discount which makes the present value of the stream of future returns plus the terminal value of the asset equal to the current market price of the asset.

Zero Balance Account: The account in which one don't have to maintain a minimum balance. It is also known as Basic Saving Bank Account (BSBA) and Zero balance Saving Account.

Zero Coupon Bond: A bond issued at a discount (*i.e.* below par value), earning no interest but redeemable at its par value, thus providing a guaranteed capital gain.